Endorsements for Worth K

This useful book helps those working in missions to understand how mission ethos and cultures can promote healthy relationships and personal growth. It utilises research data obtained from 40% of the world mission force, and should be required reading for everyone involved in world mission.

Dr. Marjory F. Foyle, WEA Mission Commission MemCa, UK

There can be few more urgent issues than recapturing the importance of long-term, whole-life-investing, mission service: long enough to learn a language properly, to get inside an alien worldview and to make real friendships, without which mission is superficial and deep-level conversion rarely happens. If we care about the God-honouring quality of world mission, then we will want to recruit and keep godly men and women. This book will help us do just that, under the grace of God.

Rose Dowsett, OMF, WEA Mission Commission Coordinator Global Missiology Teams, Scotland

If we long for a harvest of "fruit that will last" around the world, then we will implement the recommendations contained in this book. It is easier to keep things the way they are. But we will honour God by taking seriously the formidable research described in these pages,

Dr. Debbie Lovell-Hawker, Consultant Clinical Psychologist and Researcher, InterHealth, UK

The global missionary community is once again greatly indebted to the writers who are a part of the WEA Mission Commission. There is no doubt that this key book on missionary retention and best practices will challenge and change not only the mode of our member care, but also training as well as the entire process of sending of our missionaries.

Dr. David Tai-Woong Lee, Global Missionary Training Centre, Korea

Worth Keeping marks a significant milestone in the crucial work of the WEA Missions Commission. This seminal work should be read and re-read by all of us who are engaged in this exciting epoch of evangelical missions.

Rob Martin, Executive Director, First Fruit, Inc., USA

All too often research is just left on the shelf to gather dust and doesn't produce the results its conclusions commend. This research has the potential to be different. It contains hard truths alongside many practical recommendations, and we ignore its message at our peril. Study it, see what changes need to be made..., but above all don't let it gather dust.

Martin Lee, Executive Director, Global Connections, UK

Worth Keeping is the most extensive and profound international study to date on the issue of retention of missionaries. The comprehensive analysis is an invaluable tool for everyone engaged in missionary work, whether sending, training or being sent. Missionaries are not "chess pieces" of lower value that can be discarded in the global mission enterprise. Mission organisations know that they are worth keeping and that, in general, long term missionaries are the most effective.

Bertil Ekström, Executive Director, World Evangelical Alliance Mission Commission, Brazil

Worth Keeping represents the outstanding efforts of a widespread, global group of scholars and practitioners who came together to prepare, research, analyze and report a strategic study on missionary retention. What sets this resource apart from anything else is its clarity, breadth, and utility. It is a must read and applies equally to both church and mission leaders, and anyone who resources mission activities globally.

Brent Lindquist, Ph.D., President, Link Care Center, EFMA Board of Directors, USA

This book will have a great impact for sending mission organisations worldwide. It will also be useful not only in wiser recruitment, but also to significantly lower the attrition rate for many missionaries. The overview for old and new sending countries in *Worth Keeping* is very helpful to all of us.

Wolfgang Büsing, German Evangelical Missionary Alliance, Germany

The Latin American Mission Movement is transitioning forward into to a new stage. The 2006 III Ibero American Mission Congress in Spain confirmed the legacy of wisdom and concern about crucial field realities. *Worth Keeping* comes to us at the perfect time to help us grapple with the critical issues related to retention and effective field ministry. This book presents a profound analysis as well as personal case studies and models that enable the emerging generations of missionaries to be more effective in global Gospel of Jesus Christ.

David D. Ruiz M., Former president of COMIBAM; WEA Mission Commission Associate Director, Guatemala

As usual the WEA MC has produced a very significant book. *Worth Keeping* is a must read for any missionary as well as church and missions leaders anywhere who long to see retention and success in mission fields. Our thanks to the WEA MC and the team behind this work. This book should be made available in many languages as soon as possible.

Younoussa Djao, Coordinator, Francophone Africa Regional Consultation (CRAF)/ New Generations Intl, Cote d'Ivoire

As the undercurrent continues to pull the Church into deeper water in the sea of short-term missions, *Worth Keeping* compels us to swim hard against it toward the shore of appropriate longer-term engagement. "Appropriate" can be a vague user-defined word. This study and analysis helps to bring clarity to missional preparation and implementation—for the sake of the senders, the sent ones, and the receivers.

Keith Sparzak, Director/Pastor of Global Outreach, Mars Hill Bible Church, USA

worthKeeping

worthKeeping

Global perspectives on
best practice in missionary retention

Rob Hay, Valerie Lim, Detlef Blöcher,
Jaap Ketelaar and Sarah Hay

Foreword by William D. Taylor

William Carey Library
Pasadena, California
www.WCLBooks.com

About the cover design:

Why the bin?

Are we suggesting that missionaries get thrown away—well yes we are: we recognize that when we do not identify and promote best practice we settle for second best and that may mean that people are lost unnecessarily!

Are we suggesting that we need to throw things away—well yes we are: we recognize that many of us are not currently following best practice, indeed we may not be certain of what best practice is, *but* if we choose to seek after it we must be prepared to discard some of our current, often long standing, practices!

The whole idea of Worth Keeping is to look for best practice in missionary retention. In this book, we present that best practice very positively and constructively, *but* we also seek to help you discern between bad and good. Indeed, going a stage further, we need the courage to choose to go for the best; rather than to simply accept what may already be okay, even good. May we have the courage to review, examine and reflect upon our current practice. Let us retain, refine and protect best practice where it already exists. But where it does not, let us fearlessly throw things away (discard "less than best" practice)… So, that's why we chose a bin!

Worth Keeping: Global perspectives on best practice in missionary retention

Copyright © 2007 by World Evangelical Alliance Mission Commission

All scripture quotations, unless otherwise indicated, are taken from the Holy Bible, New International Version. ©1973, 1978, 1984 by the International Bible Society. Used by permission of Zondervan Publishing House.

Published by William Carey Library
1605 E. Elizabeth Street, Pasadena, California 91104
www.WCLBooks.com

William Carey Library is a ministry of the U.S. Center for World Mission, Pasadena, California.

Printed in the United States of America

ISBN: 978-0-87808-515-6

Library of Congress Cataloguing-in-Publication Data

Worth keeping : global perspectives on best practice in missionary retention / edited by Rob Hay ... [et al.] ; foreword by William D. Taylor.

p. cm.

Includes index.

ISBN 978-0-87808-515-6

1. Missions. 2. Missionaries. I. Hay, Rob.

BV2063.W67 2007

266.0068'3--dc22

2007011333

Contents

Section C

Case Studies

Foreword

To be read

William D. Taylor, Global Ambassador, World Evangelical Alliance

As we get started—brush strokes on a broad canvas

Welcome to volume six of our singular series, "Globalisation of Mission," another example of a world mission resource that bears the mark of scores of researchers and writers from many nations—a truly globalised book.

At the end of the day, in our global service to the Triune missional God and as leaders, we all battle hard to balance three dimensions and values: the people entrusted to us, the human and spiritual task before us, and the organisations that converge the first two. In the global, cross-cultural mission movement, it means that we invest in people, seeking their highest good, believing in them, challenging them even in the hard character issues, and releasing them for ministry, even beyond our own gift mix, leadership and organisation. It means that people are central to both God's mission and ours, and that we do not use them to advance our own structures, organisations or self-image. This book addresses the three dimensions—people, task, and organisation—and calls us to keep them in the right perspective.

In this Foreword, as back in 1996, when I began editing *Too Valuable to Lose: Exploring the Causes and Cures of Missionary Attrition* (Ed., William D. Taylor, William Carey Library, 1997), my mind travelled the globe, tracking some of our personal friends. Our core of respected friends committed their lives to mission and invested years to language and culture learning as they gained credibility for the Great Story to be told. They went with the longest-term dreams possible. A good number of them are still there, perhaps in different contexts and assignments, but still in cross-cultural mission. Most of them served in the "tough" areas of the world—from Europe to central China; from the Middle East to Central Asia—serving creatively under tremendous pressures. Their names (using pseudonyms and changed geographies to protect them) and faces are before me even on this January 2007 night.

Where are they now? Is their heart still passionate for God and his Great Narrative mission? Harold and Marion: nine years in a Russian speaking context; superb work; now back in their home (passport) country preparing for a radically different career in international economics; but both committed to the living God and his historic mission. Magdalena: returned from a rough set of years; married; I have lost touch with her. Mark and Mary: back in homeland after health crisis and abusive, toxic leadership by an executive who treated people like objects. It took them three years to recover and return to health but now they serve from a very different perspective in their passport country.

As I write this paragraph I gaze at a picture of Dorothy and Roger now in their 12th year serving in a Francophone-European Muslim context. Hard slogging and long-term commitment characterise their lives.

While writing this Foreword, my wife, Yvonne, and I visited some long-time friends from many years, Jack and Deborah, with a 35-year-long trajectory in one of the most difficult people groups of Europe. They are long-term church planters with unusual insight into their people but they are also questioning existing models of church for Europe. Deborah recently was diagnosed with a voracious cancer and their future is now uncertain.

Tomas and Andrea recently spent a half day in our home. In their mid-twenties, they declare commitment to "career missions" (a category not used much in mission) and the desire to go into a tough African context. I think of Ruben and Sarita, Latin Americans (I baptized him years ago) now in India long-term. I note the radical discipleship of a young single Latin woman medical doctor, "lost" in the interior of Mozambique. She recently reminded me that it was after I had spoken in her church in Central America that she had made her decision for mission, and that I was partially responsible for her life!

Sadly, I know of too many who went out with high dreams and expectations, some very gifted and highly trained, others with less raw material, who were sent prematurely by a pastor or mission group; and now they are back "home". But they are alienated from their former vocation, and some even from friends and churches; some struggle with deep spiritual doubts. One returned home and married a Buddhist. One couple slipped into universalism. What really happened here? Do we send too many people too early, without appropriate screening, training, supporting and shepherding? Yes, we do; let's be frank about it.

Yvonne and I receive as many as 110 missionary news/prayer letters in a year. We read them all. We appreciate the honest letters that invite us to travel behind the scenes into the heart and health battles, the struggles to learn language and culture, the yearning to see the Gospel come alive, and the times of joy and grief. We are tired of triumphalist letters dedicated to proving what people are "doing" for God, with endless reports of high performing children who weather every season of life with excellence. Reality, honesty, authenticity… that is what is needed.

The personal, human narrative is core to the reality of this book. We trust that as you read it, you will discern the hearts of researchers and writers, honestly grappling with tough issues of attrition, retention and best practices of sending teams—agencies and churches. We must see people as too valuable to lose and truly worth keeping. But we will probably have to change some of the ways we have been doing mission and missions.

Too Valuable taught us a lot about attrition: preventable and unpreventable, expected and painful. We also learned, in too many cases, of attrition that should have taken place but did not, to the detriment of national church, sending church, ministry and colleagues! Retention in and of itself is not the prime virtue. What's "worth keeping" are the people who should stay in cross-cultural mission, even if their geography and assignments change, even if they return home for a needed "upgrade" of skills and gifts in order to more effectively serve Christ in other cultures and geographies.

As I consider this new book, a statement from a quote from Chapter 16 summarizes much of what drives me:

> "We do not consider the reduction of missionary attrition as an end in itself, nor do we aim to increase missionary retention at all costs. Missionaries can also stay for too long and hinder the maturing of the national church and the development of local leadership. But places hardened to the gospel will only be reached by the gospel through dedicated, experienced long-term missionaries that have carefully learned the language, adjusted well to the culture, live a simple lifestyle, and maintain trusted relationships while being supported by a caring community and an organisational structure with lean management and effective leadership. This brings together the two biblical issues of shepherding and good stewardship."

Singular features of this book

You hold in your hands the report and findings of a huge amount of research and reflection. It's too valuable to lose. It's worth keeping. It requires real work to mine its riches: to discern the meaning of numbers; to enter into the life stories of the case studies; to compare research results from the older and younger sending countries; to apply the findings to your church or agency or school. This book is not a quick read; but rather it's a working tool to be treasured and heeded. We have focused on the mid-term to longer-term cross-cultural mission force, not on short-termers who require a very different kind of research project.

Let's start with the cover, pregnant and provocative. Some of us did not like it at first because we said "Hold it! Missionaries are not for the rubbish bin! This sends the wrong message!" No, we are not trashing missionaries, but we must toss into the bin some of the established (even treasured) principles and practices that do not generate personal and organisational health. And this book, as no other, provides a map to identify what kind of mission ethos and culture promote healthy relationships that enable our mission partners not only to survive but to thrive—however long the sovereign Spirit keeps them there.

The Mission Commission, World Evangelical Alliance, for twenty years has generated internationally relevant publications designed to identify and address grassroots as well as global needs in the mission community. Some of our books emerge from consultations, such as missionary training and attrition; others are generated as the outcome of a long-term research project; yet others are produced by missiological teams from both Global South and North, to deliver a resource to serve the global mission enterprise. Our teams serve as "reflective practitioners". These are women and men of both action and reflection, doers and thinkers, committed to serve and who, in thoughtful ways, ask Biblical, theological and missiological questions. Our goal is to shape and transform the way we think and do mission in the world today. We pray that these resources will leaven the hearts and minds of church and mission leaders in every sending country of the world.

This new publication is the result of a long-term research team and project (the research process itself taking two years), working in 22 nations (with usable data from 20), and representing both Global North and South. It is a distinct sibling of its predecessor, *Too Valuable to Lose,* which analysed data from 14 nations of South and North. In 1996 we sensed the future need for a follow-up research project to evaluate changes in these 14 nations, but we wanted to go beyond the parameters of attrition. Thankfully, some of the key players of the '90s significantly shaped the second study, particularly Dr. Jonathan Lewis and Dr. Detlef Blöcher. God also brought to the new team gifted younger partners such as Valerie Lim, Jaap Ketelaar and Rob Hay. Without Rob's dedication, we would not have the book.

No other publication exists with this kind of cross-cultural, international research that comes from an evangelical, missional perspective and commitment. Secular and United Nations studies like this require countless millions of Euros and large numbers of professional researchers. The WEA Mission Commission completed ReMAP II primarily with dedicated volunteers—an amazing kingdom investment. The Mission Commission provided initial leadership and limited funding, but it was the combination of our global colleagues, along with the sending Spirit of God, who brought it to completion.

Together, *Too Valuable to Lose* and now *Worth Keeping* give you the invaluable comparison between OSC and NSC nations—Old (older) Sending Countries and New (newer) Sending Countries. Valerie Lim provides us a more complete explanation of these terms in her superb chapter on the research project and process. The richness of the case studies strengthens the book by their quality and diversity; and this feast awaits you, the reader.

You will learn of some singular mission challenges emerging out of the NSC contexts: issues of filial piety in Asia and some African nations; care of aging parents in the missionary family budget; the vital importance of family blessing into mission; the role that the demonic and evil supernaturalism plays in the lives of mission candidates and how to address these realities.

Our Primary Readers

This book is designed to serve and shape church and mission leaders: pastors with missional hearts; church mission pastors; mission agency leaders—from top strategic levels down through operational ones and across the whole range of disciplines: recruitment, personnel, finance, and member care providers in the home offices or as field leaders. Mission mobilisers will be challenged to reshape the way mobilisation is to be done. The results also challenge those committed to Biblical/theological/missiological education because too often the curriculum remains sacrosanct and unaffected by global field realities. Dedicated missionary trainers will fully appreciate *Worth Keeping*. Field missionaries form a large readership family, for the book invites them to evaluate not only themselves, but also their sending agency and leadership. Our friends dedicated to holistic member care will find their voices heard in the book. Our colleagues doing business as mission or serving as bi-vocational cross-cultural servants will dig into the resources to improve those creative models of mission.

How to read a gold mine

Who you are determines how you approach the book and how you will use the insight you gain.

But here are some suggestions to help you read the book.

First, start with the cover, mull it over and let it mull you over. What does it say? What does it not say? How could it be misinterpreted? What cover might you have suggested or created for the book?

Then study the table of contents. Discern the structure of the book, and don't forget the resources at the end. Peruse the index to see what primary themes are discussed.

Third, carefully read Section A, starting with the graphics code to help you understand the book. Don't forget the icons, and remember the meaning of the "scoring circles". Detlef Blöcher's profound chapter sets the background of ReMAP II, summarising the main findings and impact of ReMAP. It shows people that research like this truly affects mission on the ground. In Chapter 3 Valerie Lim presents the ReMAP II project methodology, an example of collaborative international research and teamwork. This chapter outlines the very innovative way in which the project was run which enabled such a large study to achieve such robust results.

Fourth, you are ready to dig into the rest of the book, either by order of chapters or according to your select interests and needs. Others may do what I did, ploughing my way from start to end, underlining what I felt was significant for my own situation.

Fifth, "ground" your reading of the more theoretical and statistical data with the reality that comes in the case studies. I found myself reflecting over my 17 years in Latin America with a mission agency, serving on a kind of "team". The case studies on leadership, organisational ethos/culture and member care were the most provocative. When my wife and I left Latin America after those years of fruitful and valuable life and ministry, I know the agency catalogued us as attrition cases. After all, we left; we attrited! But the key, as we all know, is not longevity nor organisational loyalty, but stewardship and the appropriate use of skill sets and gift mixes within the ongoing call of the travelling Spirit of God.

Sixth, be sure to check out the websites we mention, especially, www.wearesources. org. A treasury of other WEA missiological findings, there you will locate the initial and comprehensive ReMAP II report, featuring the 20 national reports and other insights, published in the June, 2004 issue of *Connections*. Download and read it at no cost at www.wearesources.org/publications.aspx. On this site you will find Detlef Blöcher's other reports from the ReMAP II data. Another invaluable site, referenced many times in this book, is the one with the rest of the ReMAP II information (and many other materials) www.worthkeeping.info.

Seventh, you will find at the end of Chapters 4-33 the discussion questions, and a matrix to be completed. These can be used by church, training and agency leaders, and contributes to the book being used as a course text.

Eighth, remember the resources section at the end, including the complete survey instrument, itself a crafted gem of cross-cultural research. Be sure to read the footnotes of this book, for you may be surprised by the kind of information you find tucked away in the small print.

Ninth, cross-reference your reading reflections. If you want to review something on missionary attrition, then cross-reference *Too Valuable to Lose*. If you read something that draws you to more resources on member care, check out *Doing Member Care Well: Perspectives and Practices from Around the World*, (ed. Kelly O'Donnell, William Carey Library, 2002). Missionary trainers will want to check out another new book, *Integral Ministry Training: Design and Evaluation*, (eds. Robert Brynjolfson and Jonathan Lewis, William Carey Library, 2006).

Finally, don't get lost in the mass of details, numbers, comparisons, research issues. Remember that the book is about people, women and men whom many of us know, love and respect. The book is a gift to the global, missional community, with the desire that it strengthen our ministry, and that we remember those who are worth keeping in these ministries until the Spirit says otherwise.

Presenting the key players—researchers and prime writers

I cannot adequately express my gratitude to the men and women who led the research project and produced this book. The original conceptual team included project coordinator Jonathan Lewis (Argentina/USA), researcher Detlef Blöcher (Germany), along with Joe Varela (USA), Seth Anyomi (Ghana) and Jim Van Meter (USA). Australian researcher, Barbara Griffin, soon joined the core group, developing a vital draft of the survey instrument prior to the first 2002 team meeting in England. Jonathan Lewis served on Mission Commission staff from 1992-2006. He was the architect of the 1994-1996 research on missionary attrition that produced *Too Valuable to Lose*. Born in Argentina as one of eight children, he is a third generation missionary who, with his wife Dawn, served from 1976-1997 in Honduras, Peru, Mexico and Argentina. The development of ministry training resources and programmes has been the predominant thread in the Lewis' ministry. We have released Jon to his first love, missionary training, serving with the Mission Commission's International Missionary Training Network (IMTN). He is also WEA's Organisation Development Consultant and continues as a Mission Commission Associate.

The ReMAP II team first listened to national mission leaders around the world and then selected a national ReMAP II coordinator for each one. These are the field servants, coming from the 20 nations that provided usable research data.

REMAP II National Coordinators

Argentina	*Daniel Bianchi*
Australia	*Barbara Griffin*
Brazil	*José Roberto Prado, Ted Limpic*
Canada	*Laurel McAllister*
Costa Rica	*Marcos Padgett*
Germany	*Detlef Blöcher*
Ghana	*Seth Anyomi, Sampson Dorkunor*
Holland	*Jaap Ketelaar*
Hong Kong	*Vanessa Hung*
India	*Pramila Rajendran*
Korea	*Dong-Hwa Kim*
Malaysia	*Philip Chang*
New Zealand	*Rachel Murray*
Nigeria	*Timothy Olonade*
Philippines	*Rey Corpuz, Bob López*
Singapore	*Valerie Lim*
South Africa	*Henkie Maritz*
Sweden	*Brigitta Johansson*
UK	*Rob Hay*
USA	*Jim Van Meter*

Detlef Blöcher and Valerie Lim were our research wizards. Nobody reads statistics better than Detlef; and his gentle, pastoral heart is exemplary. Valerie's quiet, stellar work generated three chapters plus the marvellous resource in the 58 case studies, without which the book would have lost its human flavour. Researcher Barbara Griffin (Australia) assisted Detlef before the international team was formed. Barbara and Detlef helped the national coordinators to create suitable questions with the appropriate wording for the final ReMAP II survey instrument. We express gratitude also to Korean researcher Dr Steve Moon who served the project in its initial stages.

Case Study authors in *Worth Keeping*

The following is Valerie's global team of case study writers. Their contribution is invaluable and we are indebted to them for putting the face of reality and people into this book. Some, such as Bibien Limlingan, wrote three case studies with great insight.

Asia	*Fi McLachlan, Paul Bendor-Samuel*
Australia	*Barbara Griffin, Alan McMahon*
Brazil	*Márcia Tostes, Antonia L. van der Meer*
Canada	*Dan Sheffield, Laurel McAllister*
Costa Rica	*Marcos Padgett*
Egypt	*Fayez Ishak*
Germany	*Detlef Blöcher*
Ghana	*Albert Seth Ocran, Thomas Oduro, Bernard Ofori Atta*
Hong Kong	*Vanessa Hung*
India	*John Amalraj*
Kenya	*Duncan Olumbe*
Korea	*Dong-Hwa Kim*
Malaysia	*Philip Chang*
Middle East	*Bob, Nancy, David Milligan*
Moldova	*Rebecca Barnhart*
New Zealand	*Rachel Murray*
Nigeria	*Nathaniel Abimbola*
Philippines	*Bibien Limlingan, Bob Lopez, Ana Gamez*
Senegal	*Ron Brown*
Singapore	*Stroma Beattie, David Wong, Ajit Hazra*
South Africa	*Henkie Maritz*
Spain	*Terry Miller*
UK	*Paul Adams, Jonathan Ingleby, Alan Pain, David Lundy, Rob Hay*
USA	*LeMei Littlefield, Paul Rhoads, Steve Hoke, Steve Richardson, Caryn Pederson, David Dougherty, Thomas Sanchez*

The book production then passed into the hands of a team led by Rob, Valerie and Jaap Ketelaar. Rob brought to the book a new way of putting the material together, and Valerie revised each case study to ensure focus. Koe Pahlka (USA) served as our keen-eyed copy editor whose desktop publishing abilities have also formatted the book. We are grateful to Redcliffe College, UK, for loaning Rob to this project. Finally, we thank William Carey Library for taking the risk to publish, advertise and distribute another WEA Mission Commission book. Here are the biographical sketches of our writers.

Lead editor/writer

Rob Hay is husband to Sarah and dad to two energetic and creative boys, Thomas and Jacob. Rob originally trained and worked as a management consultant in public and private organisations before working overseas as Health Services Director for the International Nepal Fellowship in Nepal. There he managed a team of 45 people from 15 nations, covering 13 professional areas, spread across seven geographical locations. He survived by having a great (and gracious) team and drinking copious amounts of sweet Nepali tea! He is now Director of Research and Partnership Development at Redcliffe College - Centre for Mission Training in Gloucester, UK (www.redcliffe.org). He also runs Generating Change, an organisation dedicated to researching and innovating in global mission, and is Editor of Encounters (www.redcliffe.org/mission), an on-line Mission Journal designed as a "UK-space for missiological reflection". He is a member of the Institute of Directors, holds an MA in Contemporary Issues in Global Mission, and is currently working on a PhD Thesis on organisational health and toxicity. More information about Rob's work is available at www.generatingchange.info and he can be contacted on rhay@redcliffe.org. He is a WEA Mission Commission Associate.

Other writers

Valerie Lim is a mission researcher in Singapore. Trained as a scientist, she holds a Master of Science degree in chemistry and a postgraduate diploma in systems analysis. Over the years, she has worked in multi-disciplinary research, project management, staff development and training at a university and a few multi-national companies. She began serving in mission research as research analyst (1993-1996) at the international headquarters of OMF International. Since 1997, Valerie has been an Associate of Global Mapping International (www.gmi.org). She represents GMI in South East Asia, where she collaborates with mission leaders and church pastors on various research-related projects, mission surveys, and prayer guides. One recent project was a CD-ROM edition of the prayer guide *Peoples of the Buddhist World* (GMI and Piquant Editions, 2006). From time to time, she conducts training workshops on research methodology and mission cartography in partnership with mission agencies or theological schools. Valerie also serves as a WEA Mission Commission Associate.

Detlef Blöcher was born 1953 in Germany. He is married to Dr. Elisabeth Blöcher and they have three children aged 23 – 16 years. With a PhD in physics, he worked as a research scientist in Biophysics at GSF (1976-81) and at the University Clinics Frankfurt (1981-1984). From 1976-81 he studied Theology at Frankfurt University (part-time) and then Missiology at All Nations Christian College, England (1984-85). The family joined German Missionary Fellowship (DMG) and served in a tentmaking role in the Middle East (medical research, 1986-90) till he was appointed as Personnel Director of their mission (1991-99) and then elected as their Executive Director in 2000. Since 1996 he has also served as an Associate of the World Evangelical Alliance-Missions Commission (WEA-MC), particularly in the ReMAP I-research project and as international research coordinator of ReMAP II. Presently he also chairs the German Evangelical Mission Association (AEM), representing some 92 evangelical mission agencies with 3000 missionaries.

Jaap Ketelaar is married to Alexandra and father of three daughters: Thirza, Ruth and Anna. After finishing his study at the Bible Institute in Belgium (now Evangelical Theological Faculty), he served as a pastor in two local churches for 11 years. After that he became a staff member and later interim-director of the Dutch Evangelical Missionary Alliance, umbrella organisation of about 75 mission- and relief-agencies in The Netherlands (three years). From his work-experience he has seen the need for organisational and leadership development in churches and para-church organisations. That is why since 2004 he has offered his services as a trainer, consultant and coach in that area. With churches he practices this as an intentional interim pastor, helping them especially in change and innovation, training and coaching, recruitment and selection in times of transition. With para-church organisations he offers custom-made organisational and leadership development programmes as a partner of several networks of trainers and consultants. His drive and focus is the joint missionary calling of all Christians and through his work he wants to catalyse and facilitate partnership between the several partners involved in the missionary process. Because of that he is also a partner of the Dutch Evangelical Missionary Alliance and an Associate of the Missions Commission of the World Evangelical Alliance.

Sarah Hay is married to Rob and is full-time Mum to Thomas (5) and Jacob (2). She is a Chartered Member of the Chartered Institute of Personnel and Development. BC (before children!) she worked for several years in the Human Resources field within the National Health Service. After a year of study on the Professionals in Mission course at Redcliffe College, she and Rob served in Nepal where she was the Personnel Manager for International Nepal Fellowship, responsible for 200 expatriate missionaries. Currently, Sarah does a limited amount of personnel consultancy in the charity sector and is a charity trustee of Gloucester City Mission and the International Nepal Fellowship (UK). She also volunteers at Redcliffe College where she is involved in pastoral care of students. She believes passionately in ensuring that mission partners are cared for, encouraged and equipped well! And never tell her you're tired if you've not taken any annual leave or R and R (Rob included)!

Jonathan Ingleby is Postgraduate Lecturer in Mission at Redcliffe College, Gloucester, UK. He lectures on subjects in missiology and world Christianity to Postgraduate level and specialises in the history of mission and missiology and in globalisation and postcolonialism. Jonathan was brought up in Portugal by missionary parents. He worked for twenty years in India at Hebron, a school for missionary children, as teacher and then headmaster. Jonathan's PhD is from the Open University. His Oxford Degree is in History and his Bachelor of Divinity is from Serampore College, India. He is married with two grown up children, and attends a local Baptist church. Jonathan is also Co-Editor of *Encounters Mission Ezine*—an online journal dedicated to exploring topical issues in mission.

 **Richard Tiplady** is British Director of European Christian Mission, a church-planting mission agency with over 150 missionaries working in 19 European countries. He also worked as a consultant to several Christian organisations including Tearfund, with assignments in Russia, Afghanistan and Pakistan. He was Associate Director of Global Connections, the UK evangelical network for world mission, from 1996 - 2002. He has written or edited several books on mission, including _One World or Many? The impact of globalization of mission_ (William Carey Library, 2003), _World of Difference: Global mission at the pic'n'mix counter_ (Paternoster Press, 2003) and _Postmission: World mission by a postmodern generation_ (Paternoster Press, 2002). A WEA Mission Commission Associate, he is also on the board of London School of Theology and the council of Global Connections. He has a BD from the University of London and an MA in Theology of Mission from the University of Nottingham. His particular interest is in the contextualisation of the Gospel into the contemporary Western context. He is married to Irene, who works for a mental health charity, and they have one son, Jamie.

Drawing to a close

For three decades I have been grappling with the meaning of finishing well, as a man, a husband, a father and grandfather, as a mission leader, as a storytelling servant of the Most High God. We know most of the reasons why men and women in ministry don't finish well: financial mismanagement, family crisis and/or collapse, sexual immoralities, power abuse in ministry, pride and ambition, the inability to turn over leadership, failing the radical tests that come in life's middle stages, burning out, departure from Biblical orthodoxy, evil supernaturalism, and coasting to the end.

I rather agree with what I wrote some years ago:

> Finishing well does not mean someone who completes his or her personal career, regardless of the vocation, whether in ministry or not, on "top of the success pile"; lauded by all as the great examples of modern ministry production. Finishing well does not mean great banquets celebrating retirement, or biographies written about you, or going on the final conference circuit sharing your secrets to success, nor having your ten-step video programs dazzling the millions. It does not mean prizes given to the spell-binding speakers, the writers of self-help books, the powerful motivational speakers, the Evangelical celebrities, the prophetically gifted ones, the great public intercessors, the international missions' mobilisers or legendary missionaries. Nor does it mean the high prizes given to parents who claim, "I praise God that all my children are on fire for God and serving Him in....."

So what does finishing well really mean? It means coming to the end of the life race with integrity, not fame. I personally have two passions in life related to finishing well, and I measure them simply. Finishing well to me means ending with integrity towards my wife and my children. At my funeral I want my family to say, "Dad loved Mom passionately unto the end, was totally faithful to her, and did not sacrifice his children on an illegitimate altar of his travelling ministry." That's my bottom line. The second passion is simply to do all I can to pack heaven with worshippers. Those two drive me to finish well.

Finishing well in cross-cultural ministry does not mean having to be a missionary for the rest of your life, nor to base in the same geography all your life, regardless of your dreams or desires or whether you are gifted for that task. The future missionary will serve with greater mobility, according to global and local needs, based on one's skill-set and gift-mix, seeking to expand the Kingdom into the tough unreached areas, and also committed to building up the church of Christ wherever. The true meaning of the Great Commission equally balances the proclamation of the Gospel and the edification of the Church.

Finishing well is best done in community. That includes our extended family, our spiritual family, our church family, our colleagues in ministry, our fellow believers from different nations and cultures, and in particular with those to whom we have entrusted our deeper life, our fellow mentors and intercessors. Finishing well also means completing in the right manner the different stages of our ministry and assignments, not just the Final Finish.

Send Me! Your Journey to the Nations, Steve Hoke and William Taylor, William Carey Library, 1999, p. 101-102.

Finishing well means the downward path of the cross and not the upward path of Christian social status. It means finishing our life with living faith in the one, true God and his Son, the Christ, empowered by the Spirit of God. It means that, at the end of the day, we are still committed to God and that Eternal Metanarrative that judges all other stories, including our own, and that must be carried to the ends of the earth and until the end of our history.

At the end of the day, the core message of *Worth Keeping* is people—children, youth and adults, women and men, single and married, all created in the image of God, called and sent into mission. They are our highest stewardship and we will serve them as long as we are able.

May God guide and bless your reading, reflection, and the implementation of best practices in mission in your church, training programme, sending structure.

Austin, Texas, USA
February 2007

ReMAP II Country Coordinators, London UK, 2002

Back row from left to right:
Jim Van Meter (USA), Daniel Bianchi (Argentina), Jonathan Lewis* (Argentina, USA), Dong-Hwa Kim (Korea), Marcos Padgett (Costa Rica), Sampson Dorkunor (Ghana), Detlef Blöcher* (Germany), Seth Anyomi* (Ghana), Joe Varela* (USA), Henkie Maritz (South Africa) with Nerina, Rob Hay (UK), Jaap Ketelaar (Netherlands), Philip Chang (Malaysia).

Front row from left to right:
José Roberto Prado (Brazil), Barbara Griffin* (Australia), Laurel McAllister (Canada), Rachel Murray (New Zealand), Valerie Lim (Singapore), Birgitta Johansson (Sweden), Pramila Rajendran (India), Vanessa Hung (Hong Kong), Rey Corpuz (Philippines), Timothy Olonade (Nigeria).

* ReMAP II Steering Committee members

Acknowledgements

ReMAP II is the largest research study ever done in the missions world and was only completed because of a huge team of dedicated and committed people who made up the ReMAP II project team. Bill has named you all in the foreword but here I acknowledge and honour you. It was an incredible achievement, an act of service to the global missions community and for me, one of the most rewarding experiences of my life, to work with you all on this project.

The case studies themselves are a team effort: Firstly, the writers of the many case studies—the book moves beyond a text and comes to life with the case studies—the stories you tell from around the world. They make the issues real. Where we can do, we name and acknowledge you but all of you deserve credit for your work. Secondly, immense appreciation goes to Valerie Lim who as case study coordinator, hunted down these stories and experiences from all over the world and then worked with the writers to refine, focus and just generally bring to life, this vital part of the book that adds so much value.

Kalun Lau, the incredibly gifted young man who, as well as designing the icons and images that make navigation easier, captured the book in an image and designed a cover that confronts, intrigues and captures the unsuspecting reader.

Koe Pahlka, who as copy editor, took some Excel tables and graphs and a load of Word files and transformed them into something that actually looked like a book—your skills, patience and encouragement made you a invaluable part of the team.

My three wise men were indispensable and unwavering rocks, for the entire life of the project: Bill Taylor, for your trust and encouragement that made me and so many others in this project, dare to step out and take responsibility—I hope we have repaid your trust. Jon Lewis; for your vision, experience, wisdom and guiding. And finally Detlef Blöcher—where do I start? He has been the brains behind so much of the project. His wisdom, expertise, and work have only been exceeded by his encouragement, faithful support, grace and patience. I and the whole team appreciate all three of you.

Jaap Ketelaar and Sarah Hay (more on her later) not only shared the load by writing significant chunks of the book, but even more by journeying with me as we wrote. Their ideas, creativity and desire to communicate, inspire, challenge and change, made this a journey travelled in fellowship and not alone.

The principal, governors and my colleagues at Redcliffe Centre for Mission Training, where I serve on the faculty, have been supportive, encouraging and gracious in releasing me to this project. The students I have taught over the last four years from over thirty nations have been a gracious and long-suffering test bed for ideas and thoughts expressed in my writing. In many respects this book is dedicated to you, with the prayerful hope that it may help your ministries to be even more effective in the years ahead, as you seek to serve the world and share Jesus Christ.

Many individuals have supported us financially and in prayer throughout the life of this project and three churches in particular: New Life Church, Libanus and the Lees Chapel, have walked with us for over a decade of ministry—may God repay your faithfulness.

I want to single out Jonathan Ingleby, who as well as writing a chapter and proof reading the entire book in his usual thorough fashion, has been for ten years, mentor, advisor and friend.

And finally, because the most important people come last, Sarah, my talented, patient, and supportive wife and Tom and Jake, my two great boys—the three of you take life beyond service and make it an exciting adventure.

Rob Hay
Gloucester, UK
February 2007

Section A

Viewing the site:

*Section A sets the scene, explains the layout of the
book, provides help in getting started, and presents
the history and background to the project.*

Worth Reading
The Blueprint

"In your hands you hold the secrets to success…"

A self-help book would begin as above, then espouse some ethereal solution to the pressing problem you may not even be aware you had! Unlike the myriad of self-help books available, this book is based on facts—and not just facts, but robust statistical results from the largest research study ever undertaken on world mission.

Why read this book?

Here are a few reasons why this study is worth reading:

✓ Forty-percent of the world mission workforce was represented in the study.

✓ The study was undertaken by the Mission Commission of the World Evangelical Alliance, a worldwide network of mission and church leaders representing mission movements in more than 70 countries.

✓ Twenty-two countries on six continents were represented.

✓ Denominational and inter-denominational agencies, as well as churches sending directly to the field, were represented.

✓ Major differences between the best and worst mission agencies were uncovered.

The missionaries in high retaining agencies average 17 years service—in low retaining agencies they average just seven years!

✓ We have written with mission practitioners, church leaders and mission agency leaders in mind.

✓ We aim to identify the best practices that make the difference between having mission agency partners who serve effectively long-term rather than ineffectively short-term.

Why read this chapter?

As we began to write, we realized that it is unlikely this book will be read from cover to cover by anyone other than the writers and editors; therefore, why write in that style? Instead, we have set out to write a reference book you can dip into; a book in which you can turn to the section pertaining to a specific issue, get a handle on it, and find help on how to address it in your organisation. It is designed with a clear layout to help you find your way around... *but*, to do so effectively you must read this chapter. This chapter is your blueprint.

> **blue·print** (blü' prīnt')
> 1. A detailed plan of action.
> 2. A model or prototype.
> 3. Something intended as a guide for making something else; "a blueprint for a house".

A blueprint helps you to know how things fit together and how to begin building what you want to see come into existence. However... a blueprint does not build for you, nor is the end product the plans and drawings of a blueprint, but it is the house, office or cathedral. In the same way, this book is not designed to be an end product, but rather a guide to good materials and building techniques. You need to identify the building blocks of best practice appropriate to your organisation and assemble them in a style appropriate to your context.

How this book is organised

Section A – Viewing the site

This section introduces you to the book and how to use it, presents the previous study (ReMAP)—what it was, what it did and what it achieved—and then gives an overview of the follow up study (ReMAP II) on which this book is based, highlighting some key findings and implications.

Section B – The building blocks

This section comprises the bulk of the book, with each chapter covering a key issue that is a building block of best practice. In the case of a particularly large or complicated issue, there are sub-chapters focused on a particular aspect. All these chapters have the same layout marked with icons to allow easy navigation. Each chapter takes you through the key facts, the supporting data, key findings from the data, real world application, and examples from around the world.

Section C – Construction... in the real world

You may decide that this study gives the building blocks for a code of best practice which you can develop appropriate to your own context, be that organisational, national or regional level. However, putting together a meaningful and workable code of best practice requires care, effort and skill. Richard Tiplady, who oversaw the development of the Code of Best Practice for Short Term Mission in the UK shares insight and techniques on how to do this. There is also a copy of the questionnaire and a full index for ease of reference.

Getting an overview

The scoring

As part of the chapter headings and data tables, a simple graphical score indicates health or ill-health in an area, according to survey results. More white dots mean greater health, more black dots mean greater ill-health; or, to put it a different way, many black dots indicate an area requiring improvement.

Example:

○○○○○○○○○○	Ten white dots indicate excellent health
○○○○○○●●●●	A score in between indicates a degree of health or ill-health
○○○●●●●●●●	
●●●●●●●●●●	Ten black dots indicate severe ill health

Icons used in this book

 The key facts: this icon indicates key points from the chapter's topic.

 The data: a table showing the statistical results in an easy-to-read style (see page 6 for more detail).

 The key findings: the important highlights of a topic or sub-topic, summarised in bullet form for quick overview.

 What it means: here the data is discussed—why is the issue important and what effect does it have on retaining missionaries?

 Case study: a case study from the real world of missions.

 In the real world: a chart to provide some clear, practical ways to put the research findings into practice for your organisation (see page 7 for more detail).

 Website indicator: a mark to help you quickly identify where to get more information (see page 7 for more detail).

The data

Each chapter displays a data table, which contains a summary of responses to questions in the ReMAP II questionnaire. We have two categories: Old Sending Countries (OSC)—Australia, Europe, and North America, and New Sending Countries (NSC)—Africa, Asia, and South America, as often the answers from these two groups were significantly different.

For most chapters in Section B, a Health Score was derived from the average rating[1] on organisational practices by adding a 5 for each very high score (5-6), and subtracting a 2 for each mediocre rating (3-4) and subtracting a 5 for each low rating (0-2). This number was then reduced to the lower full digit and displayed in the data table as the number of white dots. In a few chapters (namely 6, 7 and 8), we determined how important a factor is for the selection of new mission candidates, so we have an "Importance for Selection" instead of a "Health Score."

The data table also highlights which factors are correlated strongly with missionary retention—this is shown with a tick.

The issue that the question asked about and the score relates to. For the full text of the question see the questionnaire in Chapter 35.

How did the Old Sending Countries rate on this issue?

How did the New Sending Countries rate on this issue?

Q. No.	Factor	OSC Health Score	✓	NSC Health Score	✓
41	Plans and job descriptions are communicated clearly to the missionary	○○○○○○●●●●	✓	○○○○○○●●●●	✓
42	There is a free flow of communication to and from the leadership	○○○○○○●●●●	✓	○○○○○○●●●●	
56	MIssionaries are assigned roles according to their gifting and experience	○○○○○○●●●●		○○○○○○●●●●	✓

The number on the questionnaire.

Does it significantly affect retention?

---

1   See page 32 for more details.

In the real world - the integral tables

Every chapter ends with an integral table. The tables are designed to stimulate seeking best practice through partnership. The question raised is: "Who can do what, when?"

Looking at the table from the top-down on the far left column are the stages of the sending process. However, the first row highlights tasks that should be done continuously.

Who? → When? ↓	Home Church	Missionary	Mission Agencies	External Partners
Continuous	➢ Disciple and mentor church members in vision for missions ➢ Let "being called" be a natural happening ➢ Have a culture of confirming people in their gifts and ministry ➢ Give trust and varied opportunities for involvement in ministry ➢ Let agency have a role in education programmes	➢ See confirmation of call by church as fundamental	➢ See endorsement of church and pastor as crucial ➢ Give input for programmes in church ➢ Provide short-term outreach opportunities as way to test calling	➢ Support in developing discipleship programmes ➢ Support by providing tools and standards for testing of calling
Recruitment	➢ Be available as a reference for candidates	➢ Be open to take time to let others be convinced of call	➢ Get church involved in test of calling	
on				

At the top, from left to right you see the missionary partners. Who might you think of when you see the broad categories of partners?

1. *Home Church:* Local Church, Church Mission Agency, Home Front Committee, Family
2. *Missionary:* Missionary, Partner, Child(ren)
3. *Mission agencies:* (Inter)National Agency, Agency/Partner on the field
4. *External partners:* Umbrella organizations (for example WEA Missions Commission or National Mission Movements), Specialists (Member Care, etc.), Training Institutes

The integral tables provide examples—they are not meant as a final answer and they are certainly not complete. In fact, they are purposely left incomplete, as we hope you start to think about what is already being done and are provoked to think of more ideas, even new ideas.

Please write about your own unique experiences and send us your case studies so we can make them available for others through the website or in a possible reprint of this book. What we really hope is that through thoughtful efforts, the link between "the missionary world" and "the church" is strengthened and the full potential of all partners is employed in strategic ways.

The website

This book has been written for church leaders, mission partners and mission agency leaders as the primary audiences. It has not been written for statisticians who want to analyse the figures, but rather for leaders and practitioners who want to use the findings to improve their own or their organisation's effectiveness in building the Kingdom of God. So if you think "standard deviation" sounds like something you could be arrested for—look no further, this book provides everything you need to use the results from the survey. It seeks to give enough data to understand the results, but not so much that you get lost in the detail.

However, the study is based on extensive statistical research and for those that want to delve deeper there are more technical details on-line at the website, www.worth-keeping.info. So if statistical data is important to you, please go online. There are many other resources and further case studies available at the website, as well as space for sharing your own examples of best practice and room to dialogue with others around the world who are reading *Worth Keeping*.

The other piece of the jigsaw

Also on the website you will find details of several studies that have been or are being conducted to find out what answers individual missionaries give when asked what issues could cause or have caused them to leave the mission field. For details of these and to take part, please go to www.worthkeeping.info/individuals

Where to start

If you want to know more about the study and its background go straight on to chapters 2 and 3. If you are ready to get stuck in with a particular issue just go to one of the issue chapters 4-33 or if you need more help logon to www.worthkeeping.info and click "Where to start."

2

ReMAP I

What ReMAP I said, did, and achieved

Detlef Blöcher

Introduction

We all know them, missionaries who departed from home with great enthusiasm, convinced that the Lord sent them—then returning after a short time with broken hearts and shattered vision, and now facing their disappointed home church and confused supporters. Why did it go wrong? What could have been done to prevent these tragic events?

At the 1993 National Missions Congress in Caxambu, Brazil, participants were shocked at the report given by a respected Brazilian missionary leader that 75% of that nation's cross-cultural missionaries quit their posts during their initial five-year term of service or don't return after the first furlough. Could a 20% per annum attrition figure possibly be true? None of the participants at the congress could confirm or refute the figure. There were simply no reliable data available.

Survey

This was the reason why the Mission Commission of the World Evangelical Alliance launched a comprehensive research project on missionary attrition called "Reducing Missionary Attrition Project" (ReMAP I). How many missionaries do actually return home and for what reasons? In addition, the new vibrant mission movement of Latin America, Africa and Asia had recently boomed. How do the new missionary sending countries (NSC) differ from the older missionary sending countries of North America, Europe and Australia (OSC)?

The staff of the World Evangelical Alliance Mission Commission (WEA-MC) designed the study process, and it was initially led by Rodolfo Girón, President of the Latin American mission movement COMIBAM and member of the MC's Executive Committee. Fourteen representative countries were selected, each with a sizeable mission force and an organised evangelical mission movement so that reliable data and a good return rate could be expected. They included countries from North America (USA, Canada), Latin America (Costa Rica, Brazil), Africa (Ghana, Nigeria), Europe (Denmark, Germany, Great Britain), Asia (India, Philippines, Singapore, South Korea) and Australia. A country coordinator from each country was chosen to administrate the survey. These leaders gathered in London (February 1995) and identified 26 specific causes of missionary attrition that they felt were of primary concern. With these issues in mind, the survey instrument was designed.

For practical and strategic reasons, the survey addressed mission leaders instead of individual missionaries for the following reasons: (1) the decision makers in their organisations are the ones who ultimately implement needed change, (2) mission leaders have a good overview and could present a more comprehensive and "aggregate" perspective, (3) working only with a single mission executive for each agency allowed the survey to be manageable, and (4) a higher return rate could be expected. Organisers understood that such a survey could also stimulate mission leaders' prayerful reflection on why they were losing valuable people from the field and could fuel their thinking on critical issues and show them practical solutions.

The researchers were aware of the different perspectives on why a missionary chooses to discontinue his/her ministry. Some reasons are explained in the missionary's prayer letter (called "stated reasons"), while additional reasons are revealed to his/her close friends/family ("personal reasons"). He/she may even believe in another set of reasons deep in his/her heart ("secret reasons"). The team or field leader may identify "leader's reasons" but only a subset may go on file ("recorded reasons"), the sending base director may believe in another array of reasons ("believed reasons") and in the mission's journal "socially accepted reasons" may be published, and the missionary's professional counsellor may identify further reasons, while the "true reasons" may be a combination of all of these—or even be different again. In fact, in most cases it is not one reason alone but often a whole range of reasons that all contribute to the decision. All of these perspectives are true insights, yet none of them are complete without the others. ReMAP I focused on the mission leaders' "believed reasons" because of the important process outcomes expected by having executive leadership involved. The study organisers urged agency leadership to collect data from members of their own organisations in ways that were both non-threatening and could help prevent unwanted attrition. Further studies are presently under way to listen to the missionaries' story and hear their voice. (See www.worthkeeping.info for further details.)

ReMAP I was designed to help missions leaders to take a "reality check" on their agencies and their national attrition and to seek for creative solutions to this costly problem. The success of the project would need to be measured by an overall reduction of missionary attrition, particularly among the mission agencies that participated in the study. This called for a follow-up study.

The second ReMAP study (ReMAP II) did indeed confirm a major improvement in attrition, particularly in the mission movements of the New Sending Countries

(NSC).[1] As in the first study, data on attrition was collected from all the participating countries and compared, but there were some major differences in the two studies. While the ReMAP I study primarily considered personal reasons for the return of missionaries (from the mission executives' perspective), the follow-up study ReMAP II ("Retaining Missionaries: Agency Practices") focused (1) on missionary retention and (2) on organisational issues: which structures and organisational practices keep missionaries in service, what makes their ministry fruitful?

ReMAP II was done eight years after the first study when the impact of the organisational changes initiated by ReMAP I would have been felt. While this encourages us to claim some credit for the overall improvement in attrition, in reality it is impossible to know how significant an influence ReMAP I actually had. The second study was not a "replication" study in the classical sense and this blurs our ability to pinpoint any cause-effect correlations. We do know, however, that the publication that stemmed from the ReMAP I study: *Too Valuable to Lose: Examining the Causes and Cures of Missionary Attrition*[2] was translated into four languages and widely used by agencies in discussing attrition. Anecdotal evidence for the effectiveness of this process driven research is also strong.

The original ReMAP I questionnaire asked the leaders of sending agencies for their practices and procedures as well as their number of returnees in the years 1992-94, and they were also asked to identify their predominant "believed reasons" for the return of their missionaries. Four hundred and fifty-five mission agencies with 23,000 long-term missionaries participated in the study and they reported 4,400 returnees in the years 1992-94—this sheer number exemplifies the scope of global missionary attrition and the need to work on this issue. The national break-down of participating agencies was as follows: Australia (44 agencies), Brazil (22), Canada (13), Costa Rica (6), Denmark (10), Germany (20), Ghana (52), Great Britain (37), India (20), Nigeria (14), Philippines (18), Singapore (7), South Korea (54), USA (114). Agencies from the New Sending Countries of Africa, Asia and Latin America (NSC) were analysed separately from those of the Old Sending Countries (OSC) of Europe and North America. OSCS and NSCS refer to agencies with low attrition, thus they receive a "S" mark for superior. OSCW and NSCW refer to agencies with high attrition, thus receiving a "W" mark for worse.

Causes of attrition

The attrition rate was calculated as the annual number of returnees divided by the number of active missionaries on the field of this agency[3]. In OSC 7.1 ± 0.3% of

---

1   Detlef Blöcher, "ReMAP II Affirms the Maturation of the Younger Mission Movement of the South," *Connections: The Journal of the WEA Mission Commission*, (Oct.. 2003), p. 48-53.

2   William D. Taylor, ed., *Too Valuable to Lose: Examining the Causes and Cures of Missionary Attrition*, (Pasadena, CA: William Carey Library, 1997).

3   The attrition rate has not been corrected for the number of newly arrived missionaries which should be subtracted from the number of active missionaries. Therefore agencies with dynamic growth or high turnover rate underestimate their actual attrition rate. Detlef Blöcher & Jonathan Lewis, "Further findings in the research data. Appendix B: Correction for rapidly growing agencies," Taylor, *Too Valuable to Lose*, 1997, p.122-123.

the active missionaries[4] (that is seven out of 100 active missionaries) leave their agency each year, which is about one out of 14 missionaries. This percentage is slightly higher than in the new and enthusiastic mission movement of NSC which loses only 6.4 ± 0.4% of its workforce each year (one out of 16 missionaries). As the aim of the study was to reduce missionary attrition, we distinguished between "unpreventable attrition" (i.e., regular retirement, death in service, completion of project) and "potentially preventable" reasons such as personal (i.e., emotional problems, immoral lifestyle), family (i.e., children's education, marriage problems), team (i.e., conflicts with co-missionaries), agency (i.e., financial problems, disagreement with leadership), work-related (i.e., personal dissatisfaction, lack of performance or training) and cultural reasons (i.e., unsuccessful cultural adjustment, language learning deficits).[5] Obviously there are more normal retirement and end of projects in OSC. Their unpreventable attrition rate (UAR) is almost three times higher (2.5 ± 0.14% per year) compared to NSC (0.93 ± 0.11% per year). Thus one third of the OSC returnees come home for unavoidable reasons, while two thirds (4.5 ± 0.2% per year) leave for potentially preventable reasons. In NSC, 6 out of 7 returnees come home for potentially preventable reasons, which amounts to 5.5 ± 0.3% per year. Figure 1 gives the break down of the groups of reasons for OSC and NSC as identified by their mission leaders (the two central columns in each set of bars). According to the executives' insights, personal reasons dominate among the preventable reasons, followed by agency- and work related reasons. Agency- and team-related reasons are more important in the new mission movement of the South which is assumed to still be maturing its mission structures and policies.

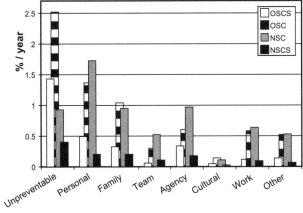

Fig. 1: Reasons for Attrition

As the aim of the study was to examine missionary attrition, agencies were grouped according to their potentially preventable attrition rate (PAR) into three blocks of equal numbers of missionaries: low (S-superior), middle (M) or high (W-worst) attrition.[6] These subgroups were compared with the full sample to identify patterns for excellence. The peripheral bars in Figure 1 (OSCS, NSCS) give the percentage of returnees of agencies with low attrition. Their total attrition rate is 3.0 ± 0.2% (OSCS) which is only 42% of that in OSC, respectively 1.3 ± 0.2% in NSCS, which is only one-fifth of that in NSC. As

---

4   The number following the "±" symbol gives the "standard error" of the average due to the stochastic nature of attrition. The average is absolutely precise, but the question arises what the average number might be if another year had been considered or another ten agencies or 100 missionaries had been added to the study. This uncertainty of the "true average" is characterised by the standard error (67% percent confidence interval).

5   Complete list of reasons (as used in the questionnaire) is given in Fig. 2.

6   This procedure is only applicable for agencies with more than 25 missionaries. Only they had a sufficient number of returnees in the three years period 1992-94 to calculate a reliable attrition rate. OSC included 233 agencies with 14,324 missionaries that provided attrition data; NSC (181 agencies with 7,183 missionaries); OSCS (41 agencies with 4,788 missionaries, PAR < 2.83 % per year); NSCS (29 agencies with 2,000 missionaries, PAR < 2.14% per year).

these attrition rates are based on the actual performance of the sizeable subgroup of low attrition agencies (one third of the missionaries in the total sample) and not on abstract definitions or theoretical circumstances, the numbers demonstrate the huge room for organisational improvement. Indeed, two-thirds of all missionary attrition could have possibly been avoided.

To our great surprise, even the rate for "unpreventable attrition" (UAR) comes down. At first this fact sounds illogical, but we need to keep in mind that the definition of unpreventable attrition includes reasons like: completion of contract, end of project, political unrest and marriage to a person outside the mission family—and these reasons are not absolutely fixed but can possibly be influenced by good member care, effective mission structures and opportunities for reassignment after the completion of a project. Figure 1 shows that low attrition agencies have indeed reduced their "unpreventable attrition" by 50%.

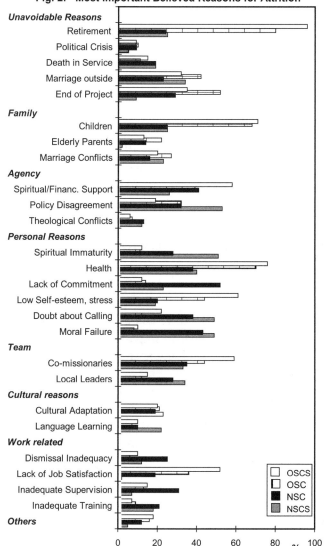

Fig. 2:   Most Important Believed Reasons for Attrition

The reduction of preventable attrition is even larger. Figure 1 shows that the personal, family, team, agency, and work-related attrition have been reduced to one fifth in NSCS (compared to the full sample NSC) and to one third in OSCS—yet agency-related attrition is more resistant to reduction in OSC.[7] These impressive facts prove that the majority of attrition cases could have indeed be prevented. Figure 2 gives the definitions of the various groups of reasons. Mission executives were also asked to identify those seven factors out of the list of 26 important reasons which they consider most important in the return of their missionary.

Figure 2 gives the percentage of all missionaries of the samples whose leaders had ticked the stated issue as one of the seven most important reasons. In OSC *Regular retirement* was considered the prime factor, followed by *Health problems, Missionary children and their education, Project end, Low self-esteem, Conflicts with co-missionaries, Marriage outside the mission, Lack of spiritual or financial support, Lack of job satisfaction, Disagreements over*

---

7   For this reason, agency-related and personal reasons have gained in relative weight in OSCS, and family reasons in NSCS.

policies and *Marriage problems*. These factors need special attention in OSC when agencies work on their policies and practices. In low attrition agencies (OSCS), *Retirement, Health problems, Missionary children, Conflicts with co-missionaries, Low self-esteem, Lack of spiritual and financial support* and *Lack of job-satisfaction* have gained in relative importance compared to OSC, while *Project end, Marriage outside the mission, Disagreement over policies, Marriage problems* and *Care for elderly parents* have lost in significance. The latter issues have been cared for well so that they are not large factors in attrition.

In NSC agencies, *Lack of missionary's commitment* was considered as the prime cause, followed by *Moral failure, Lack of spiritual and financial support, Health problems, Doubt about calling, Conflicts with co-missionaries, Disagreements over policies, Lack of supervision, Project end, Spiritual immaturity, Relational problems with local leaders at the place of service, Dismissal by agency, Missionary children, Normal retirement* and *Marriage outside the mission*. These are the greatest challenges to NSC missionaries and the leaders have to wrestle with these issues. This list is completely different from that for OSC and it mainly exposes inefficient candidate selection and lack of personal support. In NSC agencies with low attrition NSCS, *Disagreement over policies, Spiritual immaturity, Doubt about calling, Moral failure,* and *Marriage outside the mission* gained in relative weight, while *Lack of commitment, Lack of spiritual and financial support, Lack of supervision, Project end, Dismissal by agency* had lost significance. Organisational issues have apparently been dealt with well so that personal issues have gained in relevance, which is related to careful candidate selection and personal support during service. These topics direct the road to excellence for NSC agencies.

How to further reduce missionary attrition

As we were particularly interested in how to reduce missionary attrition, mission executives were also given a list of 12 important issues (listed in Figure 3), and asked (a) to select the three factors they believed to be most effective in *further* reducing their missionary attrition and (b) to identify the three factors which they felt to be the least important factors on the list of 12 important factors. Figure 3 gives the percentage of missionaries from the samples whose mission leaders selected the mentioned factor to be one of the three top factors to further reduce their missionary attrition.

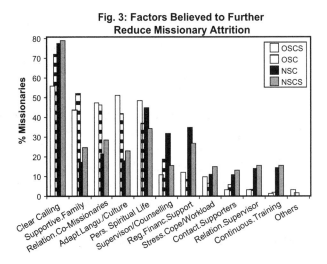

Fig. 3: Factors Believed to Further Reduce Missionary Attrition

In OSC, *A clear sense of God's calling into mission service* is considered as the most important topic, named by the leaders of more than 70% of all OSC missionaries in the survey. It was followed by *Supportive family, Good relationships with co-missionaries,*

Ability to adapt to different culture and learn new language and *Maintaining a healthy personal spiritual life*. In the low attrition subgroup OSCS, *Calling* is still the prime factor yet with a smaller percentage (apparently it has been dealt with effectively and thus lost in significance), while *Adaptability to a different culture and learning language* and *Maintenance of personal spiritual life* have gained in significance.

In NSC agencies *Clear calling* is considered most important, followed by *Maintenance of personal spiritual life*, *Regular financial support* and *Supervision*. *Good relationships with missionary colleagues*, *Supportive family* and *Adaptability to language and culture* come next, yet with a much lower rating than in OSC. In the low attrition subgroup NSCS, *Clear calling* has received an even higher rating at the expense of *Maintenance of personal spiritual life*, *Regular financial support* and *Supervision*. The latter have apparently been dealt with well in these agencies. The rating of NSCS appears to lean more towards that in OSC.

In order to further pinpoint the most important issues, we subtracted the percentage of missionaries whose leaders had rated an issue as one of the three less important issues out of the 12 stated issues (3Min) from the percentages of 3Max, resulting in a differential percentage of missionaries (3Max-3Min) which runs from 80% to −80%[8]. Figure 4 gives the results which further highlight the prime role of *Clear calling*, followed by *Supportive family*, *Relationships with co-missionaries*, *Adaptability to language and culture* and *Maintenance of personal spiritual life*. These are the five big issues in OSC, and they are also the most important issues in the low attrition agencies OSCS, although in revised order. *Adaptability to language and culture* and *Personal spiritual life* had gained in relevance at the expense of *Calling* and *Supportive family*. The latter have apparently been dealt with so well that it will not yield in further reduction of missionary attrition.

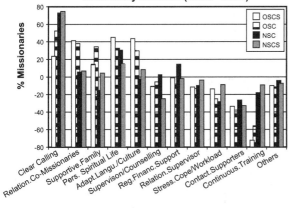

Fig. 4: Factors Believed to Further Reduce Missionary Attrition (3Max - 3Min)

In NSC agencies *Calling* is even more dominant, followed by *Maintenance of personal spiritual life*, *Regular financial support*, *Good relationships with missionary colleagues* and *Supervision*. In the low attrition subgroup NSCS *Maintenance of personal spiritual life*, *Supervision* and *Regular financial support* have apparently been solved so well that additional investment in these areas would not further reduce their missionary attrition. Yet, *Supportive family*, *Adaptability to language and culture*, *Relationship to superiors*, *Stress cope-ability* and *Continuous training* have gained in relative weight. These issues need careful consideration as agencies work on their organisational development.

---

8   Negative numbers are obtained when more mission leaders considered it as one of the three less important factors (3Min) than as one of the three most important factors (3Max).

In order to further reduce unwanted missionary attrition we explored correlations between various agency characteristics and preventable attrition (PAR).

Agency size

Figure 5 gives the preventable attrition rate (PAR) as a function of agency size, demonstrating that small agencies lose a huge percentage of their workers.[9] PAR falls with agency size, reaching the baseline at an agency size of 50+ active missionaries. This correlation is observed in OSC and NSC. Further studies have shown that small agencies have less structure and expertise, but not to the extent to explain this huge difference in attrition rates. It appears that a "critical mass" of missionaries for survival on the field, a balanced mix of gifting and experience in a ministry team, and specialisation in services in the home office are required to be effective. We believe that this impressive fact directs us to the biblical concept of cooperation and fellowship in ministry that the Lord has commanded us (John 17:21, 1 Cor. 12:4-6, Eph. 4:1-6, 1 Peter 4:10).

Fig. 5: Agency Size

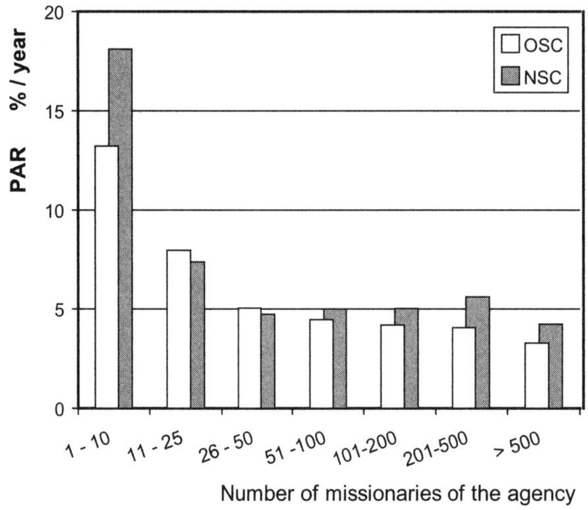

(PAR % / year vs. Number of missionaries of the agency; legend: OSC, NSC)

Agency age

Figure 6 gives the preventable attrition rate (PAR) as function of the age of the agency. It is evident that young agencies have an increased attrition rate as they lack experience and have not yet developed their way of operation. PAR comes down as the agency matures, yet old agencies (>100 years) have again an increased attrition rate as they may lose their original vision, dynamic and enthusiasm.

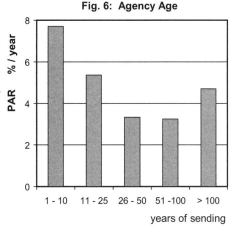

Fig. 6: Agency Age

(PAR % / year vs. years of sending: 1-10, 11-25, 26-50, 51-100, > 100)

Candidate selection

Agencies were asked for details of their candidate selection procedure and in particular whether or not they consider 13 specific areas of life (listed in Figure 7). This diagram gives the percentages of the missionaries of the samples that had been checked on this issue during their application procedure. The chart proves that the basics like *Calling*, *Doctrinal position*, *Physical health examination*, *Acceptance*

---

9   The unpreventable attrition rate of small agencies was also three times higher than in large agencies in OSC (6.8 ± 0.9 % vs. 2.4 ± 0.1 %) and NSC (2.0 ± 0.5 % vs. 0.8 ± 0.1 %), so that agencies with fewer than ten missionaries lose a fifth of their work force each year.

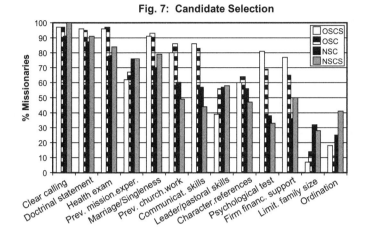

Fig. 7: Candidate Selection

of present family status (marriage/ singleness), Previous experience in church work and *Communication and relational skills* are considered by most agencies, yet some agencies have deficits regarding *Character references, Psychological and personality testing* and *Communication skills.* OSC agencies have somewhat more rigorous procedures than NSC, and low attrition agencies (OSCS, NSCS) invest significantly more in their candidate selection than the total samples.

Careful candidate selection also proved to be one of the decisive areas for reducing missionary attrition. Figure 8 gives the average preventatable attrition rate (PAR) of agencies that had (or not) considered the mentioned area of life as part of their application procedure. The diagram proves that *Health Examination, Missionary's calling, Acceptance of the present family status (marriage/singleness), Character references, Firm financial support of the home church/supporters* or applied *Psychological or personality testing* are critical areas and agencies that did not check them suffered an increased attrition rate.

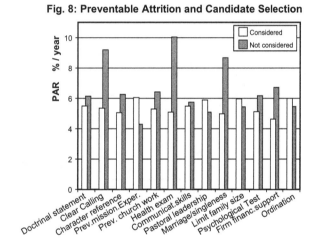

Fig. 8: Preventable Attrition and Candidate Selection

This fact is also demonstrated in Figure 9, giving the average preventable attrition rate (PAR) depending on the number of areas covered in the agency's selection procedure. Again it proves the significance of careful candidate selection: agencies with little or careless candidate selection suffer greatly increased preventable attrition.

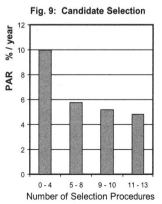

Fig. 9: Candidate Selection

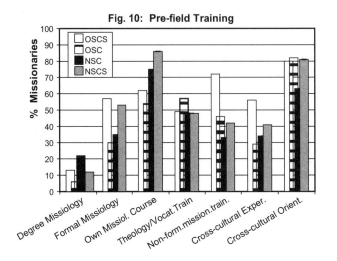

Fig. 10: Pre-field Training

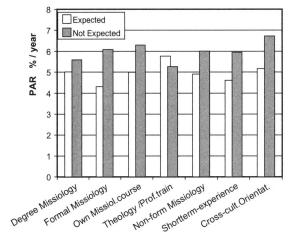

Fig. 11: Preventable Attrition and Pre-field Training

Pre-field training

Another critical area is pre-field training. Figure 10 gives the percentage of all missionaries of the samples whose agencies expect the mentioned pre-field training for acceptance of new missionaries.[10] Most agencies provide their *Own missiological course* as well as an *Orientation programme*, yet missiological training is not always required. It is obvious that agencies with low attrition have higher requirements regarding missiological training. This evidence is further emphasised in Figure 11, which gives the average preventable attrition rate (PAR) of agencies that do or do not expect this type of training from their new missionaries. The results show that missiological training and cross-cultural experience are of great value for mission longevity. Figure 12 shows PAR depends on the total number of training units (mentioned in Figure 11) expected by the agency from their new missionaries and again proves the correlation between high training standards and low attrition (consider overlap in the training modules of Figure 10).

Care for missionaries on the field

Figure 13 shows the percentage of field missionaries of the sample that are provided with a certain service on the field. Most of the missionaries (nine out of ten) get *Supervision on the field*, yet not all are supplied with the other provisions. *Annual leave*, *Effective missionary team*, *MK-schooling* and *Member care by a person other*

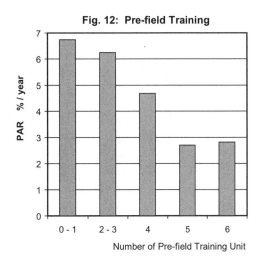

Fig. 12: Pre-field Training

---

10   It remains a mystery to me why Theological training and Professional training had been put into one group.

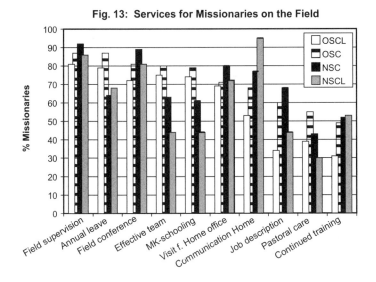

Fig. 13: Services for Missionaries on the Field

than field leader are more important to OSC agencies, while NSC agencies put stronger emphasis on *Regular communication with home churches*, *Field conferences* and *Annual visit from the home office.*

In general NSC agencies provide the same amount of services to their missionaries as OSC, and low attrition agencies do not provide more than the total group. It appears that services on the field in themselves do not keep missionaries in ministry, unless thwey are predated by careful candidate selection and pre-field training.

The effect of member care is shown in Figure 14, giving the preventable attrition rate (PAR) in dependence on the amount of total staff time invested in member care for NSC. It is obvious that agencies with little member care suffer very high preventable attrition. PAR declines with the investment in member care up to a time—8% of the total organisational time (at home and on the field). Beyond this value, PAR increased again. Can there be a 'too much' member care? Indeed, if mission teams are too much concerned about their internal relationships at the expense of their ministry and looking out for unusual emotional feelings they may even cause what they expect. Agencies known for their intensive member care may also be approached by unsuitable candidates and their home office may be inclined to accept them trusting on the good care on the field, but in most cases such graciousness will not pay off. In addition we need to keep in mind that we just estimate the amount of member care, but not its quality.

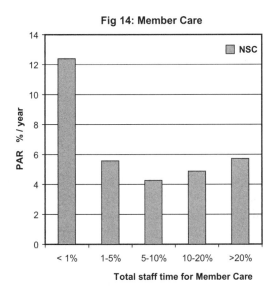

Fig 14: Member Care

Summary

The ReMAP I study has been one of the first global studies on missionary attrition, particularly in comparing the older and newer mission movements. It has identified a number of critical areas in candidate selection, pre-field training, leadership, organisational structure, and member care that have a tremendous impact on missionary attrition.

The characteristics of agencies with very low return rates can serve as models. Their example will direct the way for reducing unwanted loss of missionaries. Member care is not a department added on to the administration, but a characteristic feature that determines the overall operations: a shepherd's heart.

Yet missionary attrition is just the "tip of an iceberg." Many more missionaries are worn out by personal concerns, frustrations and disappointment that deplete their energy and joy and reduce their effectiveness—but they may not have the courage to face reality and go home. Therefore, the issues mentioned above have a much wider scope than just missionary attrition. They relate to the effectiveness of all missionaries.

Moreover, we do not consider reduction of missionary attrition as an end in itself, unless the missionary is really productive in a vital ministry. Missionaries can be ill-placed or be unsuitable for a given task and in need of reassignment or to be brought home with grace and dignity. Wounded and tired missionaries need restoration and our full compassion. Missionaries can also stay for too long and thus hinder the development of local leadership instead of moving on to a new ministry. Mission agencies need specific criteria for completion of a project and a clear exit-strategy before even starting a project.

What ReMAP I did

Statistics are of limited value. They serve to provide information to decision makers so that they can make organisational changes and improvements. In the example given in the introduction statistical information was desperately needed to clarify what turned out to be disinformation that was very discouraging. To their relief, ReMAP I showed Brazilian mission leaders that their national annual attrition rate was actually $8.5 \pm 0.9\%$ and not the 20% as claimed by that speaker (some agencies have indeed lost 20% per year but these are individual agencies and/or exceptional years). Still, the national attrition rate was of great concern as their preventable attrition rate, PAR, was 50% higher than the global average. Follow-up on the study encouraged mission agency, Bible school, and church leadership to prayerfully discuss their procedures and practices, and to implement needed change. The result of putting the spotlight on attrition is found in the follow-up study ReMAP II, where the Brazilian national preventable attrition rate was down to 2.6%, one-third of what it was eight years before. This statistic points to the massive improvements—improvements that are saving the mission careers of at least 250 Brazilian missionaries each year. ReMAP I claims modest credit for these marvellous results.

The ReMAP I study developed a survey tool for in-house attrition studies used by various agencies to analyse where and when they lost their valuable missionaries and to take appropriate action.

Without a doubt, the ReMAP I study drew great attention to the key issue of missionary agency member care and has given a tremendous boost to those concerned about these issues around the world. A Mission Commission Member Care Network (MemCa) was spawned with the development of various national and international member networks and the publication of numerous member care resources. Their internet site offers (www.membercare.org) a number of resources. Only by the mutual sharing of expertise has this been possible.

Likewise, the agencies' minimal requirements in missiological training have grown in the past eight years as ReMAP I has highlighted the importance of missionary training. In 1994 only 6% of the OSC missionaries were expected to hold an academic degree in missiology. In 2002 it had increased to 23%. And the percentage of missionaries expected to have formal missiological training increased from 29% to 35%.

Attrition issues have spotlighted the need for whole person or "integral" missionary training. Integral training concepts of including substantial informal and practical missionary training have been developed, especially in the newer sending countries. Increased international attention has been focused on this through another Mission Commission affiliate, the International Missionary Training Network (www.missionarytraining.com). ReMAP I has also promoted the continuous training of missionaries. Many leading missionary institutions have developed long-distance programmes for academic and practical missionary training and flexible units adaptable to the needs and time frames of missionaries. Missionaries are not trained once for life, but are growing into a lifestyle of life-long learning.

ReMAP II shows that candidate selection procedures have grown tremendously in the past eight years, especially in NSC. The percentage of missionaries asked for character references has grown from 54% to 99% in the past eight years. 92% (instead of formerly 77%) have physical examinations and 64% (instead of 37%) received psychological testing. Similar evidence is found in the areas of calling, ministry experience in their home church and acceptance of the present marital status—and also for OSC. Statistical information helps agencies understand the critical areas that need to be clarified before the acceptance of a new missionary.

One real benefit of international studies such as ReMAP I and II is the level of co-operation that must be evoked to carry it out both internationally and on a national scale. These relationships don't end when the study is finished. Thus, national alliances are strengthened as agencies work together. The German Evangelical Mission Alliance (AEM), for example, has recently set up payroll services for smaller mission agencies to provide the extensive expertise to cope with the constant changes in labour laws and social security. Without a doubt, both ReMAP studies have brought significant cohesion to participating national mission movements.

It is difficult to tell which of these improvements has been the direct result of the ReMAP process, yet the bottom line is that over the past eight years the missionary attrition rate in NSC has dropped by 50% and also remained low in OSC in spite of the global trend towards shorter appointments and frequent career changes. This is an example of how process focused mission research can draw attention to critical issues, stimulate organisational development, and ultimately foster change leading to greater effectiveness in extending the Kingdom of God. ReMAP I has certainly helped keep many more missionaries in service and make their ministry even more fruitful, releasing blessing to the nations of the world and honour to God.

3

ReMAP II
Project Methodology

An example of collaborative international research and teamwork

Valerie Lim,[1] Singapore

This chapter describes the methodology for the ReMAP II project, which was a multi-national collaborative effort by a team of researchers who conducted a mission survey simultaneously in 22 countries on six continents. The continued interest and positive impact of the ReMAP II findings around the world have been partly due to its robust project methodology,[2] which has been openly commended by other researchers.[3]

ReMAP and ReMAP II

In 2002, the Mission Commission of the World Evangelical Alliance (WEA-MC) commissioned the ReMAP II project. As the name implies, ReMAP II was the second of two projects.

The first project was simply known as ReMAP, an acronym for "Reducing Missionary Attrition Project" and its main objectives were to:

- Identify the core causes of missionary attrition,

---

1 Valerie Lim is a Research Associate of Global Mapping International and an Associate of the Mission Commission of the World Evangelical Alliance. She was the Singapore coordinator for the ReMAP II project. Trained as a scientist, Valerie worked for many years in multi-disciplinary research, project management, staff development and training in the manufacturing industry and a local university. Over the years, she has participated in several collaborative projects with researchers from different countries.

2 A paper on ReMAP II methodology was presented by the author during the Fourth International Lausanne Researchers' Conference in Cyprus in April 2005. The session on "ReMAP II Research Process and Key Findings" stimulated lively discussion among the researchers. Many commended the ReMAP II project's careful planning and the cooperation of its multi-national research team.

3 Dr. Todd M. Johnson, Director of the Centre for the Study of Global Christianity at Gordon Conwell Theological Seminary, was at the conference. He has described the ReMAP II survey as "one of the most comprehensive and careful surveys of missionaries ever done." He suggested "Frontier missions advocates should look forward to more research results from the WEA ReMAP II study." *International Journal of Frontier Missions*, Vol. 22:4, (Oct. – Dec. 2005), p. 151.

- Determine the extent and nature of the problem,

- Explore solutions to the problem, and

- Deliver products and services to mission agencies and churches worldwide that would help reduce undesirable attrition.

ReMAP involved a survey conducted in 14 missionary-sending countries between 1994 and 1996. A common survey form had been developed, and it was used in each participating country. In April 1996, an international workshop on missionary attrition was held at All Nations Christian College, UK, and key findings from ReMAP were presented. Subsequently, a book[4] was published in 1997 with many articles about missionary attrition and helpful suggestions on how to prevent avoidable loss of mission personnel.

The ReMAP survey was designed as a qualitative study, which limited its potential for in-depth analysis of some issues. Some questions remained unanswered, such as:

- What helps missionaries to grow into fruitful ministry?

- What helps missionaries to stay in service for the long term, in spite of changing circumstances and needs?

- Which organisational structures and practices provide effective support to missionaries and provide the best environment for productive ministry?

- What constitutes effectiveness in ministry?

These and other questions were on many minds when leaders in the Mission Commission of the World Evangelical Alliance prepared for ReMAP II. While the previous study ReMAP had focused mainly on missionary attrition and personal reasons for the early return of missionaries from the field,[5] the new study ReMAP II would centre on missionary retention and agency practices.

Hence, ReMAP II or "Retaining Missionaries, Agency Practices." In ReMAP II, the main objectives would be to:

- Identify the "best agency practices" that contribute to missionary retention,

- Promote these "good practices" in the global missions community, and

- Provide tools for mission agencies to strengthen missionary retention.

But why study "missionary retention"? Jim Van Meter explains the reasons as follows: "The retention of personnel is all about stewardship. It is about retaining people for good reasons. It is about the blessing of making appropriate changes to practices for the sake of the kingdom of God. It is about minimizing turnover due to inappropriate reasons. All for the purpose of fulfilling the call of God upon the individuals as well as the organisation. The (ReMAP II) project highlights those

4 William D. Taylor, ed., *Too Valuable to Lose: Exploring the Causes and Cures of Missionary Attrition*, (Pasadena, CA: William Carey Library, 1997).

5 Detlef Blöcher and Jonathan Lewis, "Further Findings in the Research Data," in *Too Valuable to Lose*, pp. 105-125.

practices and services of mission agencies that contribute most to the retention of good people, while minimizing avoidable turnover."[6]

Preliminary planning for ReMAP II

Long before the ReMAP II project began, much preliminary planning occurred between January 2001 and May 2002.

In January 2001, the leadership team of the WEA-MC (Dr. William Taylor, Dr. Jonathan Lewis and Dr. Bertil Ekström) met together with Dr. Jim Van Meter, and they outlined the direction of a follow-up study on ReMAP. They set up a steering committee comprising Dr. Seth Anyomi (Ghana), Dr. Detlef Blöcher (Germany), Dr. Jonathan Lewis (Argentina), Dr. Steve Moon (Korea), and Dr. Jim Van Meter (USA), thus representing five continents.

The committee members corresponded by e-mail for several months. Then, they met face-to-face for two days during the WEA-MC meeting at Port Dickson, Malaysia, from 2 to 3 May 2001 to develop the survey strategy and focus. After that meeting, Dr. Barbara Griffin (Australia) joined the team, which now represented six continents.

The steering committee developed the following strategy and focus for ReMAP II:

- The ReMAP II project would be a quantitative study that would survey mission agencies (not individual missionaries).

- The survey would be facilitated through evangelical national mission movements (NMM) in order to achieve maximum impact. Thus, only those countries with an active and functional NMM could be considered as potential participating countries.

- By collaborating with the NMM in a participating country, the WEA-MC sought credibility for the study as well as high response to the survey. The NMM would assist in the entire survey process: distributing the questionnaire, providing clarification about questions, arranging for translation of the questionnaire (if necessary), doing follow up on non-respondents, checking for the completeness of responses, as well as assisting in the data entry.

- In each participating country, the survey would be conducted by individuals (country coordinators) who know the mission agencies including their organisational structure. The national country coordinator would conduct interviews with the executives of missionary-sending agencies. A survey tool (ReMAP II questionnaire) would guide the information gathering on the existing organisational practices.

- The intention of ReMAP II was not simply to conduct a survey. The ReMAP II project also sought to initiate change within missionary-sending agencies.

---

6 Jim Van Meter, "Distinctive Practices in High Retention USA Agencies," in *Connections: the Journal of the Mission Commission of the World Evangelical Alliance*, Vol. 3:2 (June 2004), pp. 26-29.

Hence, the outcomes of the survey would be reported to each participating agency, so that the findings could stimulate its organisational development.

• In ReMAP II, we would work from a perspective of the "Kingdom of God." We would not glorify an agency or a country for its excellent performance, nor would we shame one with poor performance, but we would identify what values or practices contribute to missionary retention. The results of ReMAP II would highlight the best practices in a significant group of high retaining agencies from all the participating countries.

Having agreed on the survey strategy and focus, the steering committee approached the national mission movements in both Old Sending Countries (OSC)[7] and New Sending Countries (NSC)[8] to invite them to participate in the ReMAP II project.

For the selection of participating countries, the steering committee decided that:

• The ReMAP II survey would deliberately be designed as a truly international study. The participating countries would come from six continents, with invitations sent to both the older NMM and the newly emerging NMM.

• We would seek to keep a global balance. Instead of accepting a maximum number of participating countries in each continent, we would select representative countries.

The steering committee eventually selected 22 representative countries from six continents. The OSC selected were Australia, Canada, Germany, United Kingdom, Netherlands, New Zealand, Sweden, USA, and South Africa. The NSC selected were Argentina, Brazil, Costa Rica, El Salvador, Ghana, Guatemala, Hong Kong, India, South Korea, Malaysia, Nigeria, Philippines, and Singapore. Each participating country was requested to appoint a country coordinator, someone who could be responsible for coordinating the ReMAP II project in the country. In most cases, this country coordinator was appointed in consultation with the local NMM.

The actual ReMAP II project involved three main phases:

• Phase I was Survey Preparation, from June 2002 to October 2002.

• Phase II was Research and Data analysis, from November 2002 to May 2003.

• Phase III was Reporting and Training, from June 2003 onwards.

---

7 Old Sending Countries (OSC) are mostly from Europe, North America and Australia. They have an average of 60 years experience. South Africa was included in this group due to its long experience in missionary sending.

8 New Sending Countries (NSC) are mostly from Africa, Asia, and Latin America. They have less than 30 years experience.

Phase One: Survey preparation

The steering committee continued working prior to the gathering of the ReMAP II project team. They designed a programme for an intensive week of discussions as well as an orientation of our team to the project's administrative procedures.

In October 2002, the newly appointed country coordinators from 20 of the 22 nations, together with five of the six-member steering committee, gathered for one week in London, United Kingdom. During the week (6–10 October 2002), the steering committee facilitated a series of sessions during which the country coordinators discussed Survey Preparation as well as the subsequent phases of the ReMAP II project.

This gathering of country coordinators was significant, because it marked the beginning of collaborative efforts by the ReMAP II team. Unlike other projects, this project began with a strong commitment towards international collaboration.

The servant leadership of the steering committee was effective in promoting teamwork. The committee encouraged open communication and a free flow of ideas, so that each individual could learn from the others. Coming from different cultures, we had to take time to listen to other views. We needed to understand our respective expectations, priorities, natural work patterns, decision-making processes, and communication styles. As we got to know one another, mutual trust and respect was built between individuals in the newly formed ReMAP II team. Everyone soon realised that we could harness our individual strengths by working collectively and by consensus.

Our sessions on survey preparation began with a presentation of the research strategy for ReMAP II, which was thoroughly discussed. Having understood the objectives for the project, the team was ready to jointly develop the survey tool (ReMAP II questionnaire). We examined a draft questionnaire prepared by prior empirical and theoretical work of the steering committee (Dr. Detlef Blöcher and Dr. Barbara Griffin). A high priority had been placed on construct validity[9] and content validity.[10] Items in the draft were based on ReMAP and other research findings on attrition. The draft comprised ten sections (from A to J) with questions on:

A. The agency and the ministry priorities of missionaries on the field

B. Pre-field screening of candidates

C. Education level of missionaries

D. Pre-field training and other training

E. Pastoral member care

F. Agency operation (with subsections on communication, orientation and continuous training, ministry, ministry outcome, personal care and family support, finances and home office)

---

9 Construct validity is the extent to which a measure corresponds to the underlying theoretical rationale.
10 Content validity is the appropriateness of a given measure as subjectively assessed by an expert.

G. Factors that contribute to on-field effectiveness

H. Factors that hinder on-field effectiveness

I. Length of service record[11]

J. Retention record[12]

We would ask mission executives about their organisational ethos, leadership practices, and personnel procedures, as well as for personnel data on missionary sending over a 20-year period. We would also ask them to identify what they considered were factors that contribute most to their missionaries' present effectiveness, and the factors that most hinder missionaries from attaining their on-field objectives. These open-ended questions would look beyond the assessment of present agency practices, and they sought the mission executives' insights and wisdom on how to improve the local mission movement and their own organisational development.

The draft questionnaire provided the framework for our consultations on the face validity and cross-cultural implications of the questions. For example, prior work had not identified "family approval and/or blessing" as a key factor during the selection of missionaries. The Asian and African country coordinators explained that "family approval and/or blessing" was a potentially important factor in missionary retention, especially where filial piety and respect of elders are strong cultural values. Thus, we included a question on this factor under pre-field screening of mission applicants. With further input from the country coordinators, the draft ReMAP II questionnaire grew to 148 questions. The majority felt that this was far too long to secure a good response.

Through a lengthy process of negotiations, we agreed on a common survey tool comprising 98 questions in an eight-paged document. Our final document (ReMAP II questionnaire[13]) reflected a consensus among all parties. It was a satisfying experience to see how the entire ReMAP II team had reached this through give and take. We were patient to consider different opinions and issues, and to evaluate our options. In the end, everyone believed our common survey tool would be equally meaningful in our different countries and cultures, within our mission movements with different states of development and respective needs.

Following this, the team spent time discussing various details for the research process and data analysis phase, including strategies for translation, administration and increasing response rate. In addition, we considered some material for the reporting and training phase, which had been prepared by the steering committee (Dr. Jonathan Lewis and Dr. Jim Van Meter).

After the meeting in London, each country coordinator returned to their home country to produce the ReMAP II questionnaire, to arrange for questions to be translated into a local language (where necessary), and to enlist local volunteers

---

11 The *Length of service record* section would obtain data on the average length of service for a specific group of missionaries who left the agency. (We later agreed to use the two-year period between 1 January 2001 and 31 December 2002).

12 The *Retention record* was a request for personnel data. Each agency was asked to provide data for missionary sending over the past 20 years. (We later agreed to use the years from 1981 to 2000).

13 The ReMAP II Questionnaire can be found in Chapter 35.

to assist in conducting the survey. In countries where translation was necessary, a "back translation" strategy was used, whereby each translated questionnaire was translated back into English and checked for clarity and meaning. In some cases, the translated draft was field-tested and further improvements were made.

The ReMAP II project team of country coordinators and steering committee continued to keep in touch with one another. A key means of communication was a special e-mail forum called 'remapii' on Yahoo Groups. Each coordinator was encouraged to report on the progress of the ReMAP II project in his/her country. From time to time, different individuals exchanged tips on how to manage any problems associated with the research process. The ReMAP II team continued praying for each other's work for many months, as they were informed by the regular news and reports posted on the forum.

Phase Two: Research and data analysis

Phase II began in early 2003 with research projects being launched simultaneously in 22 countries around the world. OSC that participated were Australia, Canada, Germany, United Kingdom, Netherlands, New Zealand, Sweden, USA, and South Africa. NSC that participated was Argentina, Brazil, Costa Rica, El Salvador, Ghana, Guatemala, Hong Kong, India, South Korea, Malaysia, Nigeria, Philippines, and Singapore.

The study was confined to missionary-sending agencies[14] that send long-term[15] cross-cultural[16] missionaries. A ReMAP II questionnaire was sent to all known evangelical mission agencies (or "missionary sending bases") in each participating country. It was accompanied by a recommendation letter from a well-known evangelical leader and contact details (such as a hotline telephone number) of the country coordinator who was available to answer further questions.

The entire ReMAP II study was conducted with utmost confidentiality to protect the identity and responses from individual "missionary sending bases."[17] To ensure confidentiality, we used a research code comprising two alpha characters[18] and four numerals[19] on the cover of each questionnaire. The research code enabled us to keep a record of questionnaires as they were mailed, and to determine those that were returned and those that were not. In a few countries, the survey was administered by the mission alliance office, which assigned the research codes, distributed the questionnaires and followed up on non-respondents. All completed questionnaires

14 "Agency" refers to a sending base that is an independent mission, a denominational mission department, or a church that sends out missionaries without the assistance of another organisation.

15 Long-term or career missionaries are expected to serve for at least 3 years.

16 Cross-cultural missionaries serve in a culture other than their own. Normally they learn a different language and/or make significant cultural adjustment. They may serve within their country or abroad.

17 Confidentiality meant that no name of church or mission agency appeared on the research questionnaire.

18 The two alpha characters used were the ISO country code for the country.

19 The first digit of the four numerals coded for the type of sending base: whether a denominational mission agency ('1'), an inter-denominational mission agency ('2'), a local church sending their missionaries independently of mission agencies ('3'), or some other type of sending base in the country. The other three numerals were issued at random from 001 onwards, so that every sending base had a unique code.

were sent to the country coordinator, who received the results and research codes without knowing the identities of sending agencies. Our emphasis on confidentiality encouraged truthful answers to the questions.

Returned questionnaires were checked for completeness and obvious mistakes or unlikely results. Data from each questionnaire yielded a dataset (corresponding to a particular agency and identified by its unique research code), which was carefully transcribed to a Microsoft Excel worksheet.[20]

Datasets from the 22 countries were eventually merged together into an international database.[21] This pooling together of data was possible due to our common survey methodology. The extensive ReMAP II database, built from the responses from 22 countries, consisted of datasets for some 600 mission agencies with almost 40,000 long-term cross-cultural missionaries.[22]

Data analysis of the ReMAP II database was facilitated by the statistical tools available to worksheets in the Microsoft Excel software. Below are two essential calculations in this study: retention rates, and weighted averages.

Retention rates

The main concept for ReMAP II is the term "Retention," which refers to the percentage of missionaries still in active ministry after a period of time 't' (that is years of service).

From the personnel data in the retention record,[23] the Annual Retention Rate (RR) for each agency could be calculated as follows: First, we calculated RR_t, which was the percentage of missionaries retained in each year of missionary sending:

$$RR_t = 10\wedge((\log R_t) / t)$$

presuming a uniform probability of coming home,[24] where R_t measures the percentage of missionaries retained on the field after t year(s) of service. Then, RR_t values were averaged for all years of sending,[25] thereby resulting in the averaged Annual Retention Rate RR, the independent variable to which all organisational factors and agency practices were related.

These calculations for "Retention Rate" allowed us to compare missionaries commissioned in different years as well as different mission agencies over the long term.

---

20 Data entry involved transcribing the answers for each agency to an Excel worksheet. A template (sample Excel file) had been prepared and distributed to the country coordinators by Dr. Detlef Blöcher.

21 Datasets from each country were forwarded to Dr. Detlef Blöcher in Germany, who later merged them to form the international ReMAP II database.

22 The response rate was between 50 to 90% of the total national mission force.

23 Each agency provided data on their missionary sending during the past 20 years. A table with six columns (from A to F) was provided, with each row representing a year's data. The six columns were: A = year of first departure, B = number of new missionaries in that year, C = number of these still in active service with agency on 31 Dec. 2002, D = number of these transferred to another agency but are still working on the field as on 31 Dec. 2002, E = number of these who left the agency for unavoidable reasons, F = number of these who left for potentially preventable reasons or were dismissed.

24 Extensive studies by Detlef Blöcher have proved that this is a reasonable assumption.

25 Not all agencies had missionary-sending data for 20 years.

For example, agency X has an annual retention rate RR of 0.97 (that is 97 out of 100 missionaries were still in service at the end of the year, while three had gone home, that is 3% attrition) which may look impressive, while agency Y has an RR of 0.90 (that is 90% retention and 10% attrition) which may not seem too bad. However, if we were to project the trends over ten years, we will notice a dramatic difference. If 100 missionaries were sent out by agency X in a given year and its average retention rate had remained at about 0.97 for the next decade, then only 74 of its original missionaries would still be in active service after ten years.[26] For agency Y, only 35 missionaries of its original 100 missionaries would still be serving after ten years.[27]

In the retention record, each missionary returning was assigned into one of three different categories:

1. Return for potentially preventable reasons (any reasons due to personal, cultural, family-related, team-related, work-related, agency-related issues),
2. Return for unpreventable reasons (normal retirement, death in service, project end, completion of assignment), and
3. Harmonious transfer to another organisation while continuing with service in the same people group. Harmonious transfers were not considered as negative events in this study because we worked from a kingdom of God perspective. Harmonious transfer meant that the missionary had remained on the field, but was serving with a different agency.

Special emphasis was put on the first category in the ReMAP II project because attrition for potentially preventable reasons could possibly be reduced by organisational development.

From these three categories, we could calculate the following retention rates:

*   RRT (or Total annual retention rate) was derived from the Annual retention rate RR where R considers all the missionaries still serving on the field (whether with the agency or with another agency due to harmonious transfer),
*   RRP (or Annual retention rate for the incremental risk of potentially preventable attrition) is similarly obtained from RR, but where R considers the retention of potentially preventable attrition, and
*   RRU (or Annual retention rate for the risk of unpreventable attrition) is likewise calculated from RR, but where R considers the retention of unpreventable attrition.

Having calculated the RRT and RRP for each agency that participated in ReMAP II, we grouped the agencies into three equal subgroups according to their Retention Rate: high (H), medium (M) and low (L). Due to significant differences in their mission movements, two separate analyses were run for Old Sending Countries

---

26 The calculation for Agency X is as follows: 100 multiplied by 0.97^{10} = 74.
27 The calculation for Agency Y is as follows: 100 multiplied by 0.90^{10} = 35.

and New Sending Countries. Standard errors were calculated for each average to indicate the uncertainty of the number due to statistical fluctuation. For these calculations, we also used the statistical tools available to worksheets in the Microsoft Excel software.

Weighted averages

In ReMAP II, we wanted to establish the relationship between "Retaining Missionaries" and "Agency Practices." Therefore, we designed some 48 questions on agency operation, and we requested mission leaders to do a self-evaluation of their own agency's practices.[28] However, mission agencies differ considerably in size: some sending bases were small agencies with fewer than ten missionaries, while others were large organisations with thousands of missionaries.

Therefore, when analysing the data collected, we had to use weighted responses. This is the only way of obtaining a meaningful average for the demographic data,[29] attrition data[30] and retention data.[31] Weighted averages were also used for the other questions. This meant that each response from an agency was multiplied by that agency's number of active missionaries. Hence, we took into account the number of missionaries actually serving within the agency's working conditions, under its leadership of specific values or convictions.

Phase Three: Reporting and training

Phase III began in June 2003 with initial data analysis and discussion of our early findings. The country coordinators met in Vancouver at "Canada 2003" conference, an international gathering of the various taskforces under the Mission Commission of the World Evangelical Alliance. Preliminary results were presented and discussed. Further data continued to be submitted and collected until December 2003. The final analysis was conducted at the end of 2003.

Country coordinators received the analysed results by e-mail. This included the retention rates for each participating agency (identified by their research code), analyses for each country, region or continent, and the global findings.

Here is a brief overview of our key findings:

- There was a strong positive correlation between missionary retention and agency practices. Some 40 specific factors were identified from our analysis of the ReMAP II international database. These factors were in the areas of candidate selection, vision and purpose, leadership, communication, personal

---

28 As evidenced by their time, effort and effectiveness rated on a 7-point Likert scale from 1 (not well done) to 6 (very well done). The 7-point scale includes "0" (not applicable).

29 Demographic data was gathered from questions 1 to 10, 26 to 39 in the ReMAP II questionnaire.

30 Attrition data of the years 2001 to 2002 was gathered from questions 97 and 98 in the ReMAP II questionnaire.

31 Retention Record was gathered in Section J of the ReMAP II questionnaire. This was a table of personnel data about missionary sending, retention over a 20 year period (from 1981 to 2000).

support, member care, ministry priorities, ministry outcomes, continuous training, finances and home office operations.

- Missionary retention involves a complex web of factors, not one factor or a few factors. Agency practices and procedures are generally determined by a composite of an organisation's ethos, values, and purposes. The character and worldview of an agency permeates all aspects of its operations. Indeed, certain factors observed in OSC and NSC expressed their history, culture, church traditions, and expectations of supporting churches.

- Although missionary retention has gradually dropped over the past twenty years, it has not decreased in the subgroup of high retaining agencies. These agencies have been flexible enough to change with the times, and to maintain their missionaries' commitment, loyalty and vision. Thus, high retaining agencies continue to be blessed with experienced staff.

- Our results suggest that adopting the best practices of the high retaining subgroup could reduce the "potentially preventable attrition" in both OSC and NSC. When the performance of the high retaining subgroup (about one-third of all agencies) is taken as our standard, then it may be possible to reduce "potentially preventable attrition" by 45% in OSC and 65% in NSC.

- In addition, adopting the best practices of the high retaining subgroup could possibly reduce what is often considered as "unpreventable attrition" by a larger percentage. The reduction was calculated to be 55% in OSC and 75% in NSC, from the actual inspiring performance of the best one-third of their mission agencies.

Since early 2004, the country coordinators have reported these ReMAP II findings at one or more workshops to mission executives and church leaders in almost all of the participating countries. During these workshops, the local mission leaders are given the opportunity to reflect on the key findings and to discuss specific efforts to strengthen their organisational practices, especially those relating to missionary sending and member care. ReMAP II results have also been presented at a few regional conferences. Numerous short reports from participating countries have also been published in national and international missiological journals.[32]

Several correlation analyses on specific issues were performed. These included: the trends observed among the younger mission movements,[33] the correlation between member care and mission retention,[34] and the trends in evangelical missionary deployment among unreached peoples.[35]

---

32 One important collection of reports was the "ReMAP II—Long-term retention of mission personnel," *Connections: the Journal of the WEA Missions Commission*, Vol. 3 No. 2, (June 2004). This issue of *Connections* contained 21 articles on ReMAP II: 2 editorials, 6 foundational studies including an overarching introduction, and 14 short national reports.

33 Detlef Blöcher, "ReMAP II affirms the maturation of the younger mission movements of the South," in *Connections: the Journal of the WEA Missions Commission*, Vol. 2 pp. 48-53, Oct. 2003.

34 Detlef Blöcher, "Member care builds up mission personnel," one of several organisational area papers available in the ReMAP folder on the website www.wearesources.org. A similar folder is available at www.worthkeeping.info.

35 Detlef Blöcher, "How shall they believe? Evangelical missionary deployment vis-à-vis the least reached peoples" in *International Journal of Frontier Missions*, Vol. 22:4, pp.147-150, Oct. – Dec. 2005.

Concluding thoughts

Collaborative work across international borders requires mutual trust and good communication as well as a willingness to learn from one another. In the ReMAP II project, our face-to-face meetings in London and Vancouver enabled the country coordinators and the steering committee to get to know each other and to understand how we could work together on a significant research project.

Collaboration is a powerful approach to strengthening our international mission partnerships between the national mission movements in different countries. The collective ability of a team far exceeds that of individual members. In ReMAP II, our combined findings from the 22 participating countries resulted in an international database, which was far larger than what we expected.

The small nations that participated experienced great benefits through our collaborative research. They had been constrained by their limited resources and expertise. However, as a part of an international team, each nation had the opportunity to participate in a research project and to learn from other nations.

Through their participation in the ReMAP II project, some country coordinators have initiated regular communication between their respective national mission movements. Such links are welcomed because they will bring mutual encouragement and development within the global mission community.

Acknowledgements

The author would like to thank Dr. Detlef Blöcher (Germany), Dr. Jonathan Lewis (USA), Dr Jim Van Meter (USA), and Dr. Barbara Griffin (Australia) of the ReMAP II steering committee for their encouraging support and valuable comments in their review of this article.

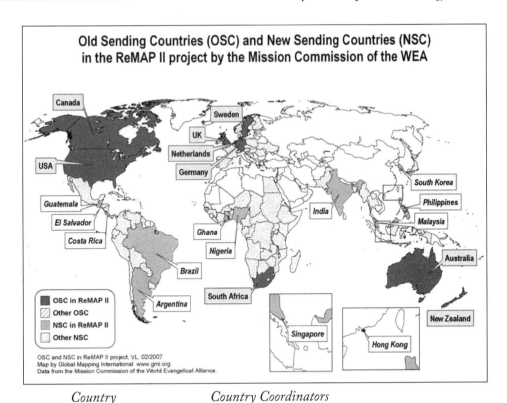

	Country	Country Coordinators
1.	Argentina	Daniel Bianchi
2.	Australia	Barbara Griffin *
3.	Brazil	José Roberto Prado, Ted Limpic
4.	Canada	Laurel McAllister
5.	Costa Rica +	Marcos Padgett
6.	Germany	Detlef Blöcher *
7.	Ghana	Sampson Dorkunor, Seth Anyomi *
8.	Hong Kong	Vanessa Hung
9.	India	Pramila Rajendran
10.	Korea	Dong-Hwa Kim
11.	Malaysia	Philip Chang
12.	Netherlands	Jaap Ketelaar
13.	New Zealand	Rachel Murray
14.	Nigeria	Timothy Olonade
15.	Philippines	Rey Corpuz, Bob Lopez
16.	Singapore	Valerie Lim
17.	South Africa	Henkie Maritz
18.	Sweden	Birgitta Johansson
19.	UK	Rob Hay
20.	USA	Jim Van Meter *

+ also El Salvador and Guatemala
* ReMAP II Steering Committee members

Mission Commission Project Coordinator: Jonathan Lewis* (Argentina, USA)

Section B

The building blocks:

Section B is the core of the book but it is also a reference section. These chapters are designed to be referred to selectively, depending on the issue you need to address. You may have opened the book already wrestling with an issue and know what you want help with, or you may want to access the facilitator's guide (www.worthkeeping.info) and take the online assessment to identify the areas you need to review. Whichever approach you take, once you decide on the chapters, accessing them should be easy as each one is laid out in a common format.

4

Agency Size and Partnerships

"Small agencies need partnerships with others"

The facts

Big is better… at least up to a certain size: 50, in fact. ReMAP II has demonstrated that very small mission agencies across NSC and OSC lose people at an alarming rate of 33% per year. Larger agencies do much better with the loss of just 6% in OSC and 1.3% in NSC.

Size appears to give an agency scope to redeploy people more effectively, and thereby avoid losing them. It also gives them a better cross-section of support services and offers significant cost effectiveness savings (just one home office staff per ten active missionaries in large agencies, compared to two home office staff per active missionary for the smallest agencies). Leaders of small agencies rated their performance much lower than did leaders of large agencies, and this was across a whole spectrum of key areas, including missiological pre-field training, orientation, team support, member care and home office operating.

ReMAP II findings call for strategic alliances. Partnerships—a buzzword in missions for some time—are now quite clearly a vital need, both specifically for the health and well-being of the individual missionaries and generally for the effectiveness of building the Kingdom.

The data

Percentage of Missionaries Serving in Agencies of this Size

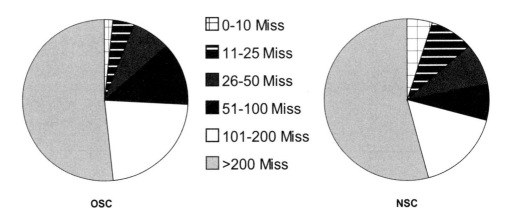

- ⊞ 0-10 Miss
- ▤ 11-25 Miss
- ■ 26-50 Miss
- ■ 51-100 Miss
- ☐ 101-200 Miss
- ▨ >200 Miss

OSC   **NSC**

The key findings

✓ Small agencies have very low retention rates and high attrition rates.

✓ Small agencies have a much higher ratio of home office staff to active missionary.

✓ Small agencies have significantly less structure and lower care facilities, but these limitations do not explain the high attrition rates.

✓ The low retention of small agencies is primarily due to their small size (limited synergies, cooperation, under critical-mass).

What it means

Detlef Blöcher

Figure 1 gives the annual percentage of returnees for the years 2001/02. It reveals a very high return rate for small agencies: they lose up to one-quarter of their work force per year (a group of 50 mission agencies with two missionaries each—totalling 100 active missionaries combined—will lose 24 missionaries each year)! This is a tremendous loss of human resources, particularly if we take into account the relational nature of the societies of many of the countries in which they are serving. These high return rates were found in NSC and OSC alike.[1] Large agencies of NSC, on the other hand, lose only 1.3% of their workforce per year. This is an extremely low percentage and much lower than that of the 5.3% in the ReMAP I study some ten years ago,[2] proving the tremendous maturing of the new mission

---

1   ...with considerable national differences which will be discussed elsewhere.

2   Detlef Blöcher and Jonathan Lewis, "Further Findings in Research Data," *Too Valuable to Lose*, William D. Taylor, ed., Pasadena, CA: William Carey Library, 1997), p. 105-125. D. Blöcher, *Evangelikale*

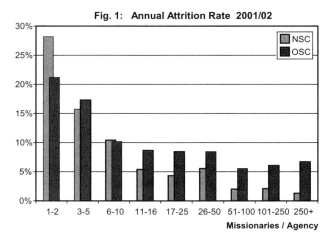

Fig. 1: Annual Attrition Rate 2001/02

movement of the Global South.[3] OSC agencies are more affected by issues such as end of contract, completion of projects, retirement of missionaries, etc., so that their return rate is 6.3% per year, a value similar to that found in ReMAP I. It is evident that the smallest possible agency for minimising the return rate is an organisation with 50 field missionaries. It appears that this allows sufficient size for meaningful specialisation in the home office as well as mutual care and sufficient diversity of gifting in the ministry teams in the country of service.[4]

The retention rate (RRT)[5] shows a similar dependency on agency size (Figure 2), increasing from 90.8% to 98.0% in NSC. All of these retention rates look impressive and the differences between them appear small, yet after ten years of service the agency with a retention rate of 90.8%[10] would only have 38% of its missionaries still in active service compared to 82% in large NSC agencies with 98.0%[10] = 82% in large NSC agencies. This means that 62% of missionaries in small agencies left the field compared to just 18% in large agencies: a factor of 3.5.[6] In OSC, a retention rate of 87.5% was found for small agencies and 94.8% for large ones. This means that after ten years of service only 26.4% of missionaries in small OSC agencies

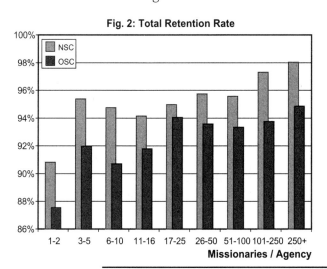

Fig. 2: Total Retention Rate

Missiologie 14 (1998), p. 93-100.

3   Detlef Blöcher, "ReMAP II Affirms the Maturation of the Younger Mission Movement of the South." _Connections: the Journal of the WEA Mission Commission._ (Oct. 2003), p. 48-53.

4   ReMAP II did not look into team size on the field, but smaller agencies generally have several smaller ministry teams.

5   Agencies reported on the number of new missionaries for the years 1981–2001 and their fate since then, whether they were (a) still in active service with their agency on 31 Dec 2002, (b) have in meantime transferred to another organisation (i.e., harmonious move to another agency or church, merger of agencies or outsourcing of projects. etc.) but are still in active service in the same country/people group, (c) returned to home country for unpreventable reasons (i.e., completion of predetermined contract, end of project, retirement, illness, visa withdrawal, appointment to leadership position in home office or agency's International Office, death in service) or (d) returned for Potentially Preventable Reasons (i.e., all personal, family, work, agency related reasons or dismissal by agency). The annual Retention Rate RRT was calculated from the percentage R of still active missionaries (a and b) after t years of service: $RRT = 10^{\wedge}((\log R) / t)$ (assuming a uniform risk of return irrespective of the length of service—extensive studies by the author showed that this is a reasonable assumption).

6   The numerical differences between Fig. 1 and 2 stem from the different concepts of attrition (returnees of a given year irrespective of their length of service) and Retention (Percentage of missionaries still in service after five or ten years of service) as well as the different time period considered (returnees of 2001/2002 versus Retention of new missionaries of the years 1981-2001).

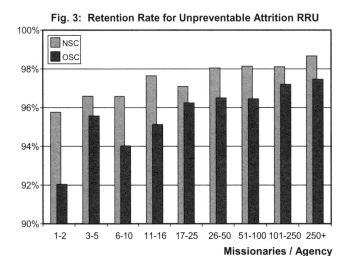

Fig. 3: Retention Rate for Unpreventable Attrition RRU

are still in active service compared to 58.9% for large OSC agencies.

Figure 3 gives the retention rate for unpreventable attrition (RRU).[7] For NSC it increases from 95.7% (very small agencies) to 98.6% so that after ten years of service 35% and 12.5% respectively have left for unpreventable causes, again a factor of three! In OSC, RRU increased with agency size from 92.0% to 97.4% so that after ten years of service 56% and 23% respectively had left the field for unpreventable reasons. This steep increase of RRU with agency size is even more surprising as small agencies are considerably younger (average age—NSC 11 years, OSC 27 years) than larger agencies (average age—NSC 31 years; OSC 96 years), so issues such as missionary retirement and phase-out of projects have less significance. Apparently many small agencies are focused on one project and/or country; they cannot (or do not want to) offer new opportunities for service after the completion of a project. This indicates the conceptual and structural limitations of small agencies in personnel deployment and long-term retention.

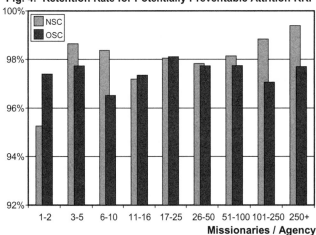

Fig. 4: Retention Rate for Potentially Preventable Attrition RRP

The retention rate for potentially preventable attrition (RRP)[8] (Figure 4) also increases with agency size from 95.2% to an impressive 99.3% (NSC), so that after ten years of service 38.5% of the missionaries of small agencies and 5.9% of the missionaries of large agencies had left the field for potentially preventable reasons, resulting in a factor of almost seven! (In OSC, RRT was less dependent on agency size, hovering around 97.7% so that the difference between NSC and OSC is most pronounced in large agencies). Thus, preventable as well as unpreventable causes decrease with agency size.

The high return rates for small agencies are even more unexpected as small agencies have up to 30 times (!) more staff per active missionary (Figure 5) serving in their home office than do large agencies (0.1 staff per active missionary) and thus provide very personal care for the sent missionaries.

---

7   Definition in footnote 5 (c).
8   Definition in footnote 5 (d).

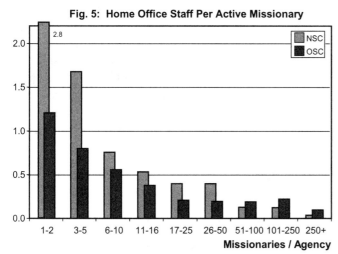

Fig. 5: Home Office Staff Per Active Missionary

The ReMAP II data also proved that small agencies have very high annual recruitment rates: in the years 1999/2000 it amounted to 40% (NSC) new missionaries per year and 21% (OSC)—however, every second one of these new missionaries left the agency within three years! Large agencies (250+ missionaries), on the other hand, had much smaller recruitment rates: merely 7.1% per year (NSC) and 6.5% (OSC), of which only every seventh missionary left the agency again within three years. Small agencies appear to operate like a "revolving door" with many new missionaries coming in and then leaving again. This would appear to be a tremendous waste of human and financial resources. For the missionary, there is the high financial investment of training and the personal cost of leaving career and home, and for the project there is the experience of personnel resignation before the worker has become effective not to mention the disappointment of the home church and supporters who become confused about God's calling.

What are the reasons for this high attrition rate in spite of the very personal family character of small agencies? The ReMAP II data shows that mission leaders from small agencies gave significantly lower ratings to their agency's performance (as compared to ratings given by leaders of large agencies) regarding a number of vital functions (Figures 6-9 are examples for NSC). These included: organisation,[9] leadership,[10] minimal

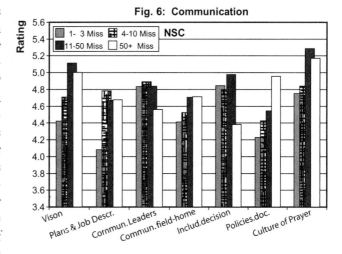

Fig. 6: Communication

---

9   NSC -8%; OSC -10%. Individual factors were: Vision & purpose (NSC -12%; OSC -8%), Plans & job description (NSC -13%; OSC -6%), Documented policies (NSC -15%; OSC -8%), Annual performance review (NSC -1%; OSC -20%), Handling complaints (NSC -26%; OSC -30%), Continuous training of missionaries (NSC -10%; OSC -14%), Appropriate amount of work (NSC -9%; OSC -6%), Ministry opportunity for spouse (NSC -13%; OSC -13%), Mutual support in missionary team (NSC -15%; OSC -23%).

10   NSC -9%; OSC -11%. In particular: Example of leaders (NSC -3%; OSC -10%), Leaders identify problems and take actions (NSC -12%; OSC -5%), On-field Supervision of missionaries (NSC -20%; OSC -25%), Risk assessment (NSC -29%; OSC -33%), but Communication with leadership (NSC +6%; OSC +2%) and Missionaries included in major decisions on the field (NSC +11%; OSC +5%) as they are small agencies.

pre-field training requirements,[11] field orientation,[12] personal care on the field,[13] educational standards,[14] staff development,[15] finances[16] and running the home office.[17] Candidate selection[18] and missionaries' ministry[19] showed little difference, however. Major variations with agency size were found in the areas of missiological pre-field training, orientation, team support, member care and home office operations. This draws our attention to the structural limitations of small agencies. These lower ratings are the more compelling as they were not assessments from outside by critical researchers applying idealistic criteria, but assessments by the mission leaders themselves.

The structural limitations of small agencies are significant, but they are not so critical as to explain the relatively huge size of their attrition rates: so we need to look for other explanations. It appears that mission agencies resemble a wood fire where burning pieces mutually heat each other and thus keep the fire burning. Set aside, a burning log will soon die out as it now loses more heat than is produced and received. In a similar way mission agencies need a "critical mass" of workers to secure a mix of gifts and experience, generate a stimulating and inspiring atmosphere, cover the various ministries and roles, provide mutual support and overcome situations of crisis.

This minimal size appears to be critical for the care and spiritual survival of the missionary. Therefore, we recommend that small agencies enter into partnerships

---

11   NSC -16%; OSC -16%; in particular: Length of theological training (NSC -10%; OSC -30%), Missiological training (NSC -41%; OSC -71%), Practical Pre-field Missionary training (NSC +20%; OSC +56%), Agency's own orientation programme (NSC -19%; OSC +300%).

12   NSC –21%; OSC –32%; in particular: On-field orientation (NSC -25%; OSC -20%), Language learning of new missionaries (NSC -15%; OSC -41%), and Ongoing culture and language training (NSC -15%; OSC -30%).

13   NSC -18%; OSC -14%. Especially: Member care (NSC -38%; OSC -21%) and Preventive member care (NSC -52%; OSC -73%), Administrative and practical support on the field (NSC -19%; OSC -16%), Mutual support in the missionary team (NSC -15%; OSC -23%), Pastoral care on the field level (NSC -19%; OSC -9%), Interpersonal conflicts resolution (NSC -15%; OSC -9%), Growth of missionary's spiritual life (NSC -21%; OSC -16%), MK education (NSC -45%; OSC -28%), Health care provided (NSC -23%; OSC -0%), Annual vacation (NSC -19%; OSC -8%), Risk assessment & Contingency Planning (NSC -29%; OSC -33%), Missionaries' continuous training (NSC -10%; OSC -14%), Re-entry programme (NSC -20%; OSC -30%).

14   Maximum educational standard: BA (NSC +25%; OSC +160%); MA (NSC -42%; OSC -50%); Doctorate (NSC +100%; OSC -50%).

15   NSC -9%; OSC -11%. Especially: Ongoing language & cultural studies (NSC -15%; OSC -31%), Development of new gifts & skills (NSC -10%; OSC -14%).

16   NSC -5%; OSC -10%: Sustained financial support (NSC -4%; OSC -9%), Back-up system for missionaries with low financial support (NSC -10%; OSC -44%), Project finances used effectively (NSC -13%; OSC -9%) and Transparency of agency finances (NSC -14%; OSC +3%).

17   NSC -14%; OSC -17%. In particular: Pre-field screening (NSC -14%; OSC -20%), Pre-field training (NSC -22%; OSC -34%), Staff prays for missionaries (NSC -17%; OSC -22%), Re-entry arrangements (NSC -21%; OSC -30%), Debriefing during home assignment (NSC -22%; OSC -10%).

18   (-2%) with the following significant factors: Character references (NSC +5%; OSC -10%), Family blessing (NSC -10%; OSC +12%), Ministry experience in local church (NSC +25%; OSC -15%), Physical examination (NSC -12%; OSC -10%), Psychological assessment (NSC -11%; OSC -11%); Contentment with present marital status (NSC -5%; OSC -11%), but Previous cross-cultural experience (NSC +27%; OSC +12%), Potential for financial support (NSC 3%; OSC +45%) and Potential for prayer support (NSC +11%; OSC +15%).

19   NSC -5%; OSC -4%. With significant changes in: Missionary not overworked (NSC -9%; OSC -6%), Ministry role for spouse (-21%) and Administrative and practical support on the field (NSC -19%; OSC -16%) having significant effects.

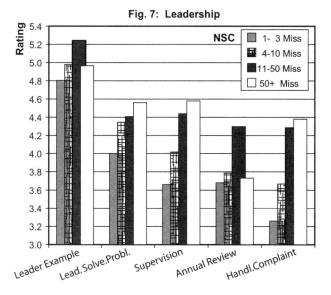

Fig. 7: Leadership

with others in the country of service. Cooperation with national churches or organisations and/or other mission agencies already on the ground would appear to be essential, particularly in the early phase of a project when a new agency is still small numbers-wise and is gaining experience of the work and the situation. By contrast, existing organisations would by now have gained experience, set up effective leadership and support structures and built trusted relationships with individuals in authority. Likewise, small agencies need a balanced team in their home office/sending base with a variety of complementary personalities, gifting and experience. This will enable them to cover all aspects of candidate selection and preparation, as well as to provide better leadership, public relations, donor relationships, care for the workers on the field, etc..

Cross-cultural mission has become highly complex in our modern world. It includes labour laws, legal regulations, international bank transfers, public relations, professional standards and missiological issues, all of which require a high level of expertise. For this reason, a certain number of workers are needed to cover the various tasks in a competent and efficient way and to create synergies. In many cases this is beyond the reach of small agencies, as it would require very high financial and personnel investment to keep up-to-date professionally and cover the various tasks with competence and efficiency. We therefore encourage small agencies to share office facilities and expertise, (e.g. sharing accountancy and personal services, counselling and other specialist staff), or indeed, outsourcing these services. In mission as in business there is a global trend towards merger of organisations—not just of small mission agencies but also of large agencies with hundreds of missionaries—in order to work effectively and efficiently and to utilise synergies. Together we can achieve much more than alone.

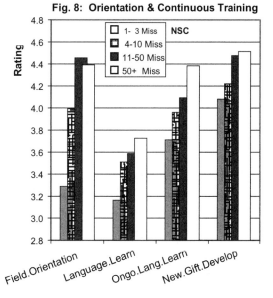

Fig. 8: Orientation & Continuous Training

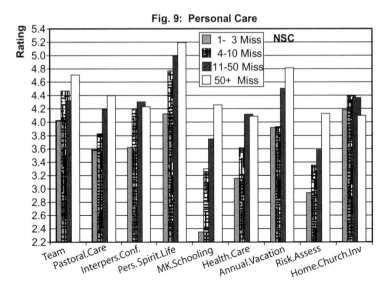

Fig. 9: Personal Care

Rating
5.4, 5.2, 5.0, 4.8, 4.6, 4.4, 4.2, 4.0, 3.8, 3.6, 3.4, 3.2, 3.0, 2.8, 2.6, 2.4, 2.2

■ 1- 3 Miss   NSC
▨ 4-10 Miss
■ 11-50 Miss
□ 50+ Miss

Team, Pastoral.Care, Interpers.Conf., Pers.Spirit.Life, MK.Schooling, Health.Care, Annual.Vacation, Risk.Assess, Home.Church.Inv

In addition, there is a global trend towards partnership, strategic collaborative ventures in the country of service, the formation of large consortiums, sometimes even hundreds of churches and agencies with common specific goals.[20] This process has been pioneered by the international agency, INTERDEV, which has been instrumental in building and facilitating many regional partnerships. It is also the aim of the WEA Mission Commission (WEA-MC), with its various task forces and working groups, who work to pool global insights and share resources. Cooperation and partnership is the key concept of the day. This involves the sacrifice of one's own aims, plans and pet ideas, and the willingness to submit and be accountable to each other, though without loss of identity. This is good stewardship and faithful service—anything else is likely to be a waste of precious human and financial resources, a duplication of existing projects and carelessness towards sent missionaries. It is HIS Kingdom, not ours!

The need for cooperation not only results from the convincing statistical evidence presented, the financial limitations of mission agencies and pragmatic concepts of mission strategists—the need for cooperation also flows from a fundamental theological and missiological principle: Jesus sent his disciples always in pairs (Mark 6:7), the Apostle Paul usually worked on his mission journeys in a team (Acts 13:13) and more than 50 of his co-workers are mentioned in the New Testament by name. In addition, Paul cooperated with churches in Antioch, Philippi, Jerusalem, and Rome. Jesus promised much blessing for common prayer (Mt 18:18) and unity among believers (Mt 18:19). In fact, this was Jesus' prayer focus (John 17:11-23). The New Testament is filled with words like: "together," "each other," "one with another," "for each other," etc. (John 13:14,34f; Rom 12:5,10; Rom 15:5-14; 1 Cor 1:10; Col 3:13; 1 Thess 3:12; 1 Thess 5:11; 1 Peter 4:10; 1 Peter 5:5). This is the Lord's calling for the church and for missions, and it is especially relevant in the complexity of the 21st century with its rapid political changes and diverse network of relationships between various churches and agencies. This fundamental concept of cooperation in missions finds its mandate in clear statistical and theological evidence. It is a call for real partnership to the honour of God.

---

20   William D. Taylor ed., *Kingdom Partnerships for Synergy in Missions*, (Pasadena, CA: William Carey Library, 1994).

DMG - A model for partnerships in missions

Detlef Blöcher,[21] DMG, Germany

Research has shown that small and young agencies have a very high risk of losing their workers. Their attrition rate is up to ten times higher than that of large agencies (with 50+ workers) due to the lack in personal support, professional administration, and opportunities for service. At the same time, small agencies need up to ten times more administrative staff in their home office (per active field missionary). This is because they need to employ staff for accountancy, administration, employment, legal issues, writing and layout of the mission journal. It is almost the same amount of work, whether you do each of these tasks for five or 50 missionaries.

Agency size is therefore a matter of effectiveness and efficiency, or to express it in biblical terminology "good stewardship." But every new agency starts small. Therefore, the question is "How can an agency survive its first ten years without losing its first generation of missionaries?"

A mission executive in a neighbouring country recently called me on the telephone. He explained that they had accepted a new mission candidate from my country (Germany) who will be sent out by their agency. They are seeking a way to channel her financial support. Is there a way other than to set up an office of their organisation in my country with all the legal work, office expenses, demands on information, public relations, etc., implied? Is there a way of partnering in missions in order to bring about her calling and sending in an efficient and effective way? His request caught my attention, because his dilemma was the reason for the existence of DMG, our mission agency.

DMG (Deutsche Missionsgemeinschaft, or German Missionary Fellowship) came into existence for the purpose of assisting German churches to send out and support their missionaries in a cross-cultural ministry by partnering with mission agencies (and churches) in the country of service. Each DMG missionary is seconded to a receiving mission organisation in the country of service, in many cases an international mission organisation that does not have its own sending office in Germany.

DMG was founded after World War II, during a time of great economic shortage and social needs: immense death tolls, towns in ruins, huge unemployment, extreme poverty, influx of 20 million refugees into Western Germany. It was a time of national grief over the atrocities of the Nazis and the horrors of war, when there were other priorities than cross-cultural missions. A number of mission agencies (mainly American) began coming to Continental Europe to proclaim the Gospel. They included Greater Europe Mission, Janz Team, and Youth for Christ.

21   Dr. Detlef Blöcher is a physicist by training and he worked in medical research at German universities and in the Middle East. From 1991 to 1999, he served as Personnel Director of German Missionary Fellowship (DMG), and since then as its CEO. He is also chairman of the German Evangelical Mission Alliance, and an Associate of the WEA Mission Commission.

At that time, Beatenberg Bible School in Switzerland was the leading missionary training centre in Continental Europe. It was also the venue for a series of mission conferences. The speakers spoke about the unprecedented opportunities for mission in Eastern Asia and Europe. They even invited Germans, their former enemies of war, to join their mission teams in order to seize the opportunities of the day.

After one of these challenging talks, Dr. Gertrud Wasserzug, the energetic Beatenberg Bible School Director, took the initiative and urged the German attendees to respond to this call in faith by forming a German sending agency. This led to the founding of DMG (German Missionary Fellowship) on the following day in 1951 at the conference centre, following the model of SMG (Swiss Missionary Fellowship) which was initiated by the same lady in the previous year.

Partnership in missions is the basis of operation for sending agencies like DMG (German Missionary Fellowship), SMG (Swiss Missionary Fellowship), and VDM (United German Mission Assistance). These agencies were founded to bridge the gap between sending churches (in the home country) and opportunities for ministry (in the countries of service). It takes a lot of effort to establish a new sending agency, to build up an administrative system in the home country, to gain the trust of sending churches, to establish a good reputation, and to develop effective structures and policies. It requires lots of experience and resources to build effective ministry teams in the country of service, to establish relationships with local government officials and/or national churches, to learn the culture and local way of doing business, to establish a relevant and appropriate project, to secure project continuity, to develop a strategy for culturally relevant church planting (to avoid merely importing our own ecclesiastic traditions) and so on.

Newly emerging sending agencies (especially those in new sending countries) can follow the example of DMG and SMG and place their own missionaries into ministry teams of existing mission agencies. Their missionaries can then focus on ministry, while enjoying the fellowship and support of colleagues of the partner agency, serving under their leadership, and receiving their supervision, advice and care.

Likewise, international agencies which want to receive missionaries from a certain sending country (where they do not have an office) may choose to partner with a national sending agency in the country (for example DMG, if the sending country is Germany). The local sending agency (such as DMG) will serve as their home-based mission link to the sending churches in the home country (in our case Germany). It will provide information on mission opportunities, conduct pre-field training, build up prayer and financial support, help the sending churches grow in competence and understanding, help to select suitable mission candidates, and choose suitable assignments. It receives the financial support and maintains donor relationships, provides employment and social security for the missionary, keeps in touch with relatives etc. The receiving organisation will provide field orientation, language acquisition, member care, work assignment, leadership, accountability, periods of rest and refreshment, etc.

The respective expectations are laid out in a written cooperation agreement (an example is given on the webpage: www.DMGint.de/dam). In other words, DMG is considered the German sending office for those international mission agencies without an office in Germany.

In the home country, only the local sending agency is visible, and the churches and the general public will know this agency. Meanwhile, several different international mission agencies can use this agency as their sending base for personnel recruitment and fundraising. This results in an efficient and lean mission sending structure.

DMG presently cooperates in this way with some 400 local churches in Germany, which currently have sent out some 330 long-term missionaries (plus 70 short-termers per year and a growing number of finishers) who serve in 70 countries under the umbrella of 102 international partner agencies. These 102 agencies have reported some 4,000 vacancies for missionary service. DMG will match a prospective mission candidate with a certain vision for ministry with an opportunity for ministry (place, ministry, team structure, organisational ethos, theological stance, etc.).

After some years, when such a newly emerging sending agency has grown in experience and size, it could decide to establish its own teams and ministries in a country of service, and it may do so. By that time, the sending agency would have already gone through a steep learning curve, possibly saving the first generation of its workers, and it would have built up its own team leadership.

Yet DMG, SMG, and other similar sending agencies have learned to appreciate such mission partnerships and chosen not to establish their "own" mission teams or projects. They have consciously decided to continue to work in partnership with other mission agencies in the countries of service. This is because they view this manner of operation as the most effective and efficient way to exercise good stewardship in doing missions. They believe that partnership in missions is commanded by the Lord for their work in global missions.

Discussion questions:

1. What are the strengths of the DMG model for synergy in missions? What are the weaknesses?

2. Could this be a suitable model for partnerships of the emerging mission agencies in Eastern Europe and countries of the South? What do you think?

3. What models of mission partnerships exist in your country or region?

4. If there are no such partnerships, what can be done to establish one or more mission partnerships in your country or region?

Sending workers by teams

Bob Lopez[22] and Bibien Limlingan,[23] Philippine Mission Association,[24] Philippines

In the Philippines, church congregations are small, with an average of 58 members in each congregation. Our mission agencies are also small, with only an average of 26 members in each agency. In fact, more than two-thirds of our missionary sending bases have fewer than 20 missionaries.

In recent years, we have observed that when small mission agencies work in partnership to send teams of missionaries to reach people groups, they accomplish much for God. Such partnerships thrive and they are able to mobilise more people for missions.

Partnership is not just a very good practice in the Philippines but also an appropriate one. It reflects a very important cultural value, "bayanihan", which speaks of community cooperation to accomplish a certain project.

What happened in the past

The earliest missions efforts in the Philippines were individualistic in nature because of territorial divisions and also, historically, the country was subdivided by the first North American Protestant and Evangelical denominations after the country was liberated from the Spaniards at the very start of the 1900s.

People groups won to the gospel were generally from the lowland people and the highland tribes of Luzon, Visayas, and Mindanao. They were the most ready for religious change, and their receptivity to the gospel was high. Furthermore, there was a romantic notion of mission going to the most economically depressed and backward areas. Much effort was directed at the most receptive areas and at animistic tribes.

Meanwhile, some people groups in the Philippines resisted almost all efforts to bring the gospel to them. They despised the spiritual legacy of the colonial powers. They are 'the neglected ethno-linguistic groups' in the most difficult places for church planting. Although there has been a very long history of individual mission efforts and zealous ministry to bring the gospel to these peoples, such efforts have

---

22   Bob Lopez serves as the National Director of the Philippine Missions Association. He also serves as a board member of the Tentmakers International Exchange, the global tentmaking "arm" of the Lausanne Committee on World Evangelisation and the World Evangelical Alliance Mission Commission. He is a member of the Global Leadership Team of the Filipino International Network. Bob has been involved in missions mobilisation, training and deployment since 1995 when he began serving with the Asian Center for Missions, eventually becoming its Chief Operating Officer. He is married to Cristina. Together, they have three adult children and three grandchildren.

23   Bibien Limlingan serves as the Research Officer of the Philippine Missions Association. Bibien has a Masters degree in Theology from the Asian Theological Seminary. She has just recently finished putting together an extensive study on all the people groups in the Philippines. She is married to Pastor Jong Limlingan and they have three daughters.

24   Philippine Missions Association is a 23 year-old organisation that serves as the missions commission of the Philippine Council of Evangelical Churches.

had very little success, only marginally affecting the people. Many workers who laboured eventually died without seeing the fruits of their labour.

How partnerships began

It was the disappointing lack of fruit that led mission groups reaching "the neglected ethno-linguistic groups" to begin exploring the option of partnering with other agencies with a similar field focus. Talks about forming a "consortium" began as far back as 1984. The breakthrough came in 1998 during the Centennial Missions Congress where the Body of Christ celebrated the first 100 years of Protestant and Evangelical missionary activity in the Philippines. During that historic gathering, the nuclei of the first few partnerships targeting the most gospel-resistant peoples were formed. We have made significant progress since then.

Over the years, frontline workers in the most difficult places began to organise programmes to encourage one another. They began planning a unified evangelistic thrust. The concept of church planting movements was espoused and embraced. They started pooling their resources together for specific resistant people groups. In the many partnerships that have formed, a church planting programme may include some or all of the following components:

- Evangelism and discipleship
- Continuing education and literacy programme
- Bible translation
- Primary health care programme
- Livelihood & skills development programme
- Community organising and empowerment
- Infrastructure and support services
- Feeding programmes
- Youth ministry
- Pre-school ministry
- Community internet cafes

How partnerships are developing in the Philippines and beyond

Today, we have seven mission partnerships working among seven of the 14 "neglected ethno-linguistic groups." During the last ten years, we have seen significant breakthroughs in ministry, and house fellowships of new believers have been formed and are increasing in number.

One of these seven mission partnerships comprises over 20 participating churches and organisations. Together, they are involved in intercession, mobilisation or fund assistance, with eight of them being directly involved in operations to reach a specific "neglected ethno-linguistic group." Their combined missionary team is closely knit and very effective in providing mutual support and encouragement. There is a strong family atmosphere within this partnership. They have won a significant number of souls in the past seven years. Other partnerships have also experienced encouraging developments. One of the most positive indicators of the church planting partnership is that we are seeing previously neglected people groups now helping to reach their own people.

One of the important factors in providing the impetus for partnership formation and other collaborative ventures is the biennial gathering of field workers based in the region where there is the concentration of the said resistant people groups. Over the past two decades, this event has provided a forum for fellowship, intercession, sharing of good practices and new initiatives. Even ministry to those who have been hurting and/or neglected can be provided during this time.

In recent years, missionary teams working within the same religious block have begun to convene nationally on a regular basis, in order to encourage, empower, and sustain one another. Highly committed frontline workers have emerged as Religious Block Advocates for the major religious blocks in the Philippines as well as champions for many of the unreached groups in Asia.

Missionary sending agencies are also mobilising missionary teams for overseas mission work, in particular for church planting in the most difficult places. Agencies will often recruit a team of six missionary families from as many churches and send them together as a team. When they are on the field, the team members in a group will provide the necessary member-care to one another. The sending agencies regularly arrange for regional conferences as part of their organisational missionary care while the sending churches back in the Philippines provide prayer, financial support, and other forms of member care.

Realising that Filipinos seeking overseas jobs were being strategically deployed in most of the least evangelised countries in the world, dozens of missions organisations began consulting with one another to explore ways to leverage this divinely engineered opportunity. As a result, these agencies organised themselves to embark on an unprecedented six-year project to raise hundreds of thousands of equipped tentmakers and long-term missionaries.

New networks aimed at missionary training, youth mobilisation, and missions intercession were organised to augment the other existing networks of member care and ministry in Muslim areas in order to serve the Body of Christ. Consultations with denominations, ministerial fellowships and mega local churches have begun so as to bring ownership of the Movement to as many as possible. Many Filipino churches in the National Capital Regions, Central Luzon, Central Visayas and Eastern Mindanao are now part of this growing grassroots movement.

Meanwhile, Filipinos in diaspora churches (outside of the Philippines) have also formed networks among themselves. We know of Filipino international networks in Europe, North America, Asia and the Middle East. We are now trying to collaborate to bring our networks closer together. If these networks can be harnessed properly, they can bring about a synergy never before realised on a global scale.

Working together in partnership is highly valued by Filipinos. We have found that this arrests the unhealthy practice of competition among churches and agencies. Partnership is essential to have a significant and sustained impact in the most difficult fields. Furthermore, it affirms the value of using gifts that the Lord of the Harvest has entrusted to every believer, church and mission organisation in a spirit of unity. May God bless our partnerships and networks for His glory.

Discussion questions:

1. Does your organisation or church work in partnership with other organisations or churches in your country when mobilising or sending your missionaries to the mission field? What factors have hindered you from pursuing such cooperation?

2. Do your missionaries on the field collaborate with missionaries from other organisations or churches? What is the nature of their partnership, if any?

3. What can be done to encourage or strengthen mission partnerships in your country or region?

4. How could strong partnerships and effective networks contribute to missionary retention?

In the real world:

A table to stimulate ideas for best practice in mission partnership. For further explanation, see page 7.

This chart has been partially filled in for you. Now you fill in the blanks.

Who? → When? ↓	Home Church	Missionary	Mission Agencies	External Partners
Continuous	➢ Create a culture of practising partnership, modelled by the leaders ➢ Teach partnership in educational programmes for young and old ➢ Make a deliberate choice to be involved in the missionary process	➢ Stimulate partnership with missionary partners ➢ Be inclusive and informative ➢ Have a team-approach	➢ Enter into partnerships with (external) partners ➢ Share needs and answers with other agencies ➢ Seek involvement of the home church ➢ Encourage and facilitate opportunities for missionaries to partner on field	➢ Serve needs of others ➢ Facilitate partnerships ➢ Teach partnership ➢ Partner (inter)nationally
Recruitment				
Preparation				
On field				
Crisis				
Furlough				
Re-entry				

5

Education

> "Highly qualified people stay longer"

The facts

In simple terms, education (equipping, training) is very helpful in retaining missionaries. High retaining agencies have almost twice as many missionaries with masters degrees and doctorates. They also have, on average, a two to three times higher minimal requirement in formal missiological training. (The value of specifically missionary focused training is discussed in detail in Chapter 9). Highly educated personnel can be more easily retained, since they have more potential to be offered and successfully fulfil different assignments within the same agency.

Agencies with highly educated missionaries also do better in the areas of professional organisation, personal care and co-operative leadership style, which (as discussed in other chapters) is good for their retention rate and their ability to attract high quality professionals to work with them. The leaders of high retaining OSC agencies underline the significance of continuous training for missionary longevity by rating their performance in that area 12 to 20% higher than low retaining agencies.

The data

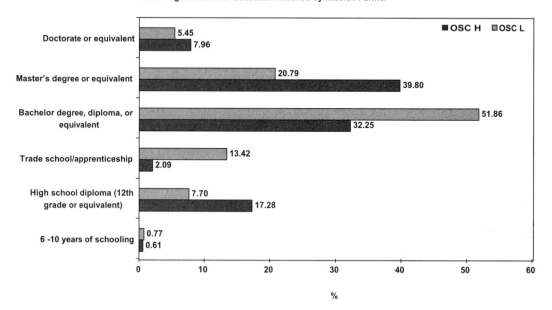

OSC - Highest Level of Education Reached by Mission Partner

	OSC H	OSC L
Doctorate or equivalent	7.96	5.45
Master's degree or equivalent	39.80	20.79
Bachelor degree, diploma, or equivalent	32.25	51.86
Trade school/apprenticeship	2.09	13.42
High school diploma (12th grade or equivalent)	17.28	7.70
6 -10 years of schooling	0.61	0.77

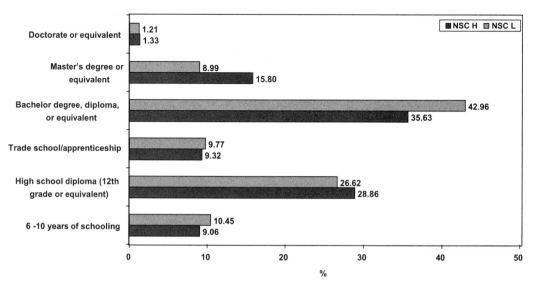

NSC - Highest Level of Education Reached by Mission Partner

	NSC H	NSC L
Doctorate or equivalent	1.33	1.21
Master's degree or equivalent	15.80	8.99
Bachelor degree, diploma, or equivalent	35.63	42.96
Trade school/apprenticeship	9.32	9.77
High school diploma (12th grade or equivalent)	28.86	26.62
6 -10 years of schooling	9.06	10.45

L: denotes low retention
H: denotes high retention

The key findings

✓ High retention is correlated with high educational standard (MA, PhD, Q31-32)
✓ In India and Nigeria there is a subgroup of agencies with high retention, though missionaries have generally only elementary or high school training.

What it means

Jaap Ketelaar

In an article in the WEA Mission Commission magazine, _Connections_ (Vol. 4, No. 2, Summer 2005), K. Rajendran, General Secretary of India Missions Association, spotlighted the importance of training for modern missionaries. Mission is changing across the world, and this impacts how missionaries are being trained. The following list is what he sees as macro-changes in world mission:

1. **The concept of a missionary is changing across the world.**

   The concept of a missionary has changed—from Western missionaries to a new category of local missionaries reaching across their own cultures, castes, ethnicities and families. From the 'long' concept of cross-cultural, meaning distance to travel, to the 'short' cross-cultural, where distance is limited so as to relate to people who are very near, yet different. From sharing the message in one specific way to sharing it in many ways to meet different needs. From full-time missionaries to tent-makers. From overt preaching intending to 'convert' people to a more holistic approach.

2. **The lessons learned from past missionaries are important for good or for worse.**

   It is important to relate God's good news in a fresh manner while retaining the good lessons learned.

3. **The challenges of missions today are different from the past.**

   For example, accelerated population growth and the use of mass media communication (visual, print, audio, internet).

4. **The demands on missionaries are higher today than ever.**

   The world is no longer an information-closed, colonised world where people are cooed into accepting Christianity. It is more important to bring people to Christ as "communities" and to disciple a "whole nation," instead of sporadic individual Christians in the mission compound. Pastoral care needs for missionaries are great and missionaries must try to relate to the society-at-large and not live a monastic style of life.

5. **The number of missions, the diverse visions, and the sheer number of missionaries are mind-boggling.**

   Multiple visions of missionary service are needed for the myriad of challenges across the world.

Has this need for continuous updated training been seen and sensed before? The context of increasing numbers of major changes in the world suggest it is important, and the data from ReMAP II has now clearly shown that it is not just important but a vital need. Looking from the perspective of retention of missionaries, the answer is stark and simple—a highly educated missionary has a stronger chance to survive and thrive in the work of God's Kingdom!

But what to think of this? Is mission something only for the elite who have both the talent and opportunity to study? This raises several questions:

- What of the "barefoot missionaries" in India and Nigeria (see *Key findings* and *In the real world*)?

- How does this relate to the findings of Christian Schwarz in his Natural Church Development Survey (1996), where he found that a theological education negatively correlates to church growth in quantity and quality?

- What about the Lord Jesus calling fishermen (Matthew 4:19) and Paul reminding the Corinthians of the state they were in when they were called ("not many of you were wise by human standards," 1 Cor 1:26). Did Jesus make a mistake?

The danger in focusing on higher education is that we lose sight of the balance that is needed. The Bible shows the importance of knowledge and education ("my people are destroyed from lack of knowledge," Hosea 4:6), but God clearly uses "unschooled, ordinary men" (Acts 4:13). God used Peter and John, both unschooled fishermen, but this did not mean they did not teach the believers (Acts 2:42). It looks like God glorifies himself through each and every believer, and yet there is a responsibility for everyone to grow in knowledge and be trained and equipped for use in God's service ("And the things you have heard me say in the presence of many witnesses entrust to reliable men who will also be qualified to teach others," 2 Tim 2:2). Every believer has received some talents from the Lord (Matt 25:15) and is responsible to give his or her "utmost for His Highest."[1] This perspective highlights the potential of every Christian and encourages all to be good stewards and further develop their God-given gifts and abilities (1 Peter 4:10).

Issues to deal with

How then, should this training take place?

Jonathan Lewis, a leader of the International Missionary Training Network (www. missionarytraining.com), uses a metaphor to describe the philosophy and character of ministry training: the metaphor of service.

---

1   Oswald Chambers, *My Utmost for His Highest*, (New York: Dodd Mead & Co., 1935).

"A Christian philosophy of training sees its foremost purpose as developing God's servants—enabling and equipping God's people to engage fully in their 'reasonable spiritual service' (Romans 12:1). The means is a transformational process that requires resisting conformity to the world's standards and attitudes, the infilling of God's Spirit, and the generation of right thinking/attitudes. It produces a lifestyle that is kingdom-centred and purposeful in service. The outcome is a 'living sacrifice' that is holy, pleasing, and acceptable to God for His service."[2]

Lewis identifies ten principles of training embedded in this metaphor:

1. The goal of the curricular process is to grow believers in the likeness of Christ and increase their usefulness in serving Him and His purposes.

2. The curriculum is an integrated process that addresses the need for growth in every area of life.

3. The curricular process understands and employs a broad range of different methods, means, and contexts to achieve its ends.

4. Training intentionally develops specific skills, right attitudes, and essential understanding for ministry competence.

5. Trainers are fellow servant/learners that are competent to guide the training process, and committed to mentoring the trainee.

6. God has a unique design for each individual that trainers perceive and help develop.

7. Learning happens in community and depends as much on interaction with fellow trainees as on the input of mentor-guides.

8. Knowledge is not a goal in itself, but when combined with obedience and practice, it contributes to understanding, maturity and competence.

9. The trainee is responsible for his own growth through obedience to God's will and diligence in practice and service.

10. The training programme and skill of the mentor-trainers is evaluated by their trainees' success as persons and in their ministry.

These principles underscore the position that training is not theoretical alone, but that the whole person should be transformed. Character-building is an essential element to the success of training and is the basis for life-long-learning[3] that is so needed on the mission-field.

---

2   Jonathan Lewis, "A Metaphor and a Model for Missionary Training," *Connections*, Vol. 4, No. 2, (Summer 2005), p.14.

3   Please refer to Chapter 23 on "Staff Development" for further discussion on life-long learning.

In his article "An Integrated Model of Missions"[4] Rodolfo Girón, President of COMIBAM, echoes the same vision and identifies a model of the development of a missionary. He calls it the process of Spiritual Formation and it starts with a person's birth:

1. *Foundational* Level 1 encompasses a missionary's *Life Foundation, Secular Foundation* and *Professional Foundation*. The *Life Foundation* describes a person's unique cultural, social and family background. God took life development into account when He chose Paul to minister to the Gentiles and Peter to minister to the Jews. Next, a person's *Secular Foundation,* shaped by High School, College, and Graduate School, becomes the basis for professional roles. This training can influence a missionary's role and can even provide opportunities for working as a professional in restricted areas. Finally, the *Professional Foundation*—professional experience gained in the secular world, gives the missionary greater awareness of the realities of life.

2. Level 2 is the *Ecclesiastical* level, training from the church. This begins with discipleship at the local church and is informal in nature. Next comes biblical training, which can also start in the local church, and provides a solid base for life and work. Theological or missiological training follows. The need for a well-rounded development throughout the earlier stages of life seems obvious, but the results of ReMAP II show that if this is lacking it is a major hindrance to retention. Leadership and ministerial experience complete this level. The best missionaries are those who have proven in their home culture that they can minister in a relevant way to other people.

3. On top of this integrated model is Level 3: the *Missionary* Level. A good cross-cultural experience or training programme helps the missionary and sending partner know if the missionary is able to adapt to another culture or community before going to the field. How good it would be if this programme could be run either in another country, another culture or in a training environment that has a strong multi-cultural community life so the missionary could really experience its challenges before going. Such programmes (language school, outreach training, etc.) would ideally be held close to the host culture where the missionary will work.

Finally, the missionary is ready to go to the field. This preparation may take a long time; however, the focus should not be on short-term success, but should aim for quality and fruit for the long-term.

Mutual learning

- Training institutes in both Old Sending Countries and New Sending Countries could develop programmes together, including an exchange programme in their curriculum.

---

4   Rodolfo Girón, "An Integrated Model of Missions," William D. Taylor, ed., *Too Valuable to Lose: Examining the Causes and Cures of Missionary Attrition*, (Pasadena, CA: William Carey Library, 1997), pp. 25-40.

- Older generations could offer themselves as mentors and coaches for younger generations.

- Umbrella organizations (national, regional and global) could function as catalysts to bring all the partners together. Each partner should display an attitude which focuses on:
  - A spirit of partnership
  - A clear picture of the different roles
  - Communication

Is higher education required for effective mission work?

Nathaniel Y. Abimbola,[5] Ethnos Christian Missions,[6] Nigeria

Note: Some names used in this case study have been changed to protect the identity of individuals working on the field.

In the early 1980s, some Christians from Shield of Faith Ministries International (SFMI)[7] in Oregon, USA, came to Nigeria. They conducted discipleship training among the young people, many of whom had only received a basic primary education.

Some of those first generation students are still being used by the Lord now at Ethnos Christian Missions (ECM). We are involved in researching new tribes, training new workers, and establishing local churches in rural areas. Therefore, we are teaching what we have been taught as well as working in new fields.

My life story

By God's grace, I was one of the students who went through the discipleship training. Please allow me to briefly share my life story. I was born in the 1950s, but I met my Saviour and Lord only on February 14, 1974. Prior to that, my life had been a spectacular manifestation of God's saving grace. I am one of three surviving children in a family of 14 children. That in itself tells a story. I received basic primary education followed by trade school, which eventually qualified me as a technical supervisor working in a top brewery. When I was called into full-time mission work, I resigned. I have not looked back since.

After completing the discipleship training conducted by SFMI, I have continued in full-time missions for about 20 years. Presently, I work with my family in a village called Baaki that has hamlets of more than four different tribes of people from

---

5 Nathaniel Abimbola was previously Field Secretary and is currently the Mission Director at Ethnos Christian Missions. Nathaniel travels frequently to oversee the ministry on various fields "because the work cannot be done from afar, and missionaries do need encouragement and visitation."

6 Ethnos Christian Missions is an indigenous missionary training and sending agency, primarily based in Ibadan, Oyo state, Nigeria.

7 Please visit the website www.sfmiusa.org for more information about SFMI.

Nigeria's neighbours. The tribal people have come here to work in farming. They are the Ditamamaris, Ajah, Fongbe and Ewe from Benin republic and Ghana, and they work for the Egbas, who are the land owners. In such a modern day Babel, conflicts frequently occur. At times, the conflicts are simply due to lack of proper understanding and cooperation, coupled with an abysmally low literacy level. But God is good. We know that He will perfect the good work He has started among them.

It is my joy to serve at ECM. The leadership team includes Moses Bola Osho (Executive Director) and Samuel Ola Deji (who leads Christian Leadership and Missionary Training Institute (CLAMTI), the training arm of ECM). Alongside other very dedicated people, we work together to fly the banner of Jesus. From time to time, trainers from SFMI come back to conduct refresher courses, and these courses are open to brethren from different local churches and other agencies.

"What are you holding in your hands? Just come with that, and the Lord will work through you, because it is neither by power nor by might but by the Spirit." This statement actually reflects the way the Lord has been working in the lives of missionaries trained by Ethnos Christian Missions (ECM). All the missionaries sent out by Ethnos are full-time workers sent out in faith, and there are no salary earners among us. But the Lord has always been faithful to meet our many needs.

Many of the very effective missionaries sent by Ethnos Christian Missions have had little education, apart from basic primary and/or secondary education. Some of the missionaries have eventually undergone leadership training at CLAMTI, the missionary training institute arm of our organisation. Thus far, we have not seen any adverse results in ministry outcomes on the field as a result of low education. Instead, a preoccupation with higher education has at times been a setback to the field work. I will illustrate by sharing about some missionaries who served at one time or the other at ECM.

The rural worker

Bamidele was a young single missionary sent overseas to work among the local tribe in a rural area. He worked hard because he knew that God had called him to serve this people. Then one day, he felt that in order to do more on the field, he needed to get his Grade II teacher's certificate as well as the N.C.E (Normal Certificate of Education). So he left the field and returned to Nigeria. For some years, Bamidele pursued his studies, and finally he obtained these educational qualifications.

When Bamidele eventually returned to the field, he returned as a married man, and his wife had just delivered a baby. He soon discovered that the work which he had begun years ago had to be started afresh. As a family, the challenges they faced were much greater than what Bamidele had endured when serving as a single person. His ministry circumstances had changed. The problems of acclimatisation had to be overcome again. This was worsened by the fact that where the rural tribes lived, the amenities he and his family had taken for granted were virtually non-existent.

The village teacher

Adaobi was a student waiting for admission to college. She saw the need for a resident teacher and missionary on a field close by her home, and so she volunteered to serve for a year. During the day, she worked at the adult literacy and children education classes. In the evenings, Adaobi went to different villages on the field. She visited each village once a week for Bible studies and prayers. When Adaobi completed the one year, she left the field. Meanwhile, three children who had participated in Adaobi's teaching were brought to the town by their parents. The children were put in the Primary Three class, which was two years ahead of where they should have been for their age. Adaobi had obtained no formal teacher training certificate, but she had nevertheless been effective in her ministry.

Soon after Adaobi left, Okon took over as teacher and missionary. Being an N.C.E certificate holder, everyone had expected a lot from Okon, but expectations were not met. The villagers started to complain that their children were no longer speaking English very well, unlike when the other teacher (Adaobi) was around. The Bible study classes in the villages, which had been started earlier stopped abruptly. This was because the new missionary would not stay long enough on the field to lead them. Within a year, Okon left to serve elsewhere.

The church planter

Wole was content with the basic primary education that he had. When he came to ECM, he received some training at CLAMTI, our missionary training institute. Then Wole immediately directed his energies towards learning the language of the rural tribe. Language learning took several years. Eventually, Wole planted some local churches. Today, we rejoice that these new local churches are sending their own leaders to attend missionary training at CLAMTI. So far, two missionaries from this tribal people have successfully completed their training.

What we discovered

In summary, at ECM we have discovered that the barest minimum of education (the acquisition of literacy) is often sufficient for our field missionaries. In fact, we have observed that higher education in Nigeria (except in the technical schools) often does not train people to be problem solvers, but merely to be consumers. In many cases, someone with practical experience in agro-industry, furniture-making or mechanical workshop, who is able to read and write, can undergo language training as well as a university graduate.

The person with practical experience may even function better on the field. This is because he would be able to use his hands or skills proficiently on the field, thereby providing a means to support himself. In addition, our mission students who undergo short training under agencies such as the Red Cross (to acquire knowledge about first aid and basic health practices) are frequently more useful to the villagers on health matters than visiting social workers. The latter may not easily diagnose the health problems caused by conditions peculiar to the field.

Formal education, however, is not being thrown to the dust. Linguistic graduates have been of tremendous use in the translation of the Bible and other gospel materials into different languages. Language translation is often a long-term investment. Material that has been translated into local languages will ensure the steady growth and maturity of the local believers. Otherwise, the local believers have to depend on local interpreters.

The educational qualification of a potential missionary need not be a big question as to his/her suitability. Instead, the firm spiritual standing of a person is more important. Whatever educational qualifications a person holds, effectiveness on the field is guaranteed only if other enabling conditions are met. These conditions would include commitment, total surrender to the Lord, and adaptation to the host community, among others. The Pharisees had marvelled at Jesus' disciples because they were not learned individuals. In like manner, God continues to use those who are totally attuned to Him, even if they are relatively uneducated.

Discussion questions:

1. What are the educational requirements for new missionaries in your organisation (agency or church)?

2. What opportunities are provided for on-going education of your missionaries?

3. What life experiences or skills could be recognised as being equivalent to (if not more important than) a graduate level of formal education?

Non-formal missiological training: does it work?

Duncan Olumbe[8], Mission Together Africa (MTA)[9], Kenya

The locations and the names of people in this case study have been changed to protect the true identity of individuals involved.

Training for mission is inarguably a major factor in the life of missionaries. The training could be formal, non-formal, or a mixture. Some people hold the view that good mission workers must have solid formal training; the more qualified they are the better. However, the sad reality is that sometimes having highly formally trained workers does not necessarily translate into effective service in the field! Other people strongly believe that the best mission training is non-formal through the development of skills and experiences in the school of life. Indeed there are several non-formally trained missionaries who have been highly effective in the field. This case study explores the experience of one African mission organisation to highlight the case of non-formal mission training.

Discipling Souls International (DSI) is a discipleship organisation in East Africa with an emerging global mission vision. Over the years DSI has sent over 50 short-term and longer-term African missionaries across Africa and some parts of Europe. How has DSI handled the issue of formal mission training?

Virtually all DSI missionaries have not had formal mission training prior to deployment. Primarily this is because requests for DSI missionaries have tended to be urgent, thus often there is little time to go for formal training. There is also the fact that DSI has had no funds for such long-term formal training of its potential missionaries. DSI also got discouraged by a number of potential missionaries who, having opted to undertake formal mission training before going to the field, ended up in other "plum" Christian jobs instead of their initial vision for "frontline" mission fields. Let's look at some of DSI's missionaries:

Silas was sent by DSI to central Africa in response to an SOS from a youth organisation in the host country who needed immediate help to strengthen their discipleship programme. There was neither time nor resources to send Silas for formal missiological training. Silas, in his mid-20s, qualified based on the non-formal in-house training, a formal short-course in basic biblical studies, and on-the-job ministry training he had received during his two years with DSI. A brief trip to

8   Duncan Olumbe is currently the Coordinator of Mission Together Africa (MTA). Duncan is also a member of the Core Team of Mission Mobilisation Task Force of WEA Mission Commission. He had been a short-term Kenyan missionary to the United Kingdom, where he worked among international students in Oxford. Then he served as the Missions Director of FOCUS Kenya (a student organisation in Kenya affiliated to IFES), where he was responsible for short-term and longer-term missionaries both to western countries (UK and Norway) and African countries (Sudan, Tanzania, Uganda, Rwanda and remote parts of Kenya). He was the Director of Commission 2004, a mission conference organised by FOCUS Kenya in Dec 2004 which brought together 2,500 participants from 29 countries mostly Eastern and Southern Africa.

9   MTA is a partnership of a number of churches and organisations in Africa who are keen to mobilise more Africans into global mission. Through networking and sharing of resources, we are seeking to catalyse mission movement across Africa. Specifically we are targeting Christian youth (for short-term mission trips), Christian professionals (for creative access areas), mission leaders (for consultations to reflect on new mission paradigms relevant to Africa), and Christian business entrepreneurs (for Business as Mission).

the host organisation and a series of orientation meetings by DSI mission staff concluded his preparation. Though apprehensive at first, Silas stepped out by faith into the field and ably set up a fully functional discipleship department in the host organisation. At the end of his service, he faithfully handed over the department to one of the nationals whom he had identified, mentored and trained for the task. Admittedly there were times when Silas wished he had a more formal mission training—especially to help him handle the cross-cultural challenges. However, with the benefit of hindsight, he is happy that God took him to the deep end of mission experience where he learnt to depend on God. Silas is now back with DSI and is yet to undertake formal theological training though he is hoping that this will soon be possible.

Kassey was another DSI missionary to a western Africa country. His role was to help mediate a healing and reconciliation process between two major Christian churches after a period of awful ethnic intolerance and cleansing. Being one of the first DSI missionaries, there was a lot of excitement mixed with apprehension at the prospect of having an African missionary serving in another African country! DSI did not have many models to copy or adapt in preparing Kassey. In his early-30s, Kassey had worked for DSI three years and had been a committed Christian worker. DSI therefore confidently chose him, given his experience. He had been through in-house non-formal staff training, the rigours of organizing one of DSI's major congresses, and had various short-term exposure trips. Much of his mission training actually took place on the field. Though he ended up playing a very crucial role in the reconciliation of the two churches, he was rather disappointed by DSI's member care.

Other DSI missionaries are Kuzila and his family of one son, the first DSI missionary family. Once again the request for the Kuzila family to go to Europe and serve among inner city youth was urgent and pretty hurried; their recruitment and commissioning process took less than five months! By now, DSI had a basic policy that any of their potential missionaries had to be people who had gone through their various in-house training programmes. Kuzila qualified on the basis of having served with DSI for close to six years, including a short-term cross-cultural missionary assignment. Once again there were neither funds nor time for formal mission training. Instead, they were given a condensed cross-cultural orientation by DSI and the host organisation. The hands-on experience proved very handy in Kuzila's ministry which turned out to be fairly significant in a largely post-modern Europe.

Bakunda is a young man in his 20s, currently serving as DSI's missionary in a southern Africa state. His preparation highlights some slight variations and additions in DSI's approach to mission training. He, like other DSI missionaries, has not received formal mission training. However, he qualified on the basis of having worked with DSI for over one year and thus had lots of informal training. However, in his case DSI was keen to offer a little more training. For example, he was enrolled into a language school to brush up his Swahili language (which he had learnt in school but he had not got sufficient opportunity for practice). He also had several informal sessions with some of the returned DSI missionaries like

Silas and Kuzila. When he finally landed in the field, he found the intense (though informal) preparation training very helpful in going about his ministry in a very difficult context. DSI has gone ahead to look for more informal mission training opportunities especially through mission conferences, consultations and relevant exposure trips. Though Bakunda would love to undertake formal mission training sometime in the future, the prospects are limited for now due to practical logistical issues.

In conclusion, time and financial constraints have made it virtually impossible for DSI missionaries to get formal training before placement. However, their previous experience, especially through in-house non-formal training (and occasionally augmented with formal short-courses) proved invaluable. However, lack of clear yardsticks in measuring the non-formal training was a major handicap. And though DSI missionaries have performed fairly well and compare favourably with formally trained missionaries, they would have valued some formal (or more intense non-formal) mission training prior to departure. Most of the missionaries have considered formal mission training after at least an initial term in the field.

Discussion questions:

1. How can emerging mission organisations (in New Sending Countries) creatively handle the lack of time and funds for formal mission training? Is non-formal training and prior ministry experience sufficient to cover for formal mission training?

2. If a non-formal training approach is available, has the programme been fully thought through and developed as an equal and viable alternative? Who should evaluate the quality of their non-formal training?

3. How does your organisation deal with mid-life crisis when middle-aged missionaries suddenly realise that although they have hands-on experience in mission, they lack academic qualifications to weather the rest of their lives?

4. How could we create an atmosphere where those non-formally trained are not looked down on by formally trained counterparts?

In the real world:

A table to stimulate ideas for best practice in mission partnership. For further explanation, see page 7.

This chart has been partially filled in for you. Now you fill in the blanks.

Who? → When? ↓	Home Church	Missionary	Mission Agency	External Partners
Continuous	➤ Appreciate and stimulate general education ➤ Appreciate and stimulate missiological education ➤ Provide Bible and discipleship training ➤ Offer place for learning experiences	➤ Commit to life-long-learning		
Recruitment			➤ Assess education ➤ Prioritise education	
Preparation	➤ Offer possibility of apprenticeship "at home" ➤ Financially support training possibilities	➤ Commit to training requirements and opportunities	➤ Create possibilities for pre-field, cross-cultural training	➤ Develop training modules and tools ➤ Offer character/competence training ➤ Partner with foreign training institutes
On field	➤ Support ongoing training	➤ Prioritise ongoing training ➤ Be responsible for own growth	➤ Offer training on the job ➤ Stimulate on-going education	➤ Assess education ➤ Prioritise education
Crisis				
Furlough		➤ Refresh and update personal and ministerial training ➤ Be involved in training candidates	➤ Give opportunities to do extra training	➤ Develop training opportunities ➤ Facilitate training opportunities
Re-entry	➤ Support new job training	➤ Be involved in training candidates	➤ Train missionaries for new job	

6

Selection

The facts

Selection procedures are vitally important for appointing people who will remain in service. This has been one of the major results of ReMAP I. At that time a significant minority of mission agencies had inadequacies in their selection procedures and ReMAP I confronted the missions world with the fact. Happily, the missions world was listening, and across almost all areas of selection, new and old sending countries are now rigorous in their screening procedures in most agencies. Still, the results of Questions 22 and 18 [Q22 Meets health criteria determined through a psychological assessment] and [Q18 Has ministry experience in a local church] raise important issues to be considered.

The data

Q. No.	Factor	OSC Importance for Selection	✓	NSC Importance for Selection	✓
11	Expresses a clear calling to missionary service	○○○○○○○○○●	✓	○○○○○○○○○○	
12	Agrees with the agency's doctrinal statement	○○○○○○○○○●	✓	○○○○○○○○●●	
13	Knows and is committed to the agency's principles and practices	○○○○○○○○○●	✓	○○○○○○○○●●	✓
14	Demonstrates mature Christian character and discipline	○○○○○○○○○●	✓	○○○○○○○○○●	✓
15	Has good character references	○○○○○○○○○●	✓	○○○○○○○○●●	
16	Has committed endorsement from his/her pastor/local church for missionary service	○○○○○○○○○●	✓	○○○○○○○○○●	✓
17	Has the blessing of their family	○○●●●●●●●●		○○○○○○●●●●	✓

18	Has ministry experience in a local church	OOOOOOO●●●	✓	OOOO●●●●●●	✓
19	Has had previous cross-cultural experience	●●●●●●●●●●		●●●●●●●●●●	
20	Has demonstrated ability to cope well with stress & negative events	OOOOO●●●●●		OOOO●●●●●●	
21	Meets health criteria determined by a physical examination	OOOOOOO●●●	✓	OOOOOO●●●●	✓
22	Meets health criteria determined through a psychological assessment	OOOOO●●●●●	✓	OOO●●●●●●●	✓
23	Exhibits contentment with present marital status (single, married)	OOOOOOOO●●	✓	OOOOOOO●●●	✓
24	Has good potential for financial support	O●●●●●●●●●		OO●●●●●●●●	✓
25	Has firm/stable prayer support	OOOO●●●●●●	✓	OOOO●●●●●●	
84	Pre-field screening prevents unsuitable persons proceeding to the field	OOOOOOOO●●	✓	OOOOO●●●●●	✓

The key findings

✓ Retention is highly correlated with candidate selection in general.

✓ The first six selection criteria (Calling, Q11; Doctrinal statement, Q12; Agency principles, Q13; Mature Christian character, Q14; Character references, Q15; Endorsement by pastor, Q16) were rated as being very important in all sub-categories of OSC and NSC, but especially by high retaining OSC and NSC.

✓ Calling (Q11), Doctrinal statement (Q12), Agency principles (Q13), Mature Christian character (Q14), Character references (Q15), and Committed endorsement by pastor/home church (Q16) were correlated with retention in OSC (and NSC, but some factors received a very high rating for performance and significance by mission executives in low retaining NSC agencies too, limiting the statistical significance).

✓ Ministry experience in the home church (Q18) was correlated with retention in OSC, but in NSC to a lower extent.

✓ Family blessing (Q17) received a high rating in NSC and was correlated with retention in NSC, but not in OSC.

✓ Physical health examination (Q21), Psychological testing (Q22), and Contentment with present family status (Q23) were correlated with retention in OSC and NSC; Potential for financial support (Q24) also Psychological testing (Q22) correlated in NSC (an unexpected result) and Firm prayer support of candidates (Q25) in OSC.

✓ The low rating of Cross-cultural experience (Q19) and Stress cope capabilities (Q20) and the absence of their significant correlation with retention was unexpected.

What it means

Sarah Hay

Properly conducted selection is a responsibility in order to ensure (as much as is possible with such a subjective process) that the right person is chosen. This responsibility is for the individual, for the agency, for the team on the ground, and for the church, both at home and on the field. Good selection results in a thriving, effective individual and in a thriving, successful team. These factors create a situation in which the missionary acts as a good ambassador for the mission agency, church members are encouraged to continue to support mission, and God's Kingdom is furthered.

In the area of selection, the inestimable contribution of ReMAP I and the book on its findings, Too Valuable to Lose[1] is clearly shown. This study and analysis extensively explored the selection process as a cause of attrition and showed that the more evaluation undertaken during the selection stage, the lower the Preventable Attrition Rate (PAR), as is seen in the adjacent graph. Almost all of the different areas suggested for screening evaluation (see Taylor, 1997, p. 114) presented the consistent message that attention to these resulted in lower attrition.

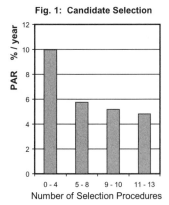

Fig. 1: Candidate Selection

In ReMAP II, these areas were explored further, and similar areas of importance emerged. The areas included: agreement with the doctrinal statement; clear call; mature Christian character; good references; and endorsement from the local church. Both OSC and NSC placed a high emphasis on these areas, and especially in OSC, these areas were significant factors in retaining mission partners. The case study from Henkie Maritz later in the chapter highlights some of these areas of best practice in selection.

The case study, "Filial Piety and Missionary Calling," by Vanessa Hung, highlights that the blessing of family [Q17 Has the blessing of their family] increases a missionary's likelihood of staying on the field for NSC. In cultures where filial piety (or a similar concept) is important, family blessing has a significant impact on whether missionary candidates can fulfil their call. Selection processes will, therefore, need to identify problems or potential problems in this area and help the candidate to find a suitable resolution, such as those suggested in the case study. Indeed, some mission agencies in NSC require financial support raised to be sufficient to provide care for the parents of the mission partners as well as the mission partners' own living costs!

---

1   William D. Taylor, ed., *Too Valuable to Lose : Exploring the Causes and Cures of Missionary Attrition*, (Pasadena, CA: William Carey Library. 1997).

OSC mission executives did not rate family blessing highly for significance and performance, and there was no correlation with retention. This is perhaps because the Western world sadly places less emphasis on family ties, and in this global village, while communication is much easier and brings people together across the distance, many individuals increasingly make decisions with little regard to the wishes of their wider family. That said, it is still necessary to discuss family issues in OSC during selection as some families do remain close and responsibilities back home can be a factor in people returning home.

In OSC, children's schooling may be equivalent to the value of looking after elders. Many parents wishing to become mission partners are concerned about school-ing—if it is to be in the same location, boarding, international, etc. Schooling is often a factor cited by a family returning home. In fact, the whole issue of bringing up a child overseas as a Third Culture Kid can be a huge concern to parents and a cause for attrition.[2] This should also be a point to consider during selection. Some agencies now advise families with teenage children to delay their departure until all children have left home or started higher education. The issue is worth investigat-ing thoroughly, for there are challenges in every choice.

A high correlation for retention was found for both NSC and OSC for selecting people who had a chance to "practice" ministry in their local church [Q18 Has ministry experience in a local church]. One reason for the correlation may be that missionary candidates can identify their own strengths and weaknesses while serving at home, and thus identify the area of ministry in which they would best be suited on the field. The selection process can help the candidate establish (if they are not already aware) where they would best be placed. NSC had a lower rating for performance and significance on this question, which might be because fewer opportunities exist for young people to be involved. Churches may need encouragement to let these future church leaders explore and assume roles with more leadership and responsibility. Certainly, if candidates are accepted and have little or no ministry experience with their church (whether in NSC or OSC), they should be encouraged to become involved as part of their preparation process.

Two surprising results were in the area of previous cross-cultural experience [Q19 Has had previous cross-cultural experience] and ability to cope well with stress and negative events [Q20 Has demonstrated ability to cope well with stress & nega-tive events]. These did not bear a statistically significant correlation with retention. Anyone who has worked overseas knows that a different culture and workplace brings many challenges and can be extremely stressful. This fact is also reiterated by the extreme rating of "work-overload" (Q61). Yet here we are merely addressing the question of whether or not this issue was an important part of selection process (and was well done) or during pre-field training or orientation, and whether or not it had major impact on the acceptance or rejection of a candidate at that time. The absolute need of stress-cope capacity for life and ministry overseas is further expounded in Chapter 18 Work/Life Balance.

---

2   See D. Pollock, "What about the missionary kids and attrition?" in Taylor, *Too Valuable to Lose*, 1997.

Our increasingly cosmopolitan, globalised world requires living daily in a cross-cultural community, so that agencies may have reflected this by rating these areas low in importance and performance for selection. While a specific cross-cultural experience may not have happened, candidates may already live side-by-side with other cultures.

In addition, evaluating whether someone has coped well with stress and negative events is difficult to assess in an application interview and this may have caused agencies to downplay its importance. Does one need to live in community with the person to assess their ability to handle stress, or can character references be relied upon? Or perhaps the question was associated with psychological testing? Was "demonstrated ability" too high a hurdle?

Whatever the reason for the unexpected result, it is known that many missionaries are severely affected by stress on the mission field. Marjory Foyle, in Honourably Wounded,[3] explores this issue thoroughly. If there is a way to uncover a candidate's strengths and weaknesses in coping with stress, it would be worth investing the time. ReMAP III (if there ever is one) should investigate these issues further.

While debating stress, it is important to note that meeting physical health criteria [Q21 Meets health criteria determined by a physical examination] and psychological assessment [Q22 Meets health criteria determined through a psychological assessment] was correlated with retention, although neither question received a very high rating. Selection needs to include health assessment, although improvements need to be made in doing this more effectively (see Chapter 7 for further discussion).

It is not surprising that Question 23 [Q23 Exhibits contentment with present marital status (single, married)] received a fairly high rating in both NSC and OSC and showed correlation with retention. Mission partners should be content with their marital status and situation if they are to relate well with others and be effective in ministry. In an age, certainly in Europe, where the law constantly tightens around areas of discrimination, it can feel awkward questioning a candidate about their singleness, but probing is important. It is often said that a person's major weakness becomes amplified when they begin a role in a cross-cultural environment away from the safety-net of home. If that weakness is their singleness, for example, it could lead to depression or even, sadly not uncommon, an affair or other inappropriate behaviour. Likewise, a couple with a weak marriage may find the tensions of living cross-culturally enough to break the marriage apart. Using this area as a tool in your selection process is essential, and it is important not only to question the candidate/s, but also to ask specific questions of the referees, their church and during the psychological assessment. Often references are work related, but many organisations now require a reference from a male friend, a female friend, the church pastor and a work manager/colleague. This gives a much broader picture of the candidate and makes the references more meaningful.

---

3   Marjory Foyle, Honourably Wounded : Stress Among Christian Workers, (London: Monarch Books, 2001).

Finances are almost always an area of concern when thinking of mission service. Perhaps it is not, therefore, surprising that both OSC and NSC gave a poor rating for Question 24 [Q24 Has good potential for financial support] because across the board (with missionaries that stay and missionaries that leave) finances often begin as a concern. What is interesting is that for OSC, potential for financial support did not show a correlation with retention, but it did in NSC. For OSC, correlation could be explained by the continuing existence of denominational mission agencies (where there is little responsibility on the individual missionary to raise their own support) and the growth of new church movements that see themselves as senders and funders (with again, little responsibility left on the individual mission partner to raise support). Many NSC agencies do not have the luxury of fully funded denominational agencies and many of their churches are starting from scratch, trying to raise the profile of missions and encourage a (generally poorer) church membership to give. Possibly, agencies in OSC are able to advise and help candidates to seek funding, while NSC agencies do not have such experience so candidates are on their own. These reason may explain why potential for financial support is correlated with retention in NSC—if you cannot find the money, it will not come from anywhere else and thus you do not go.

Conversely, the issue of prayer support, [Q25 Has firm/stable prayer support] showed correlation with retention for OSC but not for NSC. Perhaps again this reflects historical influences. Have OSC agencies been cushioned by the wealth of the church population in general and therefore prayer (and "praying the money in") is more important for selection, while NSC agencies do not have that cushion and therefore the harsh reality of no money (thus no service) overrides the need for a firm prayer base at home? Or perhaps given that there is not only the absence of a correlation with retention in NSC but also a low rating of this issue, do they start support raising only after acceptance as new missionaries, so that it is not a matter of candidate selection? Is prayer support so important and self-evident to NSC that they do not put high priority to it in their selection procedure? Do OSC also, again through historical and bureaucratic reasons, have need for organised prayer groups and promises of prayer while NSC are free from such past baggage and simply assume that people will pray for them anyway? This is speculation, but it is an interesting difference. Without doubt, however, in whatever way it is organised, prayer is absolutely vital in preparing for and carrying out God's work.

In conclusion, pre-field selection procedures are vital in recruiting suitable people who will stay on the field. As Henkie's case study states, the selection process often takes six months or more, and candidates may balk at this lengthy process. But it is in their best interest, as well as the agency's, to follow this thoroughly in order to answer as many doubts and issues as possible, form realistic and shared expectations, prepare and then enable a suitable, effective mission partner to stay on the field.

Selection of mission applicants

Henkie Maritz,[4] World Mission Centre[5], South Africa

Note: the names used in this case study are fictitious, to protect the identities of persons involved in these real-life events.

Josh was shocked when his application to Serving in Mission South Africa (SIMSA) was not accepted. Josh felt called to serve as a missionary in Africa. He had a heart for the children who have been orphaned by HIV/AIDS and war. He dreamt of building an orphanage in a specific country. However, SIMSA was clear on the outcome: "We agree that Josh has a worthy cause, but building an orphanage is not within SIMSA's vision for that country at this time. We have recommended Josh to another country where SIMSA has a vision for orphans or to join another organisation."

Susan is an exemplary Christian with a sincere heart for the nations. She felt God's calling on her life and she sent an application to the SIMSA office. In her application form she revealed that she had received counselling in the past. During her lifestyle interview, Dr. Louw asked deeper questions about traumatic past experiences, her family life and childhood. For the first time in her life, Susan broke down and admitted that she had been raped as a teenager. SIMSA guided Susan on a road to healing before any further steps were taken with regard to her entering the mission field.

These two examples emphasize the importance of an effective selection process. One can only imagine the conflicts and issues that could have occurred, had either Josh or Susan been sent to the field without these issues being picked up during selection.

SIMSA regards the careful selection for mission applicants as their primary reason for being so effective in the field. The process is very long but thorough. The time taken from application to acceptance may be a minimum of six months. This indicates the thorough and deep selection process to which SIMSA is committed.

Selection is an area of good practice in many effective mission agencies in South Africa. The following are common features of the selection process by such agencies:

1. Validating missionary's calling and vision

    The mission agency's leadership will validate that the mission applicant has a clear calling from God and that his/her vision and goals fall within the vision of the organisation and the vision of the respective field. Validation is not

---

4   Henkie Maritz is a Software Engineer. Since 2000, he has worked part time at the World Mission Centre in South Africa. Besides assisting in organizing certain events, he was Country Coordinator for the ReMAP II study in South Africa. The study gave him a deep appreciation for missionary sending organisations and the challenges they face.

5   World Mission Centre is a missions mobilization organisation that mobilizes the local church in South Africa for missions

easy to achieve, and it frequently requires a process of intense interviewing and mentoring to help the applicant discover their dreams and visions. The local church should have input to highlight how they have been involved in determining the applicant's calling and vision. In some cases, applicants have been redirected to other organisations due to a vision that does not match that of the original organisation.

2. Education and training pre-requisites

    A lack of the pre-requisite education (e.g., two years of Bible school and missions training) does not necessarily lead to an unsuccessful application. In most cases the mission organisation will walk the road of equipping and training with the applicants.

    Mission organisations have found that requiring further education and training will effectively test the commitment and determination of mission applicants.

3. Local church support

    Part of the selection process involves establishing a partnership with the applicant's local church. Operation Mobilization South Africa (OMSA) is a mission organisation that is totally committed to the local church, and it involves them from day one. For OMSA, sending a missionary involves a partnership between the person, his local church and the mission organisation. Should an applicant not belong to a local church, the applicant will be turned down.

4. Doctrinal assessment

    SIMSA's selection process makes provision for a basic assessment early on as well as a more thorough assessment later. Some applicants have been turned down after the basic doctrinal assessment. In one case, the applicant was unsure about her own salvation. In another instance, the applicant's doctrine of salvation was totally contradictory to the doctrine being proclaimed on the field.

    Why conduct doctrinal assessments? The reason is to achieve unity of truth being lived and proclaimed by the organisation's missionaries. This assessment brings the applicant's theology to light. It is used to highlight doctrinal issues that must be addressed and resolved before the applicant can be accepted.

5. Psychological assessment

    The example of Susan mentioned earlier highlights the importance of a proper psychological assessment as part of selection. Some areas typically covered in such an assessment are:

    *   Issues of sexuality in the applicant's past

    *   Involvements in drugs

    *   Previous involvement in non-Christian spiritual activities

    *   Police records

The purpose of psychological assessment is to discover personal issues that must be addressed before the applicant can continue with the selection process. (See Chapter 7)

6. Medical assessment

    A positive medical assessment result is of utmost importance in preventing known health problems arising when the missionary is on the field.

7. Character references

    Checking an applicant's character references serves to confirm and reinforce the reasons for an applicant being accepted or turned down. If an applicant is accepted, it also helps to identify strengths, weaknesses, their motives and how they are perceived in work and social settings.

Ultimately, the selection process is about getting to know the applicant in all areas of his/her life, so that the right people are sent to the right places (mission organisation and field) at the right time (when the person is ready and when God releases them to go).

In closing, here is a statement of this good practice as defined by some South African mission leaders: "We set high selection standards, but remain flexible enough to allow the guidance of the Holy Spirit."

Discussion questions:

1. How does your organisation conduct selection of its missionary applicants?

2. What areas are normally covered during selection? What other areas would you include in the future?

3. Does your organisation have mission field problems that could have been prevented during selection? If so, which and how?

4. If problems were discovered during selection, what would be some good practices to resolve them?

5. What is the role of the local sending church during the time a person resolves his/her problems (prior to acceptance into missionary service or to subsequent return to the ministry either at home or on the field)?

Filial piety and missionary calling

Vanessa Hung[6], Hong Kong Association of Christian Missions, Hong Kong

In the Chinese Culture, filial piety is a very important virtue. Adult sons and daughters have obligations to stay at home to take care of their parents. One of Confucius' sayings was: "As long as one's parents are alive, one should not leave home." Thus, aging parents can be a roadblock to those who have received a missionary calling from God. Is there anything the local church can do to solve such a dilemma?

Mandy received her calling from God, but she has an aged mother. She is the only daughter in the family. She had taken care of her mother all her life, after her father died many years ago. Nevertheless, she must respond to her calling. What could she do? She shared her burden with her local church. Their solution was to form a support group comprising some church members who would look after her mother. Mandy was relieved and left for the mission field. Since she left, members of the group took turns to visit her mother. They continued Mandy's routines such as taking her mother out for "dim sum" (Chinese meal) once a week. Even though her only daughter was overseas, Mandy's mother lived happily because she acquired so many surrogate sons and daughters who looked after her. Meanwhile, Mandy did not have to worry for her mother because she knew her church family was providing for this concern.

Tommy was the only son of his family. His father died when he was very young. His mother had worked very hard to bring him up. He had lived with his mother all his life, even after he got married. When he received his missionary call, his mother was very old, her health was not very good, and she could not live by herself. It was very difficult for Tommy to leave her alone. What could he do? Tommy shared his burden with his church. Grace, one of the church members, had a heart for missions. The Lord did not call her to mission, but she was determined to help Tommy pursue his mission dream. She decided to move to Tommy's home and to care for his mother while he went to the mission field. That solved the problem, and Tommy set out for the mission field.

Chan was an eye doctor, and his wife Kwan was a physiotherapist. God put missions on their heart. They planned to go to Afghanistan. At that time, Afghanistan was ruled by the Taliban Government. The leaders were Islamic fundamentalists and nationalists. They had banned all kinds of television, music and sports since the time they came into power. When Chan and Kwan's parents heard that they wanted to be missionaries and were headed for Afghanistan, they were shocked. After much prayer and solicitation, their parents finally agreed to let them go. Both sets of parents knew what kind of country Afghanistan was, so they were very worried for their children's safety. Because Afghanistan was an underdeveloped

---

6   Vanessa Hung graduated from Columbia International School in 1993 when she received her Master of Arts in Mission. Since then, she has served in the Hong Kong Association of Christian Missions as mission researcher. She has conducted several missionary research projects in Hong Kong, and she has a good understanding of Hong Kong mission churches and their missionaries.

country at that time, and the Government tended to shut off the country from the outside world, it was difficult for the outside world to communicate with people living or working in the country. What could the church do to help? In this case, the missionaries' church arranged for a satellite phone service for their parents. The parents could talk to their children over the phone once a month. That helped a lot, and it greatly alleviated the burden of both the missionaries and their parents.

Discussion questions:

1. Does your agency or church consider filial piety issues during the selection of missionary candidates for overseas assignments? If so, what policies or practices have been established to assist missionary candidates to resolve problems related to filial piety and/or family blessing? If not, should such issues be considered in the future?

2. Should the financial cost of caring for elderly parents be built into the support budget of the missionaries?

In the real world:

A table to stimulate ideas for best practice in mission partnership. For further explanation, see page 7.

This chart has been partially filled in for you. Now you fill in the blanks.

Who? → When? ↓	Home Church	Missionary	Mission Agencies	External Partners
Continuous				
Recruitment	➢ Have a culture of identifying candidates ➢ Serve as a clear reference for agencies ➢ Provide opportunities for pre-field orientation at home and on the field ➢ Provide special support in prayer, finances, mental or family issues	➢ Be open for feedback and (negative?) advice ➢ Be honest and transparent ➢ Be willing to take time for tested calling	➢ Be clear about expectations of profile and ministry ➢ Be clear and honest about your agency to candidates ➢ Get local church involved	➢ Provide tools for assessment ➢ Be available for assessments
Preparation				
On field				
Crisis				
Furlough	➢ Get missionaries involved in mobilising and selecting candidates	➢ Be available for sharing experiences ➢ Be available for advice ➢ Look for potential missionary candidates	➢ Give opportunities for missionaries to help in selection	
Re-entry				

7

Selection
Health and Psychological Assessment

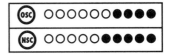

 The facts

The selection of suitable mission partners is complex, includes different components, and is highly correlated with retention. Part of the selection process is the use of physical and psychological assessments to determine a candidate's suitability in physical and mental health. These two types of assessments were highly correlated with retention, both for OSC and NSC.

 *The data*

Q. No.	Factor	OSC Importance for Selection	✓	NSC Importance for Selection	✓
21	Meets health criteria determined by a physical examination	○○○○○○○●●●	✓	○○○○○○●●●●	✓
22	Meets health criteria determined through a psychological assessment	○○○○○●●●●●	✓	○○○●●●●●●●	✓

 The key findings

✓ Rating of physical health exams (Q21) was highly correlated with high retention in NSC and OSC.

✓ Psychological testing (Q22) was rated significantly lower than health exams (Q21) and proved to be correlated with retention, especially in NSC.

What it means

Sarah Hay

The medical examination has been part of candidate selection for a long time, reflected by fairly high ratings for performance and significance by mission executives in both OSC and NSC. Later in the chapter, Dr. Stroma Beattie, from OMF International, outlines a very clear "best practice" example of how medical examinations can be carried out and what type of problems and complex issues may arise. As she states, "No-one is immune from ill-health." Thus, the purpose of these examinations is not to eliminate everyone who may be at risk of ill health (because potentially no-one could go), but to identify the *level* of risk. Dr. Beattie reminds us that "it is a difficult matter to place someone with known health problems in a situation which will aggravate their health." If potential problems are identified, solutions can be examined and a new mission partner can receive guidance in placement so as to serve as effectively as possible—as long as the risk to their health is not too great.

While the ratings were quite high, there was certainly room for improvement in their use. NSC may have a problem with finding medical experts who are aware of the medical issues faced on the field. For both OSC and NSC, lay-people may have difficulty interpreting the medical opinion. When given medical advice, agency personnel can be tempted to interpret it themselves or possibly even disregard it (which could be valid, but care should be taken to connect the missionary partner with an on-field medical advisory team).

Part of the key to the success of OMF International's medical procedure is that there is communication between home and field. The medical advisors should have experience in missionary health and be in contact with relevant medical personnel on the field to establish further information, such as the country's health care capacities and specific drug availability. A particular health issue may not be accommodated in one country, but could be in another. This can be established with informed knowledge and communication. Best practice dictates that medical advice be listened to and carefully, confidentially considered as part of the selection procedure. No-one is helped when someone is sent to the field if their health puts them at risk and drains resources, especially human resources, from the team. In our own experience—ignore medical advice at your own peril!

Psychological assessments are a new issue in missionary selection (though not in the secular world, having been used for over 50 years). The low rating by NSC may be a reflection of the relatively recent introduction of psychological assessments in some agencies or that other agencies do not use them at all. The medium rating given by OSC may reflect the reality that some organisations still do not use psychological assessments or do not feel they provide the information necessary to determine whether the candidate actually meets the requirements. There is still, in some quarters, a suspicion about these assessments; in other quarters perhaps ambivalence. Some organisations feel that having a candidate live with them in community for a period of time during pre-field orientation is sufficient to form an opinion of that person's coping mechanisms and psychological well-being. However, such an experience, though different from normal life perhaps, will not generate the same huge stresses of moving, living and working on the field. It is important that a professional experienced in dealing with psychological issues and aware of overseas placement stresses is involved in the assessment. From our own anecdotal evidence, a number of people suffering stress, burn-out or other psychological problems were people for whom no psychological assessment had been received because their agency did not, or would not, use them.

To alleviate some of the suspicion and help those of us who are not professional psychologists/counsellors, it is helpful to understand something about psychological assessments. Psychological testing is often called occupational or psychometric testing, terms used to describe specifically designed tools to measure areas such as intelligence, personality and ability. Tests can be used for different situations, such as team building or selection. The Chartered Institute for Personnel and Development (CIPD) in UK describes them as follows: "Psychological tests are tests which can be systematically scored and administered, which are used to measure individual differences (for example in personality, aptitude, ability, attainment or intelligence). They are supported by a body of evidence and statistical data which demonstrates their validity and are used in an occupational setting."

An organisation should establish a policy on test use that takes into account issues such as: at which stage tests should be incorporated into the selection process; who will carry out which tests; what weight will be given to the results in terms of decision-making; confidentiality and record-keeping; and who will give what feedback. One of the important reasons for carrying out tests is to help a candidate identify their own issues for development or training (see Dr. Barbara Griffin's case study) so the way in which feedback is given is important. As already mentioned, these tests must only be administered, scored and analysed by trained people and so, when deciding what tests to use, an agency should seek advice from the trained individual or organisation. CIPD advises the use of more than one test (see examples of tests in case study). It must also be stressed (as Dr. Griffin highlights in the case study) that a selection decision must not be made solely on the basis of a psychological assessment. There is no right answer to such a test—indeed people often worry that they will fail the test because they did not have time to answer all of the questions, but tests are often designed not to be finished. Tests are meant to help inform the decision of selection when used alongside other parts of the selection process, e.g., interview and references. A reference and interview may allude to an individual preferring to work alone and a psychological assessment could be used to clarify this. A suitable placement where the individual will not be required to work in a large team could then be identified.

A brief word should be mentioned about a relatively recent development—on-line psychological testing. Currently in UK, only 5% of companies are using this method, but according to CITP, it is likely to increase. On-line testing would obviously be an attractive option for organisations that have no access to a trained professional or organisation to conduct the tests on their behalf. However, there are a number of concerns, not least who is actually behind the test on-line and was the test conducted under test conditions. The British Psychological Society has identified three main conditions under which tests take place: uncontrolled and unsupervised (the test taker registers and does the test on the open internet); controlled but unsupervised (the organisation registers the candidate, ensuring their identity, but does not supervise the tests in terms of environment or time); and controlled and supervised (a qualified test user logs in the candidate and ensures that timing and test requirements are met). The International Test Commission is producing International Guidelines on Computer-based and Internet Delivered Testing. In the meantime, it is advised to only use such tests if there is no other alternative, and to ensure control and supervision where possible.

A number of agencies also require their mission partners to undergo a physical examination and psychological assessment during home assignment and upon final re-entry. This is partly to ensure that the individual is still medically and psychologically fit to return. The testing also helps to identify needed medical treatment. Additionally, this procedure has the added benefit of helping an individual identify further training or development needs they may have and whether they need further de-briefing or counselling to help them assimilate their mission experiences and be ready to return to the field or home.

Organisations need to assume moral and ethical responsibility for sending out a whole family because it is not sufficient for just the post-holder to be fit! William Carey may have been the father of the modern missionary movement, but the health of his family and the psychological state of his first wife, Dorothy, was clearly a secondary issue and his family suffered terribly. If a candidate's spouse or child is at risk, either physically or psychologically, that needs to be taken into account (see Chapter 6 and David Pollock's chapter in *Too Valuable to Lose*). A number of organisations now conduct assessments for the whole family (certainly for children over seven years old). This is a big step forward.

Some may be reading this chapter because they want an answer to a specific medical or psychological dilemma: "I have a candidate who is 55 years old and has high blood pressure—should they be accepted?" "What about a candidate with a history of anorexia, or a family history of depression?" It is impossible to come up with a tick list of who to send or refuse because each candidate will have different factors affecting their health, not only from their own background, but also from the type of role and place that they may be sent to. Only by considering all of the factors can an informed decision be made.[1]

The excellent case studies provided below attest to the importance of health and psychological assessments. If mission agencies are to improve on their selection and retention record, this area must be given attention. Trained testers, their results and recommendations must be used as part of the selection process for a candidate's acceptance, identification of placement, and role.

---

1   For an approachable and yet thorough overview of such issues, see *Honourably Wounded: Stress Among Christian Workers* by Marjory Foyle (London: Monarch Books, 2001).

Candidate selection and medical matters

Stroma Beattie,[2] OMF International, Singapore

OMF International, formerly the China Inland Mission, has been sending missionaries to East Asian countries for 140 years. In the early days, candidate selection was a fairly straightforward affair, often relying on personal interactions between potential new recruits and agency leaders such as the visionary founder, Hudson Taylor.

The story is told of Taylor turning down one Scottish gentleman on two occasions, although he tried to convince Taylor of his call to serve in China. On a third occasion, when the persistent Scot caught him at the end of a meeting, the man again tried to impress Taylor with his sense of call. The Scot quoted Jeremiah—"The lame shall take the prey." Taylor acknowledged that there was plenty of "prey" in China at that time (using this vivid metaphor for evangelism) and that the man, with his wooden leg, was certainly lame enough. Therefore, Taylor relented and accepted him for service. The story ends with a comment: "In those days, candidate councils and selection processes were yet to be developed."[3]

Nowadays, candidate councils and selection processes are well established. As a missionary-sending agency, OMF International has set policies and practices for the health screening of all new workers and their families. In a typical year, OMF handles more than 150 applications for missionary service. (This does not include those who apply for service of less than one year.)

Missionary applicants complete a detailed medical questionnaire as part of their candidature. They and their families then undergo a full physical medical examination, some baseline medical investigations, and a psychological assessment. Depending upon the sending country, these assessments are done by OMF International's own Medical Advisers or in partnership with groups which specialize in missionary health, such as Edinburgh International Health Centre (UK) or International Health Management in Toronto (Canada). With all these assessments, the results are not seen as "pass/fail" examinations, but rather one part of what a former OMF International Director for Personnel has described as "the Holy-Spirit directed art of candidate selection."

Reports from the medical assessments and recommendations of the home-side Medical Adviser are sent to OMF's International Headquarters in Singapore. There, the International Medical Adviser (IMA), an experienced missionary and full-time doctor, makes a formal medical recommendation to the agency leaders

---

2 Dr. Stroma Beattie has post-graduate qualifications in family and travel medicine. After a further year in psychiatry, she moved to South Korea with her husband in 1991 as OMF missionaries. Full-time language study was followed by medical and missions work. She moved to Singapore in 1998 to become OMF's International Medical Adviser.

3 A.J. Broomhal, *Hudson Taylor and China's Open Century*, Book Three: "If I Had A Thousand Lives," (London: Hodder and Stoughton and Overseas Missionary Fellowship, 1982).

regarding the health and suitability of each candidate to serve in the receiving country.[4]

For some, the medical histories are straightforward and the assessments simply lead to basic advice such as pre-field immunizations. For others, new problems are detected or complex issues come to light:

- A candidate takes regular medication. Is this medicine available in the country of service or can it be legally and reliably sent into the country?

- A routine investigation has revealed an abnormality but the underlying cause is unknown. Should the person proceed or wait until it is fully diagnosed in the home country? Will the new condition impact the candidate's medical insurance? Could the medical problem mean that the person's much-needed emergency medical evacuation insurance will be restricted?

- What about a person with insulin-dependent diabetes who wants to work in a remote area where there are no facilities for effectively storing insulin?

- A family has a young child who has just been diagnosed to have learning difficulties. Should they be placed in a bilingual situation during the child's critical language learning years?

In such situations, besides interacting with the Medical Adviser in the home country to obtain further details, the IMA consults with the relevant Field Medical Adviser (FMA), another medical missionary usually living and working in the specific country where the candidate hopes to serve. This FMA usually has a much greater knowledge and awareness of the country's health capacities, the local health risks and the everyday pressures which new workers face.

The IMA then gives advice to OMF's leadership regarding the individual's fitness to serve. This is a professional medical judgment based on several factors. These include an awareness of the specific medical conditions the candidate may have; an understanding of the cross-cultural pressures they will face; a knowledge of the specific field situation and the likely ministries which will be involved; an appreciation of the support infrastructure, if any, which colleagues might be able to offer; the nature of the local medical facilities; an assessment of the possible need for medical evacuation or particular insurance considerations; the dynamic of the couple or family offering for service as well an assessment of what level of risk it seems wise to take.

Usually, the medical recommendation is positive. Sometimes, the recommendation is to reconsider designation, possibly moving a potential new worker from a remote area which has very limited medical resources to one which has some basic emergency medical care and will provide the kind of back-up that the new worker with their specific medical problem needs. On rarer occasions, it is felt that the condition precludes field service and the individual or family unit would be best to focus on ministry in their home country.

---

4   For more details, please refer to the case study "OMF's medical advisory service - a model for medical member care" in Chapter 16 on Member Care.

Whatever the advice, the agency leaders (in both the receiving and sending countries) along with the individuals will pray through the recommendation to discern the Lord's guidance and make a final decision regarding acceptance of each candidate. Usually the medical advice is followed. However, at times, the leaders and a candidate decide to proceed despite a negative medical recommendation. At such times, it is then the role of the Medical Advisory team to help provide appropriate care for the new worker.

For some, this idea of involving medical expertise and professional advice (it might be termed pragmatism or common sense) in the process of discernment of a spiritual issue such as missionary call is sometimes seen as potentially meddling with God's sovereignty. For many, it is seen as prudent stewardship. At OMF International, we see called and willing Christians as our very best resource for the task of world mission. No task-force would place unfit team members on the front-lines where they would be personally subject to immense stress and potentially preventable premature repatriation.

The aim of the whole process of medical and psychological candidate screening is to provide sound professional medical advice which will serve the best interests of the candidate and in turn the agency. As a side benefit, the screening provides baseline information on medical and psychological matters which can be used to help the new worker when fresh health problems arise.

No one is immune from ill-health. Everyone on the field is willing to care for sick colleagues when the need arises. However, it is a different matter to place someone with known health problems in a situation which will potentially aggravate their ill-health. As well as placing them at significant personal risk, it may also absorb the time and energy of colleagues, diverting everyone from their ministries, as they seek to deal with a health crisis which was to some extent predictable.

The screening process is designed to enable the new worker to better serve effectively in the area to which they have been called. This enhances the local ministry, protects the work of the team in the area and enables the agency to maintain an effective taskforce.

Clinical summaries for discussion:

1. A 66-year old retired pastor is hoping to serve in a remote Bible college in the Philippines. He has high blood pressure, diabetes and kidney problems. He has had heart trouble in the past. What would you advise?

2. A childless couple is hoping to serve in Mongolia. They plan to leave in two months but they have just realized that the wife is pregnant (eight weeks). She has had one miscarriage in the past. They have been married eight years. What would you advise?

In each of the above situations, the questions to be asked include: Where and for how long do the individuals hope to serve? (For a short-term placement, greater risk-taking might be acceptable.) What are the local medical facilities like? What about the living conditions? What are the likely stress levels they would face? How about the diet? What level of physical exercise is demanded? What about their ministries? Would they be isolated or part of a team? Would they be insured?

For the pregnancy: Could a pregnant mother be evacuated? (Some airlines limit the carriage of pregnant women.) What are the facilities for the baby, should it be born prematurely?

Other questions to be considered are the following: What level of risk is acceptable to them? To their families? To their sending churches? To their agency? To their colleagues in the receiving country? Who will pick up the pieces if things go wrong? Should there be a fuller medical assessment? Should they delay their departure?

Missionary selection and psychological assessment

Barbara Griffin,[5] University of Sydney, Australia

During the early 1990s, "Agency A," an organisation in Australia with a church planting focus, was thrilled with the rapid increase in applications for overseas service. At that time their selection process did not include psychological assessment. However, the following two incidents motivated the Director to implement its use.

David's profile

David was accepted as a new worker with Agency A for a position with a church planting team in a country whose people were known for their outgoing, loud, "collectivist" nature. In this culture, high importance was placed on spending time with family and friends, often in animated conversation, and emotions were freely expressed. David, a computer programmer, was a highly intelligent young man with a gift in teaching/preaching. Eighteen months into his initial three-year term, the Australian Director of Agency A received a letter from David's field leader documenting David's poor performance, including an apparent lack of ability to relate to nationals, an aloof attitude to co-workers, and overall poor adjustment. He eventually returned to Australia and resigned from the agency. A subsequent personality profile indicated that David was:

---

5   Dr. Barbara Griffin is an organisational psychologist based in Sydney, Australia. Previously, Barbara and her husband were full time workers for WEC International for 22 years. She is currently on the academic staff at the University of Sydney and also works in private consulting. Barbara lectures in psychometric testing and selection for the senior undergraduate psychology programme and for the coaching psychology unit at the University of Sydney, and offers training in stress management, personality and generational differences to several mission agencies. Barbara also conducts the psychological assessments of candidates for a number of different mission agencies and denominational groups in Australia.

- Strongly reserved with a preference for solitary work
- Serious, prudent and restrained
- Highly self-reliant and individualistic with a low preference for group-oriented activities and decision-making.

Discussion questions:

1. Had David's profile been known before his acceptance, which of the following do you think are valid options when considering his application? Why/why not?

   - Not accept David
   - Redirect him to a different ministry
   - Give David feedback on his results, highlighting the strengths, challenges, and differences with the "typical" national personality
   - Further question his referees and pastor about his ability to overcome his natural preferences and interact well with others
   - Ask him to spend a period of time in a home church situation to develop his interpersonal skills
   - Organise for a formal mentoring relationship to be available on the field
   - Accept David and trust that his personality would change once he was on the field
   - Accept David but warn the Field Leader about his personality

Miriam's past

Miriam, a bright, vivacious, and outgoing young woman applied for cross-cultural work with a team ministering to urban poor. Miriam wanted to work in the day care centre for children, many of whom had been the victims of physical or sexual abuse. Her pastor spoke highly of her Sunday School teaching ministry and other referees were generally positive, although one mentioned that Miriam could be moody at times. Several months after arriving on the field, Miriam became significantly depressed, cried frequently, withdrew from her colleagues, often missed work, and according to her housemate, spent much of the day in her room sleeping. The Field Leader discovered that Miriam had begun self-harming behaviours and arranged for her immediate return to Australia. On arrival, she was referred to a psychologist who found that Miriam had experienced several episodes of depression in the past and had self-harmed on a number of occasions during her teenage years. Miriam disclosed that she had been sexually abused as a young child. She had never received professional help for her problems.

Discussion questions:

1. What effect could Miriam's experience have on the missionary team? On the local believers? On her supporting church? On the sending agency?

2. Had Miriam been assessed before her initial acceptance by Agency A, what do you think would be the best practice in handling her application?

Three main objectives

The use of psychological assessment for missionary selection has three main objectives: (1) screening for evidence of clinical syndromes/emotional vulnerability, (2) helping the agency to maximise the fit between missionary and his/her overseas placement, and (3) providing a development/training opportunity for the individual. These objectives are achieved by use of standardised psychometric tests together with interviews.

The stories of Miriam and David illustrate how achieving the first two objectives of psychological assessment can reduce missionary attrition. See Schubert[6] and Richardson[7] for a discussion on how the presence of untreated or inadequately controlled psychopathology might be exacerbated under conditions of stressful cross-cultural adjustment. Just as importantly, the linking of personality characteristics with required job behaviours aids in the assessment of how well a person will "fit" a field situation (see Allworth & Griffin,[8] Griffin & Hesketh[9]).

However, it needs to be impressed that it is inappropriate to make decisions regarding a missionary applicant solely on the basis of the psychological assessment. Agency personnel should consider information provided by a trained psychologist in the context of the whole selection process which can include assessment of training, doctrine, past experience, references, call etc.

When using psychological assessment, it is also important that good ethical practice is adhered to. For example, the agency needs to clarify issues regarding confidentiality of reports, competency of the psychologist, and feedback of results to the candidate. Assessments conducted under conditions of best practice can be a powerful learning experience for the candidate, increasing their self awareness and providing goals for future growth and development.

---

6   E. Schubert, "A suggested pre-field process for missionary candidates." Journal of Psychology and Theology, 27, (1999), pp. 87-97.

7   J. Richardson, "Psychopathology in missionary personnel," In K. O'Donnell, *Missionary Care: Counting the Cost for World Evangelisation*, (Pasadena, CA: William Carey Library, 1992). pp. 89-109

8   E. Allworth and B. Griffin, B, "The application of psychological assessment to executive coaching." in M. Cavanagh, A.M. Grant, and T. Kemp, T. eds., *Evidence-based coaching: Contributions from the Behavioral Sciences (Vol. 1)*, (Bowen Hills QLD: Australian Academic Press, 2005)

9   B. Griffin and B. Hesketh, "Counselling for work adjustment," in S. D. Brown & R. W. Lent eds., *Career Development and Counselling: Putting Theory and Research to Work*, (New Jersey: John Wiley & Sons, Inc., 2004)

In the real world:

A table to stimulate ideas for best practice in mission partnership. For further explanation, see page 7.

This chart has been partially filled in for you. Now you fill in the blanks.

Who? → When? ↓	Home Church	Missionary	Mission Agencies	External Partners
Continuous				
Recruitment	➤ Be supportive of physical and psychological assessments ➤ Be available for information about the bigger picture of a candidate's history	➤ Be open for feedback and (negative?) advice ➤ Be honest and transparent ➤ Be willing to take time to confirm calling	➤ Use physical and psychological assessments ➤ Have professionals yourself or seek them as partners ➤ Have an eye for the bigger picture	➤ Provide tools for assessments ➤ Be available for assessments
Preparation				
On field				
Crisis				
Furlough	➤ Be supportive of physical and psychological assessments ➤ Be available for information about the bigger picture	➤ Be open for feedback and (negative?) advice ➤ Be honest and transparent ➤ Be willing to take time to confirm calling	➤ Use physical and psychological assessments ➤ Have professionals yourself or seek them as partners ➤ Have an eye for the bigger picture	➤ Provide tools for assessments ➤ Be available for assessments
Re-entry	➤ Be supportive of physical and psychological assessments ➤ Be available for information about the bigger picture	➤ Be open for feedback and (negative?) advice ➤ Be honest and transparent ➤ Be willing to take time to confirm calling	➤ Use physical and psychological assessments ➤ Have professionals yourself or seek them as partners ➤ Have an eye for the bigger picture	➤ Provide tools for assessments ➤ Be available for assessments

8

Selection
Calling and Tested Call
in Previous Ministry

The facts

Calling to missionary service—that historical foundation upon which so much pioneer mission work in the past seems to have been built—is as important today for keeping missionaries on the field as it ever was. In OSC, mission agencies explore calling as a priority area in selection and its rating has a strong correlation with retention. In NSC, calling is also given very high priority in most agencies (see Key findings for an explanatory note). In addition, testing the call in the local church through endorsement of the leadership also received high ratings, experience in ministry received somewhat less. Both factors were correlated with retention in OSC and NSC alike.

The data

Q. No.	Factor	OSC Importance for Selection	✓	NSC Importance for Selection	✓
11	Expresses a clear calling to missionary service	○○○○○○○○○●	✓	○○○○○○○○○○	
15	Has good character references	○○○○○○○○○●	✓	○○○○○○○○●●	
16	Has committed endorsement from his or her pastor/local church for missionary service	○○○○○○○○○●	✓	○○○○○○○○○●	✓
18	Has ministry experience in a local church	○○○○○○○●●●	✓	○○○○●●●●●●	✓
19	Has had previous cross-cultural experience	●●●●●●●●●●		●●●●●●●●●●	

The key findings

✓ Calling (Q11) received an extremely high rating for significance and performance in OSC and NSC.

✓ Mission executives from high retaining agencies gave even higher rating of calling (Q11) in OSC (NSC not significant because three Indian agencies with very high retention gave extremely low rating of calling which dragged the average down and increased the standard error of the sample—otherwise we would have found a positive correlation in NSC too).

✓ Ministry experience in a local church (Q18) was rated significantly lower than calling (Q11).

✓ NSC agencies gave much lower rating of ministry experience in a local church than OSC (young people not given so much opportunity to exercise their gifting in NSC churches with strong leadership?).

✓ Rating of church experience was correlated strongly with retention in OSC and moderately in NSC.

What it means

Rob Hay

"Calling is outdated now."

"Calling is not important like it used to be, is it?"

These are the type of comments we get as we travel around, spend time with, and listen to missionaries, personnel directors, mission leaders and others. We reply "Was a sense of call important to you?" "Yes" they reply. "It was and is vital. Without it, we would have left long ago." We have yet to meet a long-term missionary who has not felt that call and a personal sense of call was utterly vital to their own missionary journey. Everyone thinks that call as a concept is no longer widespread, and yet everyone believes it is vital for them personally. We have added it to our growing collection of missionary myths, alongside, "No one serves long-term anymore." ReMAP II totally blew away the idea that call is an outdated, irrelevant concept. Instead, call is vital to retention and prioritised in most mission agency's selection processes.

However, knowing what "a call" is proves a much harder question to answer. In ReMAP II, we only asked if a call was important, we did not ask for a definition. In another study, as yet unpublished, the question was asked "Describe what motivated you to go into mission (if you use the word "call" please explain what this means to you)." Just as in ReMAP II, everyone interviewed subsequent to completing the online survey said how important a clear understanding of God having led them to the field, was to them remaining on the field—especially through the hard times. In answering that question they also gave a very clear insight into what constitutes a call. In short, the answers were wide and varied, often practical as well as spiritual: e.g., "God spoke to me through my Bible readings... and my church confirmed the call and affirmed my gifts, skills and suitability." A call is often a mixture of different things—different ways God has been speaking, different focuses. Calling to geographic location, region or country is relatively rare today. Instead, calling is more often to a people group. Calling increasingly refers to the use of a skill or vocation, gifting or experience in God's service, not unlike the parable of the entrusted talents (Mt 25:14ff). It appears to matter little (as far as retention is concerned) what the call is to and what it consists of. What is important for retention is to have spent time (individually and with others) being certain of God's desire for you to do something and/or go somewhere, to the extent that you can look back to that experience and hold on to it during the hard times.

During selection, asking a candidate to articulate their call or explain their motivation for ministry is important, but so is verifying and testing that call. In OSC, it is common to seek character references and most agencies do so. This correlates to retention. In NSC it does not. Some colleagues from NSC have suggested that references hold little value for them as people often write what the candidate would want written rather than an accurate assessment of their character. Additionally, it might be that in NSC, the sending church has a more direct role in the selection and sending of a missionary so that a "written endorsement" may not have such relevance.

The endorsement of the missionary's home church and pastor [Q16 *Has committed endorsement from his/her pastor/local church for missionary service*] seems of more value in NSC (affecting retention in both NSC and OSC) as well as that the candidate actually has ministry experience in their local church at home [Q18 *Has ministry experience in a local church*]. The committed endorsement of the pastor and local church may have an added contribution for retention beyond confirming the call of the candidate. If the church and pastor confirm the call to the mission agency it seems likely that the church would feel a greater obligation or responsibility to support in prayer and finances. Certainly our very interesting two-part case study on the Millers (at the end of this chapter) highlights how straightforward it was to raise finances when the missionary service was seen as a natural development after previous ministry in the local church.

Sending a missionary couple to Spain

Paul Adams,[1] Banstead Baptist Church, UK

Terry and Christine Miller are our missionaries in Spain. Although they are missionaries with European Christian Mission (ECM) and living 973 miles away from Surrey (near London, UK) as the crow flies, they are also Assistant Ministers at Banstead Baptist Church (in Surrey), so our whole church feels involved in their work. But how did the Millers get to work in Spain? The obvious answer is, "God led them." But that is not the whole story.

Let me explain how our church sees our responsibilities in training and sending missionaries. We believe that church leaders have a responsibility to lead in the mission process, and not simply to accept passively what a few keen minded mission-enthusiasts believe they ought to be doing.

We see our church in Banstead as a "mission training church." Second Timothy 2:2 has become our training-purpose statement: "And the things you have heard me say in the presence of many witnesses entrust to reliable men who will also be qualified to teach others." Our fellowship grew from a shared conviction about the importance of Bible-based evangelism, biblical discipleship and the need to equip a fresh wave of Gospel ministers. In other words, we are here to share the Gospel, make disciples, and train them to do the same—anywhere. We are not interested in building a mega-church for our own satisfaction, but we do want to work with the Lord in the building of a world-wide church for His glory, by training others and sending them out. We keep watching every serving member, providing opportunities for discipleship instruction and ministry training, encouraging them not to stand still but to keep growing in faith and service. This is an intentional approach and one that is maintained by the leadership with vigour and enthusiasm

So how did this work with Terry and Christine Miller? They came to us as Assistant Ministers. It was clear that both of them had a heart for the lost, and were experienced in leading individuals, couples and small groups to understand the Gospel. Like other Assistant Staff, they came on a limited period contract. In other words, we expect them to move on, and we wanted them to go to the next ministry opportunity better equipped to do the job and better able to train others.

Terry and Christine were with us for six years. During that time, it became clear that their gift/skill set would probably not be best suited to a traditional UK church environment, but more to a pioneering environment where people had time to make relationships. They also believed in including their children in a family ministry lifestyle, which is not common in UK churches. They loved working with small groups of people, one-to-one, and young families.

---

1   Dr. Paul Adams is the Senior Minister of a growing church in Banstead and also a medical doctor. He is a lively biblical communicator, and widely experienced professional trainer and chairman of BeaconLight, where he also teaches.

There were many short-term ministry opportunities in this country, but the question for us as leaders was, "Do long-term opportunities exist for the Millers in the UK or is God calling them abroad?" They had already served short-term in Albania and in Nepal—both places leaving Christine with health problems, and I think that coloured their view of overseas service. The only place abroad they had travelled to which had not made Christine ill was Spain. Her father had even worked there as a seasonal minister in Barcelona while Christine was in her teens. They loved the way of life there and the laid-back local street culture that really suited their relationship style. But still, the mission field had not really become a possibility.

After six years, the church leaders felt the need to focus on the Miller's future. The leadership prayed and sought the Lord about their next step in ministry. The Millers prayed. One Sunday, a Visiting Mission Staff member preached a sermon that stirred the couple. Christine looked on the internet and was impressed by the approach of European Christian Mission (ECM) to a modern style of church planting strategy; and Spain seemed attractive. I too thought about Spain—it just seemed to be the natural culture where they might feel at home—and the relationship style of church planting shown on the ECM website seemed just right for them.

By the time I met with Terry and Christine for a "serious chat," the conclusion was obvious and subsequently the leadership encouraged them to pursue this opportunity. But as their Senior Pastor, I had responsibilities too. I had separate discussions with the mission in the UK and with the field leader. I wanted to ensure, as far as I could, that this would be right for them and not a blind alley. At each turn there seemed to be confirmation of a match. I was invited to attend the selection board and subsequently, I visited the field before they left for Spain.

My trip to the field assured me that they were equipped to do the work, but they needed to learn the language from scratch. Could they do it? We contacted a Spanish phonetics expert who spent a week with them at home here and she assured us that she thought they did have an aptitude for the language, which was also most encouraging for them. The whole leadership team was reassured that they were on the right track.

The time came to depart. The church was then presented the challenge of supporting them. We might have simply transferred their salary from "home staff" to "mission staff" budgets, but we needed to replace them at the church. So, to cut a long story short, in six weeks there was sufficient money in cash and pledges to keep them on the mission field for three years! You see, they were known, loved and respected. Their ministry had made a difference to people in the local church here in Banstead; this really encouraged people to want to give and pray and communicate with them…

We in Banstead have been privileged to be a part of Terry and Christine's pathway to the mission field and they continue to be a part of our church life here. Our experience of them and another couple, now in Madagascar, is that the best way to train a missionary is to have them on the staff of the home church. In fact, we now think that if we are not willing to have them as a part of the home staff we probably should not send them! But there was one thing we had not prepared them for—cockroaches! That required fresh supplies of divine grace directly to Spain.

The call to Spain

Terry Miller,[2] Spain

Unlike many overseas missionaries, we didn't have an initial "call to Spain." Neither was there a specific time when we received a Bible verse or other means of direction which suddenly changed our thinking about our future ministry.

Our sense of "call to Spain" grew out of theological convictions and desires combined with experiences of God's grace in our lives. As we pushed forward and sought God's wisdom, Spain became an increasingly open door.

If all that sounds very spiritual it may be helpful to flesh it out a bit…

Shortly after we met as a couple, it was clear that we shared an important conviction: that God is glorified most when people put their trust in Jesus. This conviction grew as we experienced God's grace with us—working in secondary schools in Kingston-upon-Thames and in the church work in Cranleigh where we saw many teenagers and adults transformed by the gospel and the Holy Spirit's power.

The "Church planting and Evangelism" course at Spurgeon's College added the desire to establish churches where there was no effective witness. However during our time at Cranleigh and Banstead a door wasn't open for such a ministry, and we were left with the question, "When would God use us in church-planting?"

During ten years of Christian ministry, we sensed that God was preparing us for something different in the long-term. We suspected that it would involve some sort of pioneering ministry: we were increasingly aware of our ability to start things well on a small scale and then to hand over to others as the ministry develops.

However, we had all but written off overseas mission, even though our two short-term trips had seen good fruit. Where was God leading us? We didn't know. Strangely we weren't concerned because we knew that whatever it was it would be just right for us, and also right for the people we would be serving. We had enough experience of God's perfect timing and provision to know that we were safe in His hands.

So how did we arrive in Spain?

Paul Adams recounts many of the details, but for us, the idea of Spain first arose from a humorous comment in a casual conversation about where we could go if

---

2   Terry and Christine Miller work in Cordoba, Southern Spain, establishing churches with European Christian Mission. Before moving to Spain their training involved two years of Christian schools´ work, ten years of church work in England in various roles, the Church Planting and Evangelism course at Spurgeons College and the Cornhill Bible Training Course.

we ever went abroad as missionaries. That comment remained with us and Spain became ever larger on our horizon. Then God unsettled us about the idea of staying in England and by filling our hearts and minds with Spain and He did it, as usual, in a creative way.

First, the Overseas Mission Directory (listing opportunities for mission service abroad) shouted to us of the need for church planters in every area of mission work in Spain. Then, independently, we looked at the websites for the different mission organizations mentioned and were both drawn to the European Christian Mission (ECM). We liked their team centred approach to ministry in Spain, and it seemed as if the job description was written just for us!

Having never heard of ECM before, we then discovered that family and friends knew missionaries in Spain. Then we were able to visit a couple who just "happened" to be on home assignment in England at the time (now our team leaders!). We arranged to take a family holiday in Spain in order to visit a missionary in the Cordoba province (in the village where we now live); and a year later returned to visit each of the five mission points in the province.

Each step of the way we received the support and wisdom of our fellow church leaders in Banstead, and continually asked God to close the door if we were on the wrong track. But instead, the door opened wider and wider! We remember driving through the mountains between two of the mission points with butterflies in our stomachs—we knew that God really did want us in Spain. It was no surprise when God also provided the financial support we needed in a short space of time.

When we arrived in Spain to tackle the language and cultural adaptation a year later, we knew that God had been preparing us for a long time through the faithful input of Christian mentors and leaders in England. We knew that He only expected of us what He had expected in every stage of our journey up to that point: to be available to be the people He calls us to be—in the place He has prepared for us —meeting the needs He lays before us and making disciples of Jesus.

So here we are…

Training programme challenges potential missionaries

Rebecca Barnhart,[3] Operation Mobilisation International,[4] Moldova

Note: This case was adapted from feature material entitled "Moldovan training program challenges potential missionaries" from the Operation Mobilisation International website. Used by permission.

Nine people cram into the old, rickety bus for the journey into the small, bleak villages. Designed to hold about 40 people "comfortably" in a Western society, the bus carries at least double that amount in Eastern Europe. While the foreigners seem a bit uneasy and wary, older Moldovan women stand unfazed, carrying on conversations as the bus bumps along the road, jolting its occupants back and forth. Thirty minutes later, the Operation Mobilisation team squeezes out of the bus.

The team begins their two-week outreach, part of OM Moldova's "Challenge into Missions" (CIM) training programme. The young Moldavians, Ukrainians and one American are ready to share the Gospel of Jesus Christ in Ustea and Ocrita rarâ, villages inhabited primarily by elderly Moldavians who have lived through the ravages of communism and are not so open to Christianity.

In groups of two and three, the team journeys on from house to house, undaunted by the physical and spiritual barriers, to share Jesus with strangers, not knowing what reaction or response they'll receive. One illiterate Moldovan woman wept as Scripture was read to her about God's love. She didn't experience that from her own children, who are physically and verbally abusive, she explained. Down the road, three elderly men and women were quite hostile to the "hypocrisy" of Christians that they had witnessed during and after Communism. However, for 30 minutes, they listened to Tania, a 21- year-old Moldovan believer, tell them about the reality of Christ's offer for salvation, despite what they have seen and experienced before.

Since 2000, OM Moldova has been training young Moldovan and foreign Christians for world missions through its CIM programme. Now held twice yearly (Spring and Autumn), participants, ranging in ages from 18 to 30 years, memorise Scripture, receive relevant evangelistic and biblical teaching, as well as practical, hands-on outreach opportunities within and outside Moldova. During the outreach weeks, which are real, pioneering, hands-on missions experiences, the teams work with local churches doing physical work, sketch board and drama, hospital ministry, door-to-door evangelism and work with children and youth.

CIM is an intensive missions training programme. It is divided into two levels: Level 1 participants are those coming for the first time; Level 2 students are returning because they are interested in pursuing full-time Christian service work,

---

3   Since 2001, Rebecca Barnhart has served as a missionary writer with Operation Mobilisation in Central/Eastern Europe and the Balkans. She has travelled throughout this area, working with OM teams and writing stories about what the Lord is doing in this part of the world.

4   Operation Mobilisation is a global missions organisation with teams in over 100 countries.

either in missions or with their church. Second level students also take on more responsibilities during CIM, serving as group leaders on the outreaches and teaching during the in-class training. They also receive additional, more advanced training.

Matthew Skirton, field leader for OM Moldova, said the three-month CIM programme is part of the language and cultural adaptation and missions training for its two-year Global Action members. Among the participants of the Spring 2003 CIM programme were two new recruits who recently joined the OM Moldova team through the Global Action programme.

Nicole, a 20-year-old American, first worked with the International Coordinating Team, Carlisle, for nine months with SportsLink before joining the Moldova team. She arrived one week before the team left on the outreach, but was already picking up some Romanian language and had been welcomed by her Moldovan team members. Other CIM participants are on their own personal journey to discover the Lord's plan for their lives.

Vlad, a Moldovan native, is a Level 2 student, who has matured deeply in his walk with the Lord after his first CIM experience. In fact, his home church was so impressed with the noticeable change in Vlad that they hosted the outreach team in Orhei, about 40km north of Chisinau. "After Vlad returned from CIM, I could see the change in him and was so excited," said Lillia, one of the church members. "I wanted us to get involved then." Being one of the leaders in CIM has challenged Vlad even further with the increased responsibility. It is also preparing him for his ministry this summer working at a children's camp. "I have no experience with children, but after CIM, I will be ready," said the 21-year-old. Vlad is hoping to use this experience in preparing for further mission opportunities, possibly to Africa. "I would like to go into full-time missions, but I don't know if it is God's will."

Matthew said CIM also helps develop and bridge relationships between OM and Moldovan churches. Pastors of some of the Moldovan students are invited to share during the morning devotion times and during the in-class training. In addition, the outreach teams are sent into villages where a supporting church is located. "This way, the church sees how their young person is involved and the impact it's making in their life," said Matthew. "It encourages the pastor, the church and other young people to want to participate in CIM in the future and helps their vision for mission to grow."

While the majority of the CIM participants since 2000 have been Moldavians, Matthew said CIM is open to anyone who can speak English, Russian, or Romanian (Moldova's official language). All training sessions are translated into the necessary languages, depending on the make-up of the students, but if more foreigners were to join, Matthew said the CIM course could be modified to include classes in the specific languages. "Language should not stop anyone from coming."

Total cost for each participant to attend CIM includes food, travel to and from the different outreaches, and housing. OM Moldova raises about 75% of what is required and each participant raises the remainder. For some students, this is quite a hardship because their families may come from poor villages and have no jobs. (The unemployment rate in Moldova is probably the highest in Europe.)

Vlad's experience through CIM has also shown him what hands-on missionary work is like. During a different outreach, this time in Romania, Vlad and his team worked with missionaries involved in gypsy ministry. "I learned a lot about the value of missionaries conforming to the culture where they work," Vlad said. "Being willing to accept another culture's way of life can open so many doors to share the Gospel."

Discussion questions:

1. What did you learn about call and tested call from the above case studies?
2. How is the call of a potential missionary generally tested by your organisation?
3. How could the leaders in the local sending church evaluate the call of a person to long-term missions?
4. What could mission agencies do to help churches evaluate the call of potential missionaries?

In the real world:

A table to stimulate ideas for best practice in mission partnership. For further explanation, see page 7.

This chart has been partially filled in for you. Now you fill in the blanks.

Who? → When? ↓	Home Church	Missionary	Mission Agencies	External Partners
Continuous	➢ Disciple and mentor church members in vision for missions ➢ Let "being called" be a natural happening ➢ Have a culture of confirming people in their gifts and ministry ➢ Give trust and varied opportunities for involvement in ministry ➢ Let agency have a role in education programmes	➢ See confirmation of call by church as fundamental	➢ See endorsement of church and pastor as crucial ➢ Give input for programmes in church ➢ Provide short-term outreach opportunities as way to test calling	➢ Support in developing discipleship programmes ➢ Support by providing tools and standards for testing of calling
Recruitment	➢ Be available as a reference for candidates	➢ Be open to take time to let others be convinced of call	➢ Get church involved in test of calling	
Preparation				
On field				
Crisis				
Furlough	➢ Involve missionaries in testing of calling	➢ Be open to serve in testing of calling as an expert	➢ Involve missionaries in testing of calling	
Re-entry	➢ Involve missionaries in testing of calling	➢ Be open to serve in testing of calling as an expert	➢ Involve missionaries in testing of calling	

9

Preparation Time

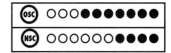

The facts

ReMAP II research attempted to determine the effectiveness of pre-field training for mission, especially its contribution to the retention of missionaries. The results show that pre-field training, especially missiological training, contributes significantly to the missionaries' ability to persevere and ultimately thrive.

Yet there are many additional questions buried in this overall enquiry, including time requirement, type of training, etc., which are often hard to define. Agencies were asked to communicate their minimum requirement for training, but this requirement may be regularly exceeded in reality. Additionally, agencies are increasingly moving away from a one-size-fits-all training requirement, making a minimum requirement difficult to define.

Results also showed clear room for improvement. Unfortunately, many OSC agencies have not made practical missionary training and/or structured cross-cultural missionary internships as an absolute requirement of their pre-field training, although their benefit has been proved in other studies. Where training did take place, it was often too much emphasis on Bible and theological education and not enough on focused mission training. Practical training was neglected. However, NSC agencies are beginning to value and use internship or apprenticeship opportunities.

The data

Q. No.	Factor	OSC Health Indicator	✓	NSC Health Indicator	✓
32	Bible school or seminary training	○○○○●●●●●●	✓	○○●●●●●●●●	✓
33	Formal academic missiological training	○○●●●●●●●●	✓	○●●●●●●●●●	✓
34	Practical pre-field missionary training	○○○●●●●●●●		○●●●●●●●●●	
35	Structured cross-cultural missionary internship or apprenticeship	●●●●●●●●●●		○○○●●●●●●●	✓
36	Mission agency's own orientation	○○●●●●●●●●		○○○○○●●●●●	

The key findings

✓ This group of questions asked the agencies for their minimal requirements of training prior to service with the agency. Their actual training standards may be much higher.

✓ The total duration of pre-field training time is highly correlated with total retention in OSC and NSC.

✓ High retaining agencies expect three times more missiological training (Q33) than low retaining agencies.

✓ High retaining agencies (for total attrition) expect twice as much theological training (Q32) as low retaining agencies, although there is no correlation to preventable attrition (RRP).

✓ Missiological training (Q33) appears to be more beneficial than theological training, as also shown in ReMAP I.

✓ Practical missionary training (Q34) and cross-cultural internships (Q35) are still too rarely required to obtain statistical evidence of their effectiveness.

What it means

Jonathan Ingleby

How much time is typically spent in preparation for field missionary work? Our data indicates that for both NSC and OSC, most of the formal preparation time (pre-field training) is spent in a Bible school or college. However, we must consider whether this is *the right sort of preparation*. Bible school training can be good, but the proportion of time allocated to it seems skewed, for reasons we will cover. Along with the right sort of preparation, how should training vary according to the needs of the missionary in question? For example, someone preparing for a relatively short-term assignment has certain training needs, and long-term missionaries who fulfil a specific role, such as theological education, would have other needs.

Because preparation time is often limited, the essentials should be the focus. Formal Missiology [Q33 *Formal academic missiological training*] proved to be much more effective preparation (correlated with retention) than Bible school training, therefore this approach should be given strong consideration.

Furthermore, pre-field preparation must consider what sort of work the missionary will do. The educational background the missionary already has when he or she enters the mission agency impacts necessary additional training. For example, medical doctors or other professionals already have many years of education and experience. Clearly, they need preparation for mission, but not as much and perhaps of a different sort than someone who is beginning their career in missions. More missionaries from the European OSC are involved in "social work," and thus are likely the professionals mentioned above. NSCs are investing more in Bible school or seminary training, which may be explained by the higher number of missionaries just beginning in their careers or training. They, therefore, need training assignments which involve getting to know people, evangelism, church planting, and learning how to put down roots.

Trainers must therefore think extensively about how they can offer *appropriate* training. They need to ask the teleological question—what is the goal, the end purpose—or in other words, they must start with the end in mind. After they determine what situation they expect the trainee to be part of and to contribute to, they should ask what sort of preparation is necessary in order to ensure effectiveness. This sounds simple, but in practice, training programmes far too often lay out a set menu, which when consumed results in a less than adequate diet.

For example, "Knowing what the Bible teaches"—an all-purpose biblical introduction—may not be as helpful as it sounds. We hear the complaint often enough that "young people today do not know their Bibles." A far more serious concern is that even when they do know their Bibles (have some formal biblical training), they may have no idea how it might be applied in a given mission situation. I remember going to a Bible study in Kathmandu and meeting a group of twenty-five missionaries. I came away with the impression that, as far as they were concerned, the Bible had very little to say about the actual work they were doing. Data from the educational section of the survey shows that academic training has a very strong correlation with retention—does this highlight the helpfulness of reflection on day-to-day praxis?

As mentioned, formal *mission* training is a good investment for future missionaries. It seems likely (though this is an argument from silence as far as the data is concerned) that more attention should be given to the practical element within training. Yet, mission and church training in the West (which has been exported globally) has been standardised as a particular tradition of ministerial formation that goes right back to the Middle Ages. This tradition includes Bible, theology, ethics, church history, religions, and then some "practical" studies such as homiletics and evangelism. Missionary training colleges often find that they have also inherited this sort of curriculum. Whether this traditional approach is a suitable preparation for the leader of a church in the US or Western Europe could be debated, but it is certainly not an adequate training for someone about to embark on cross-cultural mission. For example, where are the courses on leadership, world trends, the social sciences, communication theory, development studies, globalisation, world religion, animism, contextualisation, cross-cultural communication and language learning?

The training of missionaries must be, mission focused, cross-cultural, and practical in the sense that it involves some sort of effective experiential learning:

a) *Mission focused* means that mission is not something we should blunder into without reflection. To an alarming degree, one still meets missionaries deeply involved in missionary work who have hardly thought at all about what they are doing. During a long-term missionary experience, I constantly encountered fellow missionaries who wished that they had had more training, understanding (with hindsight) that it would have helped them be more purposeful about the missiology of their work and ministry. Indeed, in regard to Question 55 [Q55 *Missionaries are provided with opportunities for continuous training and development of gifts and skills*], where mission partners are offered opportunities for ongoing learning, we see a strong correlation with retention. This is discussed in more detail in Chapter 25.

b) *Cross-cultural preparation* is simply not an optional extra. Of course, we know that the gospel has to be contextualised and that missionaries have to learn to live cross-culturally, with the huge demands that this makes in terms of communication (language learning, cultural awareness) and personal identity (what can I give up and still be me?). But the cross-cultural aspect is even more challenging than that! Missionaries also often work in cross-cultural teams. These teams, according to mission agencies, are the number one contemporary challenge.[1] These teams will become a more frequent experience as mission is increasingly globalised. Are we ready for that? Has our preparation given us the necessary skills?

c) Finally, our training must include more *experiential learning*. The little learning circle, beloved of Liberation theologians, *experience-reflection-action*, has now become an important part of learning theory everywhere, and rightly so. Even missionaries in training must have some experience on which to reflect, a point well made in the accompanying case study from Dan Sheffield. The absence of a structured cross-cultural missionary internship or apprenticeship as part of the OSC training must be rectified. *Practical* pre-field missionary training needs a much

---

1   Research conducted by the Marketing Team at Redcliffe College, Gloucester, UK, conducted by telephone interview with Personnel Managers in the UK during 2005.

higher profile. NSCs are experimenting with new forms of training, including On-the-job training, but because these are not mandatory, we were not able to assess them to a significant degree. Likewise, the internship programme, while included, was largely unique to the USA and although helpful there it could not be compared in other countries.

The conclusions have strong practical implications. People who have been well prepared perform better and stay longer on the job. What is the best sort of preparation? Evidence suggests that we need more targeted missionary training and that we have inherited forms of training which are not always helpful. We need opportunities for reflective learning, on-going training, and cross-cultural preparation. We need more experiential learning included in our preparation programmes, especially in OSC.

Preparing people appropriately

Jonathan Ingleby,[2] Redcliffe College, UK

This is a true story—the names have been changed.

When I first met Alan Chalmers he was a comparatively young man who had already been appointed as the "acting" leader (he was soon to be given the permanent job) of a large mission group somewhere in South Asia. He was responsible for about 800 people, comprised of both nationals and missionaries and involved in a number of holistic ministries. It was a tough task. A once friendly local environment was becoming increasingly hostile. Civil war threatened. Government could not make up its mind whether it wanted the missionaries or not. People were being asked to leave unexpectedly and it was difficult to find replacements in good time. The team itself was very mixed—not just nationals and expatriates, but mission partners from all over the world. As well as cultural differences, there were the usual theological disagreements and personality clashes. Meanwhile the mission needed to maintain the high standards it had always set.

Alan shared with me some of his concerns. Not least of these were his doubts about whether he had the necessary skills to do the job he had been catapulted into. I tried to reassure him. He was clearly a born leader with a good understanding of the magnitude and complexity of the task ahead of him.

We spoke for a while about his preparation for the job. He admitted that, formally, he had none. He had attended a missionary training college for two years, and

2   Jonathan was Head of Mission Studies at Redcliffe College, Gloucester, UK for 15 years until his "retirement" in Summer 2006. He continues to lecture on subjects in missiology and world Christianity to Postgraduate level and is an expert on the history of mission and missiology and in globalisation and post-colonialism. Jonathan was brought up in Portugal by missionary parents. He worked for twenty years in India at Hebron, a school for missionary children, as teacher and then headmaster. Jonathan's PhD is from the Open University and looked into the way that education was used as a missionary tool in India during the long nineteenth century (c. 1789-1914).

felt that the time there had been very worthwhile. One obvious gap, however, was that he never had any training for the job he was actually doing. He had learned a good deal of theology, been prepared for some of the inter-cultural dimensions of his missionary life, thought about evangelism and church planting, and deepened his own spiritual life. He was grateful for all of these things. What had not happened was any sort of leadership training. Apart from what he had learned by observation "on the job" so far, he had never thought seriously about managing a team—leading, selecting, assessing, training, team building, resolving conflict and all the rest. He had never thought about the biblical basis of leadership as such, about the ethical implications of leadership or about the particular demands of leading a cross-cultural team. When I say he had never thought about it, I do not mean that Alan had no wisdom or insight on any of these subjects, but he had never been given the chance to reflect upon them in an ordered and systematic way and to draw upon the wider wisdom of others who had done so.

My story has a happy ending. Alan, by all accounts, rose to the challenge before him. He did this so well that it puts in doubt the whole moral of this story. Innate ability combined with life experience was enough. Was it the case that he did not need training in leadership in the first place? Perhaps, or perhaps he would have been an even better leader if he had the chance to study. Besides, we are not all like Alan. Some of us need all the help we can get if we are to make a half decent job of the leadership roles we find ourselves thrust into.

Adequate preparation

Dan Sheffield,[3] The Free Methodist Church, Canada

For several years now, I have served in a leadership position with The Free Methodist Church in Canada, as Director of Global and Intercultural Ministries. We are seeking to lay a foundation for Canadian mission initiatives, including entering new fields and sending our own missionaries.

One of the first policy documents that we developed concerned Adequate Preparation of long-term, cross-cultural ministry personnel. We have articulated a policy that focuses on laying proper foundations with the few, rather than seeking to recruit and process the many. The lessons that I have acquired over the years, as I will describe, are central to our policy and practice.

When I started as a young adult in the early 1980s to seriously consider cross-cultural ministry, I naturally wanted to make it happen expeditiously. Therefore,

---

3 Dan Sheffield is the Director of Global and Intercultural Ministries for The Free Methodist Church in Canada. From 1983 to 1990, Dan was a missionary with WEC International, involved in mission education and recruiting, as well as theological education in Egypt and South Africa. Then he served for three years as an associate pastor for evangelism and discipleship at a church in Canada. From 1994 to 1999, he and his family with Free Methodist World Missions (FMWM, USA) planted a multi-cultural urban congregation in South Africa. Dan served as International Urban Ministry Facilitator with FMWM since 2001 and as mission director for the FMC in Canada since 2003. Dan views developing competent cross-cultural workers as one of his most significant priorities.

I did a one-year missionary internship with The Shantymen, a Canadian home mission agency, where I lived and worked on the West coast of Vancouver Island among fishermen and loggers. This experience created several impressions: everyday people are looking for meaning and answers in their lives, understanding your ministry context makes all the difference, and being adequately prepared is at least half the task.

Following this experience, I did a year or so of training in graphic design before offering myself to WEC (Worldwide Evangelization for Christ). For some reason, they allowed a twenty-year-old into their six-month Candidate Orientation Course. At the time, most mission agencies might have expedited an unproven, uneducated, single young adult into a short-term assignment, but not into their long-term programme.

But WEC took me where I was and worked with me. During the extended orientation course, WEC leaders covered such topics as spiritual warfare, cross-cultural communications, unreached peoples research, evangelism, and church-planting, but they also drew us into the ethos and functional structures of the organisation in a communal environment. At the end of six months, I was a "WEC-er."

Then the WEC director, Ken Getty, sat me down and said, "Dan, if you really want to be most useful in ministry, we think you should go to Bible college before heading out overseas."

So off I went to Winnipeg Bible College (now Providence College) to sit at the feet of mission professor, Jon Bonk, for two years. A foundation was laid in Bible study skills and knowledge, theology, ministry theory and practice, church history, cultural anthropology, and missiology. My cross-cultural ministry experiences were also foundational. I spent nine summers working in Christian camping as a choreboy, counsellor, programme director, and church youth leader. I did a short-term assignment in Mexico with Operation Mobilization. I got married. My wife is a nurse, a former Navigator associate worker, and a graduate of the WEC candidate programme. Then we left for Egypt with a two-year-old child.

What were some of WEC's Good Practices?

1. They interacted with individuals and their call in a relational paradigm rather than an organizational one. A missionary is made to feel like part of a family and valued for her contribution.
2. They wanted evidence of spirituality and character through assessment in a communal environment.
3. Language, culture, and cross-cultural communication skills were taught and expected of competent missionaries.
4. They required sound biblical and theological skills.

After eight years with WEC, which involved experience in Egypt and South Africa, my wife's health situation led us to resign from WEC. I took on a pastoral assignment back in Canada with The Free Methodist Church. At one point, we wondered if we were another statistic on the attrition list.

Then four years later (in 1994), a call came from the Free Methodist Mission based in Indianapolis. We were invited to consider a church-planting/community development assignment in South Africa.

Our stepping out of active cross-cultural ministry had been due to my wife's health and my need to have hands-on pastoral ministry experience. Now, my wife was capable of another overseas assignment and I had gained four years of pastoral experience. So, we responded positively. Besides the normal application and screening process, we were given four days of orientation and sent to South Africa.

Our retention (that of my wife and myself) in cross-cultural ministry until today (2005) has had little to do with Free Methodist Mission personnel procedures.[4] It has had a lot to do with the adequate preparation we received through the WEC process. We knew the "why, what and how" regarding the mission task from the early foundations that we had received. We understood the significance of culture and language immersion, as well as the signs of, and the steps through, culture shock.[5] I must admit that I learned the way through "ministry shock" from the pastoral assignment.

What have we learned about adequate preparation and retention over the years?

1. Start with the person and craft a developmental process, rather than offering a standard one-size-fits-all process.
2. Spirituality and character need to be identified and affirmed by leaders in a local church context.
3. Hands-on ministry experience in one's own cultural context is required.
4. Harmony with the church or mission's ethos, value base, and operational approaches is required.
5. Biblical and theological foundations are required.
6. Social sciences and intercultural communication foundations are required.
7. Cross-cultural and intercultural experience of at least one year is required prior to making a long-term commitment.
8. Potential church planters require pastoral experience in their own cultural context first.

We are now seeking to develop these good practices regarding adequate preparation for our Canadian Free Methodist mission personnel. Instead of feeling inadequate to the task, our missionaries will develop competence in cross-cultural ministry skills, which I believe is a significant factor in missionary retention.

---

4 In the 1990s, the Free Methodist Mission had a 50% attrition rate.

5 Dan Sheffield and Joyce Bellous, 2003, "Learning to Be a Missionary: The Dreyfus Model of Skill Acquisition applied to the development of cross-cultural ministry practitioners," WEA Resources: www.wearesources.org/publications.

Discussion questions:

1. What are some best practices for adequate preparation mentioned in this case study?

2. How does your organisation currently prepare new missionaries? Are new missionaries being trained and prepared by those who have a personal awareness and understanding of the pressures and challenges of cross-cultural ministry? If not, what can be done to increase the awareness in trainers of the practical skills required for effective cross-cultural ministry?

3. Due to the changing nature of mission work in many places, how does your organisation evaluate the overall preparation of new missionaries to ensure that the preparation is balanced and relevant for each field? Who does the evaluation, and how could the preparation process adapt to changing field needs?

Changing our training to gain commitment during preparation

Alan Pain,[6] BMS International Mission Centre, UK

In August 1999, BMS World Mission, known at the time as Baptist Missionary Society, completed its purchase of the former St. Andrew's Hall in Selly Oak, Birmingham. BMS's intention was to refurbish the premises and to develop their own mission training centre, which they named International Mission Centre (IMC).

BMS had felt a growing need to take control of their mission training, which had become increasingly fragmented with potential mission personnel training for short periods of time at a variety of locations. In addition to a lack of clarity regarding standards, there was little opportunity for selected candidates to "bond" with BMS during their training. The original vision for IMC expressed the hope that it would provide "appropriate, effective, adaptable training" for all those who were to serve overseas with BMS: long-term workers, Action Teams (a well-established gap-year programme), other short-term teams, and a growing number of solo volunteers. The word "flexibility" summed up what BMS leaders had in mind for the new venture in mission training.

Our new training center

Inevitably, the establishment of a new centre for mission training was not without its controversy, but the prevailing view within BMS was that the existing situation for its own mission training could not be allowed to continue. There was a strong

---

6   Alan Pain is director of IMC, the International Mission Centre of BMS World Mission in the UK which trains people for cross-cultural mission. Alan specialises in biblical studies and missiology.

conviction that the availability of the St. Andrews Hall premises offered a timely opportunity which was not to be missed.

Now fully refurbished, IMC can accommodate 65-70 people and seeks to be a high-quality residential centre which meets BMS's needs for mission training as well as for selection events and other committees. The size of the premises means that IMC also welcomes non-BMS groups, large and small. They come for their own mission training or to share in IMC courses, all of which helps to shape and to refresh its corporate culture.

What the training includes

At the beginning of 2006, the core business of IMC remains that of training those who are to serve in cross-cultural mission with BMS. For example, training includes:

- A one-year foundation course in mission studies for newly-accepted long-term workers. This includes two significant personal projects and a February placement, which most people take overseas.

- A month's training in September as well as a selection weekend prior to six months overseas, for our Action Teams.

- Two weeks of de-brief and training in April for the Action Teams before an eight-week tour of British churches. There is also a couple of days final celebration in June and a reunion weekend just before Christmas.

- Three Volunteer Preparation Weeks each year, designed for the varied and highly-skilled people who offer BMS short-term service up to two years.

- Selection, training and de-brief/reflection weekends for our Summer Teams, Church Teams and Medical teams.

- A new BMS programme for Mid-term volunteers (2-4 years) is the latest challenge, for which a three-month term is likely to become the normal period of training.

The new mission center and BMS

It is still too early to assess the long-term effectiveness of IMC for mission training, but several aspects of its existence have been noted:

- IMC *is* BMS, and all sorts of people come to regard it as home. This makes a big difference to their commitment to BMS and has begun to influence some short-term workers back to longer-term service. Hopefully, in time, it will also increase the average length of service of long-term (career) mission personnel.

- IMC training is purpose-built for the needs of BMS. Its courses are prepared with the sole aim of providing effective preparation for those who are to serve with BMS. Other Senior Staff from the BMS international headquarters in

Didcot, Oxfordshire, UK, make regular visits for teaching and consultation, which has become an important addition to the year.

- With IMC in place we can be sure that all those serving overseas will have been trained in issues such as child protection, security and health. We can also tackle areas of particular interest to BMS.

- IMC training is evaluated regularly, and changes are made in the light of evaluation, without the restrictions of external accreditation or separate college authorities. The challenge of IMC is to reach the original vision, "… a centre of excellence for the formation of mission workers." That is part of the reason why we prefer to talk about "Centre," "Director," "Mission Personnel" instead of using the academic language of "College," "Principal," and "Student."

- IMC tutors are colleagues of those in training, with a vested interest in their progress and their future. The relationships established at IMC can prove extremely useful in the early days of overseas service, especially when the going is tough for newly-arrived mission personnel.

- The training year provides a unique opportunity to develop relationships with BMS home staff, most of whom work at the headquarters in Didcot. It is very reassuring for them to make the move overseas knowing that they are by now far more than names to those who have administrative, financial and pastoral responsibility for them.

- By the time new mission workers move to their locations, they have already established strong relationships with their BMS Regional Secretary. This partnership of responsibility has already proved its worth and can be decisive for the longer-term survival of mission personnel, especially if the early months of service prove unexpectedly tough.

For example: In November 2002, a young American OM worker, Bonnie, was murdered in Sidon, Lebanon. The effect of her death was particularly traumatic for a small group of Christians working in Sidon. A young woman from BMS was part of this group. Becky (pseudonym) was in Sidon for language study prior to taking up a teaching post in Beirut. She had been part of this group for just two months and had developed a close friendship with Bonnie. Very soon after Bonnie's death, Becky relocated to Beirut and 19 months later, she came back to UK to be with her father who was terminally ill.

Becky had become an integral part of BMS, mainly through her year of training at IMC, and this made a huge difference to the way BMS was able to cooperate with her home church in caring for her through a very rough couple of years. IMC has been part of this support for Becky, and has been able to work with colleagues in other situations for the understanding and encouragement of former "students" (we never use the word!)

Becky has now returned to work with BMS in South Central Asia where she has made an extremely positive start in a new country with a fresh challenge of language, culture and people.

Discussion questions

1. What did this organisation (BMS) do to improve its preparation of new mission workers?

2. What changes could be helpful within your own organisation or church, so that new missionaries are better prepared for cross-cultural ministry?

In the real world:

A table to stimulate ideas for best practice in mission partnership. For further explanation, see page 7.

This chart has been partially filled in for you. Now you fill in the blanks.

Who? → When? ↓	Home Church	Missionary	Mission Agencies	External Partners
Continuous	➤ Identify and affirm the need for competence, character and spiritual skills ➤ Offer hands-on pastoral and ministry experience ➤ Provide a biblical and theological foundation ➤ Create a culture and practice of coaching and mentoring			
Recruitment			➤ Inform candidates about preparation requirements	
Preparation	➤ Form a Home Front Committee that supports missionaries broadly ➤ Support practical preparation ➤ Develop relationships with the family who stay behind	➤ Be willing to take time for the right preparation ➤ Work on a Home Front Committee	➤ Have a personal and relational approach ➤ Use programmes that fit the individual ➤ Use tools to develop competence, character and spiritual skills ➤ Offer orientation to the mission agency ➤ Include missionary kids in preparation	➤ Develop appropriate practical learning tools to be used ➤ Offer communal environment to prepare candidates ➤ Facilitate cross-cultural experiences ➤ Offer theological and missiological training ➤ Offer specific job training ➤ Develop tools for preparation of missionary kids
On field				
Crisis				

Who? → When? ↓	Home Church	Missionary	Mission Agencies	External Partners
Furlough		➢ Be involved in preparing candidates		
Re-entry		➢ Be involved in preparing candidates		

10

Orientation and Continuous Training

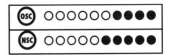

The facts

Orientation is usually thought of as the most vital part of preparation, and yet, in OSC, language and cultural learning far exceeded orientation in correlation to retention. Significant difference exists between NSC and OSC, most likely because NSC missionaries are often sent to near-cultures, where less language and cultural adaptation appears to be required. In OSC, continuous training and development of new gifts and skills is strongly correlated with retention, although there is a correlation found in NSC as well.

The data

Q. No.	Factor	OSC Health Indicator	✓	NSC Health Indicator	✓
52	Effective on-field orientation is in place for new missionaries	○○○○○●●●●●	✓	○○○○○●●●●●	✓
53	Language learning arrangements are provided that enable new missionaries to learn the local language well	○○○○○○○●●●	✓	○○○○●●●●●●	
54	Ongoing language and culture training are actively encouraged	○○○○○○○●●●	✓	○○○○○○●●●●	
55	Missionaries are provided with opportunities for continuous training and development of gifts and skills	○○○○○○●●●●	✓	○○○○○○●●●●	✓
85	Pre-field orientation prepares missionaries for adjustment to cross-cultural life and ministry	○○○○○○○●●●		○○○○○○●●●●	

The key findings

- ✓ On-field orientation of new missionaries (Q52) was positively correlated with retention in OSC and NSC, yet the correlation was not as strong as expected (usually considered extremely important).

- ✓ Initial language and cultural learning (Q53) was rated even higher than orientation (Q52) in OSC for performance and significance and clearly correlated with high retention (for preventative attrition RRP—yet not so much for total attrition, RRT).

- ✓ NSC mission executives gave a much lower rating to Initial language and cultural learning (Q53) than OSC, probably as many NSC agencies are working in near cultures where language learning is not so relevant.

- ✓ In NSC, Initial language and cultural learning (Q53) is even negatively correlated with retention (it is assumed that NSC agencies are working in a near culture, where language learning is not so relevant, have higher retention rates than those working truly cross-culturally)

- ✓ In OSC, Ongoing language and cultural studies (Q54) received the highest rating in this block of questions and it was highly correlated with retention for preventable attrition.

- ✓ In NSC, Ongoing language and cultural studies (Q54) again was negatively correlated with retention (as many agencies are working in near cultures)

- ✓ Continuous training and development of new gifts and skills (Q55) received high rating and proved to be correlated with retention, especially in OSC, and particularly regarding preventable attrition RRP in OSC.

What it means

Sarah Hay

On-field orientation is positively correlated with retention. However, the correlation was not as strong as anticipated and the agency's pre-field orientation showed no correlation with retention. The overall aim is to prepare individuals to learn the local language (where necessary), survive culture shock, and settle into the host country or culture so as to be able to live and work effectively and without undue stress.

The method, timing and content of orientation will vary, but generally, the mission agency will carry it out. The case study by Rachel Murray (see the case study following—Collaborative orientation in New Zealand) gives an interesting example of a group of agencies who carry out orientation together. This is a good use of resources and provides a depth and breadth to the issues covered. Orientation, however, should not be confused with mission or Bible training that takes place at a college (see Chapter 9).

If we consider orientation in two distinct categories of pre-field and on-field, it is interesting to look at the ReMAP II results. Q85 [Q85 *Pre-field orientation prepares missionaries for adjustment to cross-cultural life and ministry*] shows that while OSC and NSC executives both believe that they do pre-field orientation reasonably well (though with room for improvement) we did not find a correlation with retention. We must assume, therefore, that there is little difference in pre-field orientation between the high and low retaining agencies—the scores suggest that all agencies must do this reasonably—at least in the leader's opinion. It is an interesting result because we have often come across individuals for whom a major stumbling block has been poorly shaped expectation as a result of poor pre-field preparation and orientation. It seems fairly common that people struggle on arrival because of a vast difference between their expectations and reality. (On a personal note, we (Rob and Sarah) did not have this problem when we went to Nepal because we expected it to be horrendously difficult, so it was, therefore, a delight to discover that it was only difficult!). Despite the lack of correlation, the scores and the testimonies we have encountered would suggest room for improvement so that better preparation can be made. Perhaps the leaders of the sending bases need to better grasp the immensity of this issue.

In order to shape expectations prior to departure, there is nothing simpler than visiting the proposed field to look and see. Cost is a factor, and many cannot afford the luxury of such a visit (especially for some NSC agencies). But a visit is highly valuable if at all possible. When we were thinking of applying to go to Nepal, International Nepal Fellowship (INF) suggested such a visit, as neither of us had been to Asia before. Finances dictated that only one of us would go, but Rob was able to visit, work a couple of weeks, and get a really good feel—not just for Nepal, but also for INF. In planning later for departure, we were reassured to know where we would live for the first three months, who would meet us, and a few important things about Nepal (e.g., Nepali pillows are like rocks, so take your own!). Friends of ours recently arranged a "look and see" visit with their whole family to the Middle East. The visit was especially helpful for the children, who were able to visit their future schools, prepare, and get excited rather than scared about the unknown. However, a short visit (especially during an unfavourable season) can also give false impressions as one's body does not have enough time to adjust to the climate, food, germs, host culture, etc.. A place that would seem unbearable can indeed become manageable on the long run.

Another helpful tool in pre-field orientation is to link up future mission partners with previous mission partners in the home country and current people on the field. These links provide a vital source of advice. If possible, link people with others in similar circumstances, e.g., family to family, so that there are commonalities. Potential missionaries are encouraged by knowing others like themselves who have been able to cope and by being able to ask specific questions. Sometimes, it is easier to ask someone in this capacity rather than someone in the agency human resources department. I remember wanting to ask about electricity and hot water availability but feeling silly. When I finally asked, it was great to know that there was electricity (most of the time) and hot water (as long as the sun shone!). It wasn't pointed out that in the winter, when you need a hot shower to warm up rather than a cold one to cope with hot monsoon, the sun was often hidden by clouds so that the solar panel didn't give you hot water! (Perhaps there is an element of being a little selective...!)

Linking with someone on the field is another very helpful activity, because it automatically provides the new missionary with someone known upon arrival. Before departure, the on-field missionaries can be contacted with questions such as availability of items and what to pack or take. In Nepal, availability changed on an almost monthly basis, and things that we originally needed to take with us were available by the time we left. These links make important connections and make a smoother journey from home to field.

Once an individual arrives on the field, the agency typically provides an intense period of orientation. The length of timing of this varies widely, especially if language training is included. OSC and NSC scored the same for on-field orientation and both correlated with retention. However, despite this correlation, the scores were poor, showing much room for improvement. Mission partners must be provided with good orientation if they are to be effective in ministry and stay on the field. The scores should be higher for what, surely, is an obvious target for improving retention: preparing people for the task and location.

We should say a word about the type of issues that should be covered during pre-field and on-field orientation. This varies between agencies and there is no hard and fast rule (see the following case studies). The agency must consider what new mission partners would be facing and what they would need to know. Review and evaluate the current orientation with fairly new mission partners and ask them to point out areas which may be missing or are superfluous. The suggestions below are simply suggestions and are not an exhaustive list. It is not important whether each suggestion is covered pre-field or on-field, but that it is covered at some point:

Pre-field

- Language acquisition skills (preparing to learn another language)
- Cultural issues such as working in an international team, with national colleagues, and national church (preparing for culture shock)
- Introduction to the agency
- Medical/health and stress issues for individuals and families, including issues such as singleness, marriage and education
- Visa application process, time-line, etc.
- Items to take
- Support raising—finances and prayer

On-field

- Language training
- Specific cultural practices and norms
- Local religious beliefs and practices
- In-country agency and/or national church matters
- Gospel contextualisation
- Developing personal faith and spirituality

Most of these issues should require no explanation. However, according to the data, language learning shows no correlation with retention for NSC nor does it receive a high score, while the opposite is the case for OSC. Many assume that the majority of mission partners from NSC go to people groups nearby, where there may be similarities of language and cultural practices, e.g., an Indian mission partner serving elsewhere in India. They go to a near culture rather than a very different culture. In these situations, language training may be unnecessary. The factor of near culture may enable good relationships to be formed regardless of language. On the other hand, near culture is still different from the home culture and these differences need to be recognised. Adjustments may come unexpectedly and even cause culture shock.

Mission partners from OSC are usually crossing culture lines to places where there is no similarity between language and cultural practice. In this case, then, language learning arrangements are vital. This is substantiated by higher scores and positive correlation. There is still room for improvement in language and cultural training.

A key to learning language is to identify one's learning style and learn language accordingly. For a dyslexic person, learning language by reading text may prove difficult and unnecessary. I (Sarah) like to learn language through grammar, spelling, and script and to have a sentence perfect before I open my mouth. Rob, on the other hand, would rather attempt a conversation straight off, regardless of correct grammar or tense, and see where he gets!

Language learning should not be rushed. Mission partners are tempted to begin their role immediately, neglecting language study, but then struggle with language later. Not having adequate language skills was a major frustration for me, particularly as I worked in an English speaking environment and did not have as much chance to practice as others. On the other hand, people undertaking pure language learning for a long period (often over two years for Arabic or Japanese) suffer the frustration of feeling childlike and useless (because they are not "working"). However, these frustrations are short-lived and worthwhile if the outcome is relative fluency in language to enable the person to be more effective in ministry.

Hopefully, the importance of orientation regarding cultural issues and religious beliefs and practices is obvious. Of major importance is to learn not only about the national culture (though that is vital), but also about the cultures of team members who might have different nationalities and the challenges that arise as a result.

There has been much written about this (e.g., *When Cultures Collide* by Richard D. Lewis[1]) and its importance should not be underestimated (see Chapter 15).

Addressing stress issues for individuals, couples and families serves to highlight an important factor that affects all missionaries. People must look at themselves and be aware of their weaknesses, which are magnified especially during stressful situations when people are away from their usual support networks (as previously mentioned in Chapter 7 on Health and Psychological assessments). Thus, if a single person finds their singleness as an emotional, stressful issue, they need to plan, before the issue compounds with other stressors on the field, how they will develop coping strategies. Single individuals will find it helpful to understand the pressures on families and vice versa so that teams can support one another.

It is also helpful for people to be encouraged to develop ways in which they can spiritually feed and care for themselves. In a different environment where church language is unfamiliar and perhaps worship styles are different, mission partners will often struggle to feed themselves spiritually until they have been on the field for a time. Indeed, mission partners often reach a plateau (or even a valley) in their spiritual lives while on the field. Helping people to learn how to maintain and grow their own spiritual life is a vital aspect of orientation and could include setting up mentoring or accountability structures.

A study undertaken by Andrea Thomas, Orientation Officer for International Nepal Fellowship, showed the value and benefit in giving opportunities for mission partners to continue their orientation. Apart from the obvious benefits of continuing to equip people for service, continued training also gives a sense of worth, value and therefore motivation. The orientation continues to build affiliation with the agency so that new missionaries can quickly feel a part of something (not apart!) (especially an issue for Generation X and beyond).

NSC did not find on-going language and cultural training to be greatly linked with retention but this does not mean that they do not need to be improving. While the language element may be less important, there is still a need for ongoing cultural training, to help with motivation but also to highlight issues where practice may be similar but still different and therefore important to deal with to become more effective. Both OSC and NSC had a mediocre score for mission partners having opportunity for continuous training and development of gifts and skills, and yet both areas were correlated with retention. The need for continuous training and orientation is important (see Chapters 23 and 25 which cover Appraisal and Continuous Development).

It is worth reiterating that orientation is a very significant tool in the retention prevention kit. The data shows that there is significant room for improvement and it is hoped that this chapter and case studies will provide a basis for revisiting your orientation programme and making some significant improvements. Not having a good orientation programme is like admitting that you are only willing to do half a job. As a fellow language student once said in our class, "Do I have to learn the

---

1   Richard D. Lewis, *When Cultures Collide*, (London: Nicholas Brealey Publishing, 2000).

future tense, can't I just stick with the present?"! Make sure that you look to the future and provide mission partners with all the orientation that they need.

Collaborative orientation in New Zealand

Rachel Murray,[2] New Zealand

Orientation is a vital and important part of how mission candidates are prepared for cross-cultural service. How orientation is carried out and what is included will have implications on the initial settling down, the on-going learning, and the long-term service of the individual and/or family.

Many agencies will use their own resources to prepare their mission personnel for service. They are large enough to do so, without the need to call on the assistance of others. However, in a country with a small population, or where there are several small agencies in one region, it would make more sense and it could be more fruitful to pool resources to orientate new missionaries.

In New Zealand, four mission agencies have combined their time, talents and resources to offer orientation in the home country to prospective mission workers. The programme, known as Discovery, was developed in the late 1990s.

The earliest programme was based on the standard six-week Orientation programme originally run by Wycliffe. Discovery was run as a two-week residential programme, usually in a Christian camp environment. Although it was run by Wycliffe, other organisations began making use of the course. For example, SIM required their candidates to attend Discovery. In time, SIM personnel became involved in running the programme alongside Wycliffe. Later, Interserve (NZ) and OMF (NZ) joined.

Each agency now contributes key personnel to teach the course, with each trainer adding value through their personal experience and expertise in various sections of orientation. Those attending Discovery include mission candidates preparing to go shortly, those in application, and those still in very early stages of thinking about their call to mission service. The participants have a variety of ministry interests: with some going out to do church planting and evangelism, while others seek to work as tentmakers in their professions.

In the early years, a large component of the orientation course had been on language acquisition. In two weeks, the participants were required to grasp at least

---

2   Rachel Murray was the New Zealand coordinator for the ReMAP II project. She was formerly the short-term mission coordinator for Interserve (NZ), an agency facilitating individuals into positions related to their professional skills for 1 to 12 months throughout Asia and the Middle East. In her role at Interserve (NZ), Rachel worked with enquirers regarding service with the agency. This included the orientation and preparation of short-termers, many of whom went on to be long term mission partners. Two of her Interserve colleagues were closely involved with the Discovery orientation course. Rachel is currently the Executive Assistant at Carey Baptist College in Auckland, New Zealand. In her new role, she assists the Principal in leadership of a growing Bible and theological college where people are trained for mission, ministry and the marketplace.

the basics of a language. Over the years, however, other factors were added to the course structure.

Today, the Discovery programme comprises a three stranded approach: language, culture and missions, and personal growth. There are daily sessions covering these three areas after a time of worship and biblical teaching.

1. Language

    At first, the focus was on personal learning styles and linguistics. More recently, the focus has changed. Instead of mastering the basics of a language, the participants discover how to learn a language. This training allows for flexibility, personal style and a variety of language groups to which the new missionaries might be exposed.

2. Culture and missions

    The focus is on working with international teams, national colleagues and the national church, contextualisation of the gospel, tentmaking, medical/health issues for individuals and families, and education.

3. Personal growth

    This focuses on issues of faith and spirituality, spiritual warfare, marriage, family, singleness and personality types (including completing a personality test such as Myers Briggs).

Being a residential course, children are cared for during sessions by child care workers. This immediately sends the message that children are welcomed and valued. The residential nature of the course means that attendees get to know each other and they begin the process of learning what it might be like to be part of a close-knit team on the field.

In early 2005, Discovery had to alter its structure to accommodate the changing nature of society in New Zealand. The two-week programme has become a one-week programme. Although this change required some consolidation of the sessions, the basic components remained. This shorter programme is better suited to the professionals who had to take annual leave from their work environment. Other reasons for the shorter course are: volunteer workers for the children's programme and catering have become scarce and the overall costs for a residential course are prohibitive for some.

In 2006, it is likely that Discovery will be altered again to become an intensive weekend course, in which the language and cultural components as above are the focus. This new course would include worship at a church of a different ethnic group on the Sunday morning.

Discussion questions:

1. Are there agencies or churches in your region or country that could work collaboratively with your organisation to offer an orientation programme for new missionaries? What obstacles might have to be overcome for different agencies to organize a common orientation course?

2. What particular aspects of the two-week Discovery course in New Zealand are most likely to contribute to missionary retention?

3. What would be an appropriate length of orientation course for your country and local culture? What are the disadvantages of a short orientation programme? What other topics could be included if an orientation course were more than two weeks?

Orientation contributes to missionary retention

Albert Seth Ocran,[3] Torchbearers Mission Inc., Ghana

Torchbearers Mission Inc. is an indigenous inter-denominational missionary-sending organisation started in 1988 in Accra, Ghana. The vision of the six founding fathers was to raise committed Christians, train them and send them to unreached people groups. This vision was pushed along through regular prayer and fasting retreats held monthly. The Lord heard our prayers and began to lead us into mission trips to the Upper East Region of Ghana.

We recruited our first missionary, Pastor James Abedingo, at Bolga in 1990. He was taken through a six month orientation programme in Accra and placed on the field in the same year, specifically to work among his own people (the Kusasis) in his village, Apodabogo, in the Bawku West District of the Upper East Region. The fact that Pastor James Abedingo has since been faithful to the call and has been on the field for the past 15 years shows how much God has helped Torchbearers from the beginning.

After Pastor James, other missionaries were recruited and they have also stayed at their stations. We have not lost any missionary from his station, so we can say we have a 100% missionary retention. Praise God! Our present missionary strength includes six couples (full-time) plus one tentmaker missionary couple in Ghana and a couple in Malawi. This excludes the five full-time office staff, also considered missionaries.

---

3   Albert Seth Ocran is the General Director of Torchbearers Mission Incorporated in Ghana. He has been serving in missions for the past 18 years. Prior to this, Albert was a Lecturer and Head of General Agriculture Department, College of Agriculture, Maiduguri, Nigeria. He studied missions at the WEC International headquarters in United Kingdom. Albert is a founding executive member of Torchbearers Mission, and he formulated its constitution, financial and other policies. In his present role as General Director, Albert supervises the missionaries and office staff, chairs and directs the executive committee, as well as conducts training and teaching of potential missionaries. Albert is also a founding executive member of the Ghana Evangelical Missions Association.

Factors that contribute to our Missionary Retention include:

1. Prayer

   We have depended a lot on prayer because we believe in the strategy of Luke 10:2b: "Ask the Lord of the harvest, therefore, to send out workers to his harvest field." We pray that God would send labourers into the harvest field and he answers by sending some to us. We pray for the sustenance of the missionaries on the field.

2. Acceptance of missionaries

   Each person that has been recruited as a missionary had been highly recommended as a faithful and committed Christian, with some experience and involvement in evangelism. We have a highly competent Board that interviews each applicant. When an applicant is found to lack some skills, a recommendation for further skills development is made to ensure that the person gains the requisite knowledge.

3. Orientation and training

   All our new missionaries go through six months of orientation and training. They will either complete:

   - Six months of the Missionary Orientation Programme (MOP), or

   - Six months of the International School of Missions and Leadership Development (ISOMALD), where they learn several subjects within the six courses: Biblical Studies, Leadership and Management Studies, Missions Studies, Cross-Cultural Studies, Communication Studies, and Ministry Skills.

   Several experienced lecturers bring their knowledge and experience to bear on these new missionaries, thereby sharpening them for effective and lasting ministry on the field. During the training, the new missionaries also have field practicums to test their knowledge and see things practically.

   One reason why our missionaries have stayed on the field is because the six months of orientation and training acts as an observation time both for the organisation as well as the missionaries. Any negative observations made by the organisation could lead to the potential missionary being asked to repeat the programme, or else they are prevented from being commissioned and sent to the field. This period of orientation and training has been our weeding stage, and we have had cases of potential candidates withdrawing voluntarily.

4. Commissioning and sending

   The public and open celebration associated with commissioning of the missionaries also encourages the missionaries in their going and staying in the field. Another factor that has encouraged our missionaries to continue to stay in the field is the fact that candidates are sent to the places where they believe they have been called by God to go.

5. Fellowship and brotherhood

   During the orientation and training programme at the organisation's office, the students and candidates have fellowship with staff and members of the organisation. Some of them even stay with members of the organisation. The fellowship brings about bonding with and knowledge of the people within the organisation and also brings to light any rough edges in the potential missionary's life that can be smoothed.

6. Spiritual maturity

   Our missionaries have known the Lord for a considerable number of years and so they have developed a regular and consistent devotional life. This enables them to effectively train and disciple leaders among the converts they make on the field.

7. Family life

   Each missionary is taught and encouraged to have a good family life. Though most of our missionaries were recruited as singles, they were encouraged to marry. At present, all of them are married. The wives are also admitted as missionaries and they go through a similar orientation and training. This makes the couple, especially the women (who may not be familiar with the organisation before marriage), understand what they are involved in, and what life on the mission field will be like.

Since our missionary couples are young, they also have young children (below 21 years) who are with them on the field. We have had a situation where one missionary couple had to move from a village to a bigger town close by, in order to find a good education for their children. They still kept on ministering to the village and other villages from their new base.

From our experience, orientation and training plays an important part in the retention of missionaries in our ministry. If the right personnel are recruited, given adequate orientation and training, sent to places where they believe God has called them, and given adequate support and care, then attrition can be minimised and we shall have many workers staying on the field to fulfil the Great Commission.

Discussion questions:

1. At present, what orientation and training is provided by your organisation (agency or church) to your new missionaries?

2. What aspects of the orientation programme could be improved? How would you do this?

In the real world:

A table to stimulate ideas for best practice in mission partnership. For further explanation, see page 7.

This chart has been partially filled in for you. Now you fill in the blanks.

Who? → When? ↓	Home Church	Missionary	Mission Agencies	External Partners
Continuous				
Recruitment				
Preparation	➢ Support the idea of pre-field orientation ➢ Make pre-field orientation possible financially	➢ Take time to orientate upfront ➢ Be honest about experiences	➢ Use pre-field orientation as way to test calling ➢ Be honest about what missionaries can expect ➢ Provide practical information as much as possible	➢ Catalyse partnership in orientation ➢ Bring partners together
On field	➢ Pray for feeling at home on the field	➢ Take time to orientate	➢ Supply language training ➢ Introduce cultural practices and norms and local religious beliefs and practices ➢ Introduction to agency matters on the field	➢ Provide tools for training ➢ Supply practical help to start living in a new context
Crisis				
Furlough				
Re-entry				

11

Spiritual Life

The facts

A healthy spiritual life is, not surprisingly, essential for missionaries and mission organisations. The overall performance rating related to spiritual life was rated highest of all groups of questions in both NSC and OSC. In OSC, they show a clear correlation to retention. Considering individual questions, the testing of the maturity of a candidate's spiritual life and the emphasis on the maintenance and growth of that spiritual life specifically are rated highly for performance and significance and correlate with retention. A culture of prayer throughout the mission agency (shown in regular prayer for the missionaries) is valued highly, and in OSC is clearly correlated to retention. Prayer and the overall grouping of personal spirituality was given a high priority for almost all NSC agencies so that there is little distinguishable difference between high and low retaining groups.

The data

Q. No.	Factor	OSC Health Indicator	✓	NSC Health Indicator	✓
14	Demonstrates mature Christian character and discipline (prayer & devotional life)	○○○○○○○○○●	✓	○○○○○○○○○●	✓
25	Has firm/stable prayer support	○○○○●●●●●●	✓	○○○○●●●●●●	
46	A culture of prayer is actively promoted within the agency	○○○○○○○●●●	✓	○○○○○○○○●●	
47	Most leaders are a good example of the agency's beliefs and values	○○○○○○○○○●	✓	○○○○○○○○●●	

58	Missionaries know how to handle spiritual warfare	○○○○○●●●●●	✓	○○○○○○●●●●	✓
74	Emphasis is placed on the maintenance and growth of personal spiritual life	○○○○○○○●●●	✓	○○○○○○○○●●	✓
86	Staff in the home office pray regularly for the missionaries	○○○○○○○○●●	✓	○○○○○○○○○●	

The key findings

✓ Issues of spiritual life received the highest rating of all question groups in OSC and NSC.

✓ In OSC, strong spiritual life was highly correlated with retention. In NSC, they received a very high rating for performance and significance even in low retaining agencies so that no correlation was found.

✓ Culture of prayer throughout the agency (Q46) was rated very high for performance and significance by mission executives and is highly correlated with retention in OSC; in NSC, this question received a high rating by all agencies.

✓ High emphasis on maintenance and growth of personal spiritual life of missionary (Q74) received a very high rating and correlated with retention.

✓ Testing of mature spiritual life of candidates (Q14) was rated very high and highly correlated with retention in OSC and NSC.

✓ Experience with spiritual warfare (Q58) had average rating and was moderately correlated with high retention.

✓ People in host culture are becoming followers of Christ (Q67) was rated very high in NSC and correlated with high retention.

✓ Home office staff prays for their missionaries (Q86) received very high ratings even in low retaining agencies (in OSC exceptionally high and correlated with retention).

What it means

Jaap Ketelaar

The fact that issues of spiritual life are rated highest of all question sub-groups should not surprise us. This reflects the importance God's Word places on this topic. The clear correlation to retention shows the worth of spiritual practice in the life and ministry of missionaries.

When Moses died, God called Joshua to be the leader of Israel. As he began in leadership, the Lord spoke very directly to him. He confirmed Joshua in his new position and promised His support. He called Joshua's to meditate on the Law day and night and do strictly what is commanded in it (Joshua 1:8), then Joshua will be successful and have a blessed life and ministry.

In John 15, the Lord Jesus teaches his disciples that without Him they can do nothing (John 15:5). To Jesus is given all authority and power and he will be with them always when they go out and fulfil the great commandment (Matthew 28:19-20), but it is crucial that they are close to him just as the branch is to the vine. This means a close and obedient walk with the Lord, connection with his Word that purifies us and gives direction, and communication by prayer to experience his presence and to move mountains in our ministry.

Knowing this, Daniel had the habit of praying three times a day with his face towards Jerusalem. In his busy life with his great responsibilities, he took time to seek the face of the Lord and find courage for the tensions he dealt with (Daniel 6:11). The church in Jerusalem (Acts 2:42) had the discipline to stay faithful in studying the Word, praying, celebrating the Lord's supper, and participating together in community. No doubt this foundation was essential as persecution came (Acts 4-5).

In ministry, one experiences much stress and many challenging situations; thus, continuous fellowship with the Lord is essential for inner rest and power to conquer Satan in spiritual battle. A disciple of Christ can never be "Too Busy Not to Pray."[1] Furthermore, they have a moral responsibility to live out the doctrine they espouse. In his book, "A Resilient Life," Gordon MacDonald writes that he owed the people he served in his church "a filled-up soul":

> "Whether they encountered me in the pulpit or on the streets of our community during the week, they needed to know that if (perish the thought) there was only one human being in their world who had some experience in the presence of God, I would be that man."[2]

Issues to deal with

But is maintaining a strong spiritual life clear and easy in practice? Apparently not, according to the survey "How spiritual are missionaries?" in *Helping Missionaries Grow: Readings in Mental Health and Missions*.[3] Questions on prayer and Bible reading, how we reconcile God and suffering, mission relationships, theological fidelity, depression, holiness (including sexuality) and the charismatic experience lead Phil Parshall to give some serious reflections and recommendations:

> "Are missionaries spiritual? The question should cause not a small amount of probing and introspection. Perhaps it is time to have field seminars on the subject. Often a close friend or colleague can be a catalyst be-

1   Bill Hybels, *Too Busy Not to Pray*, (Downers Grove, Il: Inter-Varsity, 1988).
2   Gordon MacDonald, *A Resilient Life: You Can Move Ahead No Matter What* (Nashville: Thomas Nelson, 2005), p. 191.
3   Kelly S. O'Donnell and Michele Lewis O'Donnell, *Helping Missionaries Grow: Readings in Mental Health and Missions* (Pasadena, CA: William Carey Library, 1988).

tween us and the Lord. Missionaries are sensing needs in their times of prayer and Bible study. Annual spiritual life retreats should be scheduled that are not encumbered with business agendas. Missions may want to consider the appointment of a field chaplain, whose only task is to minister to missionaries. Such a person could be shared among several smaller missions. Tension and depression continue to be major problems. Mission leaders should seek to alleviate continuous pressure points. Regular vacations and changes in routine are vital. This survey indicates intellectual stagnation on the part of many. Reading programmes, team seminars, and furlough study should all be incorporated into the normal flow of missionary life as should the provision of relevant, accessible mission journals such as Connections[4] and Encounters,[5] both aimed at practitioners of mission rather than closet academics. There are journals available in other languages—details of these can be found on the *Worth Keeping* website in Chapter 11. Busyness should never be allowed to become an excuse for the neglect of one's personal growth."[6]

Busyness and the pressure of the ministry are a serious danger and threaten to weaken the strength of missionaries and their ministry. In *Missionary Care*, Kelly O'Donnell stresses even more forcefully the importance of a person's relationship to God. Examining the life of Abraham and Sarah, he looks at five core issues for missionaries and concludes:

"The missionary's relationship with God is the pre-eminent issue. It is important to be aware of the numerous challenges of missionary life and to make sure that missionaries are supported as they face these. But ultimately, these are secondary issues, which must be understood in light of the missionary's need for obedience, perseverance, trust, perspective, and testing. This makes strengthening and encouraging a person's relationship with God the central component of any member care programme."[7]

How is this done? How can a missionary maintain his spiritual life so he will grow and be "On mission with God," as Avery T. Willis, Jr. and Henry T. Blackaby put it in their challenging book of the same name?[8]

The key factor is developing discipline. A disciple needs discipline and a missionary is a disciple. Because of all the pressures he or she is under, maybe a missionary needs discipline even more than a Christian that stays working in his own Jerusalem. This means making choices and sticking with priorities. Taking time with Jesus, studying the Word, and asking God for sanctification, help with challenging people, and the ability to obey his will, etc., are crucial. Gordon MacDonald describes the way he practices these elements daily:

---

4   See www.worldevangelical.org/commissions/missions.htm for details.
5   See www.redcliffe.org/mission to access this free online journal.
6   O'Donnell and O'Donnell, *Helping Missionaries Grow*, p.81.
7   Kelly O'Donnell, ed., *Missionary Care: Counting the Cost for World Evangelization*, (Pasadena, CA: William Carey Library, 1991), p. 44.
8   Avery T. Willis, Jr. and Henry T. Blackaby, *On Mission with God: Living God's Purpose for His Glory*, (Nashville, TN: Broadman & Holman, 2002).

"I try to rise early and seek God's heart. And how is such time used? I worship and, occasionally, write prayers of praise and exaltation. I read (Scripture and meditative literature). I pray. I give thanksgiving. I reflect on the events of the previous day and finally, I try to focus on what I think God is saying about the use of today's hours and write down my intentions."[9]

Mission agency leaders have a responsibility to help the missionary maintain a strong spiritual life (see quote from Phil Parshall). A missionary can and should work on personal discipline, but to receive support and encouragement from the mission agency—for personal spiritual discipline to be an expectation—would make a tremendous difference. Clearly, agencies see the importance of praying for the missionary. This is encouraging and there is clearly a correlation with retention. Along with this, agencies have a very important role in creating an environment and culture that helps missionaries make personal spiritual life top priority. Aaron and Hur held up the hands of Moses (Exodus.17:12) so he could pray, but they also found him a stone, so he could sit. Praying only is not enough; facilitating the circumstance for a missionary to function well and grow is also integral. (See Chapter 18, *Work-Life Balance*, for further discussion.)

Mutual learning

- Is this a topic in which OSC can learn from NSC, considering the fact that even low retaining NSC agencies underline the importance of having and maintaining one's spiritual life?

- What about the generational differences between (in the West) Builders, Boomers, X-ers and Y-ers? The form may change, but the principles stay the same. We cannot do without a close walk with the Lord.

- Husbands/wives, parents/children can help and support each other through encouragement and providing opportunities and time for each other to spend time with the Master. Singles could look for "kindred spirits" or accountability partners. What can men learn from women and vice-versa in this?

---

9   MacDonald, *A Resilient Life*, p. 191.

Development in the spiritual life of a single missionary

Rachel Murray[10], New Zealand

Just as we grow and develop in our physical lives, our Christian growth is important for expanding the understanding of our faith. We are exhorted to move from spiritual immaturity, the basic foundations, to a more solid maturity and understanding (Hebrews 5:12-6:3). Without exception, we are *all* encouraged to grow. However, for those in Christian leadership, spiritual growth is a responsibility, and expectations are often higher. Whatever the form of leadership, there is generally an accepted understanding that the leader must not only have the appropriate skills for the role, but also be in a spiritual position to model, guide, encourage and lead others to their own spiritual maturity.

By its nature, cross-cultural mission exists not only to spread the Good News of Christ through proclamation and demonstration, but also to encourage the spiritual growth and development of those who have heard and accepted Christ as their Saviour. Missionaries are commissioned to do just these things in all corners of the earth, whether they are involved in relief and development work, pastoring a church, evangelism or education. However, if they themselves are not growing spiritually, then an important factor and basis for their involvement in this work has been compromised.

Michelle[11] lived in an Asian country for 17 years. Working with an international agency, she was involved in theological education of women; initially as a teacher and then in leadership of the college. She had a six-month home assignment every three years and a one-year home assignment after ten years on the field. She has since retired back to her birth country.

Working in a college environment that was "faith-based," where people shared similar values, it would be easy to assume that maintaining one's spiritual life would be easy. But the wider Islamic context and culture, where Michelle was based, presented its own challenges. Never married, Michelle lived in a country that was patriarchal in nature and where marriage and family gave status and security. Politically, there were periodic upheavals which created uncertainty and instability. Simply living where she did was not always straightforward.

Adjusting to these differences, coping with the difficulties, and becoming accustomed to the diversity of the culture was challenging. Learning to be open and appreciative of alternative ways of "doing," re-examining and expanding expecta-

---

10 Rachel Murray was the New Zealand coordinator for the ReMAP II project. She was formerly the short term mission coordinator for Interserve (NZ), an agency facilitating individuals into positions related to their professional skills for one to twelve months throughout Asia and the Middle East. In her role at Interserve (NZ), Rachel worked with enquirers regarding service with the agency. Rachel is currently the Executive Assistant at Carey Baptist College in Auckland, New Zealand. In her new role, she assists the Principal in leadership of a growing Bible and theological college where people are trained for mission, ministry and the marketplace.

11 The missionary's name has been changed.

tions and boundaries often without support structures—all of these things meant that Michelle had to develop a stronger personal faith than she may have done in her birth country. Through a growing awareness of this new culture and its customs, which was far different from her own, Michelle learned to appreciate the strengths and weaknesses of both cultures that were now part of her life, including which aspects did or did not approximate Christian standards. She had to think on what it truly meant to be more Christ-like and to live as Christ would in these situations.

Michelle attended church communities which communicated in the local language. This alone presented challenges until she was fluent enough in the vernacular. These congregations had been influenced by the churches that had founded them. Worship styles were therefore not totally unfamiliar from Michelle's church community in her birth country, but the combination of mixed cultural practices and formality was often stifling her spiritual growth. Unfortunately, orientation sessions in her host culture had no impact on how she could adjust to new practices of church and fellowship.

Retreats were organised on occasion by the local leadership of her agency. With little biblical input, Michelle felt these tended more towards a "time-out" than an opportunity to grow spiritually through solid teaching. Her own initiatives of personal retreats at local centres gave her more memorable opportunities for development. They could be timed and focused on her own needs and relationship with God—a personalised occasion rather than a packaged one that could not so easily provide for the individual.

Michelle's work brought her in contact with people, issues and the culture on a daily basis—all of which challenged her to think about how she presented herself to others. She was, after all, in this country as a "mission worker" and her actions would portray her beliefs and the God that she served. The challenges which faced her through interactions with others and the issues of daily life in that context became some of the most influential factors in her growth as a person. Therefore, for Michelle, much of her growth came out of circumstances and pressures in her overseas context.

The unstable political situation of the country was ongoing and could create a sense of mistrust amongst even close friends. Michelle found herself a confidante on a number of occasions, due to the assumption that foreigners understood and respected issues of confidentiality. While difficult, Michelle came to see that such conversations with local people have helped her own spiritual growth. She had the opportunity to hear, think through, and deal with issues that she may not have otherwise.

Over the years that Michelle was in Asia, retreats, spiritual direction and more eclectic practices became more common. While it was not unheard of to have "days out" for prayer, they were not used widely enough. Today, Michelle now sees some benefit in retreats during home assignment or on the field, but she also notes two dangers; a) a "one-size-fits-all" mentality that can creep in, and b) an underlying assumption of missionaries having deep psychological issues due to their time in the field.

Michelle has not been under spiritual direction either on the field or now that she has retired from cross-cultural service. For her, having established personal spiritual practices prior to leaving for Asia helped her to continue what was best suited to her needs and to her relationship with God. This foundation meant she did not need to start something new in a context that already required a large amount of energy in adjustment and challenge in the initial years. A key feature for Michelle was her teapot… taking time to be with God in prayer, the reading of Scripture and reflection, for the duration of drinking three cups of tea: an established, proven practice that works for Michelle's personality and situation. In addition, pre-departure training at a Bible College for two years helped shape and develop Michelle's spiritual thinking, while reinforcing practices and beliefs prior to leaving for the field.

Relationships with others were vital to Michelle's spiritual life. Prayer partners were an important part of maintenance and growth for her. However, as is common in cross-cultural work, the transient nature of the mission community meant regular changes disrupted patterns and established practices. Friendships with national colleagues were founded on a shared faith, providing opportunities for prayer and discussion where all were learning. Michelle's role in the college where she worked included the mentoring of younger staff. Through sharing and encouraging others in their lives, Michelle found this a point of growth for herself.

In Michelle's situation, much of her spiritual growth was based on her own initiatives rather than through those of the agency she was with. She knew what would work best for her in her relationship with God. Practices she had established prior to her departure to Asia formed the foundation for her growth while overseas. She was also open to allow the issues and situations of others to teach her and to therefore develop her own spiritual life. These elements saw her through 17 years of positive mission service and beyond.

Discussion questions

1. Michelle did not see spiritual development as different from our growth as whole people. Is this a fair comment? If so, how do we ensure that our spirituality does not become a separate entity?

2. Whose responsibility is it to ensure that spiritual growth is taking place, whether on the field or at "home"? How can agencies best serve missionaries in their spiritual growth in their different contexts, with different personalities and family situations, according to their own needs and requirements? How do we avoid the "one-size-fits-all" approach?

In the real world:

A table to stimulate ideas for best practice in mission partnership. For further explanation, see page 7.

This chart has been partially filled in for you. Now you fill in the blanks.

Who? → When? ↓	Home Church	Missionary	Mission Agencies	External Partners
Continuous	➢ Provide discipleship training at a young age	➢ Commit to discipleship	➢ Provide specifics on missions in discipleship training	➢ Support developing discipleship training
Recruitment			➢ Test for a mature spiritual life	
Preparation				➢ Provide discipleship for missionaries as part of theological training
On field	➢ Provide pastoral support (visit, internet pastor) ➢ Intercede regularly in prayer	➢ Commit to discipline in work/(spiritual) life balance ➢ Communicate needs/ answers to prayer	➢ Create right environment to make spiritual life a top priority ➢ Pray from the Home Office ➢ Provide a personal mentor/coach	
Crisis	➢ Intercede in prayer ➢ Provide pastoral support			
Furlough	➢ Support a focus on spiritual refreshment	➢ Go on a retreat	➢ Protect personal/ business agenda	➢ Organise conferences for missionaries on furlough
Re-entry			➢ Debrief (internally)	➢ Debrief (externally)

12

Spiritual Life
Spiritual Warfare

The facts

Spiritual life generally may have received the highest rating of all the broad areas surveyed, but the specific area of spiritual warfare received a significantly lower rating. High retaining agencies rate the importance of how to deal with spiritual warfare higher than low retaining agencies in OSC and NSC alike. However, the NSC gave a higher rating for spiritual warfare than OSC.

The data

Q. No.	Factor	OSC Health Indicator	✓	NSC Health Indicator	✓
58	Missionaries know how to handle spiritual warfare	○○○○○●●●●●	✓	○○○○○○●●●●	✓

The key findings

- ✓ Missionaries know to handle spiritual warfare (Q58) was rated significantly lower than other questions of this block in NSC and OSC.
- ✓ Spiritual warfare (Q58) was moderately correlated with retention in NSC and OSC.

What it means

Jaap Ketelaar

NSC rates spiritual warfare higher than OSC, which is not surprising in light of each region's historical treatment of Satan and their understanding of animism in its many forms. In NSC countries, the power of satanic forces is experienced in daily life, and mission agencies know its relevance. In contrast, evangelicals in OSCs have historically struggled to understand the day-to-day reality of Satan. Following the Enlightenment period, belief in spiritual powers that have personalities and one leader, Satan, or as he was known "the devil," was minimised or even ridiculed. These attitudes have continued to this day, which is perhaps why this area receives only a moderate rating. Or, perhaps the rating is an acknowledgement by OSC mission leaders that their missionaries have too little experience in countering spiritual warfare and that they need to give them better preparation.

In Holland, someone made a comparison between several theological universities, and he said that at one university (liberal) Satan walked in Dutch wooden shoes, so his presence was very clear. At another, he walked in fine Italian shoes, and at the third, he walked in socks. In the last case, he was there, but you could hardly hear him and the students seemed to forget about him. In the OSC, it would seem he walks in socks. However, it is dangerous when Christians minimise Satan. Neglecting this biblical and practical truth has consequences, one of which is shown in the reduced retention rate of agencies. Those that have a high retention rate see the importance of spiritual warfare, while low retaining agencies rate this topic lower.

The surprise in the data was that, in both OSC and NSC, spiritual warfare rates lower than other topics in ministry. Why is this? In Ephesians 6, Paul draws our attention to the spiritual reality we are part of and the importance of fighting the spiritual battle. Perhaps field missionaries see the topic differently? Perhaps mission executives realise the significance of this topic, but recognise the lack of equipping and experience of their missionaries or the limits of their pragmatic dealing? It seems that not only can OSC learn from NSC, but that both can learn from Scripture and in the grassroots reality of the demonic at work today in all arenas and nations. Would our total, global retention rate go up if we radically understood the reality of spiritual warfare and integrated this reality into our policies and practices?

Issues to deal with

It is fundamental that the right balance be struck between correct biblical and theological framework of this area and daily practice on the field. A combination of both is required as Paul Hiebert articulates in his chapter from *Global Missiology for the 21st Century* on "Spiritual Warfare and Worldview":

"Much literature on spiritual warfare has been written by missionaries who are forced to question their Western denial of the spirit realities of this world through encounters with witchcraft, spiritism, and demon possession, and who base their studies on experience and look for biblical texts to justify their views. These studies generally lack solid, comprehensive, theological reflection on the subject. A second viewpoint is set forth by biblical scholars who seek to formulate a theological framework for understanding spiritual warfare but who lack a deep understanding of the bewildering array of beliefs in spirit realities found in religions around the world. Consequently, it is hard to apply their findings in the specific contexts in which ministry occurs."[1]

In this chapter, we want to stress the importance of this subject and the need to develop our understanding of spiritual warfare in our personal life and ministry. Three points of knowledge are fundamental:

1. We have to know (of) the enemy

    Paul, in Ephesians 6:10-20, teaches what Daniel heard in Daniel 10:13, 20-21: we live in a spiritual reality. Lucifer, a prominent angel called to bear God's light is, in his disobedience towards his Creator, trying to ruin God's creation and the people that want to follow Him. In his ministry, Paul is aware of this fact (2 Corinthians 2:11). That is the reason why he looks at things from a spiritual perspective and responds appropriately in whatever he does in his ministry. In an article on "Strategic Prayer," John D. Robb puts the strategy of our enemy in the following words, applicable for both New and Old Sending Countries:

    "Both Satan and his powers are dedicated to destroying the human beings who are made in the image of God. Satan is the master deceiver, the author of idolatry, who seeks to dominate the world by undermining faith in God, twisting values and promoting false ideologies. He infiltrates institutions, governments, communications media, educational systems and religious bodies, using them to seduce humankind over to the worship of money, fame, success, power, pleasure, science, art, politics and religious idols. Socio-spiritual forces of evil clench societies in a dark, destructive grip in two related ways. The first is by openly idolatrous and cultic covenants and the second through false patterns of thinking which blind people to the reality of God and the hope He brings."[2]

    If this is right, all parts of integral or holistic mission need spiritual back-up!

2. We have to know ourselves

    In this spiritual battle, there is only one way to survive: standing firm in the faith. 1 Peter 5:9 says, "…because you know that your brothers *throughout the*

1   William D. Taylor, *Global Missiology for the 21st Century: The Iguassu Dialogue, Globalisation of Mission Series*, (Grand Rapids, Mich: Baker Academic, 2000), p. 163.

2   Ralph D. Winter and Steven C. Hawthorne, eds., *Perspectives on the World Christian Movement: A Reader*, 3rd ed., (Pasadena: William Carey Library, 1999), p. 146.

world are undergoing the same kind of sufferings", (emphasis mine). Dr. Neil T. Anderson, in *Victory Over the Darkness,*[3] emphasizes knowing who you are in Christ as your strength. This requires daily discipline (1 Corinthians 10:12) and a close walk to the Lord.

3. We have to know our God

   Jesus promised his church he would be with them always, to the very end of the age (Matthew 28:20). To Jesus has been given all authority in heaven and on earth (Matthew 28:18). With his resources and promise, the Church is able to triumph, personally and in its ministry. In Ephesians 6:10-20, Paul writes about the importance of spiritual armour, and note that there is only one offensive weapon: the sword which is the Word of God (cf. Matthew 4, Jesus engaging in spiritual warfare). The interesting thing in this is that we are called not to fight Satan as our primary objective, but to live and work for God and when Satan comes on our way we deal with him. This however does not mean things will go our way all the time. In these days of tension between the "now" and "not yet," the church must engage with suffering (see the examples of triumph and persecution in the book of Acts). Therefore, it is crucial that the saints persevere and are faithful to their Lord.

Personal encounters with spiritual warfare

Alan McMahon,[4] Operation Mobilisation, Australia

I was taught in theological school that demons do not exist, having been dealt with by Jesus on earth and by the early Church. Then I went to serve in my first parish located in the outback of Australia, about the time when the book "The Exorcist"[5] was published. I was curious. If there are no demons, then what does the priest cast out? So I bought a book, read it, and then laid it aside. I had been taught differently, so I wondered if this was just another error of Catholicism.

Some weeks later, while sleeping in a room next to my kitchen, I was suddenly woken up by the sound of someone smashing the furniture in the kitchen. Being alone in the house, I was terrified and pretended to be dead, so that whoever it was if he came into my room would think I was dead. After the smashing had stopped and my heart beat returned to normal, I got out of bed to assess the damage. Nothing was out of place. I looked into each of the 13 rooms, under all the beds, in the cupboards, checked the locks on doors and windows—all were secure.

I returned to my bed and again the smashing returned. I leapt out of bed. But the moment I entered the kitchen, the smashing sound stopped. Then I thought of the

---

3   Neil T. Anderson, *Victory Over the Darkness: With Study Guide* (London: Monarch, 2002).

4   Alan McMahon is an Australian who has spent 12 years serving on the Doulos ship, a ministry of Operation Mobilisation. He has taught Spiritual Warfare in every port where the Doulos has visited, as well as in other situations. According to Alan, the ignorance of demonic presence and their activity is one major cause for Christian workers to return home from the field.

5   The Exorcist is a horror novel written by William Peter Blatty first published in 1971. It is based on a supposedly genuine 1949 exorcism Blatty heard about while he was a student in the class of 1950 at Georgetown University, a Jesuit and Catholic school.

book "The Exorcist." I returned to bed, sitting up waiting, and the sound returned. Immediately, as in the book, I said, "Demons, in the name of Jesus get out of this house and never return." I went to sleep and I was never disturbed in the house again.

On the Doulos ship, we constantly warned our crew *not* to collect wooden souvenirs from Africa and India because the custom is generally for the witchdoctor to pray over the wood before or after the carving. But of course, "Westerners don't believe in these things." Crew members would from time to time return with wooden objects. The captain, with some others, would then have to go to the engine crew quarters to cast out demons that had pressed down on sleeping men, immobilising them, and trying to choke them. The men could do nothing to help themselves. We always had to throw all the wooden souvenirs overboard for on-going victory.

One evening, after I had spoken at a Spiritual Warfare conference in Malaysia, an Indian couple came and asked if I would pray for their daughter who was troubled by a demon from time to time. Many pastors had prayed for her without relief. I said I would, but explained that I did not have spiritual authority in this area. They would need to bring their pastor who would have that local spiritual authority. On Saturday afternoon, they returned with the daughter and pastor. I asked questions of the parents and the girl. As we spoke, the girl was quite normal and relaxed.

This was her story. She had gone to the cemetery to look for her cousin who was a grave digger. When she found him, he was almost finished with his grave digging and suggested she go and look at a nearby grave of a European family of five. All of them had been killed in a car accident. As she looked at the grave, her heart empathised with the five-year-old boy who died in the accident. She had mentioned this child a few times in our conversation. That was the clue I had missed. We prayed for her, then they went away without relief.

Later that night before sleeping I prayed, "Lord why didn't we have victory? What demon is it?" The Holy Spirit revealed to me, "It is the child's familiar spirit who entered her when it saw how she felt sorry for the lad." Immediately, I phoned the pastor and told him what it was, that she needed to renounce the demon, then they were to take authority and cast it out by name. Six months later, when I went back to that town on a follow-up visit, I sought the pastor and learned she had been delivered after they prayed as suggested.

An American couple was transferred by his company to work in Malaysia. The man had previously served as a deacon in a large church. The couple looked at the churches in that city and joined one that didn't have a pastor, accepting an invitation from the elders to a leadership role. Not long afterwards, the husband's mother died in the USA. So, the whole family went home for the funeral. He was very close to his mother and suffered a lot of grief.

Back in Malaysia, when he went to his usual hairdresser, he poured out his grief. She applied "black magic oil" obtained from a Malay folk-healer on his head. Soon after, he stopped going to the weekly Bible study group. Then he began to miss going to church, saying he was "busy at work!" But he was actually having an affair with the hairdresser. Meanwhile, his wife thought he just needed time to get over his grief.

Some months later, when his wife and children were in the USA for school holidays, the hairdresser moved into the home and she planted "black magic oils." When they came back, his wife soon discovered her husband's affair. Although the man loved his wife and children, he felt helpless about his relationship with the hairdresser. His wife discussed the matter with the church elders. They told her "search the house for black magic items." Her response was "we don't believe in that rubbish." To which they said, "You had better believe. Go home and look." But she ignored them.

Then one day, while cleaning her daughter's doll house, she saw a matchbox and inside were two vials of oil. Remembering what the elders had said, the wife showed them to an Indian servant in the house next door—a believer—who said, "That's black magic. You must destroy it or it will break up your marriage." She took the matchbox to the elders who told her the same thing. They destroyed it and told her to go and look for more. So she searched and found a jar of oil in the bathroom. When she showed it to the elders, all of them agreed that it was black magic and it had to be destroyed. Sadly, what they did was not enough. The marriage eventually ended, and the man has continued living with his hairdresser.

When I stayed in Singapore, I once went sightseeing with a Filipino friend visiting from Manila. Among the places we visited was the oldest temple where the "monkey god" demon has his headquarters. I went straight into the compound but my friend did not follow behind me. He had stopped to give a donation to the temple and to sign the visitors book. I scolded him that he would support the temple. While we stood opposite the entrance to the monkey god temple, suddenly there was a heavy tapping on my left shoulder. I looked around but nobody was there. I said to my friend, "I think we should get out of here." His reply was "Yes, the presence of evil is very strong right here."

We left the temple and went to a crocodile farm. Within five minutes of our arrival, my friend said, "I feel ill. Would you take me back to the hotel?" I took him back and went home to finish my message for Sunday. Soon, I also became very ill. My doctor treated me for cholera for many weeks, but the medication did nothing to help. Eventually, he cleared me to return home to Australia, where for three weeks I was prayed for by many. Finally, after preaching at a healing service in Sydney, the leader prayed for me and the demon left and I was healed. When I returned to my cell group in Singapore and shared, the Bishop's wife remarked "Alan, you live and learn the hard way don't you!" I asked, "What do you mean?" She replied that no local Christian would ever go into a pagan temple. "If our visitors want to visit a temple, we will warn them and leave them at the gate."

Those were some of my encounters. In closing, I would encourage you to remember that Jesus is Lord. Therefore, we should not go around looking for or blaming demons for unusual events. Although God may sometimes permit spiritual attacks, our focus should always remain on Jesus. We should focus on what God has done in Christ for us, and the fact that "the Lord is faithful and He will strengthen and protect you (us) from the evil one." (2 Thess. 3:3). God does provide His wisdom and knowledge when we look to Him.

Discussion questions:

1. What did you learn about spiritual warfare from these stories?
2. How can we help new missionaries to be better prepared to handle spiritual warfare?

In the real world:

A table to stimulate ideas for best practice in mission partnership. For further explanation, see page 7.

This chart has been partially filled in for you. Now you fill in the blanks.

Who? → When? ↓	Home Church	Missionary	Mission Agencies	External Partners
Continuous	➢ Teach the reality of spiritual warfare to old and young ➢ Be obedient in following the Lord ➢ Be a Bible-based church, faithful to the Lord ➢ Be a praying church ➢ Teach and practice deliverance from evil	➢ Be faithful and live sanctified ➢ Know how to handle spiritual warfare in personal life and ministry	➢ Be a praying agency ➢ Have insight into the spiritual dynamics of the ministry	➢ Support ministry through education and training on how to handle spiritual warfare ➢ Offer opportunities for rest after warfare: retreats, etc. ➢ Offer a ministry of prayer for Kingdom workers
Recruitment				
Preparation				
On field				
Crisis				
Furlough				
Re-entry				

13

Personal Care

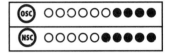

The facts

Personal care covers a wide range of issues concerning the ability of individuals to function well and fulfil the ministry role to which they are called. They include family issues, social and spiritual needs, health and safety considerations.

The area of personal care is very important, with strong correlation to retention in both OSC and NSC. This correlation runs across the majority of factors (nine of 14 survey questions in OSC, and ten in NSC), although there were interesting differences in responses between OSC and NSC.

The data

Q. No.	Factor	OSC Health Indicator	✓	NSC Health Indicator	✓
42	There is a free flow of communication to and from the leadership	○○○○○○●●●●	✓	○○○○○○●●●●	
62	Opportunities are provided for a ministry/role for the spouse	○○○○○○○●●●	✓	○○○○○○●●●●	
63	Missionaries have adequate administrative and practical support on the field	○○○○○○●●●●	✓	○○○○○○●●●●	✓
71	Missionary teams are effective in providing each other with mutual support	○○○○●●●●●●		○○○○○○●●●●	✓
72	Effective pastoral care exists at a field level (preventative and in crises)	○○●●●●●●●●		○○○○○●●●●●	✓
73	Interpersonal conflicts are resolved in a timely and appropriate manner	○○○●●●●●●●		○○○○●●●●●●	✓

74	Emphasis is placed on the maintenance and growth of personal spiritual life	○○○○○○○●●●	✓	○○○○○○○○●●	✓
75	There are satisfactory schooling opportunities for missionaries' children	○○○○○○●●●●		○○○○●●●●●●	✓
76	Health care services for missionaries/missionary families are satisfactory	○○○○○○○●●●		○○○○●●●●●●	✓
77	Time for an annual vacation or holiday is provided	○○○○○○○○○●	✓	○○○○○○○●●●	✓
78	Risk assessment and contingency planning is in place in all fields	○○○○○○○●●●	✓	○○○○●●●●●●	✓
79	Home churches are encouraged to be involved in the life and ministry of their missionary	○○○○○○○○●●	✓	○○○○○●●●●●	✓
87	Re-entry arrangements/ programmes are provided for missionaries commencing home leave	○○○○○●●●●●	✓	○○○●●●●●●●	
88	Formal debriefing is undertaken during home leave	○○○○○○○●●●	✓	○○○●●●●●●●	

The key findings

✓ Overall, issues of personal care were highly correlated with retention in NSC and OSC.

✓ Effective teams (Q71), Pastoral care on field level (Q72) and Interpersonal conflict resolution (Q73) were correlated with retention in NSC, but not so much in OSC (unexpected result). In OSC, this group of questions was also rated significantly lower than in NSC (individualistic culture?).

✓ Time for annual vacation (Q77) was rated extremely high and correlated with high retention.

✓ Involvement of home church in life of missionary (Q79) was rated very high in OSC and correlated to retention (current missiological paradigm in OSC); it was rated significantly lower in NSC and there was only a mild correlation with retention (RRP) in NSC (logistic and financial limitations in NSC?).

✓ Risk assessment and contingency planning (Q78) was clearly correlated with retention, in NSC even more than in OSC.

✓ Access to Health care (Q76) was rated in OSC significantly higher than in NSC, yet in NSC we found a stronger correlation with retention.

✓ Children of missionaries' schooling opportunities (Q75) was rated higher in OSC and was correlated with retention (for preventative attrition RRP) in NSC, but not in OSC (taken for granted in OSC?).

✓ Administrative and practical support (Q63) received a very high rating in NSC and was moderately correlated with high retention in NSC and OSC.

What it means

Rob Hay

The area of personal care covers factors that concern the support and well-being of the missionary, their spouse and family. Ensuring that people's functional needs are met and that their relationships are healthy and supportive allow them to function well as people and ministers. Maslow's Hierarchy of Needs is a widely accepted theory of motivation which may help illustrate these results.. Simply put, Maslow identifies five levels of needs that should be met to allow one to be functioning highly (summarised by Peter K. Gerlach):

Level 1: Reduce current physical discomforts first: hunger, thirst, pain, air, warmth or shade, smells, balance, noise, light, and rest (sleep). When those are satisfied, then...

Level 2: We try to fill our need to feel safe in the near future. Safety comes from trusting that our level-one needs and protection from local dangers will be reliably met in the coming days and weeks (our safety zone). In our society, that translates into believing that we'll have a dependable source of money to buy those securities. The safety zone is short for some people, longer for fear-based (wounded) others. Maslow suggested that when we feel comfortable and safe enough, we then try to fill...

Level 3: Our need for companionship—our (basic) need to feel accepted by, and part of, a group of other people. We need to feel we belong to (are accepted by) a family, tribe, group, or clan. The alternative is feeling we're alone in the world, which is not only lonely, but less safe. ...then we focus on filling...

Level 4: Our need to be recognized as special and valuable by our group. We need to be more than just a featureless face in the crowd, we need to be known and appreciated. ...then we are free to achieve...

Level 5: The need to be self actualized. A key reason people value Maslow's ideas is the universal longing to be fully ourselves. That implies we each have unique talents and abilities that we long to develop and use to benefit the world if all our other need-levels are filled well enough, often enough. Then we can become creative, energized, centred, focused, and productive and live "at our highest personal potential."[1] (or in Christian

---

1   From Peter K. Gerlach, "What Causes your Behaviour? Building on Dr. Abraham Maslow's Hierarchy of Needs", From the website Stepfamily in Formation, http://sfhelp.org/02/needlevels.htm, last accessed December, 2006.

terms, as whole as we can be this side of Christ's full re-creation and renewal).

The fifth level of Maslow's Hierarchy is work or creativity related, but the hierarchy suggests that you cannot function well at Level 5 until the lower level needs are met. Personal care touches the lower levels, but serves as the foundation that enables one to work/minister well.

The data from the personal care questions seems to affirm Maslow's theory. Factors in personal care correlated with retention in OSC or NSC. However, while some survey questions received a reasonable rating of priority, many did not—the overall rating of four and five for OSC and NSC respectively was one of the poorer areas examined.

Some areas will be discussed in more detail in later chapters. For OSC, re-entry [Q87 *Re-entry arrangements/programmes are provided for missionaries commencing home leave*] and debriefing [Q88 *Formal debriefing is undertaken during home leave*] are important for retention and an area in which further work is needed. This specific area is discussed in Chapter 33.

OSC and NSC share strong correlations with retention in support structures [Q63 *Missionaries have adequate administrative and practical support on the field*], and spiritual life [Q74 *Emphasis is placed on the maintenance and growth of personal spiritual life*], holiday/vacation provision [Q77 *Time for an annual vacation or holiday is provided*], safety [Q78 *Risk assessment and contingency planning is in place in all fields*] and home church involvement [Q79 *Home churches are encouraged to be involved in the life and ministry of their missionary*].

Given the difficulties over work/life balance that we discuss in detail in Chapter 18, it is not surprising that the presence or lack of practical and administrative support on the field (Q63) [Q63 *Missionaries have adequate administrative and practical support on the field*] should correlate strongly with retention. Many missionaries also increasingly see themselves as specialists desiring to make best use of their skills and therefore perceive administration as a distraction. The low rating in OSC or NSC suggests that the home offices (they were the respondents in ReMAP II) feel frustrated or limited in their ability to provide as much support as they would like or perceive necessary.

Time for an annual vacation received a very high rating and correlated with high retention. However, when seen in the light of the rating given to Question 61 [Q61 *Missionaries are generally not overloaded in the amount of work they do*] (discussed fully in Chapter 18) we should perhaps have asked the additional question, "Do missionaries use all the holiday/vacation allowance provided?"

The ratings and correlation for Questions 71, 72 and 73, [Q71 *Missionary teams are effective in providing each other with mutual support*], [Q72 *Effective pastoral care exists at a field level (preventative and in crises)*] and [Q73 *Interpersonal conflicts are resolved in a timely and appropriate manner*], were somewhat surprising and so are discussed in detail in the subsequent two chapters.

Perhaps explainable, but also surprising, Question 76 [Q76 _Health care services for missionaries/missionary families are satisfactory_] was rated highly by OSC and yet correlated strongly with retention in NSC. This may suggest that across the majority of OSC agencies there is an acceptable/workable level of health care access. In recent years, insurance companies in OSC have been requiring health care access or Medevac as a prerequisite for any insurance cover. With insurance provision being less widespread in NSC, any lack of local access to health care may result in return (and often permanent return) to the sending country—the only option. Effectively, access to health care appears to be taken for granted in OSC, whereas access does not seem to be the norm in NSC and, therefore, where it is present, it can make a significant difference to retention. Question 75 [Q75 _There are satisfactory schooling opportunities for missionaries' children_] had a similar result and again appears to be an "expected norm" in OSC agencies.

Personal care of our missionaries

Antonia Leonora van der Meer,[2] Evangelical Missions Centre, Brazil

In Brazil, there is a growing understanding about the personal care needs of our missionaries. More agencies and churches are seeking to care for and listen to their missionaries. In spite of our limited resources, we are encouraged that Brazilian missionaries are receiving better member care than they did ten years ago.

Having previously served as a missionary, I have considerable interest in the personal care of missionaries. I was a Brazilian missionary in Angola between 1984 and 1995, when that country was at war and under Marxism. Five other Brazilian missionaries were in Angola when I arrived. That number grew to around 30 about ten years later.

During that time, pastoral visits were something we rarely experienced. In 1991, the father of a missionary made a pastoral visit to us. Everyone looked forward to his visit, and a retreat for Brazilian missionaries was organized. The retreat was the very first time that Brazilian missionaries serving in Angola could share their fears, frustrations and questions in an atmosphere of trust and mutual encouragement.

Eventually, I returned to Brazil to serve at the Evangelical Missions Centre. I proposed that retreats should be organized for missionaries on furlough or after re-entry in order to offer them restoration and renewal. A Brazilian pastor and psychologist shared the same vision, and so in 1996, we began the retreats. Later, in 1999, the Brazilian Member Care Association was founded to serve missionaries in several other ways.

---

2   Antonia Leonora van der Meer served in Angola between 1984 and 1995, where she saw much suffering among local people and among missionaries. She has been serving at the Evangelical Missions Centre for ten years. At present, she is Director of the Mission Training Program, and one of the leaders of the Brazilian Member Care Association. She has just completed her doctorate, and her dissertation was on "Understanding and Responding to the Needs of Brazilian Missionaries Serving in Contexts of Suffering."

Missionaries from a variety of agencies and denominations, with field experience on all continents, have taken part in the Personal Care Retreats. Some of these missionaries were sent by leaders of agencies and churches who recognized the value of such retreats; some attended on their own.

The retreats are one week-long with a programme that is built around the need to renew their personal walk with the Lord. Each retreat has a flexible and un-crowded agenda. It is a time to consider issues like: reevaluating our calling; the pain of re-entry; physical and emotional care of missionary families; finding a rhythm of work and rest; and the specific struggles of couples and of singles. The retreats have been a healing experience for missionaries to be together, to be listened to by people who understand, to have a relaxed time together without high demands or expectations, to see how similar their experiences are, and to be free to weep.

Most missionaries leave a retreat feeling restored and renewed. Some open their hearts on the first opportunity, while others only on the last day. For those with more severe problems, we will ask them for permission to involve their agency or a professional to obtain further help.

We have also been able to organize some Personal Care Retreats in Angola and Mozambique for Brazilian missionaries on the field.

Let me share a few lessons we have learned from the retreats and our interaction with missionaries.

Special care for singles and families

Singles need special pastoral care. They need to know and understand the reality of life on the field, both the dangers and the challenges. They need help to integrate well in teams, where all can contribute and be respected as partners in ministry. Single missionaries often feel lonely, but they can learn to support each other.

Couples will also need pastoral care for their families, which are subject to high stress levels when living in a foreign country and culture. It could be helpful to organize special conferences for missionary couples or families, so that they can feel free to express their need for help.

Furlough and re-entry

During furlough, the time spent at home is not easy for many missionaries. They do not expect to have problems in adapting back home, but many will discover how foreign and insecure they feel, and how little people at home understand their struggles.

Missionaries generally arrive home feeling very tired from their work on the field. They expect to rest and to be renewed, but not all churches understand these expectations. Some churches will cut their support, while some will organize a packed agenda. These churches do not realise how important it is to continue supporting their missionaries, and to offer time for rest and relaxation.

Other churches and agencies, however, receive their missionaries well. They provide care for their needs and give special attention to their children. Many missionaries need help in their process of reintegration. Churches can give practical help (such as with shopping and banking) to make the reverse culture shock less painful.

Missionaries may also arrive home with many pains to deal with. They will seek opportunities to speak to their local church and its leadership (but of course not on the day of their arrival!). The leaders of their sending church and agency should be ready to offer pastoral care. They need to listen to the missionaries, find out individual struggles and pains, and determine what kind of help should be given

Life on the mission field

While our missionaries are on the field, it is necessary to offer pastoral care so that they may overcome any difficulties that arise. Ninety percent of Brazilian missionaries feel assured of receiving regular prayer support. It is also important for each missionary to receive pastoral visits and this is becoming a more common practice in recent years.

Discussion questions:

1. In what ways does your organisation respond to the need for spiritual renewal and rest of your missionaries:
   a. At home during furloughs and after re-entry?
   b. While they are serving on the mission field?

2. Would it be possible for different missionary-sending agencies in your country to work in partnership to improve pastoral care services to missionaries? If yes, what could be done to provide better personal care to your country's missionaries serving on the same field?

Caring for the missionary family

Márcia Tostes,[3] Antioch Mission,[4] Brazil

Laurindo and his wife Andreia were sent to West Africa in 2001, with their two young girls (aged three years and two years). Two years later, around Christmas time, they were having a hard time with their oldest daughter Ada. They tried to explain that financial support from home had not been enough. For that reason, they could not afford any Christmas presents. Ada was very disappointed. She asked, "No Christmas presents? Not even from Aunt Antioquia?" Ada was actually referring to Antioch Mission's special Christmas gift to each missionary child

---

3 Márcia Tostes has been serving as a missionary with Antioch Mission for the last 20 years. She is currently the Director for Training and Pastoral Care. She and her husband, Silas, trained at All Nations Christian College in England, where she gained a vision for pastoral care. Since then, she has specialized in Family Therapy.
4 Antioch Mission is a Brazilian inter-denominational mission agency. It was founded in 1976.

(which had not arrived yet). She feels so closely related to her parents' sending agency that she lovingly refers to our agency as a person!

Sadly, it has not always been like this at Antioch Mission. Some families had suffered the consequences of being pioneer missionaries in our early years, due to minimal resources and support.

Because of the experience and knowledge received from outside member care groups, Antioch Mission has developed a "Caring for the Family" programme that includes:

1. Family Training: In our Mission Training Course,[5] we have a specific subject on missionary family. The course covers topics such as Family life cycle,[6] Missionary life cycle[7] and its implications, focus on the family as a whole, focus on the children, and how to maintain bonds with family and church back in the sending country. We spend a special weekend with teenage family members to address issues such as loss and change, cultural adaptation, etc.

2. Suggestions for Choice of Education model: It is important for the family to understand the pros and cons of different models of education so that they can make the best choices for their children. A missionary family needs to understand that these choices affect the future, so education planning should start in the early years. If wise choices are not made, families will return earlier.

3. Family Brief and Debrief: As the family prepares to leave for the mission field, they are called to a family briefing. We include some exercises to help them prepare for the pain of leaving. For example, each person is asked to write down what they would like to take to the field country. For young children who cannot write, they are asked to draw the object. We then talk about the things they identified. When there is something identified that is not possible to bring, questions are asked in a creative way about how they will cope with this and what alternatives there are. On one occasion, a child said that he would like to take the local church to the field. Talking this through, he decided that it would be impossible to take all the tiles, windows, benches and so on. Talking a little bit more, it became clear that what he was really going to miss were the worship services and songs in Portuguese. He then decided that if he took some CDs, and if the church could send him more CDs during the year, he would have an easier transition.

4. Family Therapist: A trained therapist available to listen to the whole family is important. This person keeps in contact with the candidates from the time of training until they reach the field. They communicate via e-mail or telephone calls.

5. Family History: During the Mission Training Course, all the candidates are

---

5   The Mission Training Course is the orientation course for new missionaries.

6   Family life cycle refers to the stages that a family goes through: a couple just married, a couple with young children, a couple with teenagers, a couple with children going to university, etc.

7   Missionary life cycle refers to the stages that a missionary goes through over the years of missionary life: from training and selection, sending to the field, furlough, second term on field, furlough, etc.

invited to explore their family history, including single and married people. Many come from broken families and have issues that need to be addressed. We ask about marital health and how the children are coping with changes as the family prepares to embark on missionary work.

6. Creativity: When working in a poorer mission context, one has to be very creative to offer care. Through creative care of missionary children, we hope to bring a sense of belonging to a large loving family within Antioch Mission.

    *   At Christmas, Antioch Mission sends a special gift to each missionary child. Our partnership with churches and Christian organisations allows us to organize special fund-raising events, such as a bazaar to sell second-hand items during our annual mission conference. All the profits from the special events are used to buy gifts, such as children's' CDs and books, for our missionary children around the world. The Christmas gifts convey a very important message to these children: they are important and someone cares for them.

    *   We have also developed a "journal" for the children, which they receive once every three months. Every issue includes a picture of one of the missionary children, with information on where they live, what they like and so on. As third-culture kids, the missionary children relate better to people who have gone through similar experiences. When they receive the journal, they can read about other children in a similar situation as themselves.

We asked our missionaries that were sent to West Africa how they feel about the "Caring for the Family" programme. They said: "The philosophy of Antioch Mission is about being a family, so we feel we have friends on the other side. Our children consider themselves as part of the mission. It is not just something that belongs to Mum and Dad. They have their little journal, their special Christmas gift, and so on. When they visit the mission headquarters, they feel at home. They feel they are important, not for being missionary kids, but for being themselves."

Discussion questions:

1. What are some problems faced by missionary families on the field which could be prevented by better member care directed to the missionary family?

2. Does your organisation have a member care programme for the missionary family? What areas are normally covered on this programme? What other areas would you include in future?

Pastoral care to Costa Rican missionaries

Marcos Padgett,[8] Seminario ESEPA, Costa Rica

Note: The names used in this case study have been changed to protect the identity of individuals and the mission agencies involved.

In September 2005, Costa Rican pastor David Sánchez and his wife travelled to Central Asia to provide pastoral care to Costa Rican Missionaries. The following is a brief report of why they did it, how they did it, and what they did.

Why visit missionaries on the field?

The mission movement from Latin America (which includes Costa Rica) is a relatively young force. The first missionaries sent from Costa Rica were sent out about 25 years ago. Much was learned by trial and error. Two key events prompted one Costa Rican mission agency to begin a programme in pastoral care.

The first event involved a missionary couple and domestic violence. The couple returned home from the field, but the problem did not get not solved until the wife turned to a government agency, where she was able to receive counselling and protection for herself and the children. The director of the mission agency, Carlo Constanza, expressed frustration that the church had not been able to help solve this dilemma.

The second event involved a couple sent out from one of the mega-churches. In time, the family returned to Costa Rica due to health problems, but they found no support from their sending church because few members knew who they were.

The above mentioned events were the catalysts for a new pastoral care project that includes:

- Preventive care (pre-field interviews and counselling)
- Corrective care (a mission centre that will provide housing for missionaries on furlough with counselling and medical treatment as required)
- Active care (pastoral visits on the field and follow-up)
- Re-entry care to help missionaries returning from the field with adjustment to their home culture

This project is still in the fund-raising stage. A proposal is being prepared for presentation to a foundation and some individuals have donated funds. Some professionals are also providing medical care and counselling, either free or at a greatly reduced cost.

---

8   Marcos Padgett is a professor at Seminario ESEPA in San Jose, Costa Rica, where he has served for 15 years. He is currently the director of the Cross-Cultural Ministries programme. Marcos was the ReMAP II country coordinator for Costa Rica.

Getting to the field

David and his wife left Costa Rica for the Central Asian country without the required visa. They had tried five times before their trip, but they were unable to obtain a visa. On the day of departure, David had almost given up hope but he persevered in faith. In answer to prayer, a fax arrived less than three hours before they left for the airport. The fax informed David that they had to go to the embassy in a neighbouring country to collect the visa.

The funds required for this pastoral visit were over US$5,000. When one remembers that a well-paid professional in Costa Rica only earns about US$1,000 per month, we can understand why the cost of the trip was a big obstacle. The total amount was eventually raised through the sacrificial giving from individuals, from churches who had missionaries on the field, and a Missions Coffee event. Tickets were sold, coffee was served and the project presented to the attendees: over $800 was raised at the event.

What did they do on the field?

David and his wife held a three day seminar using _The Peacemaker_ material by Ken Sande. Originally, this activity was planned for only the Costa Rican missionaries. However, due to the great need, other missionaries from Latin America were also invited and many attended the seminar. The venue was in a central location at a hotel run by a Christian, who allowed them the use of the facilities for free.

After the seminar, David and his wife visited in the homes of each Costa Rican missionary family and spent three days with each family. They were not there to supervise or inspect the ministry of the missionary. Their purpose was to find out how the missionary was doing and to help deal with personal issues and problems. This trip has confirmed the urgent need for pastoral care on the field.

Recommendations from a pastoral care trip

1. Remember, the purpose for pastoral care is to see how each missionary as a person is doing. A pastoral care trip is not to measure ministry results.
2. Be merciful and pastoral. A pastor cares for his sheep, even if he has to scold or correct.
3. Allot sufficient time for pastoral care.
4. Do not skimp on resources: invest what it takes to give good pastoral care.
5. The visitor needs to have the gifts of pastoring.
6. Make ministry and pastoral care to the missionary the priority; do not go as a tourist.
7. Have the necessary tools, or know where to find them, in order to minister effectively.
8. Prepare well before you go.

9. Get lots of prayer support and be ready to persevere through difficulties.

10. Take extra money. Be prepared to handle a delayed flight, an unexpected charge, or some other emergency.

Discussion questions:

1. Could several churches or organizations in your country share resources and work in partnership to provide better pastoral care to the missionaries serving on the same field?

2. What are the advantages of a pastoral visit to missionaries on the field? How often should a pastoral visit be made? Who should make the visit? What could be done in preparation for and during a pastoral visit? What follow-up may be required after the pastoral visit?

In the real world:

A table to stimulate ideas for best practice in mission partnership. For further explanation, see page 7.

This chart has been partially filled in for you. Now you fill in the blanks.

Who? → When? ↓	Home Church	Missionary	Mission Agencies	External Partners
Continuous				
Recruitment				
Preparation			➢ Pay attention to the whole family	➢ Make available a therapist service for families ➢ Facilitate partnership in sharing knowledge and resources
On field	➢ Provide financial and material support ➢ Provide mental support ➢ Provide pastoral support, regular communication, or visits ➢ Provide prayer support	➢ Take care of work/life balance ➢ Be open about needs	➢ Have a policy of not overloading missionaries	
(Crisis)				➢ Provide debriefing opportunities
Furlough				➢ Provide counselling and medical treatment in mission centre ➢ Provide debriefing opportunities ➢ Organize retreats
Re-entry	➢ Support practically and pastorally			➢ Provide debriefing opportunities

14

Personal Care
Team Building and Functioning

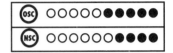

OSC	○○○○○●●●●●
NSC	○○○○○○●●●●

The facts

The missionary team is considered an operating norm for much of the mission world, and yet we find that the effectiveness of those teams is questionable. OSC demonstrates individualism and less regard for mutual support and conflict resolution than NSC, and effectiveness in teams is not strongly linked to retention; in NSC, effectiveness in teams is linked much more strongly. Overall, the results do show that OSC and NSC wrestle with the same issues and share the same struggles and weaknesses in team building and functioning.

The data

Q. No.	Factor	OSC Health Indicator	✓	NSC Health Indicator	✓
42	There is a free flow of communication to and from the leadership	○○○○○○●●●●	✓	○○○○○○●●●●	
57	Missionaries are given room to shape and develop their own ministry	○○○○○○○○●●	✓	○○○○○○○●●●	✓
63	Missionaries have adequate administrative and practical support on the field	○○○○○○●●●●	✓	○○○○○○●●●●	✓
71	Missionary teams are effective in providing each other with mutual support	○○○○●●●●●●		○○○○○○●●●●	✓
73	Interpersonal conflicts are resolved in a timely and appropriate manner	○○○●●●●●●●		○○○○●●●●●●	✓

The key findings

✓ The rating of Effective missionary teams (Q71) indicated a weak correlation with retention in OSC and a stronger one in NSC (community oriented society).

✓ In NSC, rating of interpersonal conflict resolution (Q73) was correlated with retention.

✓ Missionaries given room to shape their ministry (Q57) received a very high rating and correlated with high retention.

✓ Missionaries given administrative and practical support on the field (Q63) received a very high rating in NSC and correlated with high retention in OSC and NSC.

What it means

Rob Hay

"A team is a small number of people with complementary skills, who are committed to a common purpose, set of performance goals, and an approach for which they hold themselves mutually accountable." Katzenbach et al. (1992)[1]

A team is characterised as a relatively small number of people (3-12) who share:

• A common goal
• The rewards and responsibilities
• Goal of team (takes precedence over individual goals)
• Needs of team (take precedence over individual needs)

The goal of the team should take precedence. This is vital, and yet missionaries are often the worst material for traditional team formation. Missionaries often respond to an individualised call and have the examples of pioneer (often solo) missionaries to follow. To allow the needs of team to take precedence, we need to coach missionaries in how this happens by teaching about sacrifice, provoking people during training to see how they will react, and making them realise that their own preferences will often be challenged and thwarted if those of the team are fulfilled.

Within the area of team building we see similarities and differences in OSC and NSC. Both demonstrated a correlation with retention on the ability for missionaries to shape their own ministries [Q57 *Missionaries are given room to shape and develop their own ministry*] and this received a good rating in OSC and NSC.

---

1   J.R. Katzenbach and D.K. Smith, *The Discipline of Teams: A mindbook-workbook for delivering small group performance*, (New York ; Chichester, Wiley, 2001)

Likewise, administrative and practical support on the field [Q63 *Missionaries have adequate administrative and practical support on the field*] correlated with retention and received almost as high a rating.

A different emphasis emerged in the area of communication with leadership [Q42 *There is a free flow of communication to and from the leadership*] where it correlated with retention in OSC, but not NSC. Both gave a fairly good rating for this, and perhaps in the highly relational communities of NSC, communication happens across most agencies and therefore would explain why we saw no significant difference in retention between high and low retaining agencies.

Another area where the relational culture may help to explain some results is with Questions 71 [Q71 *Missionary teams are effective in providing each other with mutual support*] and 73 [Q73 *Interpersonal conflicts are resolved in a timely and appropriate manner*]. Neither of these correlated with retention in OSC and this may be due to the highly individualistic nature of those societies. People in OSC are often fiercely independent and reluctant to rely on others, and many are strongly entrepreneurial in nature. This would certainly begin to explain the significantly lower rating this received in OSC compared to NSC.

This result does, however, appear to be contradictory to the research on generational issues which suggests that the Western boomer generation (born between 1946 and 1965) was very team orientated, demanding that they be allowed to function in team settings.[2] However, the same research also suggests that the same generational cohort are also highly outcome-focused. Perhaps this factor, particularly when combined with the strong protestant work-ethic, overrides the priority of team functioning in the reach for high performance and satisfaction of personal goals, aspirations and self-worth. Certainly, later generations also have been noted to have a need for relational work, but perhaps with a different emphasis (as Richardson's case study discusses later in this chapter). One question we did not ask was the average age of mission partners in each of the agencies surveyed. This would be a helpful area to explore in further research to make more sense of these findings.

In NSC, relational values often dictate that a prerequisite to being able to work and function with someone to achieve a goal is the establishment of a meaningful personal relationship. In Asia, I learned the importance of drinking tea with the government officials I worked with. Spending time asking about their family and feelings was vitally important, but strange to a Westerner used to a work environment where such discussions were seen, at best, as luxuries for when time was plentiful, or at worst, distractions from the work in hand. Likewise, the fact that any conflict must be resolved as a matter of priority—to the degree that resolution supersedes the importance of the task—is a reality in NSC, although there was recognition that doing this was difficult, as NSC rated themselves at four and, even lower, OSC at three.

---

2   Richard Tiplady, *PostMission : World Mission by a Postmodern Generation*, (Carlisle, Paternoster Press, 2003).

Defining "team"

One issue that often seems misunderstood is the difference between a group and a team. If a collection of people have little in common other than their geographic location (something that often occurs in mission where there are diverse individual ministries happening in one place) those people are more of a group than a team. A team needs to have some commonality, some shared focus to glue them together. In its absence, it is usually better to recognise that you have a group and not place expectations of team behaviour upon them.

When forming a team, consider:
- How much time can be devoted to team building?
- How committed are the members to becoming a team?
- How many members will be included?
- Are they all in the same place?
- How much history does the group already have?
- Is that history positive or negative?
- How strong and credible is the leader?

You can use different team formation tools:
- Myers Briggs (MBTI)
- DiSC
- Belbin
- Strength Finders

Stages of group development

Bruce Tuckman[3] developed a four stage model of group development. He labelled the stages Forming, Storming, Norming and Performing:

Forming: Often, people are present in the group because they have been asked or told to be. At this first stage they begin to understand why they are part of the group, but their role and responsibilities often remain unclear till a later stage. The leader is usually directive at this stage, guiding and answering questions. During this stage, processes, if known, are often ignored as they are imposed rather than accepted and the boundaries of the group's freedom and the role of leader are all tested.

Storming: This stage is characterised by a turbulent vying for position within the group. Each individual is establishing their role, demonstrating their expertise and making their value in the group clear to all its members. Sometimes if a leader is not appointed some will vie for a leadership role and indeed an appointed leader is often challenged in this stage. Also, during this stage the purpose of the group

---

3   Bruce Tuckman, "Developmental sequence in small groups," *Psychological Bulletin*, 63, 1965, pp. 384-399.

begins to be clarified. The danger at this stage is that cliques can form and dealing with the people issues, while crucial, can easily distract and the group can lose the purpose of its existence.

Norming: After the turmoil and uncertainty of the storming stage, this stage is less disturbing because people have established their roles in the group and their value to it. However, this is the stage where the working practices and processes are agreed upon so there is still preparatory work to do. This is not a highly productive performance stage—that is the next step. At this stage, however, leading and facilitating the group as they develop these processes is easier and usually welcomed by the group. Often leadership begins to be shared at this stage too.

Performing: Because the norms and practices of the group and the strengths and weaknesses of the individuals are already established and accepted, the group at this stage moves forward with a shared vision. The group makes decisions and is normally autonomous. When disagreements occur, they are constructively resolved within the group. There is an equal care function that happens because the group members recognise that individual health and performance is a vital component of group health and performance.

Tuckman added a fifth stage ten years later:

Adjourning: This is the process of un-forming the group—breaking up the group. Letting go of the group structure and moving on. If it is done well, people let go while feeling good about what has been achieved by the group. This stage, by its nature, can for many people involve insecurity and a sense of bereavement—especially those that dislike change. It needs to be managed carefully, conscious of people's personalities, sensitivities and the group's history.

Third dimension teams

Steve Richardson,[4] Pioneers, USA

The Dixons are veterans of 35 years of ministry to a large unreached people group in Southeast Asia. They testify to the benefit of missionary teams on their field.

Prior to the mid-1980s, they had witnessed dozens of well-intentioned missionaries who came, stayed for a short time, and then returned to their homeland. Then, beginning in about 1985, a different pattern emerged. Young people continued to arrive, but most of them stayed. In fact, whereas the Dixons had laboured virtually alone among this people group for almost two decades, today there are approximately 80 international workers from different agencies who have joined in the harvest.

---

4   Steve Richardson serves as the president of Pioneers-USA. He lives with his wife, Arlene, and four children in Orlando, Florida. The Richardsons led church-planting teams in Southeast Asia for more than ten years. The element of team, and specifically third-dimension teams, significantly impacted their work among unreached peoples.

What had changed? One common distinguishing factor was that new arrivals after 1985 were persons affiliated with organisations that prioritised, or were seriously endeavouring to develop, a *team* approach to ministry. The organisations nurtured a strong sense of community among their personnel on the field.

Research on missionary attrition has shown that "a low sense of organisational connectedness" is an important factor contributing to the early departure of missionaries. If we lose our workers due to inadequate relational ties, perhaps we can keep our workers if we excel in team building.

Defining the objective: What is a missionary team?

When members of the mission community speak of "team," they normally refer to one of three different concepts of teamwork. For the sake of clarity, we may call these First Dimension, Second Dimension, and Third Dimension teams.

First Dimension Teams are groups of people who identify with one another on the basis of shared ministry calling and/or geographic and organisational affinity. Such "teams" consist of missionaries who happen to be with the same agency, or who work in the same area. They will normally share the same overarching goal.

An "Iron Man" sports event would be analogous to this kind of team. Team mates compete together in the same race, but with little interaction. Strategic cross-pollination of ideas, experience, and resources is limited. Members tend to be individually task-focused, decisions and leadership selection occurs democratically, and elected leaders may wield authority somewhat hierarchically. The system tends to be policy-oriented, as there is little opportunity or desire for communication. In this model, it is important that members have been equipped for survival and effective ministry *before* they get to the field.

Second Dimension Teams add a common ministry strategy to the mix. Members are interdependently task-focused as they work out priorities together. Decision making tends to be more consensus-based. People are forced to grapple more with each others' personalities and gifting, and working in concert takes on added significance. Musicians in an orchestra illustrate this kind of teamwork. While Second Dimension Teams reflect a deeper level of interaction and mutual commitment, they are still largely dependent on outside life-support systems for their member development and nurture needs.

Third Dimension Teams introduce a deeper interactive commitment among the members of the team—a desire for ongoing mutual development and encouragement. Such teams are interdependently task *and* member focused. Jesus exhibited this kind of love and concern for the members of his team. He ministered to the multitudes, but never lost sight of the twelve. He was interested in developing them as people, while training and equipping them to do the work of the ministry. These teams will eventually develop their own integrated and holistic life-support system, whereby they detect and meet their own needs: be they spiritual, practical, or strategic.

Third Dimension Teams behave more like a basketball team. Players rarely know what will happen next, but are able to fashion an appropriate response to any situation. Persons from varying backgrounds and representing various levels of preparation can be incorporated more readily.

If we define "team" in this way, then ReMAP II findings suggest our retention statistics will steadily improve.

Generational observations

Developing Third Dimension missionary teams is important for us, especially as we consider the kind of people who now make up the "harvest force." Youth of today have been described as the "with" generation. We have found that the "third dimension" concept of team is powerfully appealing to them.

Today's missionary recruits want community. We find that people wanting to serve the Lord today are not only asking "what" and "where" but "with whom?" One woman recently mentioned that she would be taking an English teaching job in Bali. "Oh, we have a team there. Would you like to be part of a team?" I said. "Why, yes!" I could sense excitement in her voice. "How do I join?" Three weeks later she joined the team.

In North America, virtually every young person I speak with about serving in missions wants to participate in a dynamic team. Surveys here show that a "sense of belonging" is more important to most people than a particular job or location.

Today's missionary recruits need community. Workers often come with emotional "baggage." What do we do with people who have had the necessary theological training and obviously have much to contribute, but carry with them emotional scars and response patterns that will take years to correct? In our experience, Third Dimension Teams are a significant part of the answer.

On the long-term church-planting team in which my wife and I served, some members had come with a great deal of personal baggage including past involvement in drugs and gangs, some had been suicidal, some had been abused as children. By God's grace and the enabling of His Holy Spirit, these younger adults are overcoming these (not to mention visa pressures, tent-making pressures, cultural and political hurdles) and this team of approximately 35 young adults continues to be a dynamic spiritual force among a major unreached people group.

Today's missionary recruits are experts at detecting genuine community (as they define it). One successful and highly respected missionary couple shared with me the trauma of their rejection by an agency some years ago, and their subsequent acceptance into a Third Dimension Team with another agency. "We felt rejected by one, and embraced by the other," they recalled. Sometimes the potential recruit may not even be able to articulate what attracts them to one group, or repels them from another. This sense of teamwork, a genuine caring, a deep valuing of each individual, is often at the heart of it. Today's agencies must grapple seriously with the concept of community among their members, both at home and abroad.

Organisational and operational implications

So how have we set about building Third Dimension Teams?

First, *teams are best built within a team-centric organisational culture.* The most effective way to restructure and reorient is for the whole organisation to begin thinking "team." Leaders, administrators, recruiters, and workers in the field must consciously integrate principles of biblical teamwork into their work.

In our experience the concept of teams needs to be written into the mission statement or core values of the agency if you are serious about developing teams. First Dimension structures tend to resist Third Dimension elements much like a body rejects incompatible transplanted organs. This does not mean that there is no need for strong leadership in a team-based organisation. On the contrary, strong and capable leadership in teams and team-oriented organisations is critical. However, the manner in which these leaders are chosen, conduct themselves, and wield their authority, is different.

Secondly, we had to *begin viewing the team as a primary locus of personnel development,* including member care. For too long we have thought of care as coming primarily from the outside, from "home." Who is primarily responsible for recruiting new personnel in your agency? For determining ministry qualifications? For mentoring missionaries and developing them with appropriate accountability over time? For crisis management? The team should play an important role in these activities, in concert with other back-up systems in the organisational structure.

Thirdly, *responsibility and authority had to be divested to teams, within the context of an inter-dependent network.* Teams must be "liberated" if they are to be truly effective. A new team had to be given the freedom to try, and to possibly fail, in order to ultimately succeed. Decentralisation of responsibility and authority is critical in a team-oriented structure. Who allocates personnel? Who fashions the ministry strategy? Who determines ministry roles and establishes financial guidelines? The first steps of empowering teams in this direction may be traumatic. Mistakes will be made by inexperienced personnel, but in time they will rise to the responsibility, and feel a greatly increased sense of ownership and belonging.

Fourthly, *leadership development, at both the team and regional levels, needed to be the primary concern of an agency's upper level management.* In any structure where responsibility and authority are decentralised, we find it is critical that leaders be mentored and equipped for the task. In a conventional structure, only a few leaders need be trained. In a team-oriented structure, many local leaders must be trained for the task. Everything depends upon the skill with which these leaders are able to facilitate the needs and ministries of the teams. While this may seem like an overwhelming task initially, tremendous energy and initiative will be unleashed in the process. In time, the organisation will have no shortage of trained, capable leaders available to assume positions of broader responsibility.

Conclusion

Over a ten-year period, the church-planting team launched in Southeast Asia in 1985 multiplied into ten new teams in the surrounding area. Today, there are 100 long-term missionaries committed to this region. The attrition rate has been relatively low, despite the fact that visas are not readily available. The application of a *Third Dimension Teams* approach has been a major contributing factor.

Discussion questions:

1. Does your organisation encourage missionary teams?
2. Do your missionaries belong to a "Third Dimension" style team? If not, what could you do to develop better teamwork on the field?

Forging a team to paint a vision

Paul Rhoads[5] and Steve Hoke,[6] Church Resource Ministries, USA

Church Resource Ministries (CRM), a North America-based agency, focused on leader development in 22 countries. Since the early 1990s, CRM had been concerned about taking better care of staff around the world. In 1999, Paul Rhoads, our Vice President for teams, who had skills in forming teams and experience in counselling and staff care, was asked to form a Staff Care Team.[7]

Rather than starting by listing needs or scheduling trips to staff "hot spots," we began by meeting together for three days every quarter in order to get to know one another, grow into an organic team, and listen to God. We committed to forging a closely knit team of like-minded people who together could create a vision for where the organisation should be and how to get there. In the context of learning each other's giftings and passions, we discussed and analysed the needs of our teams and individuals and possible solutions.

We began by spending time together in out-of-the-office settings to build relationships and teamwork before we even approached the issue of what we would *do*. By spending sufficient time together, having fun, building memories, ministering side-by-side, sharing our passions, spending time in prayer, waiting on God, thinking and talking together over a range of staff care issues, we built deep spiritual linkages and unity: we began to love and trust each other. Out of the transparency emerged trust, and out of trust we began to explore issues such as accountability, care, and support systems.

---

5   Paul Rhoads, currently Executive Vice President of Church Resource Ministries (CRM), served as the founding director of the Staff Development and Care Team, and now directs CRM's ministry teams around the world.

6   Steve Hoke is Vice President of People Development, focusing on staff training and spiritual direction.

7   Refer to our case study "Shaping a Staff Development and Care Team" in Chapter 23 on Staff Development.

Only after a year of prayer and consultation were we able to craft the following purpose statement: *We are called to resource team leaders in creating and nurturing grace-filled, safe communities for holistic staff development and care, as well as assisting staff in the areas of spiritual formation, ongoing development, and personal care as needed.*

Coming to clarity on our shared vision allowed us, now as a cohesive team, to consider other care models. We started with Kelly O'Donnell's article on "Doing Member Care Well," in which he suggested a way to structure the variety of missionary care.[8] Toward the end of the first year, we began designing a structure to meet the particular strengths and needs of our organisation. Our structure emerged from the functions we had identified, and it morphed frequently as we learned by doing.

We would nurture both individual and family spiritual formation, encourage ministry development as well as provide personal and family life-cycle care. Our goal was simply to obtain healthy leaders and effective ministry.

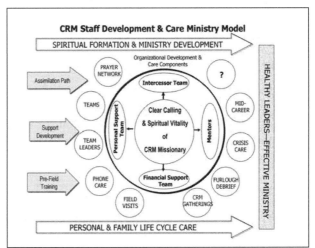

Figure 1:

Central in our model was helping each staff member form four support systems or teams of people recruited personally to sustain them over the long-haul (see Figure 1: CRM's Staff Development & Care Ministry Model).

1. First, an **intercession team** of 25 or more was critical to their initial support raising and long-term cross-cultural ministry.

2. Second, the **financial support team** was readily understood for their sustaining role.

3. Third, a small group of **close personal friends** was identified for regular communication and nurture.

8   Kelly O'Donnell, "Doing Member Care Well," *Evangelical Missions Quarterly*, Vol. 37 (2001), pp. 212-222.

4. Finally, a **cluster of mentors** they could access from a distance, both inside and outside of the organisation, was identified to help them in areas of spiritual formation, ministry skills, and personal development. Although we did share the depiction of the model with existing staff, we found it was most helpful for our own planning and ministry.

What did CRM learn about team formation and expansion?

We learned that BEING team must precede DOING care ministry. Team must precede Task. Form must precede Function. Having a team of called and gifted staff to analyse, pray, and respond to staff needs is critical. Even a small team (we started with six) can do a great deal of transformative, proactive and reactive member care. Inclusion of new team members must be very intentional and gradual, but should not be resisted once the initial team gets "formed." We wonder how we did without such a team for the first 19 years of the organisation's life!

At CRM, we want to be attentive to approaches and trends that are on the horizon that will impact individual staff member's health and the wider network. Forming a Staff Development and Care team allowed us to build on strengths and include the giftings of others as needed. It was easier to respond and incorporate fresh ideas as a team than it had been for one person to constantly sift and respond to ideas and trends in care and training. Gifted teams are better suited to "morph" into responsive shapes than individuals already overwhelmed with responsibility.

Discussion questions:

1. Does your organisation form teams for specific ministries? If yes, discuss the strengths and weaknesses of existing teams.

2. How are team members usually recruited? How could recruitment be improved if you became more intentional about inviting key people to become a part of the specific team you are forming?

3. What are the important things to keep in mind when recruiting and forming a staff development and member care team?

4. Why should BEING team precede DOING ministry? What activities can strengthen the relationships within your teams?

In the real world

A table to stimulate ideas for best practice in mission partnership. For further explanation, see page 7.

This chart has been partially filled in for you. Now you fill in the blanks.

Who? → When? ↓	Home Church	Missionary	Mission Agencies	External Partners
Continuous	➢ Promote a culture of teamwork ➢ Teach about team-approach		➢ Promote a culture of teamwork	
Recruitment	➢ Check history of teamwork		➢ Ask: Who is needed for what team?	➢ Assess personality and team role
Preparation			➢ Pre-formed teams move to the field	➢ Provide team training and team building ➢ Teach about team dynamics
On field	➢ Emphasize being a team with the missionary	➢ Seek team members ➢ Create environment of encouragement and accountability		
Crisis				
Furlough			➢ Debrief on team functioning	
Re-entry				

15

Personal Care
Conflict and Teams

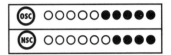

The facts

Teams are the operating reality for much of mission work today and offer an energy, flexibility, and skill set that is hard to duplicate with solo workers or pioneers. However, with teams also come huge challenges. The same diversity that can spark ideas and complement skills can also give rise to tensions and conflict. Across OSC and NSC alike, agencies are struggling to operate effectively in these team contexts.

The data

Q. No.	Factor	OSC Health Indicator	✓	NSC Health Indicator	✓
44	Missionaries are included in major decisions related to the field	○○○○○○○●●●		○○○○○○●●●●	
48	Most leaders identify problems early and take appropriate action	○○○○●●●●●●	✓	○○○○○○●●●●	✓
51	There are documented and adequate procedures for handling complaints from missionaries	○○○○○●●●●●	✓	○○○○○●●●●●	✓
71	Missionary teams are effective in providing each other with mutual support	○○○○●●●●●●		○○○○○○●●●●	✓
73	Interpersonal conflicts are resolved in a timely and appropriate manner	○○○●●●●●●●		○○○○●●●●●●	✓

The key findings

- ✓ Rating of interpersonal conflict resolution (Q73) correlated with high retention (for total attrition) in NSC, but not in OSC. Was this due to a more relational society?
- ✓ Procedure to handle complaints (Q51) is highly correlated with retention in OSC and NSC.
- ✓ Leaders identify problems and take appropriate action (Q48) is clearly correlated with retention in OSC and NSC.
- ✓ Missionaries are included in major decisions on the field (Q44) was negatively correlated with retention in NSC.

What it means

Rob Hay

Despite more recent occasional dissenting voices, the majority of the mission world is now operating on the basis of teams. This is believed to be a healthy progression from the older model of lone pioneers. Of course, some missions from their earliest days have had teams (the Apostle Paul and his team, the Serampore Trio, the Cambridge Seven and the Ecuadorian 5, for examples). In recent years, however, those teams have become less homogenous and more multicultural. Mixtures of people from different cultures, geographies, and languages make for one of the most challenging situations in contemporary mission, but also one of the most exciting, brimming with potential.

Teams are challenging because people struggle with difference. Homogeneity—being with our own people, speaking our language, eating our own food—feels more comfortable. "Normal," balanced people sometimes become nationalistic and patriotic in the extreme when they reach the mission field. We naturally retreat into what we know and are familiar with.

Of course, conflict also occurs in homogenous teams (perhaps your home church would be an example?). But conflict in a multicultural team may be interpreted through cultural terms or be caused by cultural difference. For example, a mission school to provide consistent quality education to local missionary kids was being planned. After in-depth discussions about the big issues—what curriculum to follow, what ages to teach—someone raised a "minor" closing point about school uniforms. The room erupted. What one person thought was a minor issue, the school uniform, became a major issue. Why? German parents found a uniform completely unacceptable due to its association with Hitler Youth and Nazism. This was truly a cultural issue.

These cultural differences are an unchangeable reality, but their impact can be minimised by good preparation. Good preparation includes understanding cultural difference and awareness of personal culture. My own training had taught me to be aware that Dutch and German colleagues generally spoke with a directness that bordered on offensive for an Englishman. However, it took my German partner's directness to explain how much I frustrated him by "speaking through flowers" and not saying what I really meant. My tact was interpreted as a lack of honesty, his honesty as harsh rudeness! Knowing your own preferences does not always mean you can avoid tension, but increased understanding can often bring increased grace.

Resolving interpersonal conflicts [Q73 *Interpersonal conflicts are resolved in a timely and appropriate manner*], received a relatively low performance rating in OSC (4) and NSC (5) and proved to be more important for retention in NSC (perhaps due to the more relational nature of many NSC societies). Do OSC cultures have very high (unrealistic) expectations, and so give a low rating even when the conflict is not sufficient to threaten their staying in mission? Or do they detach work issues from personal relationships more than those in NSC? In either scenario, the data shows need for further improvement.

Teams can be a source of conflict, but are also a source of support [Q71 *Missionary teams are effective in providing each other with mutual support*]. NSC countries reflected a stronger retention correlation and a much higher rating for team support. Again, perhaps the relational aspect of NSC cultures influences the results. The results could also reflect the relative youth of the agencies in NSC. Historically, OSC agencies used family structures to shape their organisations, only losing this quality relatively recently as size and age increased.

Organisations that handle complaints appropriately [Q51 *There are documented and adequate procedures for handling complaints from missionaries*] and have leaders who tackle problems proactively [Q48 *Most leaders identify problems early and take appropriate action*] have strong correlation with retention across NSC and OSC alike. But, overall, NSC and OSC performed poorly in these areas. Urgent attention is needed.

We should clarify that we are not advocating that the aim should be the absence of conflict. Conflict is healthy, and helpful in creating new ideas, challenging established norms, and fostering a deeper and truer understanding of each other (compare Acts 15:36-41). Lencioni, in his excellent book "The Five Dysfunctions of a Team"[1] says, "... teams that trust one another are not afraid to engage in passionate dialogue around issues and decisions that are key to the organisation's success. They do not hesitate to disagree with, challenge, and question one another, all in the spirit of finding the best answers, discovering the truth, and making great decisions."

---

1   P. Lencioni, *The Five Dysfunctions of a Team: A Leadership Fable*, (San Francisco, Jossey-Bass, 2002).

Serving two masters

Thomas Oduro,[2] Ghana

Note: Agency names and the names of people in this case study have been changed to protect the true identity of organisations and individuals involved.

In some countries, the process of missionary sending and receiving can be rather complex. At times, a small Christian organisation or young church on the field may make a request for a missionary to come and assist its fledgling ministry. The organisation or church will approach a missionary sending agency to send someone. Due to the limited immigration quotas for residential permits which are issued to foreign workers, that sending agency could in turn depend on other agencies to obtain the necessary immigration papers. When the missionary eventually arrives on the field, the person may find that he is obligated to serve two or more organisations. Such situations can result in considerable conflict between the different parties, as seen in the case study below.

Apollo Resource Centre (ARC), a faith based organisation, felt the need for a missionary to help fulfil its mission. However, because the Centre was not socially influential, it could not secure a residential permit for the prospective missionary. Leaders of ARC nonetheless applied for a missionary from Kingdom Association (KA), a sending agency.

The sending agency, KA, agreed to send a missionary provided that ARC could secure a residential permit. Leaders of ARC, consequently, contacted Peter Educational Institute (PEI) to facilitate the securing of an immigrant quota ("work permit") for the missionary. Leaders of the two institutions agreed to share the ministry of the missionary, an agreement that was perceived as good by KA and the prospective missionary.

As a result, Rev. Juan Davies from Nicaragua was sent to Niambonia to serve the two institutions. He arrived on the field with his wife. On arrival, Rev. Davies was made to understand that his priority was to ARC, the institution that initially made the request. ARC asked Rev. Davies to do a field survey to determine the need for teaching those who were in Christian ministry but without any formal education. He was also asked to create a curriculum and train those who would subsequently train the untrained ministers. Peter Educational Institute, the institution that secured the immigrant quota, asked Rev. Davies to teach at their school, an established educational institution with a curriculum, teaching time-table, etc.

After one year, both institutions began complaining to each other about Rev. Davies because his commitment fell short of expectations in each institution. When asked

2   Dr. Thomas A. Oduro is the Principal and a Lecturer at Good News Theological College and Seminary, Accra, Ghana. As head of the Seminary since 1994, Dr. Oduro has requested missionaries from many mission agencies. (The Seminary is interdenominational so it is open to many mission agencies). He ensures that they are integrated into the Ghanaian community, guiding them in cultural studies and practices. Prior to being appointed Principal, Dr. Oduro worked with other missionaries. Over the years, he has met with heads of mission agencies about their concerns and observations.

by the two institutions, he told them on separate occasions that, "When I am not here, then I am there." The leaders hardly believed what the missionary told them. They did not know how to make Rev. Davies more serious in his commitment. Neither did they send any complaint to the sending agency. They simply decided to advise and tolerate him.

Meanwhile, the negative attitude of the leaders of the two institutions toward the missionary soured their relationship. Rev. Davies felt disappointed, but he did not know how to heal the relationship. The unhealthy relationship continued until someone hinted to the leaders of ARC that Rev. Juan Davies and his wife had formed Grace for Needy Children Foundation (GNCF), a Non-Governmental Organisation. A website for GNCF confirmed this allegation.

The Apollo Resource Centre asked the KA to withdraw or replace Rev. Davies for breach of trust. KA did not respond to the request to withdraw Rev. Davies, so ARC decided to sever its working relationship with Rev. Davies. The authorities of Peter Educational Institute, on hearing of the dismissal of Rev. Davies, quickly changed their attitude towards him. They wrote to the KA to express their willingness to work with him.

Leaders of ARC perceived the attitude of PEI as a betrayal and taking advantage of a volatile situation. Rev. Davies, on the other hand, became bitter against the leaders of ARC because he felt that his missionary career had been tainted and was in jeopardy. He blamed ARC leaders for failing to approach him and ask him about the website, etc. before writing to the sending agency. ARC leaders, nevertheless, saw Rev. and Mrs. Davies as missionaries who came to Niambonia with a hidden agenda, that of enriching themselves.

Meanwhile, KA, the missionary sending agency, kept a tight lip and observed the impasse.

Discussion questions:

1. Each organisation had different expectations of this missionary. What could the missionary sending organisation have done to minimise conflict and misunderstanding on the field?

2. What are some other types of conflicts that missionaries from your organisation have faced on the field? What can your organisation do to help each missionary better manage such conflicts?

3. How could your organisation train your mission workers to develop culturally appropriate conflict resolution skills?

In the real world

A table to stimulate ideas for best practice in mission partnership. For further explanation, see page 7.

This chart has been partially filled in for you. Now you fill in the blanks.

Who? → When? ↓	Home Church	Missionary	Mission Agencies	External Partners
Continuous	➢ Have clear teaching on how to handle conflicts		➢ Have clear procedures to deal with conflict ➢ Deal with problems early and take appropriate action	
Recruitment	➢ Check conflict/conflict resolution history of candidate			
Preparation		➢ Understand own strengths and weaknesses		➢ Provide training in conflict resolution
On field		➢ Be willing to deal with conflict constructively	➢ Be open for external help	➢ Offer mediation services
Crisis				
Furlough				
Re-entry				

16

Member Care

The facts

ReMAP II has confirmed the significance of member care, personal support and organisational development in missionary longevity. The study has shown that both preventative member care and reactive crisis intervention are important. OSC and NSC agencies have greatly improved the quality of their member care in the past ten years. In particular, the NSC mission force has grown tremendously in organisational structure and effectiveness, and attrition rates have dropped steeply. High performance OSC agencies have retained their excellent retention rates over the past 20 years, offsetting the modern trend to shorter assignments and higher attrition rates. Likewise, high retaining NSC agencies have exceeded their earlier excellent performance.

The data

Q. No.	Factor	OSC Health Indicator	✓	NSC Health Indicator	✓
37	Estimate the % of total time spent in pastoral care of missionaries (including both home and field workers)	○○○○○○○●●●	✓	○○○○○○○○●●	✓
38	Estimate the % of budget/total finances spent on pastoral care	○○○○○○●●●●	✓	○○○○○○○○○●	✓
39	How much of these resources are preventative member care?[1]	○○○○○○●●●●	✓	○○○○●●●●●●	✓
72	Effective pastoral care exists at a field level (preventative and in crises)	○○●●●●●●●●		○○○○○●●●●	

---

1 Prevention, personal development, support, etc. (vs. responsive, crisis resolution).

The key findings

✓ There is a clear correlation between time (Q37) and finances allocated for member care (Q38) with high retention in NSC.

✓ OSC invests only half of the amount of finances and staff time into member care as NSC (Q37 and 38).

✓ The amount of preventative member care (16–33%) (Q39) is low compared to curative crisis intervention (84–67%).

✓ There is a correlation between proportion of preventative member care (Q39) and high retention in NSC.

✓ There is need to distinguish between the amount of member care and its quality.

✓ Effective member care on the field level (Q72) is clearly correlated with retention in NSC and mildly in OSC.

What it means

Detlef Blöcher

What makes missionaries strong, healthy and flexible so they can stay fresh, grow in their personalities, remain spiritually vibrant, and be resilient so as to overcome crises and challenges? Member care has a major impact on missionary health and longevity, and ReMAP I and ReMAP II have provided empirical evidence of this.

Member care implies a full range of services, including pastoral care, personal encouragement, team building, spiritual refreshment, and professional counselling in critical incidents. Kelly O'Donnell[2] illustrates ways member care can be provided by using the picture of a Roman Fountain with several levels of water basins and water running from one level to the next.

1. In the centre (and at the top level), there is the *Master Care*: the Lord himself taking care of his children.

2. *Self-Care* flows next. As the Apostle Paul expressed it, "Take care of yourself and the flock" (1 Timothy 4:16). Each missionary is responsible for his/her own lifestyle and spiritual health.

3. *Mutual Care* is one person taking care of his/her colleague (John 13:14, 34; Romans 15:5; Galatians 6:2; 1 Peter 4:10). Mutual Care includes the care of expatriates and nationals.

4. *Sender Care* is provided by sending churches and mission organisations.

---

2   Kelly O'Donnell, "Going Global: A Member Care Model for Best Practice," in Kelly O'Donnell, ed., *Doing Member Care Well: Perspectives and practices from around the world,* (Pasadena, CA: William Carey Library, 2002), pp. 13-22.

5. *Specialist Care* includes Pastoral Training, Family Care, Counselling, and help from Medical and Financial Professionals. Lastly,

6. *Network Care* describes the cooperation of Care Centres: Connecting, Consulting, Catalysing.

Member care in OSC and NSC

The ReMAP I study showed (Figure 1) that mission agencies with little investment in member care suffer a very high attrition, confirming the significance of member care. Furthermore, the attrition rate falls with increasing care for missionaries. Thus, member care really contributes to retention. Yet, there are also indications that agencies with very intensive personal care may have an increased return-home rate. Can there be a too much member care? Can something good possibly weaken the missionaries' resilience, foster a self-centredness and feeling of entitlement?

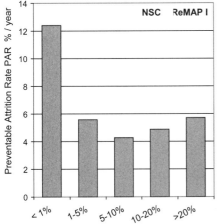

Fig. 1: Preventable Attrition and Member Care

To answer these questions, member care was studied in more detail for ReMAP II. The second study found that OSC agencies invest 7% of their total staff time (in the home office and on the field) in member care, that is to say one in 12 missionaries serving their colleagues full-time (or a corresponding number serving part time). NSC agencies dedicate double the amount of staff time to member care (14.4 %), or one in seven NSC missionaries caring for their colleagues. This confirms the earlier findings of ReMAP I, and recognises the relational structure of societies in the majority world.

ReMAP II also showed that agencies allocate 4.3% (OSC) and 9.8% (NSC) of their total budget to member care. This percentage is somewhat lower than the percentage of their total staff time, as the overall budget normally includes project and other costs other than personnel costs—and possibly not all salaries are included in budget due to many mission partners raising personal support.

The majority of member care resources are dedicated to curative crisis intervention (69% in OSC and 79% in NSC), whereas only 31% in OSC and 21% in NSC are allocated to prevention, i.e., strengthening the missionary's personality and spiritual life. This indicates that member care is still considered primarily a reactive emergency service for wounded missionaries and prevention remains underdeveloped.

NSC agencies with high retention assign twice as much of their finances to member care than low retaining agencies, and also double the finances toward preventative member care (23% vs. 11%). In this way, they invest four times more finances in prevention[3] than do low retaining agencies. This vast difference mirrors the difference in their ethos and practices.

---

3   8.7 % x 0.23 = 2.3 % vs. 4.3 % * 0.11 = 0.5 %

Member care and missionary retention

The central concept of the ReMAP II study is retention; that is, how many missionaries out of 100 are still in service at the end of a year. Ideally, the answer would be 100%, but in practice the rate is lower. Figure 2 shows the retention rate of OSC-agencies when varying amounts of member care are provided.[4] The results indicate that agencies with little member care lose almost twice as many workers for potentially preventable reasons than those with a reasonable level of member care (3% vs. 1.6%).

A difference of 1.4% per year appears small, but there is much more at stake. Missionary retention is merely an indicator. Retention is like the tip of an iceberg, with the majority of the effect hidden under the waterline. There are many more workers ineffective, worn down by the continued stress of cross-cultural mission, yet without the courage to return home. Missionary retention, on the other hand, reflects missionaries' sense of vibrant spirituality, inner peace, personal fulfilment, job satisfaction and spiritual fruitfulness.

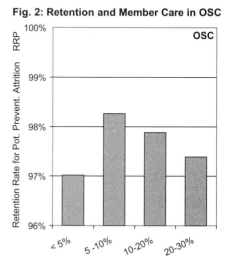

Fig. 2: Retention and Member Care in OSC

Retention Rate for Pot. Prevent. Attrition RRP

Percentage of Total Staff Time for Member Care

Too much member care?

Can there be "too much" member care provision? Can something good turn into something negative? Could excessive member care erode missionaries' resilience and personal growth? Indeed, there is anecdotal evidence that the attrition rate rises after a field visit of a professional counsellor. We need to acknowledge that some missionaries are assigned the wrong task; others may lack the required gifting, skills, training or experience. These missionaries need to be reassigned, false placements corrected, and wounded missionaries restored or brought home safely and with dignity. Yet visiting counsellors can also jump to hasty conclusions without considering the options of personal growth, inner healing or reassignment within the country of service. Happily, there are a growing number of Member Care Centres for Missionaries in various countries,[5] which allow missionaries to avoid the stress of reverse culture shock while seeking healing. Western agencies have a tendency to send home too many missionaries as soon as problems occur. By this, they prevent local believers from witnessing and experiencing effective conflict resolution and restoration.

---

4   Considering potentially preventable reasons for attrition only.

5   A comprehensive list is given in Kelly O'Donnell, ed., *Doing Member Care Well: Perspectives and practices from around the world*, (Pasadena, CA: William Carey Library, 2002), pp. 529-550.

Member care at the expense of organisational structure

The ReMAP II data shows that mission agencies with very intensive member care programmes gave a significantly lower rating to organisational issues like: Mission statement, Clear goals, Missionaries' pre-field training (especially in Missiology), Effective orientation of new missionaries in the place of service, Language study, Supervision, Effective administrative support, Sustained and adequate financial support, and Maintenance of spiritual life. Apparently those agencies strongly emphasised their member care programme to the neglect of other organisational issues. A good member care programme will not keep missionaries in service if the organisation does not have careful candidate selection, good pre-field training and effective leadership. In addition, fragile candidates possibly choose agencies with an extensive member care programme, or an agency's recruitment office may let some fragile candidates slip through, trusting on their member care programme. Finally, we need to consider that ReMAP II merely monitored the quantity and not the quality of the member care programme.

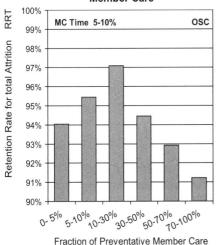

Fig. 3: Retention Total and Preventive Member Care

Retention Rate for total Attrition — RRT

MC Time 5-10%   OSC

Fraction of Preventative Member Care

Preventative member care

The effect of member care was further explored by analysing the subgroup of OSC agencies with member care time of 5-10% (the amount that showed the maximum retention rate) and examining just the preventative member care—strengthening of the missionaries' personality and spiritual life (in contrast to reactive crisis response and restoration of wounded missionaries). Total annual retention rate (RRT) shows an inverted u-type curve that falls towards both ends (Figure 3). Agencies that invest in preventative member care or in reactive crisis intervention to the neglect of the other, experience a reduced retention rate. Apparently, both types of ministries are needed: preventative member care (personal growth, spiritual life, healthy relationships, team building, etc.) as well as effective help in crises and the restoration of wounded workers. Figure 3 also shows that the optimum allocation appears to be around 25% for preventative member care (when considering total attrition).

However, when we consider preventable attrition only (RRP, Figure 4), we

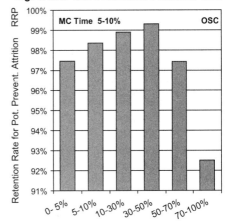

Fig. 4: RRP and Preventative Member Care

Retention Rate for Pot. Prevent. Attrition — RRP

MC Time 5-10%   OSC

Fraction of Preventative Member Care

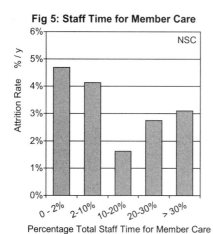

Fig 5: Staff Time for Member Care

Percentage Total Staff Time for Member Care

find a u-type with its maximum higher, at 40 % preventative Member care. Apparently, preventable attrition is reduced particularly by preventative member care.

Potentially preventable as well as unpreventable attrition are both affected by preventative member care. At first, the latter seems irrational, as "unpreventable attrition" sounds as though it cannot be affected. However, unpreventable attrition was defined in ReMAP II as retirement, death in service, illness, loss of visa, completion of contract, end of project, and appointment into leadership position in the mission. These factors are not all unchangeable, but may be affected by preventative member care. When a missionary stays physically, emotionally and spiritually healthy, his/her immune system is strengthened, he/she makes wise decisions, and he/she can be a part of a caring ministry team and a stimulating environment in which the whole person can grow. Health builds on health, and when the project is completed or one assignment comes to its end (unpreventable attrition), the missionary might be open for a new task. He or she may even continue with ministry after reaching retirement age.

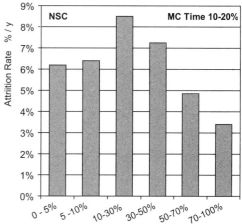

Fig 6: Attrition and Preventative Member Care

Fraction of Preventative Member Care

For NSC agencies, we find a similar result,[6] and Figure 5 shows the curve for total attrition of the years 2001/02.[7] As indicated before, NSC agencies optimally invested 10-20% of total staff time in member care. The analysis for preventative member care (Figure 6) again shows an inverted u-curve with a maximum at 25% preventative member care. When considering preventable attrition only (Figure 7), the optimum is found at roughly equal proportions of prevention and restoration.

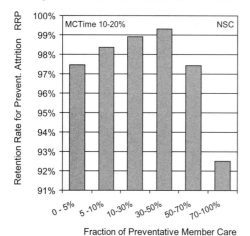

Fig. 7: RRP and Preventative Member Care

Fraction of Preventative Member Care

---

6   The result has a lower magnitude, as RRT and RRP are generally higher than in OSC so the effects become smaller. In addition, the recent trend towards organisational development in NSC and general reduction in attrition are partially levelled in the long-term analysis covering 20 years.

7   Covering only the time span 2001/02.

Member care changes

A comparison of results with ReMAP I, shows that the attrition rate in OSC and NSC is now significantly lower than ten years ago. This happened despite the global trend toward shorter assignments. The last ten years have also seen a tremendous amount of organisational development of many mission agencies, especially in NSC,[8] and particularly regarding the quantity and quality of member care. Further support has come from an international network of member care specialists, creating a wealth of member care resources, including online resources (e.g. www.membercare.org, www.missionarycare.org, www.missionarycare.com) as well as a global network of member care facilities.

This general trend toward better member care is reflected in the agencies' organisational culture as shown in ReMAP II. Leaders of NSC agencies with high involvement in member care (> 20% Time in member care) have a much higher rating for almost all organisational parameters (Figure 8). In particular, they gave 15 – 30% higher rating for the issues: Missionary teams provide mutual support; Effective pastoral care on the field level; Resolution of interpersonal conflicts; Sustained and adequate financial support; Annual vacation; Contingency plans; Adequate medical care and MK-schooling options. Leaders of OSC agencies with good member care had an higher rating in: Supervision on the field; Handling complaints from missionaries; Language and cultural studies; Sustained and adequate financial support; Maintenance of missionaries' spiritual life; Involvement of home church in

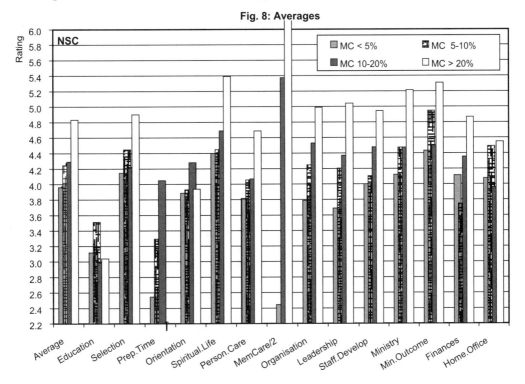

Fig. 8: Averages

---

8   Detlef Blöcher, "ReMAP II affirms the Maturation of the Younger Mission Movement of the South," *Connections* (Oct 2003), p. 48-53.

the missionary's life and ministry. It is believed that all these factors help to reduce the early return of missionaries.

Excellent personal care has great significance in our rapidly changing modern world. Many ministry locations are today shaken by natural disasters, ethnic conflicts, violence, corruption, social injustice and extreme poverty, putting missionaries under constant stress. Member care is not an option but an obligation. It is an integrated way of caring for our missionaries that infuses all principles and practices—not an additional component in our agency besides strategic planning, administration and public relations. Member care is a comprehensive way of thinking and caring. Missionaries are our most precious resources. They are the human vessels through which God's grace and love, righteousness and truth is revealed in our needy world. They are set to be examples for new believers to follow (2 Thess 3:9).

The leader must assume responsibility to care for missionaries so that they stay healthy and robust, recover after defeats, receive comfort in crises and receive assistance through changes. Home office, team, and field leaders must exhibit a shepherding function for those entrusted to their care. The standard is the example of our Lord Jesus Christ (John 21:16; Acts 20:26). This fundamental understanding is expressed by the Apostle Peter:

> "Be shepherds of God's flock that is under your care, serving as overseers, not because you must, but because you are willing, as God wants you to be; not greedy for money, but eager to serve; not lording it over those entrusted to you, but being examples to the flock." 1 Peter 5:2-3

We do not consider the reduction of missionary attrition as an end in itself, nor do we aim to increase missionary retention at all costs. Missionaries can also stay for too long and hinder the maturing of the national church and the development of local leadership. But places hardened to the gospel will only be reached by the gospel through dedicated, experienced long-term missionaries that have carefully learned the language, adjusted well to the culture, live a simple lifestyle, and maintain trusted relationships while being supported by a caring community and an organisational structure with lean management and effective leadership. This brings together the two biblical issues of shepherding and good stewardship.

Member care helps missionaries to grow spiritually, expand their resilience and durability, maintain their physical and emotional health, build effective ministry teams, encourage and care for each other, communicate effectively, develop a consultative leadership style, and develop flexibility to adjust to ever changing needs and challenges.

Church-based missionary care

Bibien Limlingan,[9] Philippine Missions Association,[10] Philippines

When the Philippines began sending missionaries many years ago, member care was hardly practiced. Churches would send out their missionaries and then forget about them once they reached the mission field. Missionaries would become disappointed because they received no letters, no visits, and no care from their sending church.

Some of our early missionaries are now mission executives. The lessons they learned through their past heart-aches, reinforce their current commitment to invest in member care. Today, member care has become "an intentional practice"[11] in most agencies and has found its way into the core values in many. The Philippine Member Care Network envisions that "Filipino cross-cultural missionaries are well cared for holistically."[12]

In general, we find three types of member care:

1. Field-based member care (missionaries care for other missionaries on the field)
2. Sending-based member care (the mission organisations provide care)
3. Church-based member care (this is a new but growing practice)

The profile below is an extraordinary example of church-based missionary care. Tanauan Bible Church (in Batangas, Philippines) has sent out and cared for five missionary families and two single missionaries for about ten years. All their missionaries continue to serve on the mission field up to the present. This church provides holistic and balanced member care. Unlike most other churches that have sent missionaries, Tanauan Bible Church is already investing monthly in their missionaries' pension plans, health plans and retirement plans.

Missionary care groups

Ana M. Gamez, Tanauan Bible Church, Philippines

When Tanauan Bible Church (TBC) started to send missionaries in 1995, we had limited knowledge about how we were supposed to take care of our missionaries from the time of their appointment, through time spent on the mission field,

---

9   Bibien Limlingan currently serves as the Research Officer of the Philippine Missions Association. Bibien has a Masters degree in Theology from Asian Theological Seminary. She has just recently finished putting together an extensive study of all the people groups in the Philippines. She is married to Pastor Jong Limlingan and they have three daughters.

10   Philippine Missions Association is a 23 year-old organisation that serves as the missions commission of the Philippine Council of Evangelical Churches..

11   Kelly O'Donnell, in his article *"Some Historical Perspective on Member and Humanitarian Aid,"* cited from http://www.membercare.org/historicalperspectives.asp, accessed 16-Feb-2007.

12   Philippine Member Care Network's vision statement.

furlough, home assignment, study leave, and the completion of their term. We only knew that we should pray for them and send our financial support based on our capability, and let our partner (the sending and receiving mission agency) take care of them.

As the years passed by, and as our church engaged in sending more missionaries, we realized that it was not enough to only pray for our missionaries and send our financial support. We realized that we should also provide the emotional, moral and practical support that they need. This may include providing food, clothing, housing, travelling needs, children's educational needs, health insurance, encouragement, visitation of families who are left behind and so forth.

We were then faced with the question: "If these are the missionaries' needs that we should provide as a sending church, is our Filipino church capable of responding to their needs? Do we have enough resources in our local church?" As a local church, we have been sending missionaries for more than ten years now. We can say that by God's grace and through a joint effort of the whole church, in partnership with the sending and receiving mission agency, we can meet these needs. We must educate our church and let them know how they can participate in fulfilling the Great Commission. If we do this I believe that we have enough resources within our church.

Let me share how we have been providing care for our Missionaries at TBC. We humbly admit that we are not experts in this area. We are still learning and doing our best to provide optimum support and care for our missionaries. It is TBC's prayer that our church-based Member Care Groups will be a blessing to many churches in Asia and the world.

TBC has several Missionary Care Groups. Each Missionary Care Group (MCG) is composed of people who have committed to support, care for and minister to the missionaries while they are on their deputation, on the mission field, on furlough, home assignment or study leave. On behalf of the missionary, they challenge and mobilize others to actively take part in the fulfilment of the Great Commission. They are also considered advocates of the missionary.

The concept of the Missionary Care Group originally came from Rev. Rey Corpuz, a former National Director of Philippine Missions Association (PMA). He came to visit our church sometime in May 1998, and he shared the concept and importance of having a church-based missionary care system. The church grasped its importance and in June 1998, we formed Spain MCG, Mindanao MCG, Vietnam MCG, and Japan MCG.

The following is our process for selecting suitable people for each MCG:

For those missionaries who were already on the mission field, the Missions and Evangelism Committee enlisted the people who already had a close relationship with the missionaries. We talked to the people, explained their responsibilities, and asked them for a commitment to be part of an MCG.

For missionaries who are in preparatory or deputation stage, we require them to follow these steps:

1. Each missionary under probation will submit a list of individuals—a minimum of six and a maximum of 12—who will serve as his/her prayer, spiritual, financial, communication, logistics & family matters coordinator/s. The availability, commitment, giftings and skills of each individual should be carefully considered in this process and they should have a genuine interest to look after the welfare of the missionaries (Phil. 2:20) and have the passion to take part in fulfilling the Great Commission (Matthew 28:19-20).

2. The Missions Board will interview the individuals selected by the missionary, to explain their would-be responsibilities, and to confirm their commitment to be a part of the MCG.

3. After the interview, the missionary will meet with the members of the MCG. They will choose a leader from among themselves who will be in charge of the group. This person will facilitate the monthly meeting once the missionary has been sent to the mission field.

4. The MCG should, in coordination with the overall church missions coordinator, decide when to meet once a month for prayer and updates. An emergency meeting is called whenever necessary. As long as a missionary is in the church, he/she is in charge of communicating with the MCG Monthly meeting, so that he/she can strengthen his/her relationship with the members of the MCG, and get to know each of them in a deeper way.

5. Members of the MCG are also commissioned during the commissioning service of the missionary.

Note: When MCG members failed to fulfil their responsibilities, we talked to them and inquired the status of their commitment. For those members who could not continue to be a part of the MCG, we looked and prayed for other church members with a genuine interest to look after the welfare of our missionaries.

Each MCG comprises several key people with specific roles and responsibilities.

*   The Prayer Coordinator(s) makes sure that the missionary is being prayed for. This person is responsible for gathering prayer requests and updates from the missionary in the host country (possibly through e-mails). The prayer coordinator will mobilize others to pray for the missionary, the adopted people group, and the host country.

*   The Communication Coordinator(s) will send e-mails/letters to the missionary regularly; share updates, issues, current events, as well as news from Christian circles of the country/place where he/she has come from. This person sends greetings or cards during special occasions (such as birthdays, anniversaries, Christmas, etc.). He/she reproduces and distributes newsletters and updates from the missionary. The communication coordinator has a crucial role in the MCG.

- The Spiritual Coordinator(s) serves as a Barnabas who will remind and encourage the missionary about his/her growth spiritually, especially during the time on the field. They will provide materials and other resources to ensure spiritual feeding of the missionary. This role includes thinking of creative ways to minister to the missionary (e.g., sending sermon cassette tapes, poems, inspirational thoughts, etc.).

- The Logistics Coordinator(s) assists the missionary during his/her pre-field preparation, time on the field, and home assignment or furlough. This includes following up on the missionary's schedules and appointments for church visitations; securing and sending materials needed by the missionary on the field as requested (e.g., books, tracts, Bibles, etc.); coordinating pick-up and send-off of the missionary at the airport; and assisting in finding a place for the missionary to live during his/her furlough and home assignment. For example, when our missionaries in Vietnam finished their term, the Vietnam MCG looked for their housing when they came back home, and prepared everything that they needed.

- The Financial Coordinator(s) facilitates easy and practical ways of sending the missionary support in coordination with the partner sending mission agency. They remind churches/individual supporters of their commitment. They may call, visit or even write to them on behalf of the missionary. They serve as a lookout for potential partners and supporters. One of our best examples is the Finance Coordinator for our Mindanao MCG. She challenged her friends to support our missionary couple in Mindanao for five years.

- The Family Matters Coordinator(s) (FMC) assists the immediate family of the missionary in matters relating to their personal and family concerns. They take care of issues and challenges faced by the family members left behind by the missionaries. This is usually discussed by the whole MCG. If the group cannot handle the issues, they will consult the Missions Committee to take the necessary action. All matters related to the missionary's family are communicated to the missionary for prayer and information. The church pastor is also informed.

Because of the important roles and responsibilities of our MCG coordinators, they are also commissioned during the commissioning of the missionaries.

There are many implications that follow from having church-based MCG:

1. The needs of the missionary (spiritual, physical, emotional, psychological, practical, and moral support) will be taken care of in partnership with the sending and receiving mission agency.

2. A specific group of people from the sending church is responsible for looking after the welfare and needs of each missionary.

3. Through their participation in an MCG, our church members are given opportunities to actively take part in fulfilling the Great Commission. Not all of us can go, but all of us can be a part of the Lord's work in mission through prayer, spiritual, emotional, moral and practical support.

4. As a church, we have been able to recruit new missionaries and empower others to go to Unreached People Groups. Two of our missionary couples, now serving in Central Asia, were former members of the Mindanao MCG and Vietnam MCG.

In conclusion, the local church, in partnership with the sending and receiving mission agency, should together provide mutual care for the missionary from the time of recruitment up to his/her retirement, so that missionary attrition will be minimized.

Discussion questions:

1. How does your church presently provide member care to your missionaries? What aspects of member care are covered?

2. Could church-based Missionary Care Groups be formed in your local church? If yes, what would be some key roles and responsibilities of such groups?

OMF's medical advisory service—a model for medical member care

Stroma Beattie,[13] OMF International, Singapore

OMF International, formerly the China Inland Mission, has been sending missionaries to East Asian countries for 140 years. From the early days, the need for medical care of its workers became apparent. Medically trained missionaries found that their skills were needed to care for colleagues also. Today, OMF International includes approximately 1,300 adults and 600+ children, representing around 30 different nationalities, 18 sending bases (Asian and non-Asian), and with members working mainly in East Asia (though some are in non-Asian contexts).

To provide medical member care to this large group, OMF International has developed a Medical Advisory Service, which provides medical advice and preventative health care to its members, their families and its leaders. This service aims to enable our workers to serve as effectively as possible and to prevent premature attrition. It seeks to provide clear medical communication between doctors, leaders and members in the various countries in order to facilitate appropriate medical care that is relevant to the specific needs of our workers.

This Medical Advisory Service is coordinated by the International Medical Adviser (IMA), a full-time missionary doctor based at the agency's headquarters in Singapore as part of the personnel department. The doctor is professionally registered with the Singapore Medical Council and runs a clinic enabling the doc-

---

13 Dr. Stroma Beattie has post-graduate qualifications in family and travel medicine. After a further year in psychiatry, she and her husband moved to South Korea in 1991 as OMF missionaries. Full-time language study was followed by medical and missions work. She moved to Singapore in 1998 where she became OMF's International Medical Adviser.

tor to provide medical services to mission personnel, to prescribe medicines and to refer patients. At the same time, the IMA works for OMF's International Director for Personnel and is involved in policy setting, candidate selection and response to emerging diseases such as Severe Acute Respiratory Syndrome (SARS) and Avian influenza ("bird flu").

The IMA leads a team of home-side and field-side doctors to provide medical care to the missionaries and their families while at the same time giving advice and guidance to the mission's leadership in major matters such as ongoing fitness for service or re-designation. The current structure involves 26 home-side doctors and 14 field-side doctors (some of the latter positions are vacant), and the team is augmented with the help of psychologists, member care consultants, counsellors and nurses.

The Home-side (sending country) Medical Advisers tend to be volunteers—busy doctors who give some of their time as part of their Christian service to assess potential new workers, organise pre-field medicals, and assist returnees or home assignees with health related issues. The Field-side (receiving country) Medical Advisers are missionaries, serving on the field, either performing their medical advisory role as part of their wider work or as their full-time ministry. On a day-to-day basis, they provide advice and assistance to colleagues in their place of service. All workers have full routine medical examinations at least every two years, following which a report (vetted by patient and doctor) is given to the mission leadership, at times giving specific advice regarding medical needs, work patterns or lifestyle issues.

Decisions regarding the medical assessment of an individual involve a team-based process. All missionary candidates undergo a formal medical examination and psychological assessment prior to acceptance as a new worker and field deployment. The International Medical Adviser receives the reports from the Home-side Medical Advisers, and then obtains any further detailed input from Field-side Medical Advisers when more is required. For example, a new worker with a chronic medical condition might feel called to a remote rural area, but the management of the condition could mean that placement in a more urban setting with better medical resources is wiser.

Such team-based decision-making will, it is hoped, lead to better medical management of a medical condition, longer field service and more effective ministry, thereby resulting in better stewardship of the person's gifts and calling. Is it wise to place a new worker dependent on a specific medicine in an area where there is no reliable supply? Should someone with a history of a chronic depressive illness be designated to a situation where the pressures of ministry might cause the condition to worsen and for suicide risk to increase? When is it possible to predict such things and when is it too difficult to do so?

Philosophically, our mission agency is committed to contextualisation. This means that members use local services where possible. However, especially in the early stages of inculturation, the assistance of a Field Medical Adviser (who speaks the local language, understands the local medical system and has lived in the country for some time) can greatly help a new worker negotiate ill-health in a foreign land. At times, as part of the medical member care system, field nurses have also been appointed who help accompany new workers to local clinics, hospitals or provide assistance when babies are born far from the natural support network of grandparents, family and friends.

Some people have asked whether this Medical Advisory Service is too luxurious a service. Are we wrapping missionaries in cotton wool? Over-protecting them? Are we so concerned about physical or psychological risks that we fail to obey God's call? Does the medical member care hinder workers from stepping out in faith, regardless of the dangers and costs?

However, others will offer an alternative view, that of stewardship. Yes, we need to take risks to engage in the task of effective evangelism and outreach. We need to respond in bold obedience, but we should also be wise in our use of resources. Called, committed people are our best resource, but often there are rather few of them. We need to take good care of them. It is hoped that in some small way, this internal preventative health care and medical advisory service enables workers to serve the Lord as effectively as possible and for as long as possible in the country to which He has called them.

Discussion questions:

1. What are the advantages of having an internal medical advisory service?

2. If your agency is not as large as OMF and cannot justify such a significant investment in medical support services, could you achieve similar benefits through partnership with other agencies?

3. How is medical member care presently provided for your missionaries? In what ways can the medical care of your missionaries be improved?

From statutory welfare measures to member care

John Amalraj,[14] Interserve (India), India

In the early 1990s, India Missions Association[15] (IMA) leaders conducted an initial survey among its member mission agencies. They discovered that most agencies in India did not have any system to care for their missionaries. Many mission agencies were being started without the necessary support structures to provide care to missionaries who were being actively recruited.

New missionaries enthusiastically left their jobs, extended families and local culture to live thousands of kilometres away. They endured learning a new language, living in a new culture, and the struggle to communicate the good news to the people around them. These young missionaries did not realize the sacrifices they were making. Often, the missionaries went without their basic physical, emotional and financial needs being met. Over the years, these young men and women got married and raised children, and their needs kept growing.

Meanwhile, their mission agency leadership, overwhelmed by the enormous challenges on the field and preoccupied with achieving ministry goals, never realized that a storm was brewing. As more of the missionaries' needs were not being met, a growing discontent developed among the missionaries. However, the missionaries rarely shared their troubles with their agency leadership, nor did they openly complain to anyone else. For the majority of missionaries, it was difficult to talk about their personal needs. This was because their church leaders and mission leadership assumed that missionaries had willingly sacrificed all their needs and that all of them were happy serving the Lord. The missionaries were often treated as spiritual heroes. Few leaders realized that in some fields, the missionaries were no longer enthusiastic. Feeling frustrated, the missionaries had already left the field mentally, even though they remained physically on the field.

In 1992, IMA published a book on "Management of Indian Missions" which discussed several management issues such as finance, law, organisation and personnel.[16] This book advocated a system for a salary structure that included provision for various allowances to meet the basic needs of each missionary and his family.

---

14 John Amalraj was trained as a lawyer. He worked for some years as a lawyer, exports company manager, and personnel manager at a group of companies in Chennai. During that time, he was a volunteer in India Missions Association (IMA) and helped to set up management standards for IMA members. In 1993, he joined IMA as the Office & Projects Manager in Chennai. Later, John pioneered the office for IMA in New Delhi in 1998, and promoted IMA in North & North East India. After four years of ministry in Delhi, John and his wife pioneered the IMA Centre in Hyderabad. Over the years, John has served in training leaders through Advanced Mission Leadership Training, coordinating IMA National Conferences, and leading many think-tank meetings. Amalraj now serves as the Executive Secretary/CEO of Interserve India and continues to be actively involved in several IMA networks.

15 India Missions Association, the national federation of missionary sending agencies and churches in India, has 208 members that represent over 30,000 missionaries. Their website is www.imaindia.org.

16 Ebe Sunderaraj and team, Management of Indian Missions, IMA, Chennai, 1992.

The book also gave suggestions for mission agencies to adopt some social security measures which were mandatory by the government.

One of IMA's leaders, K. Rajendran, prepared a critique of twenty-five years of Indian Missions as part of his doctoral thesis. He documented in detail the various stresses faced by missions and individual missionaries and the urgent need for better care.[17] This 1998 publication became the cornerstone in creating awareness about member care among Indian mission leaders.

Two national conferences

Also in 1998, India Missions Association organized a national conference[18] in Nagpur for mission leaders of all its members. During this conference, the issue of "Missionary Welfare" was openly discussed for the first time. Suggestions on how to understand the needs of the missionary and respond to them were discussed. In the following year, during the national IMA conference, the main theme was member care for missionaries. Several seminars were organized for mission leaders to discuss issues on pastoral care and counselling, managing family in mission life, health care for missionaries, and people formation (an emphasis on life-long learning).

After these two major conferences in 1998 and 1999, the mission scene in India witnessed a change toward the understanding of missionary needs. Missionary welfare was no longer regarded as an unspiritual term. Many missions intentionally introduced both statutory and voluntary welfare schemes for their missionaries. Mission leaders corporately evolved various welfare programmes that included statutory provisions like a provident fund, gratuity, life insurance, medical expense reimbursements, special financial help for the family of missionaries who die while in service, pension funds, post retirement home, etc.

Some evidence of the change was seen when mission agencies began advertising the missionary needs in their newsletters, for example the need to mobilize funds for missionary children's education, Christmas gifts, continuing education scholarships, etc. Missionary Upholders Trust (MUT), a member mission agency of IMA, started the vision of regular mission support for cross-cultural missionaries sent from North India by raising their support primarily from their own family members and friends. MUT also took the lead in evolving various corporate schemes for missions at large.

---

17 K. Rajendran, "Which Way Forward Indian Missions?" _SAIACS_, Bangalore, 1998, pp 97-121.

18 The annual IMA National Conference facilitates the executives and leaders of the missionary organisations and churches in India to come together under one roof. The objective is to impart a national vision, information, corporate thinking, skills, ethos and synergy to missions and leadership. This event is the platform to raise and discuss national missiological issues and help in formulating a national outlook, strategy and set national goals.

Recent initiatives

In early 2000, India Missions Association encouraged an existing network that had previously focused on welfare to take on a more holistic approach, and this network became known as the Member Care Network.[19]

In 2002, a national consultation on member care was organized. Regional consultations were also organized for mission leaders to create awareness about the best practices in member care. Several articles in the quarterly publication of India Missions Association highlighted the need for member care. Special one-day seminars for CEOs were organized, and these enabled them to talk about their own personal needs. Training programmes on developing inter-personal skills and family life seminars were facilitated around the country for the benefit of the missionaries belonging to the mission agencies of India Missions Association. In 2005, IMA hosted the first gathering of missionary children from different mission agencies.

After five years of efforts to encourage better member care, Indian mission leaders now go beyond just providing financial benefits. They now provide more personal care in terms of counselling, family seminars, and training in inter-personal skills. Better member care has required the equipping of second-line leaders in various skills to meet the needs of the missionaries they supervise.

Today, mission leaders are beginning to corporately address these issues in their own context. Grace Counselling, another member mission agency of IMA, provides training in counselling skills for mission leaders at various levels. Sharpening Your Interpersonal Skills (SYIS) seminars are being held in different parts of the country, through the coordination of IMA in partnership with several mission agencies.

Looking back at the last fifteen years of mission history in India, we should laud the efforts of India Missions Association to create awareness and evolve policies to care for missionaries. Such awareness about member care has made a significant impact on the Indian mission scene. In the past, mission leaders were not willing to discuss issues related to missionary welfare. But now, we have an environment where all issues related to member care are being addressed on a corporate level. Better member care has transformed many Indian mission agencies and reduced attrition rates on the field

Discussion questions:

1. Discuss the good practices for member care in India. Which of these practices would you encourage in your own organisation?

2. How could the national missions movement in your country help to create better awareness about member care for missionaries and their families?

---

19 India Missions Association has about ten networks that address the various challenges of Indian Missions. The IMA Member Care Network led by Pramila Rajendran has been active in the last five years to create awareness of missionary needs and help missions to formulate policies to care for missionaries.

In the real world

A table to stimulate ideas for best practice in mission partnership. For further explanation, see page 7.

This chart has been partially filled in for you. Now you fill in the blanks.

Who? → When? ↓	Home Church	Missionary	Mission Agencies	External Partners
Continuous			➤ Seek partnership with home church	➤ Promote member care education
Recruitment				
Preparation	➤ Start missionary care groups	➤ Name members for care group ➤ Learn to be open and accountable		➤ Provide training tools on member care
On field	➤ Provide spiritual, physical, emotional, psychological, practical and moral support ➤ Take care of family that stays behind	➤ Be as open as possible to inform about needs in life/work	➤ Facilitate communication	➤ Provide medical support
Crisis			➤ Manage crisis	➤ Be available for debriefing
Furlough		➤ Debrief positive and negative experiences	➤ Provide debriefing	➤ Be available for debriefing
Re-entry	➤ Provide a practical and pastoral welcome		➤ Provide debriefing	➤ Be available for debriefing

17

Organisational Values

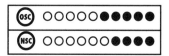

The facts

Organisational values give an agency its character and shape how it operates. Both OSC and NSC rated favourably (overall rating of five and six out of ten respectively) over twenty-one survey questions. Over half the factors showed a high correlation with retention, which is not surprising as people bond with their agency over organisational values. Missionaries identify with the organisational values of an agency; thus, the values shape the nature of the relationship between the organisation and the missionary and can indicate the strength of that relationship.

The data

Q. No.	Factor	OSC Health Indicator	✓	NSC Health Indicator	✓
40	Vision and purpose are shared and understood throughout the agency	OOOOOOO●●●	✓	OOOOOOO●●●	✓
41	Plans and job descriptions are communicated clearly to the missionary	OOOOOO●●●●	✓	OOOOOO●●●●	✓
42	There is a free flow of communication to and from the leadership	OOOOOO●●●●	✓	OOOOOO●●●●	
43	There is effective communication between sending base and field	OOOO●●●●●●	✓	OOOOOOO●●●	✓
44	Missionaries are included in major decisions related to the field	OOOOOOO●●●		OOOOOO●●●●	
45	Policies are well documented and understood	OOOOO●●●●●	✓	OOOOOOO●●●	✓
46	A culture of prayer is actively promoted within the agency	OOOOOOO●●●		OOOOOOOO●●	

47	Most leaders are a good example of the agency's beliefs and values	○○○○○○○○○●	✓	○○○○○○○○●●	
48	Most leaders identify problems early and take appropriate action	○○○○●●●●●●	✓	○○○○○○●●●●	✓
49	Good on-field supervision is provided (quantity and quality)	○○○○●●●●●●	✓	○○○○○●●●●●	✓
50	Leaders conduct an annual performance/ministry review with each missionary	○○○●●●●●●●	✓	○○○●●●●●●●	✓
51	There are documented and adequate procedures for handling complaints from missionaries	○○○○○●●●●●	✓	○○○○○●●●●●	✓
54	Ongoing language and culture training are actively encouraged	○○○○○○○●●●	✓	○○○○○○○●●●	
56	Missionaries are assigned roles according to their gifting and experience	○○○○○○●●●●		○○○○○○●●●●	✓
60	Missionaries are committed and loyal to the agency	○○○○○○●●●●		○○○○○○○○●●	✓
61	Missionaries are generally not overloaded in the amount of work they do	○●●●●●●●●●	✓	○○○○●●●●●●	✓
62	Opportunities are provided for a ministry/role for the spouse	○○○○○○○●●●	✓	○○○○○○○●●●	
64	Missionaries regularly evaluate and seek to improve the agency's ministry	○○●●●●●●●●	✓	○○○○●●●●●●	
71	Missionary teams are effective in providing each other with mutual support	○○○○●●●●●●		○○○○○○●●●●	✓
78	Risk assessment and contingency planning is in place in all fields	○○○○○○○●●●	✓	○○○○●●●●●●	✓
80	Missionaries usually receive sustained financial support that is adequate for their needs	○○○○○○○●●●	✓	○○○○●●●●●●	✓

The key findings

- ✓ The average rating of organisation values is highly correlated with retention in OSC and NSC.
- ✓ Documentation of policies (Q45), Vision & purpose (Q40) and Clear plans & job description (Q41), Good on-field supervision (Q49), Good leadership (Q47-48), and A clear procedure for handling complaints (Q51) are clearly correlated with retention in OSC and NSC.

✓ Leaders solve problems (Q48) was rated very high in NSC and clearly correlated with retention.

✓ In OSC, Free flow of communication with leadership (Q42), and Inclusion of missionaries in decisions (Q44) correlates with retention.

✓ Opportunities for service of spouse (Q62) was rated very high in OSC and was correlated to high retention in OSC.

✓ Risk assessment and contingency planning (Q78) was correlated with retention in NSC and OSC.

✓ Missionaries are committed and loyal to agency (Q60) was correlated with high retention.

What it means

Rob Hay

There are many aspects of an agency's function that contribute to its organisational values. Collectively, these aspects have a significant influence on retention. Organisational values are often the defining factor in whether an organisation thrives or flounders, whether its staff are growing and productive or constrained and just surviving. Questions can be grouped into several areas, each of which has a significant impact on organisational values: Clear Boundaries, Good communication, Effective leadership and Valuing of people.

Clear boundaries

Questions 40 [Q40 *Vision and purpose are shared and understood throughout the agency*], 41 [Q41 *Plans and job descriptions are communicated clearly to the missionary*], 45 [Q45 *Policies are well documented and understood*] and 51 [Q51 *There are documented and adequate procedures for handling complaints from missionaries*] are included in the area of clear boundaries and all are highly correlated with missionary retention. Boundaries are essential in an organisation to give people freedom to operate. Does that sound contradictory? Let us explain.

To make best use of the people in a hierarchical organisation, functions and tasks should be delegated as much as possible. Everyone needs to understand clearly what they are allowed to do, what their manager is allowed to do and what their subordinate is allowed to do. In this way, they know when to act without reference to their manager as well as what tasks should be delegated. In Asia, I found this to be vitally important. To do the job of a subordinate in the hierarchy was to deny their ability and reduce their dignity. To do a task of your manager's was not viewed as helpful or taking initiative (as it is sometimes perceived in the West), but challenging to their authority and status.

In an environment of team-work and *flat* structures, some make the mistake of thinking that boundaries have less importance. In fact, boundaries may be more important in this environment than in a hierarchical structure. In teams, people usually operate with more autonomy than in a hierarchical structure or change roles depending on the work in hand. True autonomy is achieved with boundaries, so that those involved know the areas in which they may act, think and innovate freely. They need to know when and who to involve if they desire to act outside that boundary. Without clear boundaries, most people spend their time inhibited because they worry whether they are acting within their role, or conversely, they may assume a task is part of another's role and not meet the expectations of their team-mates.

Therefore, having clear job descriptions correlated very highly with retention. NSC and OSC had a performance and significance rating of seven out of ten on this factor—a good rating, but given its importance, one that could be improved. Furthermore, a clear vision and purpose, [Q40 *Vision and purpose are shared and understood throughout the agency*], helps people to know what the priorities of the organisation are and how to align their own work in support of those aims and purpose. On this factor, agency leaders gave a rating of just under eight out of ten in NSC and OSC, indicating that they feel that the vision and purpose is shared and understood.

Missionaries and agency leaders need to know, "*Where am I going, how do I get there, and what behaviour is acceptable in my effort to get there.*" The "where am I going?" is the vision and purpose, the "how do I get there?" are the plans and job descriptions, and the policies of the organisation set out "what behaviour is acceptable?" to achieve the vision and purpose. For example, in Nepal we needed to import items, particularly medical equipment that was not available in country. This meant getting expensive items through customs. The quick way to do this was to pay a fee to the customs officials, who would then ensure that your items were processed immediately. Alternatively, not paying the fee could mean waiting weeks or even months. We needed the equipment to meet the aims of the organisation (running medical camps among the country's poorest people), but the organisation's policy was not to pay these fees as they were viewed as bribes. Policies are important for they reinforce the common behaviour required in an organisation.

In NSC, Question 45 [Q45 *Policies are well documented and understood*] received a rating of seven out of ten. In OSC, this question received a rating of only five. Perhaps OSC agencies can learn from NSC about this function? Or perhaps there are higher expectations of what constitutes a clear policy in OSC agencies? Agencies should talk, explore and learn regarding this important issue.

Good communication

Questions 42-44 [Q42 *There is a free flow of communication to and from the leadership*, Q43 *There is effective communication between sending base and field*, and Q44 *Missionaries are included in major decisions related to the field*] cover organizational communication. Communication is a value across many areas, but prioritising communication as an organisation makes a values statement. Organizations effectively say, "*We consciously communicate and put energy and effort into making communication happen.*"

To say that good communication can just happen is a myth! As the number of people in an organisation increase, the obstacles to communicating increase exponentially. Communication must be both conscious and proactive. Systems for communicating must be developed and space in which to communicate must be created. To choose communication, especially amidst busy ministry schedules, indicates that it is an organisational value. Priority on communication affects all aspects of the organisation and the lives of the leaders. For more discussion on this area see Chapter 20.

Effective leadership

Much investment, effort, and perseverance must happen to make an effective leadership. As the data shows, the workload in our organisations is very high. Since creating and maintaining effective leadership takes time, we must limit the volume of work done in order to provide time to mentor, develop and raise leaders. Tough decisions are required to lead well rather than just provide leadership that allows survival.

The Bible says, *"Without vision, the people perish (Proverbs 29:18, KJV)."* Leaders provide vision and set the agenda. The quality of leadership determines whether the organisation is growing and thriving, or whether it is regressing and dying. For organisations to function well and encourage healthy people, effective leadership must be an organisation value. Across the four questions on leadership, Questions 47-50, the data shows a high correlation with retention. The OSC, has a rating of only four out of ten; the NSC, only slightly better, at five out of ten. These ratings are discussed in detail in Chapters 21 and 22.

Valuing of people

We often say "people are our most valuable resource," but in mission, this really is true; we have very few other resources. Business organisations often have large development budgets, significant building infrastructures and the latest information technology equipment. Mission does not. Often mission organizations have very few material resources and must stretch them thin. Yet, mission does have people who are called and committed to the ministry or work.

A question I often ask mission boards is, "What organizational structure do you have?" In OSC, many mission organisations used to function as large, extended families, even having parental figures at the head of the organisation. In recent times, due to increased size and complexity, many have developed a business type of organizational structure. This is a concern for a number of reasons:

- The average business is responsible for the well-being of their staff for just eight hours per day; mission involves being responsible for the daytime and night-time of a missionary.

- In business, the relationship between the individual is based on a financial contract. The business pays a competitive rate to get a good level of service and loyalty from the individual. In mission, the relationship is clearly not based on a financial contract. In fact, missionaries often raise their own financial support, and that support is a basic allowance rather than a competitive rate.

There are other issues, but these two alone highlight some key differences. Mission must function on a contract other than financial. People know they are valued when they are allowed to feel fulfilled and use their gifts effectively [Q56 *Missionaries are assigned roles according to their gifting and experience*]. They know they are being valued when they know they are being used and not abused [Q61 *Missionaries are generally not overloaded in the amount of work they do*], and when they know both partners in a marriage are valued [Q62 *Opportunities are provided for a ministry/role for the spouse*]. Further care is demonstrated when their safety is ensured and risk level limited (to the extent that this is wise and prudent—see Chapter 16 for a discussion on when care becomes counter productive for retention) [Q78 *Risk assessment and contingency planning is in place in all fields*], as well as when their financial needs are met adequately [Q80 *Missionaries usually receive sustained financial support that is adequate for their needs*]. And finally, value is demonstrated when opinions and views are sought to shape their ministry and the ministry of the organisation [Q64 *Missionaries regularly evaluate and seek to improve the agency's ministry*]. Some of these issues received low performance ratings and require more work for they are all correlated with retention in OSC, and many in NSC as well.

One area of encouragement in these values was Question 46 [Q46 *A culture of prayer is actively promoted within the agency*]. This question correlated with retention in OSC and received a very high rating across NSC and OSC alike. Given the high rating in NSC, the lack of correlation to retention in NSC may reflect that this is a key value in all NSC agencies and so we saw no significant difference between high and low retaining agencies on this issue.

Collectively, organisational values showed the highest correlation with retention of all the areas and we need to take seriously the challenge of nurturing meaningful organisational values in our organisations. Values are not the same as a mission statement in that while a mission statement may change over time in response to external pressures, values remain constant, to the point of bankruptcy. For example, if honesty was a value and external pressure was exerted to not follow some key legislation, the organisation would be allowed to die rather than compromise that value. Applied another way, if a value is to make sure missionaries are not overworked, consider the project in which you know you need ten people for effectiveness. Supposing, after trying everything to find ten people, only six are found. You will not require the six workers you have to contribute 150% of their working hours to complete the project, but will instead deem the project not feasible because it compromises one of your key values. (See Chapter 18 for a detailed discussion of work overload issues.)

Core values keep us there

Caryn M. Pederson,[1] Pioneers, USA

At Pioneers, our core values are the heart of our movement. Some people are drawn to the concept of teams, others to the partnership with local churches, while still others to our ethos of grace. If new recruits catch this pulse that drives us forward, then that same pulse will keep them dreaming, working, and pioneering to reach the forgotten peoples over an extended period of time, regardless of the cost. As their ministries reflect this same heartbeat, they will give life to the cultures they serve and invite others to join them in obeying the Great Commission.

Each of our eight core values are an integral part of who we are (refer to our website www.pioneers.org for more details), but three values in particular impact retention: ethos of grace, teams, and passion for God. This triad of core values contributes positively to retention.

Grace

One leader in Asia tells a story of grace:

> Before coming to the field, Brad ran a successful business in the US. After a year of trying to learn a new language, he felt frustrated. Brad has dyslexia. His agonizingly slow progress in learning the language raised the obvious but unspoken question in some minds about his ability to contribute to the work. With great perseverance, Brad was able to acquire enough language to work with some local Christians, who also spoke some English. Together they began developing a ministry that would use mass media to impact the thinking of the focus people group. Year after year, their failures seemed to outnumber their successes.

> Brad has the gift of dreaming big dreams and thinking entrepreneurially 'outside of the box.' Some were sometimes sceptical. They would ask, 'Why are you dreaming up another huge project? What became of the last one? When are you going to follow through on something, so it bears some fruit?' Others however, including his team leader, saw the potential in Brad's vision, and the lessons being learned through each 'failed' project.

> Through God's grace, earnest prayer, and permission to keep pressing ahead, Brad was able to establish an indigenous organisation (of ten staff and a national director) that bridges the gap between mass media events and church planters around the country. This has resulted in a number of house fellowships among unreached peoples.

---

1 Caryn Pederson serves as the director of communications for Pioneers-USA and is author of *Batik: A glimpse of the heart* (Bottom Line Media, 2004), which tells the stories of Indonesian believers.

Brad's story is just one example of how grace from God and each other may be the single largest contributor to missionary retention. Grace breeds perseverance. Whether it comes through a leader's willingness to allow his people to pursue their dreams, or in a team's willingness to walk in love, there are results. In Brad's case, taking the risk not only brought retention, but multiplication—the establishment of new house churches.

Teams

The platform for grace is teams. Third dimension teams (teams that not only work together toward a common goal, but are involved in each other's lives) provide the glue for long-term ministry investment in hard, pioneering environments. The accountability and community that such teams provide infuses "staying power." Just as interpersonal relationships can be a strong reason for attrition, when hallmarked by grace they can radically influence retention.

On one international team, relationships were strained between two members, an Australian and an American. The dissension was so strong that team meetings became difficult. The area leader who assisted them in conflict resolution writes, "When we sat down, it ended up being a discussion that lasted several hours. For the first few hours, my assistant and I basically just listened… and listened. When the time was right, I began to probe a little. Eventually, it became clear that what was being attributed to 'worldview' was actually more about personality. When I gently confronted them on this, they began to see the situation for what it was."

"Two years after this episode, I met a friend of the one who was confronted. He said, 'My friend told me about you. He said you're a good listener.' What a blessing that was to me! It again pointed out the importance of listening and being committed to team." This leader's experience illustrates that listening is a crucial form of love. What we are known by (John 13:35), also keeps us on task.

Passion for God

Over and above the influence of a team, and its ethos of grace, is our passion for God. Making disciples of all nations is spiritual work at every level. Therefore, our passion for God and His purposes will be the single greatest factor in retention. Workers who keep Christ as their first love will persevere. They will work in settings that only make sense in light of Christ's sacrifices on their behalf. When the Lord lives through them, long-term work is accomplished, even if other core values in the retention triad (grace, team, passion for God) are absent.

One Pioneers team in Asia meets every morning for prayer. It allocates one day a month to prayer and fasting. In addition, a significant part of weekly team meetings is also devoted to prayer. Intercession equipped this international team to weather difficulties in a way that otherwise might not have been possible. In another location, after one missionary reached proficiency in the local language, he began spending his language learning time in prayer. Within a month, local friends began to suggest to him the very things they would not hear before. This clear answer from God brought fresh energy to his work.

Each of our core values when well-lived will influence retention, but the combined ethos of grace, team, and passion for God creates a three-cord strand. Together, they keep Pioneers' workers on site, on task, and expectant for what He will do.

Discussion questions:

1. What are the important core values in your organisation? Why are they important to the identity and functioning of your organisation?

2. How would you strengthen these core values and/or develop other values within your organisation?

Crafting core values of a new ministry team

Paul Rhoads[2] and Steve Hoke,[3] Church Resource Ministries, USA

Church Resource Ministries (CRM), like other agencies, has organisational values that shape its ministry. In this case study, we will share how taking time to forge a list of shared team values helped our new Staff Development and Care Team (SDC)[4] focus its energies on carefully selected priorities. These priorities enabled the SDC team to develop a range of holistic member care ministries within CRM with limited resources.

Organisational Values guide an organisation's ongoing behaviour and future ministry decisions. More importantly, values help to create an organisational "*ethos*," the fundamental character or spirit of an organisation's culture.

We identified three essential characteristics for our new ministry team:

1. Safety, trust and confidentiality would be modelled by the Care Team members. If the team maintained confidences and created grace-filled environments at conferences and in individual encounters, an ethos of personal safety would begin to spread. Then our missionary staff would feel safe in sharing their needs and weaknesses with the team.

2. Spiritual growth would be maintained by Care Team members themselves. If we want to facilitate greater intimacy with God, we had to be growing spiritually ourselves.

2　Paul Rhoads, currently Executive Vice President of Church Resource Ministries (CRM), served as the founding director of the Staff Development and Care Team, and now directs CRM's ministry teams around the world.

3　Steve Hoke is Vice President of People Development, focusing on staff training and spiritual direction.

4　For more details, please refer to our case study "Shaping a Staff Development and Care Team" in Chapter 23 on "Staff Development."

3. An environment would be created where women felt easily and naturally included, and where they had an increasing voice in the life of the organisation. It has not always been natural to include women as full ministry partners. Therefore, we wanted to be very intentional in our planning and decision-making.

Life-ministry values describe a ministry team's unique beliefs, core convictions, and guiding assumptions about life and ministry. Such values are the result of our character insights, ministry insights drawn from Scripture, and unique experiences acquired over a lifetime.

In our very first meetings of the new Staff Development and Care Team, we began praying and engaged in dialogue regarding what our Core Values were and should be. We continued these "values discussions" through each meeting into the second year. Midway through the second year, we began to shape a list of core values to direct how we focused our energies.

Staff Development and Care Team Core Values

- Our primary value as a team and for our ministry is a vital relationship with God, and thus we value the spiritual formation of each member. Eph 4:13

- Recognising that each person's relationship to God is worked out horizontally, we value safety, openness, and vulnerability. Eph 4:15

- We value a caring community: each person caring for him or herself appropriately; each person giving and receiving care from his or her CRM team and national community appropriately. 1 Cor 13

- We value growth and a developmental perspective impacting all facets of life: spiritually, life stages, leadership, team relationships, and professional growth, from recruitment to retirement. Luke 2:52

- Recognising that our staff work in a variety of cultural contexts, we seek to care for and help them live and minister in a healthy but culturally sensitive manner. Matt 28:18-20; Acts 1:8

- We value "sent presence": our physical presence with our missionaries – our emotional presence to them – our prayerful presence for them; and ourselves as resources. John 1:14

- We value lightness and joy: because Jesus carries our burden, we can be playful, and enjoy one other and God. Psalm 16:11

- We value a community where healing, personal growth and asking for help are essential elements of Christian maturity. James 5:13-16

We value openness to truth: the recognition that God is calling me to grow and to take our development into Christ-likeness seriously. Ps 51:6

The process of identifying core values

When a group of people, however like-minded and Spirit-filled, come together to identify the core values by which they will conduct ministry, differences will emerge like popcorn from a hot kettle. Each area of reflection can be a potential hotbed of discussion and disagreement.

Differences were encountered between the spiritual gifts of our team members. The mercy-gifted want to emphasise the care function. The teaching-gifted want to focus more on the proactive delivery of training and equipping.

Differences in experience will also play a part. Those with wider experience shape their inputs to focus on those needs which they perceive as most critical in the immediate. Others may strive for an ideal balance.

Different members come with different training backgrounds, and these backgrounds will influence their approach. The leader must therefore be sensitive to how these differences can be shaped and blended to contribute to a richer mix of ideas and outcomes, rather than degenerating into disagreements and divisions.

During our discovery journey, we had to learn how to blend our different perspectives on a spiritual formation paradigm for member care and development into a shared understanding. In order to minister effectively alongside each other, we had to work through our differences on a variety of issues. These included: the importance of incarnational presence, the dynamics of spiritual transformation, the ingredients of balanced spiritual health, the goal of care and nurture, the role of the team leader and member care giver, and shaping factors such as suffering, etc.

After months of prayer and interaction, we were able to hammer out a spiritual formation paradigm which linked the various components and dynamics involved in Christian spiritual formation. Prayer was essential. We would stop for prayer at regular intervals. Prayer kept us listening for the Spirit's voice in the midst of our human deliberations. More than once we would take an hour of silence from group discussion, allowing each person to get alone with God to get a clearer sense of what He was saying to us.

It takes considerable effort to shape a values-based organisation. How a group of individuals goes about becoming a ministry team, and how it prayerfully and carefully moulds essential values into its ministry style can be critical to its success.

Discussion questions:

1. How do your organisational values shape and influence how specific ministries develop on the field?

2. Who should be involved in the formation of core values for your ministry teams?

3. How might a more values-centred philosophy of ministry influence or reshape the ethos of your organisation?

In the real world

A table to stimulate ideas for best practice in mission partnership. For further explanation, see page 7.

This chart has been partially filled in for you. Now you fill in the blanks.

Who? → When? ↓	Home Church	Missionary	Mission Agencies	External Partners
Continuous	➢ Be a purpose-driven congregation ➢ Make gifts the basis for ministry ➢ Be involved in the life and ministry of missionaries	➢ Missionaries are committed and loyal to their home church and agency	➢ Home churches are encouraged to be involved in the life and ministry of the missionary ➢ Policies are well documented and understood ➢ Most leaders are examples of the agency's beliefs and values ➢ A culture of prayer is actively promoted throughout the agency ➢ Vision and purpose are shared and understood throughout the agency	➢ Provide consultancy to work on vision and strategy ➢ Help to determine values ➢ Train and coach in transition periods
Recruitment				
Preparation				
On field				
Crisis				
Furlough				
Re-entry				

18

Organisational Values
Work-Life Balance

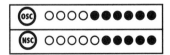

The facts

Work-life balance is one important area within organisational values In general, the field of missions has a major work overload problem. The problem is not unique to the task-orientated West or some Asian nations, but increasingly affects the Global South as well. Work-life overload affects people through physical exhaustion, and long term, leads to stress, depression, and lack of spiritual vitality. Work-life overload can reduce the ability to evaluate, reflect, and think creatively in order to improve current responses to life and meet the challenges of the future with creativity and energy.

The data

Q. No.	Factor	OSC Health Indicator	✓	NSC Health Indicator	✓
41	Plans and job descriptions are communicated clearly to the missionary	○○○○○○●●●●	✓	○○○○○○●●●●	✓
45	Policies are well documented and understood	○○○○○●●●●●	✓	○○○○○○○●●●	✓
47	Most leaders are a good example of the agency's beliefs and values	○○○○○○○○○●	✓	○○○○○○○○●●	
48	Most leaders identify problems early and take appropriate action	○○○○●●●●●●	✓	○○○○○○●●●●	✓
49	Good on-field supervision is provided (quantity and quality)	○○○○●●●●●●	✓	○○○○○●●●●●	✓
50	Leaders conduct an annual performance/ministry review with each missionary	○○○○●●●●●●	✓	○○○●●●●●●●	✓

56	Missionaries are assigned roles according to their gifting and experience	○○○○○○●●●●		○○○○○○●●●●	✓
57	Missionaries are given room to shape and develop their own ministry	○○○○○○○○●●	✓	○○○○○○○●●●	✓
59	Missionaries are committed to their ministry	○○○○○○○○○●	✓	○○○○○○○○○●	✓
61	Missionaries are generally not overloaded in the amount of work they do	○●●●●●●●●●	✓	○○○○●●●●●●	✓
64	Missionaries regularly evaluate and seek to improve the agency's ministry	○○●●●●●●●●	✓	○○○○●●●●●●	
70	Missionaries experience a sense of fulfilment in their ministry	○○○○○○○○●●	✓	○○○○○○○●●●	✓
71	Missionary teams are effective in providing each other with mutual support	○○○○●●●●●●		○○○○○○●●●●	✓

The key findings

✓ Apportioning an appropriate amount of work (Q61) is rated low for performance and significance in OSC and only somewhat higher in NSC—evidence of a tendency toward work overload.

✓ There is a moderate correlation between apportioning of work (Q61) and retention—in OSC more than in NSC.

✓ Missionaries given room to shape their own ministry (Q57) and Commitment to their ministry (Q59) received very high ratings and are correlated with high retention.

✓ High rating of Missionaries' sense of personal fulfilment (Q70) and correlates positively with retention, however, this could lead to the risk overwork.

✓ The assessment indicates that work-life balance remains a challenge.

✓ Surprisingly, Assignment of missionaries according to gifting (Q56) was rated higher in NSC than in OSC.

What it means

Rob Hay

One of the most critical areas of mission ministry is the work-life balance of missionaries. Missionaries face tremendous needs, and they have a very high commitment to their ministry, as verified by the results of Q59 [Q59 *Missionaries are committed to their ministry*]. That missionaries are in fact overloaded with work is demonstrated by Question 61 [Q61 *Missionaries are generally not overloaded in the amount of work they do*], which received the lowest rating for significance and performance by mission executives of any of the questions, and yet correlates with retention—the rating being one out of ten in OSC and four out of ten in NSC. Since it was globally one of the poorest ratings, overwork cannot simply be attributed to cultural tendencies, such as workaholism and presenteism,[1] which you might expect in the US, UK or Japan. A similar trend is found in NSC agencies, although they come from a less achievement-driven culture. The "shame culture" in some NSC may contribute to overwork in that unsuccessfulness is not an option, leading missionaries to prove their success to their home church and friends, and contributing to enormous pressure.

Perhaps the influence of the Protestant work ethic affects both OSC and NSC contexts in this area. The ReMAP II study contacted Protestant missions movements. These evangelical missionaries have been known to value action over reflection, and "doing" mission over "being" mission—a value known as the Protestant work ethic. It would be interesting to compare a similar group of Orthodox and Catholic missionaries, who are known for valuing reflection and a sense of who they are as children of God more highly. The Protestant work ethic should not be underestimated as a significant and enduring influence on the lives and ministries of missionaries. Certainly, that agencies rated themselves highly on Question 70 [Q70 *Missionaries experience a sense of fulfilment in their ministry*] would be an encouragement were it not for the very poor rating of Question 61 [Q61 *Missionaries are generally not overloaded in the amount of work they do*]. Together, the two issues raise serious concerns about the degree to which many missionaries' gain a sense of self-worth and value from what they do rather than who they are. Their identity may lie in their ministry and in the outcome of their ministry rather than in Christ.

The issue of work overload also has an effect on leadership, evidenced by the moderate ratings of Questions 48 [Q48 *Most leaders identify problems early and take appropriate action*], 49 [Q49 *Good on-field supervision is provided (quantity and quality)*] and 50 [Q50 *Leaders conduct an annual performance/ministry review with each missionary*] (see Chapter 21 for more discussion of this).

Questions 57 [Q57 *Missionaries are given room to shape and develop their own ministry*] and 59 [Q59 *Missionaries are committed to their ministry*] both received a very high rating, and correlated very strongly with retention. While it is encouraging that missionaries appear to be given freedom to develop and manage their own ministry, there should be an awareness that this independence might need to be tempered by other factors for their health and well-being. Specifically, there should be caution that, though people may choose to work many hours because they enjoy their work, the overwork may cause health strain and family imbalance. In this, missionaries need leadership and accountability to help them grow and work without compromising other values.

---

1   This phrase was coined by the accountancy firm, Price Waterhouse Coopers (PWC), who undertook major work in 2001 on the issue of work-life balance. They used the term presenteism to describe an organisational culture that equates effectiveness with time spent at one's desk or place of work.

However, there may be other motives for overwork. For those who are in faith missions—meaning that they raise their financial support from churches and individuals—there can be a psychological effect of living on income provided by others. Marjory Foyle, author of *Honourably Wounded,*[2] believes this to be one of the most significant causes of stress among missionaries. In my own interviews with missionaries, there is often an unconscious feeling that, to be worthy of the financial support they receive, they must live at the level of their poorest supporter and work as hard as their most workaholic supporter—obviously an almost impossible combination of demands. Teaching and preparation on the biblical mandate for living on gift income is necessary, as well as holding out good examples from missionaries who do this well.

Avoiding overload has direct implications to other areas of best practice. The ReMAP II study shows the need for an ongoing cycle of reflection, action, reflection. In other words, time must be available to "be," not exclusively focused on action. The analysis of Question 64 [Q64 *Missionaries regularly evaluate and seek to improve the agency's ministry*] highlights that agencies struggle with this. This question was strongly correlated with retention, and yet received a rating of just two out of ten. Likewise, team support is important for retention (Question 71 [Q71 *Missionary teams are effective in providing each other with mutual support*]), yet there must be time and energy available for this. If the sole focus of available hours of a missionary is ministry, team support will suffer.

Avoiding overload or presenteeism—the idea of just being present for work without regard for effectiveness—requires proactive top-down action. Senior leaders need to prioritise it, integrate it into the core values of the organisation, and perhaps most crucially, model it in their own lives. Work overload not only affects the individual missionary, but also the overall organisation in its ability to meet objectives. Price Waterhouse Corporation (which studied presenteeism) has shown that achieving a healthy and sustainable work-life balance can significantly affect the profitability of a business.[3]

How much is overwork limiting the effectiveness of our mission agencies? What could we be achieving by getting workaholism under control in our organisations? One area to begin addressing is "management missiology," a fixation on numbers, goals and achievements. Along with numbers analysis, there should be a clear emphasis on understanding why a particular ministry should be initiated or continued, instead of just how it can be accomplished more efficiently. The question, "To what extent does this programme really contribute to the long-term growth of the Kingdom of God in this country?" should be asked. Reflection, undertaken regularly and systematically, would help decisions about whether a ministry had fulfilled its strategic God-given purpose. In this way, its cessation may be planned in a constructive manner. Without regular reviews, ministries tend to die a slow death—because reflection on sometimes difficult and painful realities is avoided.

---

2   Marjory F. Foyle, *Honourably Wounded*, (Thousand Oaks, CA: Monarch Books Paperback, 2001).
3   In pilot studies within British Telecom, they achieved an increase in the region of 15% profitability.

Leadership and management must function in a way that protects the individual from him or herself. Only by doing this do both get maximum benefit. Clear communication of expectations and clear policies (as highlighted by Questions 40 [Q40 *Vision and purpose are shared and understood throughout the agency*], 41 [Q41 *Plans and job descriptions are communicated clearly to the missionary*] and 45 [Q45 *Policies are well documented and understood*]) on issues related to workload, such as working hours, vacations and sabbaticals, can be very important. We discuss these issues further in Chapter 20.

The importance of this issue is not just in operational areas. The mission agency will only maintain its relevance and effectiveness if it can change and respond to remain relevant in a world that is continually accelerating its pace of change. To do this, time must be allocated to research, reflect, watch, listen and innovate. Space in the busyness of ministry needs to be created for the development of ideas, some of which will come to nothing and must not be seen as failures, but rather part of finding the right way forward. Space in the busyness of ministry allows reflection, which in turn allows a quick response to what is going on the world because the important questions are already being asked. Without a quick response, many organisations miss opportunities because they are focused on an area that should no longer be taking up attention. In a fast changing world, active listening to God is vital. Attention on watching the world and seeing where the wind of God's Spirit is blowing ensures that we can raise the sail and move in that direction. Perhaps in too many cases, the effort required is such that by the time we react, the Spirit has moved on in another direction and place. Instead of having the wind of the Spirit in the sail of our organisation, we often get out the oars of human effort and insist on rowing, long after God has moved on elsewhere.

Setting goals

David Wong,[4] Haggai Institute,[5] Singapore

The subject of Goal-setting is a part of the core curriculum and a pillar of the Haggai Institute training programme.[6] It is the only subject that is taught throughout the seminar. The reason is that every other subject taught needs to be converted into goals. Setting goals takes place throughout the seminar.

---

4   Rev. Dr. David Wong is the Vice President of International Training at Haggai Institute, overseeing the training programme in both Hawaii and Singapore. He was Director of Training for Hawaii from 1994 to 2000, where he served as an overseer, faculty member and mentor to hundreds of Christian leaders from over 100 nations who trained in Maui each year. Prior to this, David had pastored a church for 17 years, taught as guest lecturer in several theological schools, and served as Deputy Dean of the Biblical Graduate School of Theology in Singapore. David completed his doctoral studies at Fuller Theological Seminary in 2004 with a paper on leadership and learning paradigms.

5   Haggai Institute has a clear focus and a specific objective: to train Christian leaders to evangelise their own people and train others to do the same. Training takes the form of a short-term seminar, residential in nature, and focused in this objective.

6   For more details, please refer to Chapter 24 for the case study that describes the Haggai Institute training programme.

Furthermore, setting goals is a concept foreign to the cultures of the Two-Thirds world. The Latin Americans are more accustomed to saying *mañana*, the Middle Easterners, *inshallah* and the Africans, *hakuna matata*. All these expressions imply the same, "Why do today what you can do tomorrow?"

To justify such attitude, Christians quote James 4.13-14: "Now listen, you who say, 'Today or tomorrow we will go to this or that city, spend a year there, carry on business and make money.' Why you do not even know what will happen tomorrow? What is your life? You are a mist that appears for a little while and then vanishes." or the words of Jesus in Matthew 6.34: "Therefore do not worry about tomorrow, for tomorrow will worry about itself. Each day has enough trouble of its own."

In answer to such, often genuine concerns, we explain that James does not speak against setting goals or planning, only against planning that leaves out God. Jesus does not speak against thinking about tomorrow, only against thinking anxiously about tomorrow.

Goal-setting can be done in full cognisance of God's ownership and sovereignty over our lives and plans. God can guide us as we plan as much as He can guide us when we execute our plans. Likewise, goal-setting takes away anxiety which the lack of goals would otherwise foster.

A set of written goals is an important key to the lasting effect of any short-term training. Not only are goals set, they are written, rewritten, worked on and reworked on, until they meet the stringent requirements of SMART (Specific, Measurable, Attainable, Realistic, Time-bound) goals. In the process, the participant becomes convinced that the exercise is more than academic. It is a personal commitment that he or she is making. Time is given in the schedule for participants to sit and write their goals, in a set format, detailing goals in areas of ministry and family, and goals for the spiritual, intellectual, physical and financial aspects of their lives.

Time is also given for the participants to articulate their goals after they are written. Each is given a minute to share a few of the goals. This serves the purposes of making a verbal commitment for one's goals, and of sharing those goals with fellow-participants for prayer. The exercise closes with the participants bringing their written goals forward to the "altar" where the Director, the Resident Coordinator and Faculty present lay hands and commit the goals to God.

Sometimes, this ritual is incorporated into the Holy Communion on the last day of the seminar. Participants solemnly bring their goals as they go forward to partake of the cup. The act symbolises a commitment to the Lord to remember and to implement the goals. One copy of the goals is left behind at the Institute while another goes home with the participant, filed as the first page in their seminar folder.

In my travels to visit alumni, I have often asked the question, "How are you doing with your goals?" I am gratified to learn that few, if any, ever forget the solemn commitment they made when they wrote their goals. Goal-setting and goal-writing have become almost a sacred ritual at the Institute.

Discussion questions:

1. What are some advantages of setting goals? What are the disadvantages?
2. How could the setting of goals in ministry help to improve the work-life balance of our missionaries?

Angela's prayer altar

LeMei Littlefield[7], OMF International[8], USA.

During our eight years in Taiwan with OMF International, we would meet each week to pray with the other missionaries in our area. Every other week, instead of meeting all together, the missionary women would get together to talk and to pray. In a smaller group, the women had a chance to share more deeply. This shared prayer time with other wives and singles helped us to develop a strong bond of fellowship and mutual support. At one of these prayer meetings, Angela shared a practical change she had made in her personal spiritual life.

Angela desired a more prayerful life. She realised that she was setting aside too little time in her daily schedule for prayer and intercession. Angela stayed in a small city apartment. She was constantly juggling her roles as wife, mother of little ones, and strategic front-line worker. One day, she sensed the Holy Spirit drawing her attention to how the television had become a distraction in her life. It was often turned on for many hours each day. And whenever the television was on, her spiritual focus would dissipate.

Angela decided to make a change. She moved the television out of the living room. In its place, she set up a simple prayer altar: a small table, a pillow to kneel on, and her Bible. Once this was set up, the prayer altar became a visual point of focus in her home. That external rearrangement enabled her to begin re-ordering her inner life. Angela began a conscious effort to prioritise personal prayer time in her daily schedule. As the days passed by, she became more regular and consistent in her personal prayer life. She looked forward to meeting with God without being distracted by her environment.

Angela's testimony sparked a conviction in my own heart. Shortly afterward, in agreement with my husband, we decided to follow Angela's example and to make this practical change in our home as well. We left the television in its place, because it was usually turned off and therefore not a point of temptation for us. We then rearranged our living room furniture in order to set up a low table in one corner.

---

7   LeMei Littlefield and her husband Michael serve at the US office of OMF International, where Michael is Director for Personnel for the OMF-US office. Michael and LeMei draw on their experiences as missionaries to Taiwan (1987 to 1997) and Singapore (1998 to 2004) to oversee the selection, training and ongoing enablement of missionaries to East Asia.

8   OMF International, formerly the China Inland Mission, has been sending missionaries to East Asian countries for 140 years. Today, OMF International has approximately 1,000 adults and 600+ children, representing around 30 different nationalities. The missionaries are being sent from 18 sending bases, both Asian and non-Asian, and they work mainly in East Asia.

We placed a cross directly above, and a kneeling cushion below. I kept a Bible there, alongside some prayer materials.

This became my "prayer sanctuary". At the time, I was leading two women's groups, and this prayer sanctuary became a lifeline. I would go there late at night after my children were sleeping, and kneel in the presence of our Lord of the universe. I will never forget the times when God met me there, revealing to me just a glimpse of the enormous depth of His love for the women I prayed for.

This prayer altar became a blessing in other ways as well. It set our home apart from those of our Taiwanese neighbors whose apartments housed god shelves with incense and glowing red lamps. Our "prayer altar" was the first thing guests saw when they came into our home.

Not long after we had set it up, an unbelieving neighbour came home with me one evening. As soon as she entered our living room, she was drawn to the prayer table. She walked over and picked up my Bible there, opening it to Psalm 68: 5, 6 : *"A father to the fatherless, a defender of widows is God in his holy dwelling..."* As she read it, her face softened in amazement. This breakthrough opened the way for us to talk about spiritual things together. God had met her at the prayer altar.

Discussion questions:

1. What are the obstacles you face in sustaining a daily quiet time of waiting on the Lord? How can we encourage and strengthen each other in our personal spiritual life?

2. How do you view the practice of setting up a designated place of prayer in the home? Would you prefer this to be in a public or private room? Why? What visual markers would designate it as a place of prayer?

3. The apostle Paul's letters reveal the supremely important place of prayer in the life of a spiritual leader. "Paul was a man of action because he was a man of prayer". [9] How could spending more time in prayer help the work-life balance of our missionaries?

---

9   J. Oswald Sanders, *Paul the Leader: A Vision for Christian Leadership Today*, (Eastbourne, UK: Kingsway Publications, 1983), page 81. Chapter 6 is titled "Paul's exemplary prayer life".

In the real world

A table to stimulate ideas for best practice in mission partnership. For further explanation, see page 7.

This chart has been partially filled in for you. Now you fill in the blanks.

Who? → When? ↓	Home Church	Missionary	Mission Agencies	External Partners
Continuous	➢ Encourage the missionary to protect work-life balance ➢ Take care of missionary kids	➢ Have spouse and family involved in ministry ➢ Take rest regularly ➢ Take care of health	➢ Leaders conduct an annual performance/ ministry review with each missionary ➢ Provide clear plans and job descriptions ➢ Provide good on-field supervision (quantity and quality) ➢ Provide missionaries with opportunities for continuous training and development of gifts and skills ➢ Ensure missionaries are not overloaded in the amount of work they do	➢ Provide training on self-management ➢ Offer opportunities to retreat for families
Recruitment				
Preparation				
On field				
Crisis				
Furlough				
Re-entry				

19

Organisational Values
Organisational Development

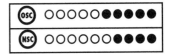

OSC	○○○○○●●●●●
NSC	○○○○○○○●●●●

The facts

A healthy organisation is not static and stagnant, but growing and developing—evolving to meet the challenges of a changing world. The importance of this ethos of growth is demonstrated by the fact that almost all of the factors related to organisational growth showed a correlation with retention. The ratings show that there is room for improvement in these areas, particularly in OSC, as NSC received a slightly higher overall rating by mission executives for performance and significance in these areas.

The data

Q. No.	Factor	OSC Health Indicator	✓	NSC Health Indicator	✓
40	Vision and purpose are shared and understood throughout the agency	○○○○○○○●●●	✓	○○○○○○○●●●	✓
41	Plans and job descriptions are communicated clearly to the missionary	○○○○○○●●●●	✓	○○○○○○●●●●	✓
42	There is a free flow of communication to and from the leadership	○○○○○○●●●●	✓	○○○○○○●●●●	
43	There is effective communication between sending base and field	○○○○●●●●●●	✓	○○○○○○○●●●	✓
44	Missionaries are included in major decisions related to the field	○○○○○○○●●●		○○○○○○●●●●	
45	Policies are well documented and understood	○○○○○●●●●●	✓	○○○○○○○●●●	✓

47	Most leaders are a good example of the agency's beliefs and values	OOOOOOOOO●	✓	OOOOOOOO●●	
48	Most leaders identify problems early and take appropriate action	OOOO●●●●●●	✓	OOOOOO●●●	✓
49	Good on-field supervision is provided (quantity and quality)	OOOO●●●●●●	✓	OOOOO●●●●	✓
50	Leaders conduct an annual performance/ministry review with each missionary	OOOO●●●●●●	✓	OOO●●●●●●	✓
55	Missionaries are provided with opportunities for continuous training and development of gifts and skills	OOOOOO●●●	✓	OOOOOO●●●	✓
60	Missionaries are committed and loyal to the agency	OOOOOO●●●	✓	OOOOOOOO●●	✓
64	Missionaries regularly evaluate and seek to improve the agency's ministry	OO●●●●●●●●	✓	OOOO●●●●●	

The key findings

✓ Missionaries regularly evaluate and seek to improve their ministry (Q64) received relatively low rating for performance and significance.

✓ Evaluation and improvement of ministry (Q64) was highly correlated with retention in OSC.

✓ There was a high rating of annual performance/ministry review with each missionary (Q50) and correlation with retention (preventable attrition).

✓ Free flow of communication with leadership (Q42) was highly correlated with retention in OSC.

✓ Leaders identify problems and take appropriate action (Q48) was strongly correlated with high retention.

✓ Continuous training and development of new gifts and skills (Q55) received a high rating in OSC and was strongly correlated with high retention.

✓ Vision & purpose (Q40) and Specific plans and job descriptions (Q41) received very high ratings and were correlated with high retention.

What it means

Rob Hay

Organisational development describes the conscious process that organisations undertake to change aspects of their focus or function. Many Western mission organisations undergo organisational development as a way of starting a significant change process. Often, the process is driven by external circumstances, such as dropping numbers of new missionaries or waning financial support by local churches or denominations, but sometimes the process is initiated for another reason, such as a new incoming director.

Interserve, is an example of an older and established mission that recently undertook a major organisational development process they called "Interserve Reloaded." Interserve has kindly shared some of the reasons why they engaged in the review and the process they used in the case study following.

A key part of any organisational development exercise is being able to take stock of the current status of the organisation—to form a realistic view of the strengths and weaknesses of the current work/ministry. Three questions give an indication of how ready organisations are to achieve a realistic evaluation [Q50 *Leaders conduct an annual performance/ministry review with each missionary*], [Q64 *Missionaries regularly evaluate and seek to improve the agency's ministry*] and [Q48 *Most leaders identify problems early and take appropriate action*]. Worryingly, for both NSC and OSC these three questions received the lowest ratings, suggesting that reflection, evaluation and proactive action are not strong current competencies.

The Interserve Reloaded case study shows reflection on knowing what they are about under the "Mission" and "Values" sections. The DMG case study illustrates how coming to a clear and meaningful vision statement can initiate an organisational development process with far reaching consequences for the organisation. Encouragingly, other questions that indicate reflection have somewhat better ratings [Q40 *Vision and purpose are shared and understood throughout the agency*] and [Q41 *Plans and job descriptions are communicated clearly to the missionary*]. Both factors are correlated with missionary retention in OSC and NSC.

Producing growth in an organisation is easier where the people within the organisation are also growing, Question 55 [Q55 *Missionaries are provided with opportunities for continuous training and development of gifts and skills*], showed that organisations recognised the need for this and were investing in their people as a result, which is considered important to OSC retention.

Finally, in any change process, and organisational development always involves change—both for the organisation and the individuals within it—workers and staff need to be continually involved so they feel they understand what is happening in the organisation and how it will affect them. Encouragingly, the rating in OSC and NSC was good in the area of communication, but given the centrality of it to any functioning, there is room for improvement—and improvement should be our aim, particularly in OSC where there is a strong correlation with retention.

As Paul and Fi (the writers of the Interserve case study) say, "Reloaded" is a work in progress. They have kindly made additional material, tools and documents from their work, available at www.worthkeeping.info and are posting updates occasionally as a "live" case study.

Reloaded: A radical organisational review

Fi McLachlan[1] and Paul Bendor-Samuel,[2] Interserve

Interserve has a long and rich heritage in the world of international mission. Started over 150 years ago by a small group of English women concerned for the plight of hidden women in India, Interserve has sought to respond to changing world patterns and adapted the way it works to meet current challenges. Interserve now has over 850 mission Partners and staff operating in more than 50 countries of the world with a focus on the peoples of Asia and the Arab world, serving in holistic mission.

'Interserve Reloaded' was the name given to the radical organisational review process begun in January 2004. This brief paper outlines why Interserve embarked on a comprehensive review and the process adopted. It should be read as a 'work in progress'.

Why an organisational review?

Knowing the time, finances, effort and potential pain required by a serious organisational review, why do it? There are a number of reasons why Interserve was ripe for an in-depth organisational review.

- The mission context in which Interserve works was rapidly changing:
  Non-western church and missions, church-to-church initiatives, lay movements - these are some of the major shifts affecting global missiology.

- The world context in which Interserve ministers was rapidly changing:

- Some of the critical issues faced include: increasing religious fundamentalism, post-modern/post-Christian humanism, increasing divide between rich and poor, unemployment, urbanisation, regional wars, people movements, HIV-AIDS.

- A number of exciting initiatives within Interserve had sprung up that challenged, in some ways, how Interserve had been working. These related to an experience of ministry through business, formation of new Interserve 'sending' Committees, new countries wanting to send workers through Interserve and work with diaspora and migrant communities.

Interserve was now a modest global organisation rather than a region-based mission. How could Interserve move from unity in uniformity to unity in diversity?

---

1   Fi McLachlan has spent all of her working life in social care and Christian organisations, becoming fascinated as to how they operate and challenged by how they can operate more effectively. She serves with Interserve as Director of Organisational Development, heavily involved in an international review and implementation plan which has resulted.

2   Dr Paul Bendor-Samuel has served as International Director of Interserve since October 2003. Paul and his wife, Liz, both of whom are medical doctors, served with their four sons for 12 years in North Africa with a Christian Development Agency. Initially involved in primary health, Paul has spent the last seven years as General Director. During this period they saw the range of roles and ministries of the agency broaden, but also experienced the thrill of seeing God at work developing a national church.

- Interserve international leadership structures were not designed to deliver the kind of leadership and services required by this growing and diverse organisation.

- The organisation was strong on decentralisation but this had contributed to a situation in which organisational units (sending and receiving countries) operated largely in isolation (silo structure). Interserve was increasingly unable to operate at both a local and global level

- The organisation had grown quite rapidly both in size and complexity. Many different nationalities from an increasingly international, rather than simply western, context worked together in a much wider range of countries. There was a growing urgency to redefine the identity of Interserve internationally

- A combination of all three factors cited above meant that Interserve internationally had neither the structures nor the processes to act strategically. Individuals were engaged in wonderful ministries but the organisation as a whole struggled to make strategic choices as to where and how to work.

In such circumstances a major, comprehensive organisational review was considered to be the only way to bring about development in an integrated, consistent and far-sighted manner.

Approach adopted

A quote from the introductory review document summarises the approach.

> "Purpose, values and vision will remain the critical components at the heart of this review. Structures are always secondary and will flow out of the former. 150 years of rich Interserve history is found principally in the purpose and values of the organisation."

The key to Reloaded has been its insistence on a process derived from Interserve's core values. These revolve around respect for the individual, diversity, participation, partnership and leadership as service. Any other approach would have failed. *If there is one transferable lesson from Reloaded it is that any major change process must be done in a manner consistent with the core values of the organisation.*

The following gives an idea of the comprehensive range addressed by the review (adapted from the work of Bryn Hughes).

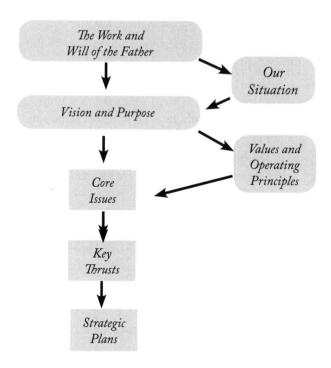

Discerning the Will and Work of the Father

> To strengthen Interserve's understanding of what God is doing in mission today.

Our Situation

> To do an organisational audit that allowed Interserve to identify perceived current strengths and weaknesses.

Vision and Purpose

> To envision the future, agreeing what kind of organisation Interserve wanted to be and to identify the specificities of Interserve's mission call in the light of the wide-ranging movements cited above.

Principles and Values

> To redefine and make explicit Interserve's operating principles and values in the light of her context and call. This includes identifying the strengths and weaknesses of the organisational culture.

Core Issues

> To identify the critical, strategic areas for organisational development that would enable Interserve, under God, to become the community it is called to be and effectively fulfil its mission.

Key Action Steps

> For each strategic area, to identify a group of action steps that will move the organisation forward.

Strategic Plans

> To elaborate the specific plans that would enable them to take appropriate and coherent action in the light of key organisational Action Steps.

Action

There were three main phases to the review

Reflection Phase: January to May 2004

This involved a widespread organisational listening exercise over five months. Two-hundred individuals and around 350-400 people in groups throughout the organisation participated in discussions and responded to four study modules on:

- The Will and Work of the Father (What's God doing today?)
- An Organisational Audit
- Our Mission
- Our Values

In addition, partner agencies, other mission agencies, supporters and churches were approached

The thoughts and ideas gathered through the responses to the modules were carefully analysed and provided the basis for a gathering of the International Council made up of country leaders in May 2004. From this meeting came a series of key Statements of Intent and the creation of five Task Forces.

Design Phase: May 2004 to September 2005

The five Task Forces addressed the Core Issues identified by the May 2004 leaders meeting. They considered:

- Leadership, Governance and Structures
- Internationalisation and Partnership
- Financial resourcing
- Communication and Prayer
- Business as Mission

The Task Forces provided initial reports in March 2005. All in Interserve were invited to study their recommendations, ask questions and make suggestions. The reports were redrafted in the light of feedback ahead of an international leaders meeting in September 2005.

In parallel, work was done throughout the Fellowship to revise foundation documents, including: Purpose, Vision, Values and Operating Principles, and Strategic Priorities.

Decisions and Implementation Phase: September 2005 onwards

The detailed proposals from the Task Forces were taken to the International Council in September 2005. These recommendations were discussed fully and amendments made. In the end there was near unanimous approval for all 77 recommendations brought to the Council.

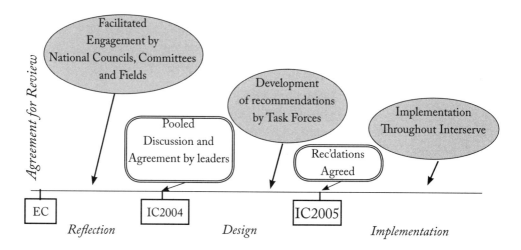

The whole process had been a focus for prayer, including a global week of prayer held during the days of the September council. The final decision making process also had an intercessory team working alongside through the final week.

Reloaded, as a review, was completed in September 2005. However, this marked the beginning of the most challenging phase, that of implementation. What had taken 20 months to complete has now to be turned into reality. As such it is still a work in progress.

Reflections on the process

Below are listed some of the beliefs about review and change that Interserve has sought to operate by.

- Name it! – Interserve decided to name the process, to define a beginning and an end, to be clear what was part of the review and what was not. Reloaded became a name on everyone's lips, and will be part of the organisational memory of Interserve.

- Involvement – if a review is to be understood and effective, it needs to involve those who will be affected by the outcomes. Around 50% of Interserve took an active part in giving feedback initially and there was opportunity to continue to do so all the way through the process. Around 50 partners, staff and council members from all parts of the Fellowship, participated in the Task Forces. People knew they were heard and their suggestions often taken up.

- Review by your values- this review process would not have succeeded in agreement on decisions of change had Interserve not operated by its own values throughout the process. Those values will now underpin the implementation process.

- Communication – review and change is less prone to raise anxiety amongst those in the organisation if people know what is happening. It was helpful to have a 'road map' for people to chart the journey. Interserve sought to do this as creatively as possible: four DVD's were made to introduce and chart progress; articles were written; a new in-house monthly Newslink publication was generated; PowerPoint presentations were made to help leaders communicate; important documents were translated to major languages to facilitate access for all. In addition, communication was two-way, with people able to have input at any point, whether to those involved in leading Task Forces or to the international leadership team. When there is two way communication, reasons for changes are more readily accepted even if the outcome is not what was hoped for.

- Make the linkages – it is important for people to see the link between their feedback and concerns, being translated into rigorous debate, research and influencing the final proposals. Right up to the final moments of decisions for change, individuals and groups were influencing thinking.

- Keep to the timeline! Reloaded required a significant period of time to undertake the First and Second Phase. But people did know it was going to end! The International Team and Task Force leaders worked hard to ensure that the time deadlines were adhered to, which meant that there was not the feeling of being in perpetual uncertainty.

- Remain God-dependent. Interserve started out with the aim of seeking to align itself with what the Father is doing. There was regular and persistent prayer for God to guide and for God to be glorified. In the September 2005 International Council, leaders were very aware that God is able to do "immeasurably more than we could ask or imagine." He did. Not only was there agreement over a wide range of challenging organisational changes, there was also a deep spirit of unity and fellowship.

Conclusion

The implementation is still a work in progress. Time will show whether the review has achieved its goal, to enable Interserve to align herself with God. One thing Reloaded has demonstrated, that despite the demands and costs, a major organisational review can build vision, strategic focus and unity whilst engaging in significant change to long held processes and structures.

Development of a vision statement at DMG leads to organisational development

Detlef Blöcher,[3] DMG, Germany

German Missionary Fellowship (DMG) was founded 55 years ago. Under the leadership of dynamic mission practitioners, it has grown from small beginnings to one of the largest evangelical missionary sending agencies in Germany. At present, there are some 330 missionaries serving in 70 countries with DMG.

At the end of 1999, there was a change in the leadership: one Executive Director retired and his successor was appointed. The new Executive Director has led the agency through a process of major organisational change.

Like many evangelical mission agencies in Germany, DMG did not have a vision statement. Therefore, the new Director immediately gathered the 12 person leadership team and initiated an extensive discussion on the agency's identity and ethos. He asked them: *Who are we?* and *Where do we come from?* During these interactions, various perceptions surfaced because people had different memories, understanding, and priorities. The leaders had to listen carefully to each other. Everyone had his/her say. Details were unpacked. Gradually, they moved towards a consensus. Then, as the next step, the leadership team identified their fundamental values and reflected on their practices. They asked one another: *What are our essentials and basic principles?* Thereafter, they worked on the agency's purpose, aim, and vision. They talked for many hours, prayed together, and listened to God's voice.

This same process was then repeated in the agency's board meetings (seven people), in the staff meetings (34 people), and in the council meetings as well. These extended discussions led to a growing awareness of their identity. After 11 months, DMG drafted the first version of a "vision statement." This document was then sent out to all 310 active missionaries and everyone was invited to provide feedback. In fact, hundreds of e-mails were returned with questions, comments, and suggested changes, and the Director answered each personally. The feedback resulted in two more drafts which were distributed and discussed openly again.

Finally, the vision statement was presented at the agency's mission council (a wider governing body consisting of some 50 people) and the document was passed without a single abstention.

The Director recalls: "The development of our vision statement took us much, much longer than expected. I had believed that it would be completed in a couple of months, but it took us two full years. Yet the time and effort was well spent as everyone got involved. Everyone had the opportunity to speak up and be heard;

---

3 Dr. Detlef Blöcher is a physicist by training and he worked in medical research at German universities and in the Middle East. From 1991 to 1999, he served as Personnel Director of German Missionary Fellowship (DMG) and since then as its CEO. He is also chairman of the German Evangelical Mission Alliance and an Associate of the WEA Mission Commission.

even if everyone's personal preference was not adopted. My personal correspondence with many missionaries has built trust between the leadership and the mission family. By the open discussion, we have grown together as a whole mission. New traditions of active participation, open communication, and joint reflection have been introduced."

The Director continues: "In the beginning, not everyone saw the significance of a vision statement. In fact, many evangelicals in our country have strong reservations about it. Many considered it as humanistic management in contrast to the leading of the Holy Spirit. It took us some time to change our organisational culture. Yet through this process we have become a learning community: listening to each other, learning from each other, respecting our differences. Our diversity is not a threat to unity. Instead, it is our greatest asset by which we can bless and enrich each other. "

With the vision statement in hand, the leaders at DMG noticed a number of discrepancies with their present structures and operations which had developed over time. Times had changed and the reasons for some structures and styles of operation were no longer valid. Others were obvious inconsistencies.

"The vision statement is not for the files, but it should be the starting point for organisational development. Form should follow function," the Director explains. The vision statement has led to a total revision of all areas of operations including their legal set-up and organisational structure. Leaders at DMG adopted shared leadership in a consultative style. They delegated responsibility, adjusted committees, introduced flexible and appropriate policies, eliminated superfluous rules, implemented new candidate selection and preparation processes, encouraged member care and life-long learning, active participation of sending churches, and initiated new mission programmes. All these changes were derived from the newly established vision statement.

For three years, everyone at DMG staff has worked on these organisational changes. "I have explained the rationale for the suggested changes time and again, in order to give everyone the opportunity to contribute to the solution," the Director continues. "In addition, we need open and detailed information so that everyone learns what is happening in the future and how the changes will affect him/her. This builds trust. It provides security and it leads to stability and peace. I have tried hard to lead people along the process, and it is worth the effort. We also need to give sufficient time for adjustment, so that people can follow and feel part of a caring community."

"I have previously witnessed unfortunate change processes in a number of other mission agencies. Often those changes were driven by external consultants who rushed through without proper staff participation. In these cases, the mission family was confronted with the decision as a done deal and they felt alienated because they could not contribute to the process. The change process in itself is as important as the final result."

The Director has challenged the mission family at DMG: "I want you all to judge my decisions and my leadership as to whether it is consistent with our vision statement." Today, the whole mission family throughout DMG continues to grow into a more caring community.

Discussion questions:

1. Does your organisation have a vision statement? If yes, think about it, and consider if it motivates your staff in their ministry. If not, why not? How could you work on it?

2. How does your mission agency introduce needed changes? Do you include your staff and missionaries? To what extent can/should they participate in the decisions?

3. In what ways are your staff and missionaries considered as experts in their field of speciality with extremely valuable insights, expertise and resources? How could your organisation tap in to their experience?

In the real world

A table to stimulate ideas for best practice in mission partnership. For further explanation, see page 7.

This chart has been partially filled in for you. Now you fill in the blanks.

Who? → When? ↓	Home Church	Missionary	Mission Agencies	External Partners
Continuous	➤ Create a culture of change ➤ Update vision and strategy regularly	➤ Regularly evaluate and seek to improve the agency's ministry ➤ Provide information and feedback from the field	➤ Identify problems early and take appropriate action ➤ Share and explain vision and purpose throughout the agency ➤ Assign missionaries to roles according to their gifting and experience ➤ Include missionaries in major decisions related to the field ➤ Create a culture where vision and strategy are continuously worked on	➤ Provide consultation to update vision and strategy ➤ Train and coach in transition periods
Recruitment				
Preparation				
On field				
Crisis				
Furlough				
Re-entry				

20

Organisational Values
Communication

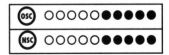

The facts

Communication has been described as the lubrication of an organisation. If it is not used liberally and regularly, movement and functions become stilted and jerky rather than smooth and problem-free. Encouragingly, the performance and significance rating given by mission executives is reasonable across this area: five for both OSC and NSC. However, given the centrality of communication, it would be wise to work hard to improve these ratings still further. Almost all of the individual ratings correlate with high retention in both OSC and NSC, and although the overall rating is acceptable, there is much variation among individual ratings which we will explore below.

The data

Q. No.	Factor	OSC Health Indicator	✓	NSC Health Indicator	✓
40	Vision and purpose are shared and understood throughout the agency	○○○○○○○●●●	✓	○○○○○○○●●●	✓
41	Plans and job descriptions are communicated clearly to the missionary	○○○○○○●●●●	✓	○○○○○○●●●●	✓
42	There is a free flow of communication to and from the leadership	○○○○○○●●●●	✓	○○○○○○●●●●	✓
43	There is effective communication between sending base and field	○○○○●●●●●●	✓	○○○○○○○●●●	✓
44	Missionaries are included in major decisions related to the field	○○○○○○○●●●		○○○○○○●●●●	
45	Policies are well documented and understood	○○○○○●●●●●	✓	○○○○○○○●●●	✓

50	Leaders conduct an annual performance/ministry review with each missionary	○○○○●●●●●●	✓	○○○●●●●●●●	✓
51	There are documented and adequate procedures for handling complaints from missionaries	○○○○○●●●●●	✓	○○○○○●●●●●	✓
64	Missionaries regularly evaluate and seek to improve the agency's ministry	○○●●●●●●●●	✓	○○○○●●●●●●	
79	Home churches are encouraged to be involved in the life and ministry of their missionary	○○○○○○○○●●	✓	○○○○○●●●●●	✓

The key findings

✓ Effective communication with leadership (Q42) is strongly correlated with retention in OSC.

✓ Effective communication between field leadership and sending base (Q43) in OSC and NSC is correlated with high retention.

✓ Missionaries are included in major decisions (Q44) has a weak correlation with retention in OSC—but a negative correlation in NSC (counter-cultural in NSC?).

✓ Policies well documented and understood (Q45) received a high rating and was correlated with high retention.

✓ Annual performance/ministry reviews (Q50) received a high rating regarding preventable prevention, and was correlated with high retention.

✓ Clear procedure for handling complaints (Q51) was clearly correlated with high retention.

✓ Missionaries regularly evaluate and seek to improve the agency's ministry (Q64) was correlated with high retention in OSC.

✓ Home church is encouraged to be involved in the life of the missionary (Q79) received a high rating in OSC and correlated with high retention.

What it means

Rob Hay

There was significant variation in the performance and significance ratings given by mission executives for questions on communication, and the variation should be understood, especially given the importance of the topic of communication. Many of the other chapters highlight the need for effective communication to make their areas function well, which is a reminder for just how important communication is.

One of the most surprising results in the study was Question 44 [Q44 *Missionaries are included in major decisions related to the field*], which received a fairly good rating in OSC and NSC, and yet did not correlate with retention in OSC and displayed a slightly negative correlation in NSC. The negative correlation in NSC could be explained by different decision-making practices being culturally normal in those countries, but in the OSC, appears to be contrary to assumptions and research. Possibly, correlation was not detectable because it is assumed that missionaries want to be included in decision-making that relates to their lives and ministry. If the assumption was widespread across high and low retaining agencies, no statistically significant difference would be evident. Given the fairly high rating in OSC, this argument could be supported from the data.

Alternatively, the lack of correlation may have resulted from the fact that mission executives of home offices were interviewed, and they are normally senior people who have built "consultation" into the structures and policies. However, they fail to recognise that the middle age generation (referred to as "Boomers" in the West), who make up the bulk of the current leadership, and the younger generation ("Generation X" in the West) who may be the majority of the active missionaries, each require different styles of involvement and communication other than that which suited the senior generation ("Builders" in the West). This underlines the need for structural reforms and organisational development.

In all of the other questions under this area there was a correlation with retention, often in both OSC and NSC. They can be discussed in three categories:

Communicating: expectations, behaviour and boundaries

Healthy human functioning happens when people know what others expect of them in terms of behaviour, work, and relationships with those around them. In the context of work, people need to know what they can and cannot do, what they are being asked to achieve, with whom they should relate, who takes responsibility for them, and for whom they should take responsibility. In the results of ReMAP II, these issues are vitally important as all correlate with retention. One area has been discussed in Chapter 18—the area of work-life balance. Generally, organisations have to encourage a proportion of their work force to work harder than they would choose to do so and that has been recognised for many years. What has only been widely recognised in recent years, is that there is also a proportion of the work force who need to be encouraged to work less, and to rest, be refreshed and have interests outside of work. In mission, there may be some people who indeed do need to be encouraged to work harder, but by far the greater number need to be assisted to work less (at least in terms of time—see Chapter 18 for an explanation of why that may actually be more productive). The communication of the vision of the organisation, the demonstration of the values of the organisation—often in how things are communicated, as much as what is communicated—can influence and affect an issue like work-life balance very significantly. Policies and procedures can encourage correct and healthy behaviour in work-rest issues as well as channelling and guiding the energy and effort of individuals towards a common shared aim (the vision of the organisation) to create a far more effective synergy than could ever be achieved or hoped for individually.

The rating of Question 40 [Q40 *Vision and purpose are shared and understood throughout the agency*] is reasonably good. However, given that this is a key function of the leaders who gave the ratings, it would be useful to explore in an organisation if the missionaries have understood and own the vision and purpose and feel that they themselves have a clear understanding of what is expected of them. There is a very clear difference between communicating something and understanding it, and organisations need to be sure that those at the grass roots of the organisation both feel communicated with and have developed the understanding of what the leadership is aiming at. Expectations need to be an essential part of the regular performance reviews with their supervisors. Question 50 [Q50 *Leaders conduct an annual performance/ministry review with each missionary*] explored this, but unfortunately received a relatively low rating. The effectiveness of communication can further be explored by taking the opportunity at staff conferences or team meetings to ask people and/or teams to describe the vision in their own words or its relevance to their area of work and ministry.

Questions 41 [Q41 *Plans and job descriptions are communicated clearly to the missionary*], and 45 [Q45 *Policies are well documented and understood*], received only reasonable ratings and there is need to improve these communication functions, for both correlate with retention. Too many missionaries lack a job description entirely (see Chapter 6 for more discussion of this), or because they are covering multiple roles, they have several job descriptions. That can even lead to contradictions between roles and cause much confusion. Job descriptions also can be out of date, which happens frequently in mission because social and political circumstances change rapidly. Often, the time from when a job is identified and the job description developed to when a person has actually been recruited and fills the job is long. The job description might be out of date or at least in need of updating before the post commences. Include a review of the job description in the regular performance interview with the supervisor (presuming the annual review actually happens and is meaningful).

Communicating: between organisations

Just as it is unusual to find an isolated missionary with no involvement in an organisation, so you rarely find an isolated organisation, with no involvement in another organisation. Often, partnerships form between mission agencies, between churches, and also between agencies and the local church. With modern communication and ease of international travel, people suppose that communication should be easier and less fraught with difficulties than in the past. However, as Marjory Foyle highlighted in a paper on the history of member care,[1] in many respects communication is harder and more stressful because of its immediacy. Historically,

---

1   Marjory Foyle, "History of Member Care," Redcliffe Consultation on Missionary Mental Health, (Gloucester: Redcliffe College, 2003).

there was often great autonomy on the field simply because of the distance and time delay involved in communications between home and field. Independent-spirited pioneer missionaries who did not want to follow the direction of the home council had the excuse of late or non-existent mail and a visit from the mission leadership was an unlikely event. While that had its own challenges, the immediacy of phone and e-mail and the ability to be almost anywhere within 24-36 hours means that leadership expects communication and decision-making authority to be sought. Conversely, missionaries expect information and consultation from the leadership.

Ensuring these expectations are met is important, but communication to and from the leadership [Q42 *There is a free flow of communication to and from the leadership*] is an area in which we are only doing moderately well. This is stronger however than communication between the sending base and field [Q43 *There is effective communication between sending base and field*], which if you read the account of the Edinburgh 1910 mission conference, is a long-standing problem. This was rated at just four out of ten in OSC, but encouragingly seven out of ten in NSC, although some NSC mission leaders made the point that they are generally sending people a shorter distance from their home-base than many of the OSC mission agencies.

Increasingly in OSC, home churches are wanting, and often demanding, a greater involvement in the life of their missionary other than simply praying and giving financial support. Indeed, in some instances they are choosing to send missionaries directly without any involvement of a mission agency.[2] OSC Mission leaders felt that they were involving the home church [Q79 *Home churches are encouraged to be involved in the life and ministry of their missionary*] with a rating of eight out of ten, whereas the NSC agency leaders felt that they were only moderately successful (five out of ten). Anecdotally, in the UK, many church leaders feel that they and their churches are not as involved in the life and ministry of their missionaries as they would like. This, like a number of areas, may be a perception issue: agency leaders think they are encouraging churches to be involved but perhaps the churches feel it is insufficient or the wrong type of involvement.[3] The poorer rating by NSC leaders may demonstrate a realistic estimation of their own ability, which takes into account that fact that many of them have more challenges in communicating, i.e., poor e-mail connections, limited resources for visits, etc..

Communicating: problems, challenges and changes

As we have said, communication overall is difficult, but to challenge behaviour, policies and practices is doubly difficult. For this reason, healthy organisations need to actively seek this kind of feedback from its staff and missionaries. Seeking feedback is still a struggle, with a very poor rating of just two out of ten [Q64

---

2   During the data collection phase of ReMAP II in the UK, some churches were contacted that had sent their missionaries directly ten years ago. Interestingly, many of them said that they had changed this policy and now partnered (albeit on a much more even footing than before) with mission agencies, as they had found the provision of a robust support network (in particular crisis member care) to be expensive and logistically difficult for the sole responsibility of the local church.

3   For an interesting model of church-agency partnership, see the case study by Paul Adams and Terry Miller in Chapter 8.

Missionaries regularly evaluate and seek to improve the agency's ministry], yet a very strong correlation with retention in OSC, though not in NSC.

Ideally, there should be free flowing communication between staff, missionaries, and leadership as well as structured processes for input into the agency leadership and direction. However, as highlighted above, this is not generally happening. If both of those channels fail to function, the fail-safe should be a robust complaints and grievance procedure to ensure that missionaries can vent their frustration before it reaches an unbearable level and they leave the organisation. Question 51 [Q51 *There are documented and adequate procedures for handling complaints from missionaries*] shows that agencies feel they are doing adequately on this issue. However, given the poor ratings on the other communication issues, this fall back needs to be further improved and become a truly fail-safe system as it has a significant correlation with retention.

Change of placement of a missionary

Vanessa Hung,[4] Hong Kong Association of Christian Missions, Hong Kong

After Jim completed his studies at Bible College, he became a pastor of a small church in a suburban town. He was well accepted by the members in his congregation, and they loved him very much.

Some years later, Jim received a missionary call from God. He had a burden for cross-cultural ministry to an unreached people group. He decided to become a long-term missionary, and he applied to Elton Mission. The church where Jim had ministered and another church in the same denomination became his sending churches. The two churches agreed to support Jim both financially and spiritually. Then, Jim started a support group, shared his vision with the people, and taught them how to support him. His support group was close to him, and he promised to write regularly to them when he left for the mission field. After a lengthy process, Jim and his family headed for the mission field.

Several years later, Elton Mission agency was searching for an administrator for the home office, but they could not find one. Then they thought of Jim, and decided to invite Jim to take up the new post at home. They approached him to consider this new appointment. After much thinking and praying, Jim agreed to come home and to take up the post of administrator. He informed his support group about his new placement.

Unfortunately, for some reason, the majority of members in both his sending churches were not informed by the support group, so they remained unaware of what was going on. It was not until Jim had returned home that many members

---

4 Vanessa Hung was ReMAP II Country Coordinator for Hong Kong. Vanessa graduated from Columbia International University in 1993, where she received her Masters of Art in Mission. Since then, she has served in the Hong Kong Association of Christian Missions as a mission researcher. She has conducted several missionary research projects in Hong Kong, and she has a good understanding of Hong Kong mission churches and their missionaries.

in the sending churches learned about Jim's new assignment. Some members were furious because they had not been informed earlier. They felt that they were not respected either by Jim or Elton Mission.

After much discussion at their Church Board meetings, both churches voted to withdraw their support to Jim. According to their church mission constitution, the churches should only support frontline missionaries who are doing evangelism and church planting. Because Jim had returned from the mission field, and he was now involved in some other work, he was no longer qualified to receive the church's support.

Sadly, our story does not end here. Members from Jim's church protested the decision that their Deacon Board had made. They loved their former pastor and they wanted to support him. Although the deacon board explained the situation to them and showed them the mission constitution, they could not convince the church members. The church members took the drastic step of withdrawing their faith promise support from their church's mission fund and they sent money directly to Elton Mission, to support their former pastor.

The above event almost caused to the church to split. It was very unfortunate that a communication breakdown led to such unhappiness in the two local churches.

Discussion questions:

The above case illustrates poor communication of several different parties.

1. What could have (should have) been done to improve communications:
    *   between the missionary and his sending/supporting churches?
    *   between the mission-sending agency and each of the two churches?
    *   among deacons on the board (before they told church members)?
    *   between the leaders of each church and their members?

2. What were the expectations of each party (missionary, agency, local church) and were these laid out clearly?

3. What went wrong with the communication process?

4. What would you have done differently if you were Jim's mission leader?

Confidentiality and trust in member care

Bob and Nancy,[5] Middle East

Working in the West as a Christian therapist, Bob had never been required to inform any church leadership or employer of a client's struggles or sinful behaviour. Unless the legal requirement to report potential or existing harm to self or others was crossed, whatever the client told Bob stayed with him. Arriving on the mission field brought a quick challenge to those ethical guidelines.

The field missionary does not live the independent, autonomous life of the Western Christian. Most serve in small team communities. Their mission colleagues may also be their church body, neighbours, and social connections. They live and work as a team, supporting each other as they reach out to the host culture community. In such a small community, the actions of one team member will significantly impact the whole team and potentially affect the team's safety, stability, witness, and reputation in the host community.

When we arrived on the field, we found that the leadership (for team, country, and field) had been providing the member care to workers for some time. As we assumed the role of member care providers, the various leaders were naturally concerned to know the progress of individuals they had previously been involved with. Leaders also felt a concern to know the spiritual and emotional health of the field members, recognising that the personal lives of the field members impacted their professional lives and that of the team as a whole. One leader told us that withholding information from him would be like asking him to steer a ship along a rocky coast without telling him where the rocks were. We soon realised that we could not function with a Western model of professional confidentiality. We would need the support and confidence of mission leadership.

During the first couple of years, we had many conversations with our field leadership. We talked about the need of each leader to know the condition of his field worker. At the same time, we explained the need for a member care provider to maintain a certain level of confidentiality in order for the worker to feel safe to seek and obtain help. We gradually learned to understand and value each other's perspective and needs, and to build our trust in each other. The leaders had not previously had a professional therapist serving on their field, and we had not previously served as on-field member care providers.

As we began our new roles, we looked around for models of how such relationships were handled on other fields. We couldn't find any other examples of anyone serving in exactly the same capacity we were entering. Together with the field leadership, we had to find our own way of doing member care as we went along.

---

5 Bob is a Christian therapist with Master's degrees in Psychology and in Marriage Family and Child Counselling. Nancy is a lay counsellor and seminar instructor. Bob and Nancy have lived in the Middle East for six years, serving as member care specialists providing counselling, pastoral care, training, and debriefing to missionaries from a variety of mission organisations.

We were given the job title of "Field Member Care Officers" and we were part of the field leadership team. We found this title affected some people's freedom to share with us. Some saw us as having the authority to punish or send workers home. Others were concerned that we would pass anything they shared with us to the field leaders.

We have revised our title to "Field Member Care Consultants." As consultants, we offer advice and insight, but we are not decision-makers. We are no longer official members of the field leadership team, although we still attend field leadership team meetings to advocate for member care and to stay abreast of developments on the field. This change has removed the incorrect perception that we had the power to punish. We have emphasised that our role is to facilitate healing and wholeness, not to bring punishment or exposure. The field leadership have been supportive of our role. They continually advocate that country and team leaders as well as field members should access our ministry freely and confidentially.

To function effectively on the field, member care providers need the complete trust and confidence of the field leadership. Without such trust, a member care provider would not be accessed by workers, nor informed about potential member care needs developing on the field, nor encouraged to develop programmes, and strengthen personal rapport with field members.

Trust was gradually built up as both sides embraced the potential of our mutual partnership. As member care providers, we could empower field members to stay long-term by addressing issues as they developed and before they became overwhelming. We could provide the resources for field workers to deal with personal struggles on the field, rather than having to return to the home country for help. Instead of seeing us as outsiders who could recommend that vital workers leave the field, the leaders came to recognise us as facilitators who come alongside to strengthen and empower the missionary, so that each person serves in wholeness with the strength to live sacrificially for the sake of the gospel.

Both the leaders and the member care providers decided that a set of Confidentiality Guidelines was essential for building trust. We developed these to address the special needs of our mission community and presented them to the leadership. The Confidentiality Guidelines were clearly defined and accepted by both the leadership and the member care providers. In developing an appropriate set of Confidentiality Guidelines, we worked through several rough drafts and discussed the concerns and perspectives of both sides. We eventually identified what behaviour needed to be disclosed and under what conditions.

All of us then agreed on the Confidentiality Guidelines, and the document became a part of our field policy. Whenever a new member joins our field, a copy of this document is given to that person.

The development of a clear set of Confidentiality Guidelines has helped to reduce tension and misunderstandings on the field.

We have gained the trust of leaders who need to know about the well-being of their members in order to lead them. This includes the leader who had been concerned about the rocks threatening his ship. The Confidentiality Guidelines have identified which rocks we would tell him about. We told him that he would need to trust us to tell him about rocks that would threaten the ship, and not about the rocks that posed no threat. This has given him a sense of security that he would not sail blindly through dangerous waters.

We have also gained the confidence of field workers. Since implementing the guidelines as field policy, we have not experienced any decrease in field members seeking us out or sharing sensitive issues with us. They know that we will work in their best interest. Disclosure, when necessary, will not be for the purpose of punishment, but rather to facilitate the access of other resources to meet the field members' needs for spiritual and emotional healing and restoration. In fact, disclosure is a rare exception and not the norm on our field.

The Confidentiality Guidelines have clearly defined the boundary for safety and support to both the field leaders and the workers.[6]

Confidentiality Guidelines

As Christians we value confidentiality and renounce gossip. We want to honour each other and protect each other from shame or humiliation by the inappropriate disclosure of things told in confidence. However, we also recognise that keeping a secret can at times be damaging to the sharer's spiritual, emotional or physical well being. At times secrecy may even place others at risk, damage the integrity and witness of the team, or even bring dishonour to the name of our Lord.

"Disclosure" is not to be seen as "telling" on someone, but as lovingly helping the person pursue the best way forward for healing and restoration and to ensure that all the resources they need to accomplish this are made available to them. The enemy works in the dark and brings bondage. What is brought to the light and love of Jesus can receive healing and grace. That is the goal and purpose of disclosure.

With this in mind it is important to clarify which topics warrant disclosure, how disclosure is to take place, and to whom.

Who must disclose: It is recognized that every field member, from associate to long-termer to Team Leader, Country Leader, and Field Personnel is a "member care provider". (From this point on referred to as the "caregiver".) We are all admonished to bear one another's burdens, and to provide mutual care for each other. With that in mind, care may include disclosure by any field member. We abhor the thought of looking for offences to "report" about each other, but also recognise that to truly love each other occasionally may mean helping each other find help and resources beyond what the person was able to find for themselves. At this point

---

6 A copy of these guidelines are provided as a word document that you can download from the website and modify for your own use. We are very grateful to Bob and Nancy for allowing their guidelines to be used as a resource for others.

disclosure, the seeking out of additional help and resources, is appropriate in the field context.

In addition:

- If the caregiver feels the need to get another opinion, they are encouraged to contact the field Member Care Consultants.

- If the caregiver is having difficulty focusing on the other people under his or her care they are encouraged to contact the Member Care Consultants.

- In the counselling process if the way forward seems unclear or stalled, the Member Care Consultants will be brought into the treatment plan.

Disclosure is to be made to either the Field Leader or the field's Member Care Consultant, recognizing that the FL and the MCC will share the disclosure with each other.

Before disclosure the individual will be notified of the need to disclose according to the agreed upon guidelines. Hopefully the field member will voluntarily disclose. If needed, the caregiver will accompany the field member to meet with the FL or MCC, but will act only as an emotional support and not a spokesperson.

Issues requiring disclosure:

1. Child molestation if either the perpetrator or the child is a field member or there is significant reason to suspect it has happened. If not sure, contact the field Member Care Consultants.

2. Adultery – emotional or physical.

3. Any ongoing sexual intimacy outside of marriage.

4. Pornography use coupled with an unwillingness to seek help from a trained therapist. This assumes the individual has a history of use and this is not just a very rare occurrence. The same applies to women involved in explicit romance novels under the same conditions.

5. The individual gives enough information to convince the caregiver that he or she will do harm to himself /herself or to another person.

6. An individual has rejected Christianity, is in rebellion, and has embraced other beliefs such as New Age, Islam, Buddhism, etc. Not just questioning as is common in PTS (post trauma stress) response.

7. Fraud or other criminal act.

In formal counselling situations the counselee should be notified of the limitations of confidentially before counselling begins. If information needs to be shared the counsellor should also clarify who will be notified and how the information will be stored. *Information needs to be kept in a secure location.*

Mission partners should sign and date the above guidelines.

Discussion questions:

1. Have Member Care Confidentiality Guidelines been developed for your current area of service (whether you are a field leader, field member care provider, field member, home office personnel, church leader, etc.)?

2. If not, what are your own personal Member Care Confidentiality Guidelines?

3. In what way does past training, experience or culture influence your personal or organisation's Confidentiality Guidelines?

4. What member care issues should be disclosed to the field leader? What should be disclosed to the agency home office? What should be disclosed to the home church?

In the real world

A table to stimulate ideas for best practice in mission partnership. For further explanation, see page 7.

This chart has been partially filled in for you. Now you fill in the blanks.

Who? → When? ↓	Home Church	Missionary	Mission Agencies	External Partners
Continuous	➤ Ensure the free flow of communication to and from the leadership ➤ Ensure effective communication between sending base and field ➤ Commit to regular communication with the missionary ➤ Teach relationships as a lifestyle	➤ Be willing to be transparent and share what is necessary ➤ Be committed to take care that communication is open and effective ➤ Allocate significant time for communication.	➤ Communicate plans and job descriptions clearly to the missionary ➤ Ensure the free flow of communication to and from the leadership ➤ Ensure effective communication between sending base and field	➤ Provide general training in communication ➤ Facilitate communication through internet, etc. ➤ Teach cross-cultural communication
Recruitment				
Preparation				
On field				
Crisis				
Furlough				
Re-entry				

21

Leadership

The facts

Leadership is the pivot point around which the organisation turns. Good leadership needs to be combined with good communication and other important aspects of organisational functioning, like direction, values etc., but leadership shapes the health of an organisation like nothing else. The author Edgar Powell has been quoted as saying, "No organisation is stronger than the quality of its leadership, or ever extends its constituency far beyond the degree to which its leadership is representative." Mission organisations are no different, as the ReMAP II results demonstrate. Fifteen out of the sixteen questions that examined aspects of leadership had a strong relationship with missionary retention. Unfortunately, for such a key area, only the character of the leader stood out as being significant, while skills and experience were rated more or less as mediocre, and we cannot afford to remain so.

The data

Q. No.	Factor	OSC Health Score	✓	NSC Health Score	✓
42	There is a free flow of communication to and from the leadership	○○○○○○●●●●	✓	○○○○○○●●●●	
44	Missionaries are included in major decisions related to the field	○○○○○○○●●●		○○○○○○●●●●	
45	Policies are well documented and understood	○○○○○●●●●●	✓	○○○○○○○●●●	✓
47	Most leaders are a good example of the agency's beliefs and values	○○○○○○○○○●	✓	○○○○○○○○●●	
48	Most leaders identify problems early and take appropriate action	○○○○●●●●●●	✓	○○○○○○●●●●	✓

No.	Statement				
49	Good on-field supervision is provided (quantity and quality)	○○○○●●●●●●	✓	○○○○○●●●●●	✓
50	Leaders conduct an annual performance/ministry review with each missionary	○○○○●●●●●●	✓	○○○●●●●●●●	✓
51	There are documented and adequate procedures for handling complaints from missionaries	○○○○○●●●●●	✓	○○○○○●●●●●	✓
54	Ongoing language and culture training are actively encouraged	○○○○○○○●●●	✓	○○○○○○●●●●	
56	Missionaries are assigned roles according to their gifting and experience	○○○○○○●●●●		○○○○○○●●●●	✓
57	Missionaries are given room to shape and develop their own ministry	○○○○○○○○●●	✓	○○○○○○○●●●	✓
60	Missionaries are committed and loyal to the agency	○○○○○○●●●●	✓	○○○○○○○○●●	✓
61	Missionaries are generally not overloaded in the amount of work they do	○●●●●●●●●●	✓	○○○○●●●●●●	✓
64	Missionaries regularly evaluate and seek to improve the agency's ministry	○○●●●●●●●●	✓	○○○○●●●●●●	
71	Missionary teams are effective in providing each other with mutual support	○○○○●●●●●●		○○○○○○●●●●	✓
80	Missionaries usually receive sustained financial support that is adequate for their needs	○○○○○○○●●●	✓	○○○○○●●●●●	✓

The key findings

✓ Overall, questions regarding leadership were strongly correlated with high retention in OSC and NSC.

✓ Example of leader (Q47) was rated very highly and it was correlated with retention in OSC. Apparently, good leaders can even offset defective organisational structures.

✓ Most leaders solve problems and take appropriate action (Q48) is rated very high in NSC and has clear correlation with retention in OSC and NSC.

✓ Good on-field supervision (Q49) was correlated with retention in OSC and NSC.

✓ Free flow of communication with leadership (Q42) was rated high in OSC and correlated with retention.

✓ Missionaries included in major decisions (Q44) showed no benefit—an unexpected result.

✓ Policies well documented and understood (Q45) received a high rating and was highly correlated with retention.

✓ Missionaries are committed to the agency (Q60) received a very high rating in NSC and showed clear correlation with high retention in OSC and NSC.

✓ Leaders conducting annual performance/ministry reviews (Q50) received a high rating and clear correlation with retention (preventable attrition).

✓ Missionaries are given room to shape their own ministry (Q57) received a very high rating and it was correlated with retention.

What it means

Rob Hay

The centrality of leadership is key to good organisational practice and a core finding of the ReMAP II data: agencies that had a high rating on all the leadership questions had high retention rates. Question 47 [Q47 *Most leaders are a good example of the agency's beliefs and values*] received a high rating in OSC and NSC. This rating reflects a reassuring fact that the vast majority of people in leadership positions in mission want to do the role well, to the best of their ability and for the greatest benefit of the organisation and furtherance of the kingdom.

One key function of leadership is the ability to make most effective use of the resources available—the most valuable of which is people. In mission, this is especially the case. Often, many of the other resources that commercial companies and public bodies take for granted—large buildings, significant infrastructure and the latest information technology—are not available to budget-constrained mission agencies. Also, people are necessarily the key resource with the work that the majority of missions focus on, namely incarnational ministry, training orientated roles, and church and government partnership approaches. Furthermore, in almost every situation that mission agencies place their people, the individuals face the challenge of limited resources and seemingly unlimited demand. The main limited resource is often their own time and energy. In these situations, leaders must help their staff manage that imbalance and reconcile the difference. Failure to do this results in stress, burnout, and wider effects on team and family dysfunction. (See Chapter 18 for discussion of work-life balance.)

Creating a successful environment

Leaders must work to create an environment in which the mission partners and teams can perform well and produce results. And leaders must proactively identify and head off problems—problems that will affect the organisation and the individuals within the organisation or stop members of the team performing at their best. NSC agencies appear to be doing this much more effectively than OSC.

Possibly NSC leaders are very conscious that their organisations are new and are generally taking very little for granted.

- Have OSC agencies become complacent?
- Are OSC agencies stuck in routines?
- How much attention is being paid to changes, both locally and internationally?

Max De Pree has said, "The first responsibility of a leader is to define reality, but the sign of a healthy leader is one who is in touch with reality."[1] Both OSC and NSC need to make improvements in this area of leadership. Reflection and evaluation help leaders understand and define reality. Leaders of high performing organisations promote reflection, utilise ideas and energy from the team, and create an environment for innovation and welcome.

Almost without exception, mission agencies in OSC are suffering from massive work overload [Q61 *Missionaries are generally not overloaded in the amount of work they do*], which necessarily makes reflection and evaluation difficult. When work is overwhelming, responding becomes reactive, so the poor rating for proactive problem-solving [Q48 *Most leaders identify problems early and take appropriate action*] is not surprising. High performing organisations make space for their workers to reflect.

Utilising ideas from the team is especially a concern in OSC. Question 64 [Q64 *Missionaries regularly evaluate and seek to improve the agency's ministry*] received a poor rating, and this is affecting retention. Again, overload is a very significant factor in this, but the difference between OSC and NSC perhaps also highlights an additional factor, namely that of establishment. In OSC, the average age of the mission agency is 60 years; in some countries like Sweden and the UK, average age is over 100 years. In contrast, the average age in NSC is just 12 years. This difference means that culture and practice are often still in the process of being developed in NSC agencies, and in OSC, they sometimes feel so well-established they might be written on tablets of stone.

Communication from the leadership to encourage innovation, participation and ownership is vital, but this quality necessitates an open channel from the workers back to the leadership. Question 42 [Q42 *There is a free flow of communication to and from the leadership*], gets a reasonable rating, but the area needs improvement. Communication, generally, and feedback and affirmation, in particular, are not at an acceptable level.[2] Even more formal communication, the annual performance/ministry appraisal, is not occurring for the vast majority of organisations [Q50 *Leaders conduct an annual performance/ministry review with each missionary*]. ReMAP I highlighted the lack of annual reviews as being a major cause of attri-

---

1   Max De Pree, *Leading Without Power: Finding Hope in Serving Community* (San Francisco, CA: Jossey-Bass, 1997).

2   The importance of this is growing as the generation known as Generation X in the West (late-20s to mid-40s) and increasingly Millenials (late teens to 20s), make up a growing part of the missionary workforce. See the discussion in Richard Tiplady's, *Postmission: World Mission by a Postmodern Generation* (Carlisle: Paternoster Press, 2003).

tion, and ReMAP II reinforces this, as it is strongly correlated with retention in OSC and NSC alike.

Empowering leaders

Often in mission situations, the distance (culturally, linguistically and geographically) from the field workers to the mission leadership is significant. Therefore, the role of the field leader is key. On-field supervision is absolutely vital for retention, and yet in OSC and NSC it received a poor rating for significance and performance by the mission executives. Is this because we do not have structures that allow these leaders to function effectively?

Research indicates that many people who go to the field do not intend to lead, but end up in some kind of leadership position. This implies that many in these key positions have never received leadership training nor have had relevant leadership experiences. More problematic, however, is the structure in which they are asked to lead. From interviews with those who have ended up in leadership roles and from occasional candid interviews with senior mission leaders, there seems to be a problem with how the field leader fits within the structure.

To be able to lead, one must know how to lead, be empowered, be given freedom to make decisions, and be given clear boundaries. Field leaders complain of having little control, influence and support. Perhaps they are not empowered because they are not considered trained or experienced enough to wield the power that the role requires. If so, that is a problem that will not resolve itself. There is an urgent need for leadership training to prepare people before they take up a leadership role, and for ongoing learning opportunities to develop their leadership skills once in the role. Since many end up in leadership unexpectedly, a case should be made for incorporating basic leadership training into a mandatory missiological course curriculum.

Leading through change

To be effective, to be faithful, and to fulfil the purposes God has set before his church, we need to be open to the challenge of change. Matthew 28 does not say, "Go into all of the first century world", it simply says, "Go into all the world." The world around us is constantly changing and so mission agencies must respond in seeking to reach out in that changed world.

Leading through change is a key skill that we cannot cover in detail here, although some aspects are covered in Chapter 19 on organisational development. However, encouraging reflection and innovation should be the daily task of the leader as he or she seeks to lead, be faithful, and develop the organisation and its people. This is known as developing a learning organisation. These organisations embrace change on a daily if not hourly basis: Can we do this better? Is there another way of doing this? Why do we do this the way we do it? This environment is hard work because one is not allowed to just go through the motions or follow procedure. However, the environment is also exciting. It actively seeks involvement, ideas and interaction. In one such organisation, I (Rob) recognised that I felt valued as a person because the organisation clearly wanted my questions, my ideas and my reactions from the very first day that I started. In reality, this meant that I shared many of the same questions that newcomers in previous years before had asked in their first few months, but I was also able to contribute new insights and a new perspective.

Leadership is a complex skill and one that mission has undervalued and under-invested in for too long. Encouragingly, organisations are beginning to recognise this. Courses are being developed and utilised, and some mission organisations now have their own leadership development programmes. These provide not only theoretical knowledge, but also practical training and a structured career path to develop individuals. In larger organisations (with a large number of leadership positions to fill), a leadership training programme allows them to move a potential leader from a junior management post, to begin to develop their skills, to a middle management post as they grow into the role. Then, when a vacancy for a role with more responsibility arises, they can move a skilled, trained, and experienced person into that role.

An idea: Newcomers to organisations can be helpful in assessing the organisation. They come with a fresh set of eyes and a mind that has not been conditioned to think in the way of the organisation. After a while, they begin to see why the organisation operates in a certain way, but some questions will bring new insights, opportunities and challenges to the status quo.

Ask newcomers to write down in a reflective diary all questions, ideas and insights. At the end of six months, they should review their diary, cross out the items that have since become obvious, and bring to their leaders anything not crossed out for discussing, sharing and perhaps incorporating.

Good leadership is servant leadership

David Lundy,[3] Arab World Ministries, UK

One of the best summaries of the characteristics of good leadership is in David Lundy's book Servant Leadership for Slow Learners.[4] He sets out eight key characteristics (summarised here by Rob Hay with kind permission).

Accessibility

Good leaders are available to their people. This availability communicates value... you value them and their work enough to take time from your own schedule to be available to them. Furthermore, in spending time with staff, a leader can model Christian life and leadership.

Affability

Good leaders need to be able to have good rapport with people—to be relationally founded. People (more in mission than many other spheres of work where there are greater resources of infrastructure, technology or other tangible non-human resources) are vital to the work we do, and leaders need to be able to relate well, listen well and work with and in their team. A key part of leading the team and empowering people in their work is affirmation. A leader must know their workers well in order to know how and when to affirm and encourage.

Vulnerability

Traditionally, team members would have only seen their leader as strong and successful, and would not have been allowed to see the leader's struggles, failures, and frustrations. In the past, to show these aspects was considered poor leadership—how could team members have confidence in their leader if doubt was admitted? Now, however, particularly with the advent of the generation in their late-20s to mid-40s, honest leadership is greatly respected. Vulnerability also communicates to team members that, just as their leader needs grace to make mistakes occasionally, so they will be given grace in their mistakes as they grow and learn.

Vitality

Leaders spend their time giving much of themselves, and they do so generously to gain a good return. However, this can only be done when they themselves have taken care of their own spiritual, physical, and mental needs. Leaders must invest

---

3   David Lundy is the International Director of Arab World Ministries and is currently serving with his wife Linda at AWM's international head-quarters in the UK. Previously, David spent seven years pastoring a church in Toronto. He also served as the Canadian Director of AWM for seven years and as the Canadian Director of Operation Mobilisation for nine years. He is the author of *We Are the World: Globalisation and the Changing Face of Missions*, *Servant Leadership for Slow Learners*, and *Borderless Church: Shaping the Church for the 21st Century* as well as numerous articles.

4   David Lundy, *Servant Leadership for Slow Learners*, (Waynesboro, GA: Authentic Media, 2002).

time in "sharpening the saw," as Lundy calls it (p 116). Without setting aside time and resources to invest in oneself, Lundy suggests that leadership will inevitably move from an empowering servant style to an authoritarian controlling one. There is a growing volume of research that supports his theory—good, high performing leaders have a good work-life balance (see Chapter 18).

Teachability

A leader needs to be continually learning, developing and improving his or her skills, whether physically, mentally or spiritually. This means standing against any temptation to believe ourselves invincible or infallible. It means not asserting, "God has told me" or "the Spirit is leading us…" as spiritualisation is often a cover for manipulation. It means consciously remaining open to learn from others, including those whom we usually lead or teach. It means understanding the potential benefit of conflict; that often out of tension, discussion and conflict, ideas that are creative, refined and full of potential are born.

Impartiality

Biblical leadership is as much about power as secular leadership, but, as Lundy explains, it is radically counter-cultural in the way power is used and viewed. Biblical leadership gives away power to enable others, rather than hoarding it to maintain position or status. Biblical leaders are called to treat all people equally. Biblical leaders are called to avoid the "perks of power"—the titles and privileges that seek to set them apart from those they serve. Biblical leaders are challenged to avoid even the success measures that are often applied, instead measuring themselves and their workers by the faithfulness with which they serve—the result of the service is God's concern. The only biblical partiality Lundy allows for is an emphasis on the poor.

Identifiability

Leaders need to culturally contextualise and be prepared for situational leadership. To do this, they need to understand and identify with the people they lead and the environment they lead in. For mission leaders, this means country contexts, but also an organisational context as each organisation has a culture. In my interviews (Rob), many say they struggled much more with adjusting to the organisational culture than the national one when they became a missionary.

Stickability

The leader's number one calling is to finish well. That should not be measured by a traditional secular yardstick but by being a faithful servant. This involves bearing pain. Lundy suggests that in order to display the other characteristics outlined, pain is inevitable for the leader. In an age where, in large chunks of the world, pain is seen as something to be avoided at all costs, this is radically counter-cultural and will need to be taught. Part of the willingness to bear pain is discipline. Alongside discipline is patience. Contrary to much of the world's pattern, leadership is a long-term job—you cannot do a good job of developing these characteristics overnight.

Discussion questions

1. How does your leadership measure up to these characteristics?
2. How does the organisation develop these characteristics among its leaders?
3. On what basis does your organisation appoint leaders and is this appropriate?

In the real world

A table to stimulate ideas for best practice in mission partnership. For further explanation, see page 7.

This chart has been partially filled in for you. Now you fill in the blanks.

Who? → When? ↓	Home Church	Missionary	Mission Agencies	External Partners
Continuous	➢ Appreciate biblical leadership in church life ➢ Assess young leaders and train them ➢ Give various opportunities to grow leaders ➢ Mentor and coach potential leaders	➢ Take time to learn about leadership ➢ Be engaged in leadership training ➢ Give feedback to leaders about their leadership	➢ Stress the importance of leadership development ➢ Assess missionaries' leadership qualities ➢ Give opportunities to grow in leadership responsibilities ➢ Mentor and coach potential leaders ➢ Have sound organisational structures	➢ Provide leadership development training ➢ Serve as mentors and coaches
Recruitment				
Preparation				
On field				
Crisis				
Furlough				
Re-entry				

22

Leadership
Good/Toxic Leadership

The facts

Leadership is a key function within all organisations. Mission agencies are no different. Good, healthy leadership is quite distinct from poor, toxic leadership. The effects of the first frees people within the organisation to thrive, flourish, and give of their skills and resources effectively to the maximum benefit of the organisation. The effect of the second, the toxic leader, is to inhibit, hold back and severely limit the performance of their team. Long-term, a toxic leader will affect the individuals within the team, who themselves will experience inhibited growth and development.

The data

Q. No.	Factor	OSC Health Score	✓	NSC Health Score	✓
41	Plans and job descriptions are communicated clearly to the missionary	○○○○○○○●●●●	✓	○○○○○○○●●●●	✓
42	Free flow of communication to and from the leadership	○○○○○○●●●●	✓	○○○○○○●●●●	
44	Missionaries are included in major decisions related to field	○○○○○○○●●●		○○○○○○●●●●	
45	Policies are well documented and understood	○○○○○●●●●●	✓	○○○○○○○●●●	✓
48	Most leaders identify problems early and take appropriate action	○○○○●●●●●●	✓	○○○○○○●●●●	✓
49	Good on-field supervision is provided (quantity & quality)	○○○○●●●●●●	✓	○○○○○●●●●●	✓
50	Most leaders conduct individual annual performance review	○○○○●●●●●●	✓	○○○●●●●●●●	✓

51	There are documented and adequate procedures for handling complaints from missionaries	○○○○○●●●●●	✓	○○○○○●●●●●	✓
56	Missionaries are assigned roles according to their gifting and experience	○○○○○○●●●●		○○○○○○●●●●	✓
57	Missionaries are given room to shape and develop their own ministry	○○○○○○○○●●	✓	○○○○○○○●●●	✓
61	Missionaries are not generally overloaded with work	○●●●●●●●●●	✓	○○○○●●●●●●	✓
64	Missionaries regularly evaluate and seek to improve the agency's ministry	○○●●●●●●●●	✓	○○○○●●●●●●	

The key findings

✓ There is a clear correlation between leadership issues and retention.

✓ System for handling complaints (Q51) was highly correlated with retention.

✓ Missionaries are given room to shape their own ministry (Q57) moderately correlated with retention.

✓ Clear plans and job description (Q41) was rated high and clearly correlated with retention in OSC and NSC.

✓ Good communication with leadership (Q42) clearly correlated with retention in OSC.

✓ Missionaries are included in decision-making (Q44) had little correlation with retention.

✓ Well-documented policies (Q45) correlated with retention in NSC and OSC.

✓ Assignment of missionaries to gifting (Q56) moderately correlated with retention in NSC (possibly taken for granted in OSC).

What it means

Rob Hay

Good leadership gives energy, vision and direction to the organisation. It creates an environment in which people want, to the best of their ability, to use their skills and experience for the good of their team and the wider organisation. Leadership communicates the big picture to staff and helps them see how vital their part is in reaching the goal. It ensures that the training, resources, and environment to perform and to achieve are in place, as well as the systems and accountability to address issues constructively.

Good leadership and management is a characteristic of a healthy organisation that keeps its staff. This is not surprising, and yet the effect of its absence is often underestimated. Using the measure of "Confidence in Senior Management," eight out of ten employees in successful business organisations believe that their senior management makes good decisions, compared to only five out of ten in less successful ones. In addition, eight out of ten employees in successful organisations say that their senior management works well together as a team, compared to only five out of ten in less successful ones.[1] Is the success of an organisation synonymous with being a good, healthy one? No it is not, but in business, to be successful you need to retain good people. In mission, retaining missionaries is not assumed to equate to effectiveness, but there is a recognition that retaining missionaries (in whom we invest significant energy and resources in training and preparing) is a vital part of being effective in the missionary task.

Leadership and management are the pivot point around which everything else works—whether well or badly. For example, fairness, which is subjective and relies on the decisions of managers and leaders for its credibility, affects the employees of an organisation directly. Misplaced benevolence, where managers avoid dealing with incompetent, negative or volatile staff, highlights a leader's failings and results in anger.[2] Having clear policies on behaviour helps to reduce perception issues in these two instances. However, ReMAP II, indicates weakness in the area of clear and documented policies [Q45 *Policies are well documented and understood*] and [Q51 *There are documented and adequate procedures for handling complaints from missionaries*]. Without these, managers are exposed to the very real dangers of being seen as unfair when we apply different behaviour to individual situations.

The role of leadership and management significantly affects all the areas of agency function. Therefore, to ignore poor or toxic leadership can be a major factor in an organisation's decline, and is to ignore reality. As Marcia Lynn Whicker says, it is "...fiddling with imperial arrogance while the organisational city is burning."[3] Reasonable significance and performance ratings are seen for Questions 42, 44, and 51 [Q42 *There is a free flow of communication to and from the leadership*], Q44 [*Missionaries are included in major decisions related to the field*], Q51 [*There are documented and adequate procedures for handling complaints from missionaries*], while Question 48 [Q48 *Most leaders identify problems early and take appropriate action*] showed a poor rating and question 64 [Q64 *Missionaries regularly evaluate and seek to improve the agency's ministry*] showed a very poor rating in OSC and NSC. Without a regular reality check as offered by meaningful review and evaluation

---

1   Bruce Karcher, *What Great Organizations Have in Common* ([cited 21/10/2005); available from http://www.discoverysurveys.com/articles/itw-051.html.

2   Anne Seibold Drapeau Robert Galford, "The Enemies of Trust," in Harvard Business Review on Building Personal and Organizational Resilience, The Harvard Business Review Paperback Series (Boston, MA: Harvard Business School Pub., 2003).

3   Marcia Lynn Whicker, *Toxic Leaders: When Organizations Go Bad* (Westport, London: Quorum, 1996).

processes, there is a serious risk that leaders would perceive a reality that is distant and out of touch with the reality and perspective of their missionaries.

Identifying toxic leadership

What does a toxic leader look like? How is a toxic leader spotted? Just as importantly, how do we spot signs of toxicity in ourselves? A toxic leader, by virtue of his or her own problems, creates an environment that frustrates subordinates and colleagues. To adequately explore this, we need to research the perspective of individual missionaries and not just the mission leaders as we did in ReMAP II. However, key questions on leadership performance received poor ratings in OSC [Q48 *Most leaders identify problems early and take appropriate action*], [Q49 *Good on-field supervision is provided (quantity and quality)*], and [Q50 *Leaders conduct an annual performance/ministry review with each missionary*]. These indicate a need for improvement among leaders, even if the missionaries respect the intention and efforts of their leaders (see Chapter 21 for a discussion of this difference).

Toxic managers are generally inconsistent: saying one thing and doing another. Their behaviour and words do not match. Decisions and direction can change suddenly and without apparent rationale. Of greatest difficulty, the toxic manager can send mixed messages so employees never know what is expected, what will be praised, and what will be punished. This problem can be reduced by having expectations clearly laid out in plans, job descriptions and policies. However, as previously mentioned, these areas [Q41 *Plans and job descriptions are communicated clearly to the missionary* and Q45 *Policies are well documented and understood*] were not strong and would benefit from further work.

The toxic manager also avoids emotionally charged situations, such as conflict or discipline and they react poorly to being challenged. They may avoid making decisions until a crisis develops. This problem can be reduced through openness in decision-making and communication. However, the survey showed slight mixed ratings for questions related to openness of communication. Questions 42 [Q42 *There is a free flow of communication to and from the leadership*], and 44 [Q44 *Missionaries are included in major decisions related to the field*] received a reasonably good rating for performance and significance, while 48 [Q48 *Most leaders identify problems early and take appropriate action]* and 50 [Q50 *Leaders conduct an annual performance/ministry review with each missionary*] showed a slightly poor rating.

In short, the toxic manager confuses subordinates, uses often subtle ways of punishment for real or imagined transgressions, creates a high degree of dependence, and is internally conflicted.

Quantifying toxicity

Whicker, in her foundational book on toxic leadership,[4] uses the work of James MacGregor Burns[5] and identifies three types of leaders and the personal character-

4   Whicker, *Toxic Leaders: When Organizations Go Bad*.
5   James MacGregor Burns, *Leadership*, 1st ed. (New York: Harper and Row, 1978).

istics and organisational impacts of each: trustworthy leaders, transitional leaders, and toxic leaders.

Trustworthy leaders are good, moral leaders. They can be trusted to put the goals of the organisation and the well-being of their followers first. They value self-esteem, the esteem of others, and self-actualisation (development of one's best personal potential) both for themselves and for their followers.

Transitional leaders are self-absorbed, egotistical leaders. They are neither uplifting in their long-term impact on others, nor purposefully malicious toward them. Rather, they are focused on the approval of others and concerned with their personal role as leaders.

Toxic leaders are maladjusted, malcontent and often malevolent, even malicious. They succeed in tearing others down. They glory in turf protection, fighting and controlling rather than uplifting followers.[6]

MacGregor Burns defines the best leadership in terms of Maslow's hierarchy. In other words, a trustworthy leader may be distinguished from their lesser transitional and toxic counterparts by using this hierarchy (see below). Psychologist Abraham Maslow devised a widely accepted, five-stage hierarchy of human needs and drives, where movement to the next higher level depends in part on satiation of a basic need at the next lower level. An individual usually progresses through the need levels as he or she matures.

Leadership Type	Maslow's Level
Trustworthy leaders	Level 5: Self-actualisation needs Level 4: Esteem needs
Transitional leaders	Level 3: Social needs
Toxic leaders	Level 2: Security needs Level 1: Survival needs

Table 2.2. Leadership Types and Maslow's Hierarchy of Needs[7]

The five levels in ascending order are: (1) survival, or basic physical needs (food, water, shelter), (2) security, or safety needs (protection from the elements and from human attack), (3) social needs (the need to belong to groups), (4) esteem needs (the need to gain the respect of others as well as to gain self-respect), and (5) self-actualisation (the need to use one's talents to the greatest potential).

Trustworthy leaders typically operate at level four or five of Maslow's hierarchy. Level four is the level at which trustworthy leadership begins. Because trustworthy leaders have considerable self-respect, they are able to command the respect of others, and continuously work to expand that respect. Trustworthy leaders have

---

6   Whicker, *Toxic Leaders: When Organizations Go Bad.*
7   Ibid., p. 32.

no need or incentive to put others down or hold others back to enhance their own self-image, since trustworthy leaders already have a healthy self-image.

They are personally motivated by self-actualisation: they want to use and expand their own talents, and as part of their leadership talent, to help others develop their talents to the highest possible degree. Level five trustworthy leaders do not just respond to the need to earn respect, even if decisions that command the respect of self and others are difficult and tough. While being concerned about the feelings and sensitivities of others, level five moral leaders have moved beyond deep concern about what others think of their behaviour.

> "Level five trustworthy leaders are driven to put their considerable talents to maximal use, so that they contribute as much or more to the organisation and society as they take back. Level five self-actualisation involves not an ethic of sacrifice, but an ethic of giving from the most fundamental part of one's being—one's talent."[8]

In contrast, transitional and toxic leaders operate at lower levels in Maslow's hierarchy. Transitional leaders operate at level three and are preoccupied with social needs (they need people to approve of them). Toxic leaders operate at level two, focusing on security needs and occasionally sinking even lower to survival needs, when employment crucial to economic survival is threatened. Driven in their own lives by lower level needs, transitional and toxic leaders lack the capacity and reserves to uplift followers that trustworthy leaders have.

Different styles but common characteristics

Toxic leaders may adopt different styles of leadership, but all toxic leaders, according to Whicker, share three defining characteristics: deep-seated inadequacy, selfish values, and deceptiveness.

Transitional leaders share these characteristics with toxic leaders, but in less virulent forms. Transitional leaders also differ from toxic leaders in that their selfish values are focused predominantly at Maslow's level three on social needs, rather than at Maslow's level two, security needs. They are, in essence, more benign forms of toxic leaders who develop toxicity unintentionally[9].

Deep-seated inadequacy

All toxic leaders have a deep-seated sense of inadequacy, fear or feel they are impostors, and worry that someday someone will find them out. The reasons for this inadequacy vary, but this characteristic of inadequacy is the hallmark characteristic of toxic leaders. This has major consequences for the behaviour and performance of the toxic leader. It can simply cause the leader to merely withdraw, lest close involvement and active participation reveal weaknesses, or at the opposite extreme, engage in frantic activity and try to control every aspect of organisational activity

---

8   Ibid., p. 33.
9   Ibid., p. 53.

in order to avoid being caught off-guard by an event or events he cannot possibly handle. Obviously, when people are placed in roles for which they are not trained or experienced and which they do not want, feelings of inadequacy are more likely.

Selfish values

Leaders who care about the organisation, its mission, its workers, and its clients, should be the ones to lead it. However, because of the toxic leader's deep sense of personal inadequacy, he or she never develops personal values that give high priority to anything greater than his own needs. However, just as good parents derive immense pleasure from the successes of the children they have raised, so trustworthy leaders derive similar pleasure from the successes of the organisations they have shaped and led. They see no conflict between the organisation succeeding and their own personal success and therefore do not feel threatened by its success.

If a leader is not coping in a role he did not ask for and with which he is struggling, almost inevitably he will be very concerned to "survive." This can manifest itself in selfishness that the individual, under normal circumstance, would never usually countenance, much less exhibit. However, having been placed in a position of leadership, he or she feels that for the sake of their ministry, they must succeed and success is defined as managing to do the job. There are expectations on them from the mission leadership, the home office, their church and their supporters—many of whom may see leaving the role as failure. This fear shapes the thinking of many mission partners who strongly feel the need to give a return on investment to the expectations of supporters.

Deception

Toxic leaders may deceive others about their selfish values and sense of inadequacy. They know they should not have selfish values: leaders are supposed to care about the organisation, its mission, and its employees. Toxic leaders care mostly about themselves and abating, soothing, and covering over their own insecurities and anxieties. They are shrewd enough to know they will be denied leadership positions, which they crave to further abate, soothe, and cover personal inadequacy, if true motives are stated. They will act in pure self-interest, but state that concern for organisational goals underlies their decisions. Very malicious toxic leaders are driven to malign and tear others down in order to feel superior, but know they cannot admit their deeds.

In transitional leaders, deception displays itself as the need to hide the inadequacies discussed above. Leadership, particularly in many mission roles, is often isolating and the possibilities of a peer group are limited if not impossible. The ability to face up to feelings of inadequacy and deal with them in a constructive and helpful way is aided significantly by sharing with people in a similar position and severely inhibited when this is not possible.

Conclusion

In conclusion, any leader has the potential to be toxic, even unintentionally (as in the case of transitional leaders), and all that possibly can be done is needed (through policies and procedures) to avoid that possibility. Once policies and procedures are in place, the careful selection, preparation and appointment of leaders is necessary, ensuring that those appointed are, if possible, trained and experienced and, if not, then they are given significant support and opportunity to develop the skills required. To maintain leaders in a healthy state, peer support networks must be actively created, giving leaders avenues of support outside of their direct responsibility, as well as opportunities for reflection and ongoing learning and development.

One vision to reach the lost at any cost

John Amalraj,[10] Interserve, India

The history of most Indian indigenous mission agencies is less than 50 years, and we are still on the learning curve. Many of our good practices tend to be leader-centric rather than agency centric. This is the story of P.G. Vargis, president and founder of Indian Evangelical Team (IET) based in New Delhi, India.

George Barna observed that, "Vision has flourished even beyond the lives of biblical characters. In our own century, there are numerous examples of people who, by human standards, showed little promise for greatness and little hope of being able to change the lives of people around the world. But these people, having captured God's vision for ministry, have lived with power and energy that undeniably transcend their natural capabilities and with an intensity of commitment that far exceeds anything they had previously demonstrated in their lives. The results of their efforts further expose the power of God at work within them."[11]

As a young man, Vargis served as an Indian army soldier in North India. Within a year after his dramatic conversion in October 1970, he asked to be released from the army. God had called him to serve as an evangelist to villagers living in the Himalayan mountains of Kashmir state. In late 1972, Vargis set out with his wife, Lilly, and their ten-month old son. They settled in Katra, a sacred Hindu pilgrimage centre, where there were no Christians. They worked tirelessly, preaching the gospel and reaching out to the people. They had no support for their ministry or family, but God always provided for their needs. After a year, they baptised dozens of new converts and planted their first church. Within three years, twelve daughter

---

10   Mr. John Amalraj serves as the Executive Secretary/CEO of Interserve India. He lives in Pune along with his wife Jessie and sons Jason and Joash. Amalraj is a trained lawyer. He served in the corporate world as HR manager of a group of companies and also in various capacities with India Missions Association until 2005. He completed his theological studies at Trinity Theological College, Singapore. Interserve India facilitates Christian professionals to be involved actively in cross cultural missions. For more details contact <isvindia@postworld.net>

11   George Barna, *The power of vision: How you can capture and apply God's vision for your ministry*, (Ventura, CA: Regal Books, 1992), p. 21.

churches were planted on the mountains. Then Vargis discerned that God wanted him to move south, in order to expand the work and start a Bible school. In 1977, Vargis moved his family to Pathankot in Punjab state.

In 1985, Vargis moved the "Indian Evangelical Team" (IET) headquarters to New Delhi. Over the years, God added many other godly men and women who shared Vargis' vision "to reach the unreached at any cost." Today, IET is one of the largest church-planting missions in India, with more than two thousand missionary pastors toiling almost all over India as well as in two neighbouring countries. Some of IET's ministries include a children's home, technical school, Bible training, film ministry, pastor's seminars, mercy ministries, counselling, publications, and crusades.

According to Vargis,[12] IET ministry has continued for over 25 years because of God's provision of all their needs. Vargis recalls how one morning, not long after he and his wife had arrived in Katra, he found his friend Joseph sitting on their doorstep. "Joseph told me that he too had resigned from the Army and had come to join me in the ministry. I explained, as we sat on a wooden box—we did not have any furniture—that I did not have even a cup of tea to offer. I suggested that he could join some other organisation which could give him regular support. Joseph said, 'When you will have a *chapatti* (Indian pancake-like bread) you can give half to me.' I took his hand in my hand and made a promise. That is the policy of IET even today. Whatever we have is divided equally."

Today, Vargis is a mentor to 18 Senior and 30 Junior leaders in IET. He has described IET's leadership team as follows: "I am a man, who is totally captivated by the vision 'to reach the unreached at any cost.' I have several leaders who are possessed by the same vision for the whole nation or their God-given area. They move so fast that it is very difficult to keep up with them. These are visionaries, my heroes. I am what I am and IET is what IET is, because of these leaders."

The leadership team oversees the work of missionary pastors. Nearly every month, Vargis will invite the leadership team and his co-workers for about three days of learning and praying together. It is a time of envisioning, with Vargis taking the lead in equipping his co-workers. He also invites guest speakers who minister regularly. This practice of gathering the co-workers ensures that all of them are continually envisioned, thereby enabling them to work as missionaries against many challenges. Only one vision grips their hearts, that is to see their precious nation of India shine with the glory of God.

Discussion questions:

1. What can we learn about leadership from the above story?
2. As a leader, what vision for ministry has God given to you and your church (organisation)? How are you sharing that vision with other leaders and co-workers?

---

12   Editorial by P G Vargis for IET 25th Anniversary, 2002, http://www.ietmissions.org/iet25.html#a.

The dysfunction in a leader breaks a team

Rob Hay, UK

John and Gail were a young professional couple with huge potential. That was the view of their tutors when they attended mission training school. Their call to mission was no passing fad. Despite John having trained seven years to become a dentist, Gail four years for her studies, then several years in their professions, they went to mission school because they recognised professional expertise was not enough. They felt a call to the Muslim world and hoped to work as tentmakers. They were highly recommended by their church, where they had been engaged in international student ministry and were faithful members.

During their time at the training school, they impressed staff with their teachable spirit and the way in which they were both natural leaders—with John being elected to lead the student committee and both often sought out by other students for advice and wisdom. They were clearly held in high regard by their fellow students. While at the training school, they investigated possible organisations where they could serve and answer the call God had laid on their heart to share the good news of Jesus Christ with Muslims in a Muslim country. They had already proved their call and ability through their work with international students. Indeed, they had seen two come to Christ.

After prayerfully considering the different organisations, they applied to a well known international mission agency who had a track record of facilitating people working as tentmakers. They would be part of a team in a small city where the organisation had placed missionaries for the last six years. They were delighted. They had recognised the importance of being in a team where they could draw mutual support and encouragement. Their reading of *Too Valuable to Lose* while they were in mission school had reinforced desire for team. God seemed to be "in this," everything was falling into place.

A few months after finishing mission school, after deputation and support raising, John and Gail flew out, excited, nervous and keen to begin. On arrival, they were met by the team leader and his wife (Bill and Jane), the most established members of the team, having been in country six years and having taken over the leadership when the founding team leader left unexpectedly with health problems. A physiotherapist by training, Bill had not wanted the leadership role, but was persuaded to take it as there was no one else willing. With only one other member to lead at that point, it did not seem a big task. In fact, the other member of the team at that point was still there, a single Dutch woman.

They arrived and unpacked. Bill and Jane helped them to settle in. They provided many meals in the first few weeks, showed them around, and helped them find language teachers. All seemed well. Then, during that first week, John asked Bill when the team meetings were held. Bill paused before replying. John noticed a look pass between Bill and his wife Jane, before he said "oh fairly soon." A couple of weeks later, John asked again about the staff meeting and got a similar response.

John and Gail decided to phone the other team member they had heard of, Lianne. She was warm and friendly, and she invited them for a meal. When they met her, she was friendly although she did seem rather tired and unenthusiastic—in some ways relieved to have them to talk to. She seemed to love the people she worked among. She was a nurse, working at the main government-run hospital in the city. In fact, she was fine the whole evening until they began talking about the team, and in particular Bill. Then she seemed to grow uncomfortable. By the time they left, the atmosphere had changed, becoming tense and uncomfortable for all.

The next day, when Bill came over, John and Gail expressed their concern about Lianne. They suggested that the team needed to help her. Bill exploded, demanding what they meant by that. Were they trying to undermine him? Why did they go to see her behind his back? Before they could respond he stormed out, slamming the door behind him. They were taken aback and sat there stunned.

For the rest of the day, they were in a daze—just doing what needed to be done: paying the electricity bill, shopping in the market, and generally avoiding the subject. At dinner time, they weren't hungry but spent some time talking and praying. They felt confused—what had they done? There was a knock on the door. It was Bill. He came in, they sat down. "I'm sorry about that," he said "ever since I took this job as leader people have tried to cause trouble for me, for the team. Lianne has issues! There is much spiritual opposition. Let's pray against it."

This was to be the first of many such experiences. Bill had blinding rages when they or anyone else questioned him. They were confused—not least when Bill would reappear, seem to apologise, then end up making them feel guilty for causing him to lose his temper. John and Gail talked with Lianne, and suggested they should contact the international office. "I did several times—they even visited us last year but I was told that I did not have a teachable spirit, that I should submit to authority," she said, bitterly.

John and Gail did contact the international office by e-mail and got no reply to the first two so then they contacted their home sending office. This time they received a reply, but it suggested that perhaps they were feeling homesick and getting things out of proportion. How, John and Gail wondered, do you get your field leader on his feet screaming across the room at you in every meeting, out of proportion?

After nine months of Bill's flip-flopping between aggression against them and then guilt-laden friendship, and with declining response from the sending office, they packed their things. They telephoned their sending office to tell them, and flew home. Their calling to mission was in significant doubt. Their confidence in God's leading and their own ability to hear that leading was severely shaken.

Three years on from this experience, after a very supportive home church taking them in and surrounding them with love and significant counselling, the story has something of a happy ending. They have now been overseas for a year with a different organisation in a similar context. Both they and their organisation are delighted with the way things are working out. They have shown their ability to adapt. John and Gail are happy with the relationship that has been built and established with this new organisation. They were completely open with the new organisation about the past events in their previous organisation. They were fortunate to have had a sending church that did not write them off when they returned unexpectedly.

Unfortunately, their first organisation still has not dealt with leadership issues on the field. Bill is no longer there, but he returned home feeling a failure, when in reality his own ministry had been very effective. It was the leadership role he had struggled with. At a recent conference, the personnel officers within this organisation confided in me their frustration at the lack of consistency and the organisations' inability to tackle dysfunction. Due to the inaction of the international office, several sending country offices had blacklisted that country and several other countries with unresolved leadership issues as places where they would not send their people.

Discussion questions

1. What might have caused Bill to struggle with the leadership role?
2. What effect does a struggling leader have on the team he is leading?
3. If your organisation is an international mission how does your organisation ensure consistency of quality between different country offices and fields?

In the real world

A table to stimulate ideas for best practice in mission partnership. For further explanation, see page 7.

This chart has been partially filled in for you. Now you fill in the blanks.

Who? → When? ↓	Home Church	Missionary	Mission Agencies	External Partners
Continuous	➤ Appreciate biblical leadership in church life ➤ Assess young leaders and train them ➤ Give various opportunities to grow as a leader ➤ Mentor and coach potential leaders ➤ Highlight experienced leaders to serve as examples for emerging leaders	➤ Take time to learn about leadership ➤ Be engaged in leadership training ➤ Give feedback to leaders about their leadership ➤ Be accountable	➤ Stress the importance of leadership development ➤ Assess missionaries' leadership qualities ➤ Give opportunities to grow in leadership responsibilities ➤ Mentor and coach leaders ➤ Have sound structures in the organisation ➤ Highlight experienced leaders to serve as examples for emerging leaders	➤ Provide leadership development training ➤ Serve as mentors and coaches ➤ Develop a Code of Best Practice
Recruitment				
Preparation				
On field				
Crisis				
Furlough				
Re-entry				

23

Staff Development

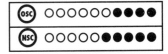

OSC	○○○○○○●●●●
NSC	○○○○○●●●●●

The facts

Staff development is important. Biblically, we are all called to be growing and learning people who are on a journey of faith and therefore will encounter change as a continual reality. To meet this challenge we must be investing in ourselves and in those from our organisations. The days are gone where simply providing pre-field training, be it secular or biblical, was enough for missionaries to be expected to go to the field and remain on the field until retirement. The good news is that agencies are, in fact, developing their people, but there are some areas of concern that need addressing, which seem to be mirrored across OSC and NSC alike.

The data

Q No.	Factor	OSC Health Indicator	✓	NSC Health Indicator	✓
42	There is a free flow of communication to and from the leadership	○○○○○○●●●●	✓	○○○○○○●●●●	
44	Missionaries are included in major decisions related to the field	○○○○○○○●●●		○○○○○○●●●●	
50	Leaders conduct an annual performance/ ministry review with each missionary	○○○○●●●●●●	✓	○○○●●●●●●●	✓
51	There are documented and adequate procedures for handling complaints from missionaries	○○○○○●●●●●	✓	○○○○○●●●●●	✓
52	Effective on-field orientation is in place for new missionaries	○○○○○●●●●●	✓	○○○○○●●●●●	✓

54	Ongoing language and culture training are actively encouraged	OOOOOOO●●●	✓	OOOOOOO●●●●	
55	Missionaries are provided with opportunities for continuous training and development of gifts and skills	OOOOOO●●●●	✓	OOOOOO●●●●	✓
56	Missionaries are assigned roles according to their gifting and experience	OOOOOO●●●●		OOOOOO●●●	✓
57	Missionaries are given room to shape and develop their own ministry	OOOOOOOO●●	✓	OOOOOOO●●●	✓
64	Missionaries regularly evaluate and seek to improve the agency's ministry	OO●●●●●●●●	✓	OOOO●●●●●●	
70	Missionaries experience a sense of fulfilment in their ministry	OOOOOOOO●●	✓	OOOOOOO●●●	✓

The key findings

✓ Effective on-field orientation (Q52) correlated with retention.

✓ Ongoing language and cultural training (Q54) correlated with retention in OSC.

✓ Continuous training and development of new skills (Q55) is correlated with retention in OSC and NSC.

✓ Missionaries regularly evaluate and seek to improve their agency's ministry (Q64) received a relatively low rating, yet correlated with retention in OSC.

What it means

Rob Hay

Staff development is investment in missionaries as individuals. A commercial company employing a staff member invests in that person's salary (usually a significant portion the total budget). There is a good return on that investment, directly or indirectly significantly more is earned in revenue than the cost of salary expenses. The employer's best interest is to invest additional money for training and development to ensure that the person is well-trained and up-to-date so as to work effectively. In mission, there is no monetary profit incentive, so it is important to prioritise staff development for other reasons, not least good stewardship on behalf of those that do provide for the salary equivalent of the missionary.

Without an annual performance review/appraisal, ensuring staff development needs are being met is difficult (and ideally, reviews should be more frequent—see Chapter 25). However, both OSC and NSC received a poor significance and performance rating for these reviews. Likewise, an individual must be allowed to stop and step back from their work periodically to assess their own performance and consider training and development requirements for the future. Question 64 [Q64 *Missionaries regularly evaluate and seek to improve the agency's ministry*] shows that individuals are not doing this (the question received a rating of just three in OSC and five in NSC). Furthermore, Question 61 [Q61 *Missionaries are generally not overloaded in the amount of work they do*] (which was rated at just one in OSC and slightly below five in NSC), revealed that time and capacity are obstacles to reflection time.

For many, the first opportunity for on-field staff development comes with orientation (see Chapter 10). This is correlated to retention [Q52 *Effective on-field orientation is in place for new missionaries*] as is language training [Q53 *Language learning arrangement for new missionaries to learn the local language*] and ongoing language and culture training [Q54 *Ongoing language and culture training are actively encouraged*], and all three received fair to good ratings.

Getting people settled in the country of service and able to communicate effectively is important to an effective ministry. However, general ongoing training and new skills development is vital for a continuing ministry where the missionary stays and serves. Question 55 [Q55 *Missionaries are provided with opportunities for continuous training and development of gifts and skills*] showed a good rating for performance and significance and correlated with retention in OSC and NSC. Mission executives rate their agencies well, but they must not be complacent. The strong correlation shows that current missionaries view ongoing training as important, and recent research suggests that it is important to the younger generation as well, so this area must be a priority. Training is particularly relevant as missionaries regularly hand over responsibilities to nationals and then take on new types of ministries in which they may have had little training and experience. Continuous training prepares missionaries for inevitable change and gives them the confidence and ability to accept new challenges.

Lifelong missionary development on the field

David Milligan,[1] Arab World Ministries (AWM)

"It's not what I expected." How many of us within mission circles have vented that thought, or heard others express it somehow? The process of realigning expected or idealistic expectations with reality can be a painful one for first-term and second-

---

1   David Milligan currently serves as AWM's International Personnel Director, with oversight of AWM's member care and member development. He and his wife have served with AWM for the past 25 years in a variety of roles. David is particularly passionate about using training opportunities to enhance self-awareness and cross-cultural sensitivity for life and ministry.

term missionaries. We are tested and challenged as we learn more about ourselves and about our new environment.

Our own sense of calling ("Maybe I got this wrong!") and suitability ("Maybe we really aren't cut out for this line of work after all!") can be put to the test by the initial challenge of language and cultural acquisition. Our eyes are opened to things about ourselves that we were not fully aware of before. Then, after a year or two of feeling like a child during the language learning process, we may feel that we are more ready to get on with changing the world. In that process though, we might have faced up to our own limitations, misplaced expectations, and possible disappointment.

Our ministry environment may also be a hurdle. The idealised draw of our calling to reach a lost world gets tested by the nitty-gritty adaptation to new ways of doing things in a radically different culture and context. Church life in a foreign land is not the same as in our home country. Opportunities for ministry need to be rediscovered in this new setting.

We need to address the rocky road of a missionary's initial two terms of service. We must ensure that new workers actually get beyond adjusting and enter into a season of effective ministry. AWM does this through ongoing training and personal development on the field. For several years now, our agency-wide emphasis has been to inculcate a mind-set of life-long learning.

A framework for life-long personal development

AWM personnel are encouraged to identify development objectives on an annual basis and to track action steps as they are completed. A user-friendly competency-based CD offers help in tracking personal development in four main areas:

1. Working with people
2. Developing ministry
3. Effecting change
4. Personal growth

This framework emphasises competency rather than curriculum. For instance, after workers have followed a course on Arabic religious vocabulary, their competency to share the basics of the gospel in Arabic is demonstrated when they actually do it.

Jane Vella, in her book on evaluating adult learning,[2] highlights three stages: learning, transfer and impact.

> "Change in skills, knowledge and attitudes from the educational experience is *learning*...
>
> The effective use of skills, knowledge and attitudes beyond the educational programme is known as *transfer*...

---

2 Jane Vella, *How Do They Know They Know?: Evaluating Adult Learning,* (San Francisco: Jossey-Bass Publishers, 1998), p. 21.

The broad, long-term measures of organisational improvement and effectiveness are known as *impact*."

When we apply Vella's model in life-long missionary development, our workers will demonstrate learning through a change in skills, knowledge and attitudes on a variety of subject matters or issues. Evidence of having learned is when our workers transfer that new learning to others in some manner. Personal and organisational effectiveness are enhanced by the impact our workers make when they transfer their learning to ministry on the field.

Relaunching our workers

To further support life-long personal development, AWM has recently established a new bi-annual training event for field workers. The premiere event took place in August 2005. Our intention is to "relaunch" our workers after their initial four to six years of service, so that their ministry assignment is well suited to their gifts and ministry passion.

This training week helps our workers to focus more specifically on issues of ministry, self-awareness and interaction with the life journeys of other participants. Through the rough and tumble of a worker's first and second terms of service, questions of gifting, best fit, and ministry passion often surface ("How do I take who I am and express my gifts and passion in ministry?"). The answers are not always readily obvious. Hence, the training week provides an opportunity for our field workers to interact with one another and to find the answers. The desired outcome is to affirm and confirm the unique ministry contribution of each worker.

While the four to six year window presents a timely opportunity to reevaluate and reassess, such an appraisal should continue regularly throughout each missionary's career, as workers mature and as the ministry settings evolve around them. An annual appraisal will allow each worker to reflect on encouragements and disappointments of the past year against personal or organisational goals and objectives. Through annual appraisal, further training needs can be identified in order to enhance the missionary's level of satisfaction and effectiveness in ministry.

Finding the best fit via annual appraisals

Annual appraisals help us in tracking the personal development and change in each missionary. One natural question during an annual appraisal is whether the gifts and passion of the worker are rightly matched with the ministry assignment. For example, a lack of motivation or productivity may indicate that a worker could be better placed in a different ministry setting. Thus, if ministry reviews are conducted once a year in the form of annual appraisals, we can help to alleviate the accumulation of dissatisfaction and discouragement.

The intended outcome is for our workers to flourish and thrive in line with their spiritual gifting and personality as much as this is possible. Objective tools to identify gifting, personality preferences or ministry strengths are of great benefit when advising workers in transition. These tools can help us to evaluate each worker's strengths and limitations. While leaders and workers may wish for an easy formula or a computer-generated answer, we need to prayerfully determine the best niche for ministry.

Emphasising the good practices in personal development and ensuring good-fit of ministry assignments will undoubtedly reduce the level of preventable loss in our ministries. At the end of the day, workers who find the right fit for ministry will remain in ministry and thrive. Those who struggle significantly in ill-fitting ministries will inevitably end up elsewhere. Good practice does not mean that we always get it right, but that we are intentionally trying to move in the right direction.

Discussion questions:

1. How does your agency encourage its missionaries to develop a mind-set of lifelong learning?

2. To what degree does your organisation (agency or church) conduct regular appraisals (or annual appraisals) to evaluate and assess each missionary's ministry and training needs, in order to enhance each missionary's level of satisfaction and effectiveness in ministry?

3. What opportunities are currently provided for ongoing training and personal development of your missionaries on the field? What else could be done to equip your missionaries as they mature and as the environment around them changes? How could partnership facilitate this?

Shaping a staff development and care team to combat member attrition

Paul Rhoads[3] and Steve Hoke,[4] Church Resource Ministries,[5] USA

- One couple, misplaced into team leadership, needed time off with counselling and care in order to recover sufficiently before returning to field service.

- One young single, after several ill-timed relational forays, needed an extended furlough in order to debrief and refocus future ministry initiatives.

- One team, experiencing the death of the national team leader, needs the presence and support of care members to listen, be alongside, and validate their year-long experience of watching a team member die.

---

3   Paul Rhoads, currently Executive Vice President of Church Resource Ministries (CRM), served as the founding director of the Staff Development and Care Team, and now directs CRM's ministry teams around the world.

4   Steve Hoke is Vice President of People Development, focusing on staff training and spiritual direction.

5   Church Resource Ministries is a North America-based agency focused on leader development in 22 countries.

At Church Resource Ministries (CRM) we are learning to look out for such member care incidents so they will not go unnoticed nor be left unattended by our team leaders. Since the 1990s, we have been concerned about taking better care of staff around the world. After attempting to launch a "Staff Care Task Force" in earlier years but with limited success, we realised we had to design something for the long-term. In this case study, we will explain how CRM has shaped a Staff Development and Care team.

What we tried between 1999 and 2003:

1. We forged a team to paint a vision[6]

   A Vice President,[7] who had skills in forming teams and experience in counselling and staff care, was asked to form a Staff Care Team. He could have started by listing needs or immediately scheduling trips to staff "hot spots." Instead, he began by building a closely knit team of like-minded people. Together, they created a vision for where the member care efforts ought to be and how CRM should get there.

2. We designed a development and care model of ministry

   We were then ready to consider member care models. We started with Kelly O'Donnell's article on "Doing Member Care Well,"[8] in which he suggested a way to structure the various components of missionary care.

   When designing the model of ministry, we considered the particular strengths and needs of our organisation. We wanted personal and family care which nurtured individual and family spiritual formation as well as ministry development. The goal was healthy members and effective ministry.

   Central to our model was four support systems or teams. Each staff member personally recruits a team to sustain them over the long-haul: an intercession team, a financial support team, a personal support team of close friends for regular communication and nurture, and a cluster of mentors they could access from a distance.

   Our holistic approach to staff care does more than merely react to member care needs. We would adopt a proactive approach to prevent problems from developing. Our efforts would involve training, with a focus on helping the team leader to become a more effective caregiver him/herself. We would constantly upgrade the team leader's skills while providing supplemental care when requested. Whenever a care issue took too much time or began to outstrip the gifting of the leader, we could be called in for assistance. In this way, we could leverage our gifting and multiply our effectiveness into

---

6 For more details, please refer to our case studies "Forging Team to Paint a Vision" in Chapter 14 on Team Building and Functioning.

7 'Vice President' refers to a leader whose rank is next below that of the President (the chief officer of an organisation) and who take the place of the President when necessary.

8 "Doing Member Care Well", Kelly O'Donnell, Evangelical Missions Quarterly, Vol.37 (2001), pp. 212-222.

qualified team leaders. We felt this was the only way a small to medium size organisation could ever hope to minister effectively to its entire staff.

3. We identified core values and our priorities[9]

We decided to identify shared team values to guide our new Staff Development and Care Team. Dialogue regarding core values began in the very first meeting, and continuing "values discussions" threaded through each meeting into the second year. A list of core values was eventually identified and they have directed how we focused our energies.

4. We began initial care efforts

The team began its care efforts, which included the following care activities:

- We launched a "Phone Care" initiative to talk to all of the staff within a three-month time span.
- We established plans to visit every staff team every year. We made additional individual visits at regional conferences.
- We created "safe places" or grace-filled environments when we were with staff. We began attending every regional staff conference as a team, and we were present to spend quality personal time with staff and schedule individual counselling or catch-up times as desired
- We refocused our Assessment process with incoming staff to proactively preclude some problems due to incomplete preparation or rushed assessments.
- We offered monthly Bible study and prayer time for staff in our office.
- We became more intentional about Furlough Debriefing and Re-entry, so that all returning staff had a chance to debrief their term of cross-cultural service.
- We offered Mid-Career Assessments to all staff who had served for more than six years.
- The biggest change was now having a team in place to **prayerfully consider** every member care need that surfaced, **before** responding. The team could evaluate each effort, rather than just one person trying to meet the entire needs of the organisation.

5. We added specialty help

Like many North American agencies, we already had a network of qualified clinical psychologists assisting us in assessments and crisis counselling. Now we could provide short-term crisis counselling for individuals and families in the field, sending an experienced counsellor to live with staff needing assistance for a week or more at a time. We began providing sign-ups for staff to meet with the counsellor during conference periods. In addition, we began to provide optional Spiritual Formation sessions at every conference, featuring

---

9   For more details, please refer to our case study "Crafting Core Values of a team at CRM" in Chapter 17 on "Organisational Values."

silent rooms, daily times for reflection, and opportunities to explore alternate approaches to spiritual disciplines.

6. We planned development and training initiatives

    In the past, our training provided for staff had been piecemeal, without a long-term plan of regular training events.

    Beginning with an annual needs assessments of all team leaders and directors, we developed a five-day curriculum for new directors, and subsequently continued an annual training event for directors each summer. The annual survey helped us focus the modules precisely on the specific needs identified by the directors in four major areas:

    *   Personal Development, including spiritual formation;
    *   Team Building and Formation;
    *   Team Vision and Ministry Development; and
    *   Organisational Communication.

    Each year we provide updated training in these four categories of a leader's responsibility.

    When the rest of our staff expressed their need for regular training for personal and ministry growth as well, the CRM-University (CRM-U) was birthed in 2004. It delivers in-house leader and skill training to our staff on a regular basis. Modules in at least four tracks are delivered as needed at annual all-staff training events: Core Staff Training (ministry basics we want all staff to master, including fostering healthy relational environments, refocusing leaders, etc.); Personal Development; Using CRM Ministry Resources; and Leader Development.

7. We started to innovate constantly

    No sooner had we launched our first initiatives, we realised that we would need to do more, and the next time around we would have to do it much better. Therefore, we developed working groups to work on specific tasks including the following: Family Care, Spiritual Health and Formation, and Staff Training. This allowed team members to specialise in one or two areas of their particular passion and experience.

What we learned (2000-2005)

1. Team formation and expansion

    Being team must precede *doing* care ministry. Having a team of called and gifted staff to analyse, pray, and respond to staff needs is critical. Even a small team (we started with six) can do a great deal of transformative proactive and reactive member care. Inclusion of new team members must be very intentional and gradual, but it should not be resisted once the initial team gets "formed."

2. Spiritual Formation

   Spiritual formation is the larger paradigm within which member care and staff development and training must take place. Regular prayer, listening and discerning must guide the team's care efforts.

3. Setting Expectations

   Forming a team to deal with staff needs can create the unrealistic expectation that the organisation should now meet every individual's every need. The team must focus on equipping leaders to become more effective care givers, while simultaneously equipping and motivating each member to own personal responsibility for their personal self-care.

4. Innovation and change

   Being attentive to alternative approaches and trends on the horizon allowed us to build on strengths and to include others as needed. We found it was easier to respond and incorporate fresh ideas as a team. Gifted teams are better suited to "morph" into responsive shapes than individuals already overwhelmed with responsibility.

5. Questions that remain

   We are exploring the following vital questions in the years ahead:
   - How can we best gauge or measure the effectiveness of our care efforts?
   - What are the most meaningful measures or indicators of staff health and effectiveness?
   - How can we evaluate the effectiveness of our training efforts?
   - How do we continue to equip team leaders to be more effective without disempowering them in their leadership role?
   - What criteria should guide the expansion of the SDC Team?

Discussion questions:

1. What pressing needs in your organisation suggest that a team approach may be required to meet those needs across the organisation?

2. Who are the people in your organisation with a heart for staff development and training? How can you invite their participation?

3. Who are the people in your organisation with a heart for improving member care? How can you invite their participation?

4. Who should be involved in the team formation process for successful implementation of a team's ministry?

In the real world

A table to stimulate ideas for best practice in mission partnership. For further explanation, see page 7.

This chart has been partially filled in for you. Now you fill in the blanks.

Who? → When? ↓	Home Church	Missionary	Mission Agencies	External Partners
Continuous	➢ Affirm God-given potential ➢ Appoint people according to gifting ➢ Teach the importance of life-long learning ➢ Create a culture which encourages personal development			
Recruitment		➢ Discover personal profile	➢ Know and work with profile of candidate	➢ Develop tools to discover gifting and experience
Preparation		➢ Create a personal development plan	➢ Emphasise personal development	➢ Provide basic training
On field		➢ Be committed to life-long learning ➢ Provide feedback about needed education	➢ Encourage and give time to keep learning ➢ Provide room to shape and develop own ministry	➢ Develop materials for continuous learning
Crisis				
Furlough	➢ Mentor and coach missionaries on home assignment	➢ Evaluate and seek new direction		➢ Provide special training modules
Re-entry		➢ Share experiences		

24

Staff Development
Leadership Development and Mentoring

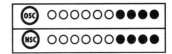

The facts

Within the broad subject of staff development, leadership development and mentoring was a significant enough area to merit exploration in detail. In OSC, leadership development correlates with retention across almost every individual rating, and in NSC the correlation is almost as consistently linked. The high rating for performance and significance of Leadership development among people served (Q69) highlights the importance placed on sustainability and indigenisation in OSC, and this was reflected almost as strongly in NSC. Leadership development seems to be something we see as needed among the people the organisation seeks to serve, but not recognised as a need internally.

The data

Q. No.	Factor	OSC Health Indicator	✓	NSC Health Indicator	✓
49	Good on-field supervision is provided (quantity and quality)	OOOO●●●●●●	✓	OOOOO●●●●●	✓
52	Effective on-field orientation is in place for new missionary	OOOOO●●●●●	✓	OOOOO●●●●●	✓
54	Ongoing language and culture training are actively encouraged	OOOOOOO●●●	✓	OOOOOO●●●●	
55	Missionaries are provided with opportunities for continuous training and development of gifts and skills	OOOOOO●●●●	✓	OOOOOO●●●●	✓
56	Missionaries are assigned roles according to their gifting and experience	OOOOOO●●●●		OOOOOO●●●●	✓

57	Missionaries are given room to shape and develop their own ministry	OOOOOOOO●●	✓	OOOOOOO●●●	✓
64	Missionaries regularly evaluate and seek to improve the agency's ministry	OO●●●●●●●●	✓	OOOO●●●●●●	
69	Missionaries are developing leadership among the people they serve	OOOOOOOO●●	✓	OOOOOO●●●●	✓
70	Missionaries experience a sense of fulfilment in their ministry	OOOOOOOO●●	✓	OOOOOOO●●●	✓

The key findings

✓ Missionaries are developing leadership among the people they serve (Q69) received the highest rating among all ministry goals in OSC and it was clearly correlated with retention.

✓ Missionaries are provided with continuous training and development of new gifts (Q55) was correlated with high retention in OSC and NSC.

✓ Good on-field supervision (Q49) was highly correlated with retention in OSC and NSC.

✓ Missionaries given room to shape their own ministry (Q57) moderately correlated with retention.

What it means

Rob Hay

Leadership development and mentoring are buzz words in mission at present. ReMAP II provided insight into whether these concepts were more than talk.

Overall, the rating given by mission executives for performance and significance in this area was fairly good, with a rating of six out of ten in OSC, and five in NSC. This is encouraging, given the strong link to retention—eight out of the nine areas correlated with retention in OSC, and seven out of nine in NSC. The strong correlation with retention demonstrates just how important leadership development and mentoring is. However, while the overall picture is encouraging, there is significant variation between individual factors.

Questions 69 [Q69 *Missionaries are developing leadership among the people they serve*], received a high rating in OSC and a good rating in NSC. This emphasis on sustainability and indigenisation is missiologically sound and practically helpful, contributing significantly to the creation of self-sustaining churches. Questions

57 [Q57 *Missionaries are given room to shape and develop their own ministry*] and 70 [Q70 *Missionaries experience a sense of fulfilment in their ministry*] both received very good ratings (eight and seven out of ten in OSC and NSC respectively), which demonstrates support of the business world principle that happy, fulfilled people are effective and productive workers.

The capacity for and quality of supervision is an area to be concerned about. Mentoring or development of people effectively takes time, relationships, and people with the experience and abilities required. The rating given to the provision of field supervision [Q49 *Good on-field supervision is provided (quantity and quality)*] received a low rating of five out of ten in OSC and six in NSC. Serious development of people must begin with the key people: leaders and supervisors. However, this result, combined with the results regarding workload (Questions 61 and 64) indicate that there is little capacity within the organisations currently to effect this change.

External help may be necessary to develop both the capacity and skills for mentoring to permeate the organisation. Research on organisations considered to be "learning organisations" suggests that developing a learning culture begins at the top level. Top level leaders must embrace the new quality initially, prioritise it, and model it for the wider staff. The high rating on developing leadership among those served (Question 69, discussed above) would seem to give hope that we do have the skills to develop leadership, but it would be prudent to explore how these skills can be produced internally as well. Reducing ministry (outward) capacity for the sake of organisational (internal) health may seem to be a difficult decision, but greater effectiveness could be achieved in the organisation by reallocating the focus of those resources for a period of time, making a good future investment.

Question 55 [Q55 *Missionaries are provided with opportunities for continuous training and development of gifts and skills*] highlights the importance of ongoing training. This was discussed in Chapter 23, but the good rating needs, for the context of leadership development, to be linked to Question 64 [Q64 *Missionaries regularly evaluate and seek to improve the agency's ministry*]. Training can be focused on a person's vocation (e.g. accountancy qualifications) or general skills development (e.g. assertiveness training), but for leadership development and mentoring, training involves giving people the opportunity to walk with other leaders, to see leaders in action, and to be intimately involved in the struggles, pondering and wrestling that leaders do as they lead an organisation.

Mentorees need to be encouraged to ask, "Why?". They need to see leaders asking "Why?". In this way, they will develop the skills essential for leaders—being able to step back from the immediate issue and take in the big picture. The results indicated that most leaders do not have the time for this type of mentoring and reflecting, especially since it always takes longer to take action while mentoring someone through that reflective process with you. As was covered in Chapter 21, leadership should be seen as a skill, vocation and indeed, a calling in its own right. Only then will we invest the kind of time and energy into developing skills in this area as we do in other, traditionally legitimate areas.

Haggai Institute – a model for training leaders in leadership and evangelism

David Wong,[1] Haggai Institute, Singapore

When John Edmund Haggai (the Founder of Haggai Institute) conceived the idea of an institute focused on leadership development for global mission, he spelled out the following approach:

- Emphasise the "How" of evangelism.

- Target credentialed and competent business, professional and religious leaders from strategic areas, including countries closed to traditional missionary endeavours.

- Select faculty, primarily from the Asia-Pacific region, Africa and Latin America, who are experts with continuously fresh, hands-on experience in evangelism.

- Require faculty members to develop their own innovative, culturally relevant materials within the curriculum guidelines.

- Employ highly interactive and catalytic teaching-learning methods.

- Motivate leaders to advance the skills of others within the community of believers by transferring what they learned, thus producing a multiplier effect leading to exponential growth in the evangelisation process.

- Prepare leaders to develop ministry resources in their countries using good biblical principles of stewardship.

In doing so, John Haggai defined the scope of the curriculum, the quality of the participants, the calibre of the faculty, the nature of the training materials, the style of teaching, as well as the follow-up to the training.

Haggai Institute has a clear focus and a specific objective, namely, to train Christian leaders to evangelise their own people and train others to do the same. Training takes the form of a short-term seminar, residential in nature, and focused on this objective.

Focus: evangelism, without compromise or offence

The focus of training at Haggai Institute is evangelism. Sadly, evangelism has fallen into disrepute. On the one hand, it comes across to non-Christians as obnoxious and arrogant. On the other, it languishes among Christians who are fear-

---

1 Rev. Dr. David Wong is the Vice President of International Training at Haggai Institute, overseeing the training programme in both Hawaii and Singapore. He was Director of Training for Hawaii from 1994 to 2000, where he served as an overseer, faculty member and mentor to hundreds of Christian leaders from over 100 nations. Prior to this, David pastored a church for 17 years, taught as guest lecturer in several theological schools, and served as Deputy Dean of the Biblical Graduate School of Theology in Singapore. David completed his doctoral studies at Fuller Theological Seminary in 2004 with a project on leadership and learning paradigms.

ful to proclaim it as "the power of God for the salvation of everyone who believes" (Romans 1.16).

The Institute calls on the leaders it trains to proclaim the gospel "without compromise and without offence." We are not to compromise the content of the gospel, neither are we to make its delivery offensive. Since most leaders of the Two-Thirds world live in countries where the majority religion is Buddhism, Hinduism or Islam, there is a strong temptation to play down the uniqueness of the gospel. Yet, syncretism (the belief that all religions are equally good and true) severs the jugular vein of evangelism. While the content of the gospel may remain an offence (I Corinthians 1:23), its presentation should never be offensive. Indigenous leaders have a distinct advantage in this regard. They know the culture and its nuances. They know what offends and they avoid offending others when delivering the gospel.

Approach: start from within, begin at the top

The best people to reach the teeming millions of the Two-Thirds world are the people of those nations. Instead of sending Western missionaries to these countries, why not train nationals to reach nationals with the gospel? The advantages they have over foreigners are obvious. They know the language and culture. They do not need visas or visa renewals to work in their countries. They remain when foreigners are forced to leave for political, economic or health reasons.

In contrast, Western missionaries take at least a year to learn the language and culture, and longer to earn their credibility among the people of the host country. The countries with the greatest need are the ones most likely to reject their application for visas. Even if approved, visas need to be renewed every so many years. Also, approximately a quarter of such a missionary force is out of circulation at any one time on account of their furlough. Perhaps most damaging of all is the perception they give: that Christianity is a Western religion, and the Church a tool of Western imperialism.

Besides starting from within a country, the approach at Haggai Institute also calls for beginning at the top. When writing out the philosophy of the training programme, Haggai's first of seven points was: "Training should focus on Christians whose leadership had already been demonstrated in the Church and in the professions."

The temptation in doing evangelism is to go where the people are most responsive and the results most immediate. Consequently, evangelism is often done among the poor, the uneducated, and the marginalised. The higher echelons of society are neglected. Such evangelism results in the gospel being seen as a crutch for those who cannot make it on their own.

For evangelism to reach a whole community, and for the gospel to make significant changes in the community (and nation), we must go to the leaders. Who can reach these leaders with the gospel? The answer must be leaders of the same or higher calibre; only they can commend the gospel as good news for both the rich and the poor, the educated and the illiterate. Hence, the approach of the Institute is to start from the top. When the top is changed, change filters down to the bottom.

Method: catalytic teaching and learning

John Haggai emphasised that, "Our training is catalytic; it is not paternalistic. It is a deliberate attempt to move away from the paternalism as perceived in the Western missionaries who came with the colonialists to many parts of the under-developed world." Such attitudes can still be perceived today, where those doing cross-cultural missions or training in less developed countries have been known to speak and act like paternalistic patrons. It is understandable, as they often have to address churches and people who are "below" them, economically, socially and intellectually.

However, the situation at the Institute is different. Since we do not train those who want to be leaders, but those who are already leaders, the participants come in at a level comparable to the level of our facilitators. Thus, the training has to be catalytic, interactive and collaborative. Participants are not there to absorb like sponges; they are there to sharpen one another like iron (Proverbs 27.17). Not only do participants sharpen one another, they sharpen the facilitators too!

The role of the facilitators is as their designation denotes: to facilitate the learning process. They are encouraged to do so in a number of ways: First, to encourage participants to ask questions and make comments. It is not rude (as it is in some cultures) to interrupt the facilitator when he is teaching. Second, to give the participants the last 15 minutes of the lecture slot for questions. That time belongs to the participants, not the facilitator. Third, to use one of the lecture slots for a workshop where the facilitator involves the participants in an activity, and then processes the learning points with them.

During question time, facilitators are urged to resist the temptation to answer all the questions themselves. They need not pose as "know-alls." They can invite answers from the participants. A question from one participant may be better answered by another participant who comes from the same region, or a similar social or political culture. Thus, we learn from one another, and not only from the teacher.

Workshops also make up an integral part of teaching. During the workshop, the facilitator takes no more than ten minutes (e.g. to give instructions), then gets the participants into an activity. It could be a game, a role play, buzz groups or any similar exercise, as long as it involves every person. It could be indoor or outdoor, preferably requiring some form of physical activity. A class lecture cannot match the catalytic impact of a good workshop. One facilitator puts it thus: "The lecture gets the head, but the workshop gets the guts."

For a workshop to achieve the purpose of interactive learning, the activity must be appropriately processed. The processing must be done by the participants while the facilitator acts only to sum up their findings. Of course, the facilitator runs the risk of watching the workshop take a direction different from what he had planned but as long as learning is achieved, the purpose of the workshop is achieved.

Finally, every faculty is evaluated by the participants. For many years, an evaluation tool was used that placed the onus of the learning process on the teaching activity. Thus, the questions asked were: Did the lecturer have an objective? Was his delivery clear? Did he sufficiently involve participants?

For participants who come from cultures where teachers and elders are highly respected, such evaluation brought unease. "Who am I to evaluate my teacher?" some had said. In addition, at the close of each series of lectures, when the faculty had delivered his final challenge, it seemed inappropriate that participants would sit back and evaluate how the faculty had taught.

If learning is collaborative, surely the participant shares in the burden of learning. The above questions are now modified to: How well did I understand the lectures? Was I able to relate the material to my needs? Was I sufficiently involved in class? Was I able to follow the delivery? Did I feel motivated to put into practice what I have learned?

Participants are more inclined to evaluate themselves as learners. It also helps in the learning process that, at the end of the lecture series, participants ask themselves, "How and what have I learned?" rather than "How has the faculty taught?"

The shift of focus means also the change of the tool's name from "Faculty Evaluation" to "Participant Feedback." Despite that, it still fulfils its purpose of helping the faculty know how he or she has taught. For example, if a participant assesses himself poorly on how he has followed the delivery, the faculty will need to ask whether he has had a part in the deficiency of the delivery process.

As the participants are there to learn, the facilitators are there for the same. Catalytic learning works both ways.

Expectation: train others

There is only one requirement the Institute expects of each candidate after the training: Each candidate must return to his or her country, stay there for at least two years, and pass the training to at least a hundred people. Every participant at the training seminar is made aware that the training is not only for him or her; it is for the people he or she represents in his nation, community, church or organisation.

Discussion questions:

1. What are the strengths of the Haggai Institute model for leadership development and training in evangelism? What are the weaknesses?

2. Could this be a suitable model for leadership development in your region? What do you think?

3. What models of leadership development and mentoring exist in your country or region? What are their strengths and/or weaknesses?

Leader development in OMF

David Dougherty,[2] OMF International,[3] USA

OMF International's leader development programme was born out of a need for added effectiveness in our ministry. In the early 1990s, a shift from an older to younger generation left us with a growing gap between current leaders and emerging leaders. To close the gap, we needed to better equip our mission leaders. Beginning in 1995, we began taking a series of steps that led to a substantial investment in leader development for OMF. Here are some of the most significant.

Support from OMF and other mission leaders

The first positive step in developing our programme came from our then General Director, David Pickard. His enthusiastic endorsement and provision of key staff was a major factor in our early success. Dr. Dan Bacon's leadership[4] and involvement was another major factor in launching our programme.

Funding for leader development

OMF has a well-known policy of not soliciting ministry funds. However, a Christian foundation offered a large grant for our ministry, which included $150,000 for leadership development. This initial funding was a marvellous provision of the

---

2 David Dougherty is a member of the leader development team for OMF International. David conducts leader training throughout Asia for OMF, as well as for several other agencies. David also serves as programme chair and facilitator for the IFMA-EFMA LeaderLink programme, which has trained almost 1,000 mission agency leaders over the past seven years.

3 OMF International, formerly the China Inland Mission, has been sending missionaries to East Asian countries for 140 years. Today, OMF International has approximately 1,300 adults and 600+ children, representing around 30 different nationalities. The missionaries are being sent from 18 sending bases, both Asian and non-Asian, and they work mainly in East Asia.

4 Dan Bacon and his wife, Lindie, joined OMF International in 1967 as church planters in northern Japan. During their ten years in Asia, they helped plant three congregations. Dan later served as the US Director for OMF for 20 years. From 1998 to 2000 Dan and Lindie moved to OMF's international headquarters in Singapore to take on the role of International Director for Mobilization. When they moved back to the US, Dan became the Director for Member Development at OMF, serving OMF members by helping them develop spiritually and as leaders. Although now reassigned since 2004, Dan and Lindie are still actively involved in leadership development for OMF and other agencies.

Lord that enabled us to invite people to participate in training events without having to charge them for programme or personal (travel and housing) expense.

We were able to develop a curriculum using a combination of high quality programmes developed by others (Leadership Challenge and Situational Leadership) as well as those we developed from our own experience. This allowed us to field test the programme and to gain essential early feedback from participants.

The positive feedback from our first programme participants was a major factor in gaining favourable attention from OMF directors, and encouragement to continue to develop the programme.

The OMF leader profile

One of the early steps in the OMF programme was development of a profile of an OMF leader. Here is an abbreviated form of that profile:

1. Influence: Godly leadership is influencing other people toward God's purposes for them primarily by setting the pace and showing the way (e.g., modelling).

2. Spiritual authority: Spiritual authority, which is rooted in Christ-like character, and Spirit-empowered competence are both essential for godly leaders.

3. Vision: A godly leader is a person of genuine vision—seeing with the eye of faith what God purposes to do.

4. Servanthood: Godly leadership is *serving* those we are called to lead.

5. Lifelong development: The formation of a godly leader involves the lifelong development of godly character, leadership skills, and strategic values.

6. Personal awareness: Godly leaders have a proper estimate of their own strengths and limitations and are confident, but not arrogant, in their calling and equipping for leadership ministry.

7. Leadership skills: Godly leadership involves developing team relationships, achieving tasks, and inspiring and motivating those who are led.

Developing the profile accomplished several major things for us. It involved a number of OMF leaders in thinking about intentional leader development for the mission. It also marked the objective that our programme was aiming toward. Each of our specific programmes is designed to help leaders move toward the profile in key areas.

Developing the profile led us to a key paradigm for all our leader development programmes. We work on a "Development Goal," "Current Progress," and "Next Steps," model that looks something like this:

Assessing current progress

The next component of our model is to assess the participant's current progress toward the goal. We use an assessment, developed by Dan Bacon, to find out where OMF members are on each element of the profile.

Establishing next steps in development

Having identified the current development level in a particular growth area, and the level we want to develop toward, the final step is determining what might be involved in moving toward the developmental goal. We use the Centre for Creative Leadership model[5] with the elements of assessment, challenge, and support.

Effective leader development programmes offer some tracking or accountability dimension to keep participants on track toward their goals. We have struggled in OMF to implement tracking. The transitory nature of the contact we have with programme participants (typically three to five days) makes it necessary to communicate with programme participants primarily via e-mail.

Identifying internal audiences for leader development

We began our programme by focusing on emerging leaders. There might have been advantages in starting with current field and international directors, but there were also strong advantages in starting with the emerging leaders. In several of our smaller fields, the current leader group merged with the emerging leader group, and we worked with all of them together.

We ultimately developed a programme which focused on three distinct audiences for leader development in OMF. These audiences included Senior Leaders (field and regional directors), Emerging Leaders (ministry team leaders), and New Leaders (those recently appointed).

Developing programmes to deliver leader development

- Our first efforts in addressing needs of emerging leaders led us to call the programme "Project: Timothy" recognising Paul's efforts at developing leaders on his ministry team.

- New leaders were the focus of the third programme. A major objective for this programme was "socialising organisational vision and values." As members move into international leadership, it is important for them to confirm their understanding and commitment to OMF's current vision and values.

- The most recent addition to our leader development curriculum is focused on "executive" leaders at the top two levels of each field, the national director and regional directors.

---

5   For more details, visit the Centre of Creative Leadership website: www.ccl.org/leadership/index.aspx

Looking ahead

The programme needs to continue to grow and develop with the needs of the organisation. With the recent appointment of a new director, her insights and vision should help us to do this. We look forward to the exciting things the Lord will do as we seek to continue to inspire OMF's 1,300 members to greater impact in the "urgent evangelisation of East Asia's peoples."

Discussion questions:

1. What are the strengths of the leader development programme at OMF? What are the weaknesses?

2. Does your organisation have a leader development programme? What aspects of your programme can be improved? How would you do this?

In the real world

A table to stimulate ideas for best practice in mission partnership. For further explanation, see page 7.

This chart has been partially filled in for you. Now you fill in the blanks.

Who? → When? ↓	Home Church	Missionary	Mission Agencies	External Partners
Continuous	➢ Teach and practice mentoring ➢ Teach and practice accountability ➢ Train to train (2 Timothy 2:2) ➢ Be examples in life and work	➢ Have a learning attitude	➢ Have a culture of seeking each other's personal development	
Recruitment			➢ Check openness for accountability	
Preparation		➢ Build relationship with agency	➢ Build relationship with missionary	➢ Offer interactive training tools ➢ Teach competence and character ➢ Develop mentoring models
On field	➢ Be involved in life and ministry	➢ Be transparent and informative ➢ Be accountable	➢ Have mentoring structures	➢ Facilitate communication
Crisis	➢ Be available	➢ Be as open as possible		
Furlough		➢ Take time to evaluate life and ministry		
Re-entry		➢ Be involved in training and mentoring		

25

Staff Development
Appraisal and Review
(Organisational and Individual)

The facts

The use of appraisals and individual reviews is highly correlated with retention. Reviews provide mission partners with the opportunity to be praised, but also to be encouraged to improve or change the ministry and to submit their own ideas and observations to help the organisation fulfil its vision and goals. The overall score shows that while both OSC and NSC have a reasonable level of effectiveness, there is still room for improvement.

The data

Q No.	Factor	OSC Health Indicator	✓	NSC Health Indicator	✓
42	There is a free flow of communication to and from the leadership	○○○○○○●●●●	✓	○○○○○○●●●●	
44	Missionaries are included in major decisions related to the field	○○○○○○○●●●		○○○○○○●●●●	
50	Leaders conduct an annual performance/ministry review with each missionary	○○○○●●●●●●	✓	○○○●●●●●●●	✓
55	Missionaries are provided with opportunities for continuous training and development of gifts and skills	○○○○○○●●●●	✓	○○○○○○●●●●	✓
56	Missionaries are assigned roles according to their gifting and experience	○○○○○○●●●●		○○○○○○●●●●	✓
57	Missionaries are given room to shape and develop their own ministry	○○○○○○○○●●	✓	○○○○○○○●●●	✓

| 64 | Missionaries regularly evaluate and seek to improve the agency's ministry | ○○●●●●●●●● | ✓ | ○○○○●●●●●● | |
| 70 | Missionaries experience a sense of fulfilment in their ministry | ○○○○○○○○●● | ✓ | ○○○○○○○●●● | ✓ |

The key findings

✓ Conducting performance reviews (Q50) was highly correlated with retention for preventable attrition in NSC and OSC.

✓ Missionaries regularly evaluate and seek to improve their ministry (Q64) was highly correlated with retention in OSC.

✓ Free flow of communication to leadership (Q42) was highly correlated with retention in OSC.

✓ Missionaries included in major decisions (Q44) received a relatively low rating in performance and significance and, in NSC, even negatively correlated with retention.

What it means

Sarah Hay

Regular appraisals and reviews have proved to be very effective in modern business. In the ReMAP II questionnaire, however, mission executives gave reviews a relatively low rating for significance and effectiveness. This may be typical for many organisations, as mentioning the word "appraisal" brings mixed feelings in many staff. Reaction to an appraisal may be one of fear, of hate, or simply indifference. I remember approaching my first appraisal, some 12 years ago, with absolute dread. My manager was a fairly high-powered, ambitious lady, and I was scared about what she may have to say. Only when a colleague reminded me that she was, at the end of the day, a human being with the same basic needs as me, was I able to relax and discover that an appraisal does not need to be a scary process! Others have said that their appraisal was a waste of time with no meaning expressed and no action resulting, thus carried out just to be checked off the list.

Unfortunately, many organisations will have an ineffective appraisal or annual review plan. Some managers give appraisals low priority and simply do not carry out the review or, worse, conduct appraisals without intending meaningful dialogue, thus achieving nothing more than discouraging the individual. Why is it that appraisals are often a low priority? Perhaps because few managers really want to manage people! Being promoted in the secular world often requires managing people as well as being good at one's profession. Yet managing people is often not something the person has trained for as a part of that profession. In the secular world, however, training is usually provided for taking on such a role. In the mission world, mission partners can end up managing a team even if this was not their desire or expectation.[1] Because of a limited workforce, there is just no other option. For such managers, appraisals represent an added burden which takes them away from their "real job" (as they perceive it in their priorities).

Appraisals are sometimes seen as form filling and time-consuming, divorced from organisational realities. Some feel appraisals favour people with easily quantifiable roles and that they discourage teamwork. Also, perhaps magnified by Christian values of encouragement and a trait of not wanting to offend (some would say not telling the truth!), some feel uncomfortable discussing issues in which a person may be struggling. And some even find it difficult to give/receive praise and thanks ("It was nothing—I only did it with the Lord's help"). (This will of course vary with different cultures.)

With all these issues, why should appraisals be done? The obvious answer is because ReMAP II has shown a high correlation between doing appraisals and retaining people. There are many reasons that could be behind this correlation. First, the rationale of appraisals is to increase an individual's (and thus an organisation's) performance or ministry success by working smarter, not harder.[2] What takes more effort: searching for a file not put away or taking it from the correct place in the filing cabinet? In the same way, staff could perform comfortably within their limited ability, or they could, with a manager's help, extend their ability through affirmation and identification of training needs. A manager's help is best expressed through an appraisal process. Appraisals are a proven way of imparting value and increased performance, which leads to job satisfaction. ReMAP II demonstrates this is not just a Western concept. Without effective, well done appraisals, retention rates will decrease.

The key principles of an appraisal are as follows:

- Review and evaluate past performance, skills and behaviour against the objectives of the job. Seek to learn from this review and improve the work where possible.
- Express encouragement and appreciation.
- Agree on future objectives and priorities.
- Identify training and development needs.
- Give opportunity for individuals to provide feedback about the team/organisation.
- Ensure awareness of the organisation's vision, strategy and goals.
- Motivate.

---

1   In research, almost 80% of missionaries who go into mission not expecting to lead end up in some kind of leadership position. Unpublished research in progress by Rob Hay, "'Your Story'—Hearing the Voices of Mission Partners," (Redcliffe College, Gloucester, UK).

2   See Chapter 18 where it is clear that there is a global work overload issue.

Appraisals are not simply a "well done" chat. Many of the questions for this section of the ReMAP II survey should be covered in an appraisal (see "The data" for the list). Objectives must be set, areas of concern explored, and, as Henkie Maritz describes in his case study, appropriate ministry fit discussed (i.e. is the person in the right role?).

In order to improve an appraisal process, best practice suggests that the appraiser should receive some basic training. A number of areas need to be addressed in preparing managers to conduct appraisals:

Preparation:
Appraisers should prepare by looking at the person's job description and previous year's objectives. Are there any reasons already known that may have prevented the individual from meeting their objectives? Consider logistical and practical issues of the appraisal, even seating arrangements.

Appraisal skills:
Skills utilised in selection interviews are transferable to appraisal interviews. For example, building quick rapport, putting people at ease, explaining the interview structure, allowing silences for reflection, note-taking, and confidentiality.

Appraisal content:
Always begin with positive feedback. Ask the individual what they feel has gone well. Ask them to self-review and even identify possible solutions to problems. (Many organisations have an appraisal or review form the individual completes prior to the interview, which helps them to prepare. Look at the website for some examples). Discuss areas of weakness or poor performance. Allow the individual time to explain their point of view and suggest solutions rather than imposing your own. Sandwich criticism with praise and appreciation so that you begin and end on a positive note and minimise feelings of despair or despondency.

Objective agreement:
Use the traditional acronym SMART. Objectives should be Specific, Measurable, Agreed, Realistic and Time bound. They should also be linked to the organisation's vision and objectives.

Training and development needs agreement:
Discuss areas for training and development, though these must be related to the role and not a wish list.

Conclusion:
It can be helpful to ask the individual to summarise the interview (so confirming that they have understood what has been discussed). The appraiser then fills in any gaps and highlights what is to happen next. Many agencies complete an appraisal form, which is signed by both parties and then passed to the next level manager. A means for appealing against the final outcome of the appraisal if the individual is not happy should also be provided.

Appraisals are, in theory, a fairly straightforward process, but there are some dangers and pitfalls to avoid. Be sure to analyse performance and not personality. Do not pre-judge or argue during an appraisal. Focus on the entire past year, rather than the immediate past. Ensure that difficult issues are not avoided, but discussed openly. These are essential for the appraisal to have credibility or a successful outcome.

Appraisals should be a two-way process of communication. Interestingly, [Q42 *There is a free flow of communication to and from the leadership*] received a fairly mediocre rating for both OSC and NSC, but was only correlated with retention in OSC. This may be due to cultural attitudes towards leadership and authority. In NSC, it may not be appropriate for an individual to question or give ideas to someone in authority out of respect. In this case, there would be no expectation of this type communication with the leadership.

Question 64 [Q64 *Missionaries regularly evaluate and seek to improve the agency's ministry*] received a poor rating in performance and significance for OSC and NSC. The rating was lower for OSC and was correlated with retention, but not for NSC. Again, lack of correlation with retention may be due to cultural expectations of leadership. Many agencies in NSC are new (average age of 12 years), so likely, many of the mission partners have been present from their agency's inception and involved in shaping the organisation. Thus, they are persons of high regard and intimidating to approach. Further, traditional teaching in the NSC is more didactic and encourages people to accept what they are taught and not challenge the norms. Or, perhaps, despite the low rating, NSC agencies are functioning well and do not need challenging to improve. In OSC, the education system encourages thinking outside of the norm and encourages the expectation to be involved in organisational decisions, etc., which would explain why a low rating would correlate with retention. OSC clearly does need to improve communication related to feedback.

Appraisals provide an opportunity to discuss training and development needs. The opportunity for training and development of gifts and skills is an important factor in retention [Q55 *Missionaries are provided with opportunities for continuous training and development of gifts and skills*], but both OSC and NSC have low ratings in this area.[3] However, setting forth unachievable training and development needs will demotivate workers and staff. Depending on the field location, cost, and so on, some training options are impractical or may need to be deferred until home leave.

The manager must avoid the common pitfall of not following through on agreed training and development needs and not referring to the objectives and actions planned until the next appraisal one year hence. Lack of follow-through undermines the appraisal process and reinforces the view that appraisals are just an annual, bureaucratic process. Follow-through should include regular, informal chats throughout the year, which allows an individual to discuss any problems in achieving their objectives and provides opportunity for the manager to discuss problems from his or her viewpoint. A major performance issue should not be a surprise

---

3   See David Milligan's case study in Chapter 23 for a good exploration of staff development.

during an annual appraisal—the issue should have been discussed well before. Open, honest and regular communication leads to a dynamic, performance-enhancing appraisal process.

ReMAP II data reveals that agencies do seem reasonably good at allowing mission partners to shape and develop their own ministry. This is important for retention. However, the ratings were not as high for mission partners being assigned roles according to their gifting and experience [Q56 *Missionaries are assigned roles according to their gifting and experience*]. More surprising was that this question did not even correlate with affecting retention in OSC, for many of us know people who were put into the wrong role and end up leaving as a result! For this reason, selection and health/psychological assessments are important in identifying a person's right place and role. The data results may reflect that all agencies are doing a poor job (so the results highlight no great differences between them), or that agencies are all doing a reasonable job (again, so no agency stands out). Thus, no correlation can be demonstrated, because there is no great difference between the high and low retaining agencies.

This chapter will hopefully inspire agencies to revitalise their appraisal system. Appraisals are a key way to show appreciation, provide help in difficulties, recognise and develop training opportunities in a world more obsessed with learning than ever, and motivate toward fulfilment in ministry.

Ministry appraisal

Henkie Maritz,[4] World Mission Centre,[5] South Africa

Missionaries need a forum where they can:

- Share their joys and frustrations
- Evaluate goals and identify the reasons why the goals have or have not been achieved
- Look ahead to define new goals and identify areas that need improvement
- Discuss the possible need for personal or ministry changes
- Devise action plans for more effective ministry

Such a forum is the Ministry Appraisal.

The essence of a ministry appraisal is to facilitate the success of the missionary, to make them feel valued, and to let them know that they are worth keeping.

---

4 Henkie Maritz is a Software Engineer. Since 2000, he has worked part-time at the World Mission Centre in South Africa. In addition to assisting in organising certain events, he was Country Coordinator for the ReMAP II study in South Africa. The study gave him a deep appreciation for missionary sending organisations and the challenges they face.

5 World Mission Centre is a missions mobilisation organisation that mobilises the local church in South Africa for missions

Marius serves with Operation Mobilisation South Africa (OMSA). He has been training missionaries for 17 years. When Peter, his leader, facilitated a recent annual ministry appraisal, it became evident that Marius needed a change. Peter helped Marius to voice his frustrations and to address his desire for personal growth. Peter discussed Marius' vision and gifts, and explored how his new desired direction could be met within the organisation. The appraisal concluded with a mutual agreement that Marius would move on to leadership and mentoring responsibilities for trainers. An action plan was drawn up in order to make this change possible.

OMSA values ministry appraisal. Through ministry appraisals, each missionary feels valued by leadership. Ministry appraisals develop a win-win partnership between the organisation and the missionary. "The missionary must first be valued by his/her leader for the achievements of the previous period. That is why it is called an appraisal."

Serving in Mission South Africa (SIMSA) is another mission agency that values ministry appraisals. For SIMSA, the purpose of a ministry appraisal is not only to evaluate each missionary's effectiveness and health (spiritual, emotional, and physical), but also to give SIMSA an opportunity to evaluate whether a ministry is still achieving its original goals and is in line with the organisation's vision.

For example, in the 1950s, SIMSA started a Christian book ministry. The goal of the ministry was to put good Christian books in the hands of non-white church members. This need was born out of the political conditions in South Africa when non-white Christians did not have free access to Christian bookstores, and when Christian books were generally very expensive. During a ministry appraisal in the late 1990s, SIMSA realised that this ministry was no longer serving a purpose, because the South African political context had changed. Thus, SIMSA discontinued its book ministry.

Ministry appraisal is a good practice which is common among the high-retaining and highly effective mission agencies in South Africa. Here are some common features of Ministry Appraisal:

1. How often should a ministry appraisal be done?

   Most mission organisations have annual appraisals for every missionary.

   Several mission organisations also have a special appraisal at the end of a term (typically at the end of four years).

2. What is essential for successful ministry appraisal?

   A personal plan for each missionary's ministry is crucial for successful ministry appraisals. Before the missionary begins the first year, a plan for his/her ministry needs to be put into place. This personal plan will outline future expectations and goals in ministry, and it forms the basis for future ministry appraisals.

   Some mission organisations use personal interviews to establish a personal ministry plan.

3. What happens during the annual appraisal?

An annual appraisal is a scheduled meeting between the missionary and his/her direct leader. This ministry appraisal meeting has the following objectives:

- To review progress made on goals set in the initial personal plan
- To discuss any problems encountered
- To discuss progress made in the areas of cultural and language acquisition
- To consider ways to strengthen interpersonal relationships
- To challenge one another in our walk with God
- To adjust the personal plan accordingly

Where there are problems, the discussion may be broadened. Either the interviewer or the missionary may add to the core areas.

4. Why conduct an end-of-term appraisal?

The end-of-term appraisal, typically done at the start of home assignment, is similar to the annual appraisal but it has the following additional objectives:

- To evaluate and review the missionary's life over the entire term
- To evaluate and decide on the overall direction for the next term should the missionary go back for another term or should he/she be reassigned to a different position

Discussion questions:

1. Does your organisation perform regular ministry appraisals of your missionaries? If not, how could ministry appraisals be incorporated as a regular event by your mission leaders?

2. What questions would you include in the ministry appraisal of your workers?

In the real world

A table to stimulate ideas for best practice in mission partnership. For further explanation, see page 7.

This chart has been partially filled in for you. Now you fill in the blanks.

Who? → When? ↓	Home Church	Missionary	Mission Agencies	External Partners
Continuous	➢ Have clear structures and goals ➢ Have a culture of reviewing ministries			
Recruitment			➢ Communicate clear job descriptions	
Preparation		➢ Be well informed about expectations ➢ Make a personal development plan		➢ Develop tools for appraisal and review
On field		➢ Seek performance and ministry reviews ➢ Be open and transparent ➢ Prepare for reviews and appraisals	➢ Conduct annual performance/ministry reviews ➢ Be open for feedback on agency's practice ➢ Offer new perspectives for development	
Crisis				
Furlough		➢ Seek performance and ministry reviews	➢ Conduct performance/ ministry reviews	➢ Conduct performance/ ministry reviews
Re-entry		➢ Seek performance and ministry reviews	➢ Conduct performance/ ministry reviews	➢ Conduct performance/ ministry reviews

26

Ministry

The facts

Ministry refers to the work that the missionary undertakes.

> "As long as it is day, we must do the work of him who sent me. Night is coming, when no one can work. While I am in the world, I am the light of the world." John 9:4-5

"Doing the work of him who sent me" is often the explanation missionaries give for why they are motivated to minister. Missionaries' ministries are varied, but the research revealed key themes that apply to all ministries and which will increase satisfaction and retention as they are improved. The overall rating for this area (six for both OSC and NSC) is quite good and this is important because there is a strong relationship between these ratings and retention in OSC and NSC.

The data

Q. No.	Factor	OSC Health Indicator	✓	NSC Health Indicator	✓
41	Plans and job descriptions are communicated clearly to the missionary	○○○○○○●●●●	✓	○○○○○○●●●●	✓
42	There is a free flow of communication to and from the leadership	○○○○○○●●●●	✓	○○○○○○●●●●	
56	Missionaries are assigned roles according to their gifting and experience	○○○○○○●●●●		○○○○○○●●●●	✓
57	Missionaries are given room to shape and develop their own ministry	○○○○○○○○●●	✓	○○○○○○○●●●	✓
59	Missionaries are committed to their ministry	○○○○○○○○○●	✓	○○○○○○○○○●	✓

60	Missionaries are committed and loyal to the agency	○○○○○○●●●●	✓	○○○○○○○○●●	✓
61	Missionaries are generally not overloaded in the amount of work they do	○●●●●●●●●●	✓	○○○○●●●●●●	✓
62	Opportunities are provided for a ministry/role for the spouse	○○○○○○○●●●	✓	○○○○○○○●●●	
63	Missionaries have adequate administrative and practical support on the field	○○○○○○●●●●	✓	○○○○○○●●●●	✓
64	Missionaries regularly evaluate and seek to improve the agency's ministry	○○●●●●●●●●	✓	○○○○●●●●●●	
66	Missionaries are developing good relationships with the people they serve	○○○○○○○○○●		○○○○○○○●●●	
70	Missionaries experience a sense of fulfilment in their ministry	○○○○○○○○●●	✓	○○○○○○○●●●	✓

The key findings

✓ The overall average of ministry related factors is highly correlated with retention in OSC and NSC.

✓ Missionaries are given room to shape their ministry (Q57) received a high rating for performance and significance by mission executives in NSC and OSC and is correlated with total annual retention.

✓ Commitment of missionaries to their own ministry (Q59) was rated high and was correlated to total annual retention.

✓ Missionaries are committed and loyal to their agency (Q60) was very highly rated in NSC (much lower in OSC) and correlated with total annual retention in OSC and NSC.

✓ Appropriate amount of workload (Q61) received a much lower rating in OSC (danger of work overload) and correlated with retention.

✓ Adequate administrative and practical support (Q63) was rated very high in NSC and it was moderately correlated with retention in NSC and OSC.

✓ Missionaries evaluate and seek to improve their ministry (Q64) correlated with high retention in OSC.

✓ Ministry opportunities for spouse (Q62) was rated high in OSC and highly correlated with retention; yet it was rated much lower in NSC and even negatively correlated with total annual retention in NSC.

✓ Assignment of missionaries to their gifting (Q56) was rated very high in NSC and much lower in OSC (higher expectations?) and was moderately correlated with retention in NSC.

What it means

Rob Hay

The area of ministry focuses on the work and ministry of both the organisation and the missionary. Ministry is distinguished from other areas in that it addresses the work the organisation or missionary does, rather than the organisational issues of maintaining the organisation.

Strength in performance and significance ratings for questions related to ministry work correlates strongly with retention. OSC and NSC alike received an overall rating for performance and significance of six out of ten. While quite a good rating, the rating shows room for overall improvement. However, individual questions that contribute to the overall rating had varied ratings, so attention for improvement can be centred in key areas.

Boundaries are a key area for effective ministry. For individual missionaries or an organisation to be effective in work, they need to know what they should be doing, where their personal boundaries are, and what the boundaries of the organisation are. Organisational values help to form these boundaries, alongside expectations and roles (covered also in Chapter 20).

Role conflict is a term for ambiguity in an ill-defined role or in a role requiring inconsistent or contradictory behaviours. For example, a leader who is responsible for performance and objectives, who is also the sole source of pastoral care for that same team, may experience conflict in carrying out these roles. Clear job descriptions can be very helpful to resolve conflict or ambiguity. Job descriptions can be restrictive—listing each and every task the post-holder must do—or they can be too broad. Regardless, they must clearly map out the boundaries of the missionary's role. If they do this and, as Question 57 asked, if missionaries are given room to shape and develop their own ministry, then research in the field of secular organisations shows they are more satisfied and fulfilled.[1] Furthermore, Question 41 [Q41 *Plans and job descriptions are communicated clearly to the missionary*], and Question 57 (as above), correlate with retention (see Chapter 20).

To be able to shape and develop ministry requires time. Time—to think, plan, reflect, read, study, and to be aware of developments in the location, the wider world and the vocational area of the missionary—is essential to develop a healthy ministry that continues to grow, change and be relevant for the needs of the contemporary context. Being able to shape ministry also requires clear overall goals [Q40 *Vision and purpose are shared throughout the agency*] and an appropriate work-rest balance [Q61 *Missionaries are generally not overworked*]. Without time to work within clear goals, the ministry will become outdated and irrelevant and the missionary will fail to develop the new skills required for the changed world (see Chapter 23 for a fuller discussion on staff development issues).

---

1   Bruce Katcher, *Employees feel like slaves* (2004), cited from http://www.discoverysurveys.com/articles/itw-038.html

High retaining agencies also look for missionaries who have a high commitment to their own ministry [Q59 *Missionaries are committed to their ministry*], while being committed and loyal to the agency [Q60 *Missionaries are committed and loyal to the agency*]. This combination is often not easy to achieve, but it does appear to contribute to retention in NSC and OSC alike. Loyalty to the agency (Q60) is proving to be slightly more challenging in OSC than NSC,[2] although agencies generally seem to have little difficulty in ensuring that missionaries have a strong commitment to their own ministry.

Formulating the right ministry role for the post-holder helps retention, and in OSC it was important to do the same for the spouse. This issue was rated at seven out of ten in OSC and was clearly seen as important in the selection and assignment process. In NSC, role for the spouse was not rated as strongly and did not have a correlation with retention. However, in NSC, making assignment decisions based on a missionary's experience and gifts [Q56 *Missionaries are assigned roles according to their gifting and experience*] was important. While this was rated reasonably well in OSC and NSC (six out of ten), the issue only correlated with retention in NSC. High expectations in OSC that this be the *normal* process and expectation probably contributed to the result, meaning no significant difference between high and low retaining agencies was evident.

Ministry adaptation

Fayez Ishak,[3] Kaser El Dobara Church, Egypt

I would like to preface this case study by applauding the many expatriate missionaries who have served in Egypt and throughout the Arab world. These faithful servants have contributed in a significant way to the budding indigenous mission movement in this region, as well as the mobilisation of a growing number of Arab workers.

Personally, I have been deeply inspired and challenged by their passion, example, and extensive influence. I am convinced that they share a rich inheritance in heaven for their labours. They have paved the way for modern mission work as it is being practised today in the Arab world, and in many cases have paid a great price.

As a representative of a Middle Eastern church which both receives expatriate missionaries and sends Egyptian workers, I would like to highlight two cases that we have observed first-hand. The first case highlights the benefit of adapting plans to fit the situation in the field. The second is a reflection on a case of passive attrition.

---

2   See the case study on BMS World Missions in Chapter 9, "Changing training to gain commitment," by Alan Pain.

3   Fayez Ishak graduated from law school. He has been an Elder and the Director of the Mission Department at Kaser El Dobara Church in Cairo, Egypt for the last 14 years. He currently supervises, encourages, and ministers to 35 missionaries in several different countries.

The positive influence of an adaptable worker

Nathan was a bright, enthusiastic young man who came to Egypt full of passion and determination to plant churches for his denomination in Egypt. Zealous for the Lord and spurred by the positive results he had seen in his home church and previous mission experience, he eagerly began working towards his goal by starting home cell groups and working with majority background believers. However, in the first couple of years, he started to see that perhaps his plans were not the best way to serve the Kingdom of God in Egypt.

Therefore, Nathan took a teachable and humble approach, asking national church leaders and others for advice and being flexible to adapt his initial plans to the context. Nathan gradually discovered both the great need for partnership and networking among the different entities in Egypt, and in the process began to develop some of his greatest strengths in bringing these diverse entities together, training and equipping them. By the end of his 12 years of ministry in Egypt, he was co-leading quite an influential church planting movement among Egyptian churches and groups.

If one were to evaluate Nathan's ministry based on his original plan and the number of churches he planted, it was a failure. If, however, one looks at the extent of his influence on the expansion of the Kingdom of God in Egypt, he was an incredible influence!

Nathan is an example of one who succeeded in the struggle between the "missionary ego," which gauges effectiveness from flashy reports or in his case the number of churches planted, versus being humble and flexible and keeping a focus on investing in the Kingdom of God.

The passive attrition of a pioneer

In most cases, engaging in mission work in North Africa requires a true pioneering spirit and a tenacious character. It could be compared to attempting to dig a garden in a bed of rocks. Keith came to this North African country with just such a determination. He was a gifted evangelist, and because of his faithfulness and resolve in building the Kingdom of God, he saw the beginning of a church formed through his ministry.

Keith continued leading this young church with the same attitude and giftings which had been so vital in early evangelism, despite his lack of gifting as a pastor. These converts were in desperate need of shepherding and discipleship in order to grow and minister in their country. However, what they met in Keith was the same bold and intense evangelist who had first led them to the Lord. As an example, in one meeting, a North African was leading the people in worship, and some of the believers began clapping their hands to the songs. Keith whistled loudly, stood up, and brusquely declared that this was *not* appropriate behaviour in the church. He sat down again, and ordered the worship leader to proceed. (I doubt he would have intervened in such a way in his home church, yet in a mission context and while trying to function in a role that was not within his giftings, this was his natural reaction.)

Sadly, though Keith had played such a tremendous role in the pioneering mission work and evangelism in this country, the national believers could not hide their joy when he left the country. This and many other factors indicated that most likely his was a case of "passive attrition". Though Keith was physically still in the field, his actions and influence were so far from the real needs and state of the believers that he ceased to have any positive influence.

One of the key lessons we can learn to aid retention is to be careful not to try to fill too many roles or to expect our missionaries to perform multiple roles which they are simply not gifted in. Often, the simple act of stepping onto an airplane and going into a mission context is all it takes for us to lay aside one of the most basic principles of Christian leadership, that is, to function within our God-given gifts. We need the humility and the wisdom to discern when the needs before us are beyond the scope of our giftings, and in such cases step down and work with others, rather than falling prey to the temptation to perform all the needed roles.

In addition, our mission organisations and churches must have reasonable expectations for our workers, and in so doing train our workers to have reasonable expectations for themselves. We cannot place someone with a pastoral heart and no gift for evangelism into a position that requires a passionate evangelist! Likewise, a servant who is clearly gifted in church planting should not be put in a place where they will be consumed solely with administrative work. A basic principle could be that a missionary should not be expected to function well long-term in a role they cannot execute in their home country.

Discussion questions:

1. How could your agency help your missionaries to become more sensitive and culturally relevant in their inter-personal relationships on the field?

2. What qualities or skills would your missionaries require in order to adapt a ministry to fit the local cross-cultural context? What training or ministry experiences may be helpful?

Resilience in ministry despite trauma

Ron Brown,[4] CMA-Canada, Senegal

The global context is changing. Many countries are now being called high security alert nations. For example, the continent of Africa has become a more violent place to live and work. At any given time, there are a number of countries involved in ethnic wars, on the brink of a coup d'état, or in turmoil of one kind or another. Inevitably, when populations are at war, people risk being suddenly displaced through political evacuations.

Working in these kinds of settings are people associated with non-governmental organisations, relief and development agencies, and missionary organisations. The uncomfortable fact is that they will very likely experience personal trauma during their time overseas. For those bringing the good news, the troubled settings in which they minister are the new frontier for the gospel. Nations in crisis need a message of hope now more than ever.

Recently, a project[5] was conducted to discover factors that contribute to the resiliency and retention of missionaries who have gone through traumatic events in their missionary career in Africa and yet continue to serve there. In this case study, some key factors were identified and analysed which seem to contribute to resiliency in western missionaries in Africa. These factors were also emphasised in the good practices of their mission agencies.

Factors that contributed to missionary retention

In the project, missionaries who had experienced various types of trauma were interviewed. These missionaries had been able to continue in their missionary calling after their particular trauma. Two questions were considered:

- What pre-trauma factors contribute to the retention of these missionaries?
- What post-trauma factors contribute to the retention of these missionaries?

Four factors that missionaries brought into their trauma event were: a strong personal "call" to be where they were, a preparedness from birth, words from God, and sturdy relationships.

Four factors which emerged after the trauma were: experiencing the "keeper" side of God, hearing authoritative leadership voices, quickly finding new ministry foci, and benefiting from functional networks.

---

4 Ron Brown, DMin, has experienced three political evacuations: once as a missionary child during the Congo Simba rebellion, in 1991 from Congo-Kinshasa, and in 1997 from Congo-Brazzaville. He and his wife Myra have worked in Africa since 1979. They are currently the regional developers for CMA-Canada based in Dakar, Senegal. Dr. Brown is a member of the International Governing Board of the Mobile Member Care Team.

5 Ronald Brown, "*Self-identified retention factors by Western missionaries in Africa who have experienced traumatic events,*" DMin project. (Trinity International University, 2005).

Three unexpected results from the trauma event were a less encumbered way of living, embracing sudden transitions as doors to new ministries, and a reshaped life for future ministry.

How agencies can enhance resilience

Further research suggested several things that mission leaders can do in order to enhance resiliency and longevity in missionaries who have gone through traumatic events. In the study, thirty missionaries who did not leave the field, despite having experienced traumas such as political evacuations, rape, car-jackings, armed home invasions and robberies were asked about factors which contributed to their resiliency and longevity on the front line.

Here are seven things the mission agencies did which their missionaries found helpful:

1. Created networks of relationships

    The good relationships that resilient missionaries enjoyed with other missionaries were most often cited as a retention factor. Their missionary sending agencies had ensured that missionaries worked on teams and provided training and coaching to nurture good team relationships. This good practice earned "post-trauma pay-off" when fellow team members helped provide a "soft landing" for each other.

    Another useful network that agencies had established was the regional network. This network was used when missionaries were evacuated to surrounding countries to find temporary shelter and safety. Agencies that plan regional gatherings will inadvertently provide for the development and expansion of a wider network of relationships for their missionaries. This larger network will sometimes pay dividends in missionary resiliency at a later date.

2. Acknowledged the trauma

    If the mission leadership does not acknowledge in some way the trauma that a worker has endured, then an elephant enters the room. The trauma suffered by a worker can have an enormous personal effect, yet the description of this same event might make a fairly minimal emotional impact on mission leadership as the e-mail describing the trauma is quickly scanned. The onus is on the leader to acknowledge the event and to actively find out how the worker is coping after a trauma.

    After a very traumatic event, one missionary family was back in their homeland for a short time. They spoke in glowing terms of their mission leader who came, along with his wife, to visit them. "It was more than an e-mail message. He came with his wife." That action spoke volumes, and they felt that the pain they had endured had been validated by the visit of a key leader. This contrasted with another family who, after a very tense and traumatic robbery, did not hear anything from their leadership. "It was as if they (the leaders) didn't care." The family felt very much on their own, and they felt hurt by the lack of leadership response.

3. Stayed in the region

   Mission teams with evacuation protocols which include a first level of evacuation to another country in the region (as opposed to a direct return to the homeland) seem to fare better after a traumatic event. According to the project data, what gives the evacuee the most benefits in survival and resiliency is the loving support of existing relationships. Personal relationships are often stronger on the field than in the homeland. The level of empathy on the field is frequently greater because it is easier to find people who have gone through similar traumas.

4. Spoke words of wisdom in love

   At crucial junctures in a missionary's life, the carefully chosen words of a leader are most welcome. One missionary had faithfully worked for twenty years in a certain country. Following an evacuation, however, she received an invitation to join a ministry team in another country. Despite that attractive opportunity, she felt committed to her original task. When her mission leader came to visit her, he said, "You have permission to leave. I think you should accept that invitation from another country." Only then was the missionary's burden lifted and she was able to change assignments without feeling guilty about abandoning her post and the project.

   It is evident from the project data that missionaries are strongly committed. They are not easily dislodged. In fact, missionaries will often regard leaving or moving as failure or betrayal of a heavenly mandate. What can override this false notion is a well-spoken timely word by a mission leader who has earned an adequate trust level. A leader like this has clearly listened and understood the situation, and therefore can, as it were, speak for God.

5. Developed a theology of risk and suffering

   According to the results of ReMAP II, mission agencies with high resiliency practice good screening procedures of mission candidates. One component of good screening should be the requirement that candidates develop their own position on risk and suffering.

   In the past, agencies would require candidates to prepare a doctrinal statement, but this document did not usually include a position on suffering. Now, as more and more candidates are placed in high security alert nations, it can be safely assumed that they will inevitably face trauma. They will be robbed, they will get sick, and they will be traumatised. Hence, candidates should be required to consider these risks and to develop their own theology of suffering.

   Developing a theology of risk and suffering before going overseas will put suffering into its proper context, and thus foster resiliency in missionaries. This is crucial for those growing up with a particular Western (and some non-Western) cultural view of suffering which says something is wrong if we suffer, so we should avoid suffering at all costs. A young mother came to the field with this typical cultural view of suffering. She thought that if she would do the right things, God would protect and look after her family and she would not suffer.

Seventy-four percent of those interviewed mentioned that they had advanced in the development of a biblical view of suffering. One quoted John 16:33, "In this world you will have trouble." Another remembered that Jesus was a man of sorrows acquainted with grief, and so we should expect suffering as we walk in His footsteps.

One mission leader believes that when agencies target unreached peoples they should expect suffering. Consequently, they need to be better prepared by putting on the appropriate armour and building a sufficient prayer base.

6. Fostered a sense of duty

    One surprising discovery in the study was to note how many missionaries referred to their farm upbringing where they learned values such as hard work, finishing a task, duty, perseverance and sticking with the project. A Vietnam veteran had also learned these core values. He brought into his missionary career the notion that one stayed at his post until the orders were changed. Quite a few workers who had suffered trauma shared this sense of determination not to run away when trouble came. They were more determined to survive trauma and to push on and get the task done. Mission executives need to consider how to identify and nurture a sense of duty in their mission candidates.

7. Affirmed the call

    Sending agencies must continue to grapple with how the concept of "the call" is expressed today. Do missionary candidates apply out of a desire to do something good in the world or because of a set of felt needs or from a sense of injustice? If so, how do those sentiments translate or morph into a meaningful conviction that holds strong during troubles and trials? How is that call developed? Where do new recruits have an opportunity to develop their sense of call?

Maybe the deeper question is how God speaks and calls people today to follow Him in mission work. Whatever the language or semantics used, sending agencies who assign people to high security alert nations must feel satisfied and confident through the screening process that new recruits are called to serve in such places. By ensuring a firm call at the beginning, and testing that conviction in ministry, we will definitely contribute to resiliency after trauma.

Discussion questions:

1. Consider the pre-trauma factors and the post-trauma factors that contribute to retention of missionaries. Which of these factors are most important in your missionaries in their ministry context? What other factors have contributed to their resilience in ministry?

2. Discuss the seven things that mission agencies can do to help their missionaries who have gone through traumatic events. Which of these good practices could be developed further in your organisation? What other good practices are relevant to resilience through suffering and trauma for your culture?

In the real world

A table to stimulate ideas for best practice in mission partnership. For further explanation, see page 7.

This chart has been partially filled in for you. Now you fill in the blanks.

Who? → When? ↓	Home Church	Missionary	Mission Agencies	External Partners
Continuous	➢ Teach commitment and faithfulness	➢ Clearly commit to ministry		
Recruitment				➢ Provide tools for assessment
Preparation			➢ Assign roles according to gifts and experience	
On field	➢ Provide spiritual and mental support	➢ Show clear commitment to agency	➢ Provide room to shape and develop own ministry ➢ Clearly communicate plans and job descriptions ➢ Provide ministry role for spouse	➢ Provide administrative and practical support
Crisis	➢ Provide a theology of risk and suffering	➢ Stay in region	➢ Provide networks for support	
Furlough		➢ Take time for rest and refreshment	➢ Do not overload missionaries with work	
Re-entry		➢ Evaluate and seek to improve ministry		

27

Ministry
Ministry Outcomes

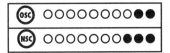

The facts

Often, to be outcome or task focused is said to be a western characteristic (with the South seen as relationship focused), and yet, mission agencies across the NSC (largely Global South) and OSC (largely the West) give a fairly high overall rating for the area of ministry outcomes. However, NSC had a much stronger correlation with retention than OSC, perhaps reflecting their passion and commitment to be involved in God's mission.

The data

Q. No.	Factor	OSC Health Indicator	✓	NSC Health Indicator	✓
65	Missionaries are actually achieving the agency's goals and expectations	○○○○○○○●●●		○○○○○○●●●●	✓
66	Missionaries are developing good relationships with the people they serve	○○○○○○○○○●		○○○○○○○●●●	
67	The people our missionaries serve are becoming followers of Christ	○○○○○○●●●●		○○○○○○○○●●	✓
68	The church on the field values the ministries of our missionaries	○○○○○○○○●●		○○○○○○○○●●	✓
69	Missionaries are developing leadership among the people they serve	○○○○○○○○●●	✓	○○○○○○●●●●	✓
70	Missionaries experience a sense of fulfilment in their ministry	○○○○○○○○●●	✓	○○○○○○○●●●	✓

The key findings

✓ The overall average rating for performance and significance of ministry outcomes was high in OSC and NSC, and it was correlated with total annual retention in NSC.

✓ Missionaries achieving their agency's goals (Q65) was rated in NSC higher than in OSC, and was correlated with high retention in NSC.

✓ People becoming followers of Christ (Q67) received a very high rating in NSC and was correlated with retention. In OSC, the rating was much lower and there was a moderate negative correlation with retention.

✓ Missionaries develop good on-field relationships (Q66) was also rated very high in NSC and OSC, so high across all agencies that there was no distinguishable correlation with retention.

✓ Appreciation of the missionaries' ministry by church in host culture (Q68) was also rated very high in OSC and NSC and was moderately correlated with retention in NSC.

✓ Leadership development among the people group (Q69) received the highest ratings in OSC. It was correlated with retention in OSC and NSC.

✓ Missionaries' sense of personal fulfilment (Q70) was rated very high in OSC (individualistic society in the West) and was correlated with retention in OSC and NSC.

What it means

Rob Hay

The encouraging result regarding ministry outcome is that agencies generally feel they are doing what they aim to do. Some might ask, "Is that result due to questions being asked of agency leaders, who might give a higher rating on this issue than the missionaries would?" This may be a valid concern, but from the writer's own research interviewing British mission partners, a similar result on ministry outcome was found. Also, in Hong Kong, the ReMAP II questions were put to individual missionaries. While the scores in general were 10% lower than those of leaders, the pattern of answers from missionaries was very similar to all the areas surveyed.

Question 65 [Q65 *Missionaries are actually achieving the agency's goals and expectations*] received a higher rating in NSC than in OSC. Is this because OSC missionaries are not interested in whether the organisation they are working with is achieving its goals? This seems unlikely, but perhaps the goals are higher due to the Western (over-) emphasis on achieving quantifiable results, thus achievement of the goals is not as easily obtainable. Emphasis on results seems to be corroborated by mission agency magazines and newsletters, where there is often (especially in the West) a focus on what the overall organisation and individual missionaries are achieving. However, the reports may have more to do with raising financial support and less with retaining missionaries.

In general, the overall focus on outcome and achieving goals is important to virtually all the OSC mission agencies surveyed. Therefore, little difference can be distinguished between the rating of high and low retaining agencies so no correlation with retention can be established. In NSC, however, ministry outcomes are correlated with retention, underlining the passion and commitment of NSC missionaries.

Yet there is one issue strongly correlated with retention for OSC agencies—Question 69 [Q69 *Missionaries are developing leadership among the people they serve*]—which seems to reflect a strong emphasis on sustainability. Rather than *doing* the mission work long-term, they are seeking to hand over or facilitate leadership from the beginning of their work. This may also be related to the perception that Westerners do not commit to a long-term placement, but often have a fixed time commitment in mind.

Question 66 [Q66 *Missionaries are developing good relationships with the people they serve*] showed a high rating for performance and significance in all OSC and NSC agencies (eight out of ten in OSC and six out of ten in NSC). This is an encouraging statistic, as all mission agencies are achieving effectiveness in on-field relationships. Therefore, there was no significant difference between the high retaining and low retaining agencies.

In further support of positive relational development, Question 68 [Q68 *The church on the field values the ministries of our missionaries*] was rated for significance and performance very highly (eight out of ten) in both OSC and NSC, and was correlated with retention in NSC. Still, there is an understanding that church-mission relationships on-field is a complex area, and there are bumps along the way as emerging churches grow to maturity, seek leadership, and develop their own identity. Because there are inevitable conflicts, the absence of a correlation with retention is puzzling and may require further research.

Question 67 [Q67 *The people our missionaries serve are becoming followers of Christ*] was another area where only NSC showed a correlation with retention. The NSC rating of eight out of ten shows that they feel they are achieving the goal of leading people to Christ. In OSC, this did not correlate with retention and was not rated as highly (six out of ten). OSC rating and lack of correlation may be linked to the lower proportion of missionaries in OSC involved in evangelism and church-planting, and a greater involvement in social and service ministries. In addition, OSC may be sensitive to accusations of proselytising (by those in their own culture) if they make conversions a major focus of their ministry, which would instill caution for focusing on this aspect.

The results clearly show that missionaries are feeling fulfilled in their work [Q70 *Missionaries experience a sense of fulfilment in their ministry*]. This question rated eight out of ten in NSC and OSC. Not surprisingly, both OSC and NSC show a correlation with retention.

Keeping records to evaluate ministry

Bernard Ofori Atta,[1] Christian Outreach Fellowship, Ghana

Note: Some names used in this case study have been changed to protect the identity of individuals involved.

Christian Outreach Fellowship (COF) is the oldest indigenous missionary agency in Ghana. Among other things, COF keeps good records for its mission personnel and their evangelism ministry. In this case study, we shall see how the keeping of such records helps COF to evaluate its ministry outcomes.

Personnel statistics:

The agency's personnel statistics for the period 1999 to 2004 show unmistakeably that the period was one of maintenance and minimal decline as Christian Outreach Fellowship sought new directions in its ministry. There were only slight variations in the number of missionaries over the period.

In 1999, we had 49 Missionaries, and this number fell to 47 in 2000. In that period, we lost Mrs. Abdul, who passed away from cancer of the liver. The other person who left service was Akay.

The worker who resigned

Akay was a teacher, and he was sent out to be a tentmaker working among the Nankansi people from a base at Navrongo. The city of Navrongo is the centre for Nankansi. It is a large market town, and the National Church Survey of Ghana shows the population as 50% Frafra (including Nankansi), 35% Kasena, 10% Dagomba, and 10% others. In other words, the Survey did not differentiate between Frafra and Nankansi. It would be difficult to do so, largely because the identity of the Nankansi has been assimilated into that of their larger cousins, the Frafra and the Kasena. Thus, hardly anybody speaks Nankansi in the streets of Navrongo.

Akay was sent to find the Nankansi. His strategy was to establish himself in Navrongo and to train disciples to reach the Nankansi to the South. He soon found that he did not have the time or the opportunities to do this effectively. He had attempted for a time to use his students, but he was teaching in a Roman Catholic Institution so he had to do this clandestinely. In the end, Akay was unable to achieve the agency's goal, so he resigned.

The couple who joined

Prior to 2000, we had not paid much attention to the Konkomba people group. The number of these people who attended church regularly, which is our yardstick for how many have been reached for the Gospel, was 2.59%, whereas their neigh-

---

1   Bernard Ofori Atta is a leader of Christian Outreach Fellowship in Ghana.

bours the Nanumba had 0.24%, the Gonja 0.47% and the Dagomba 0.78%. Even though the Konkomba were low down on the priority list when looked at statistically, it was realised that these belligerent people were in dire need of the Gospel of peace. We (at COF) also realised that they were strategic in that many of their number were to be found in neighbouring Togo, where they are known as the Hwla People Group. By reaching the Konkomba in Ghana, we could establish a base and a core of Church-planters to take the Gospel to the Hwla in the Republic of Togo. We engaged the hard-working couple Charles and Naomi to minister among these people. Thus, we were back to 49 Missionaries by the end of 2001.

Meanwhile, our numbers increased by another three when three single male missionaries took on marital partners. This brought the number of our missionaries up to 52 at the end of 2004.

Our field assistants, church-planters, and volunteers

During this period (from 1999 to 2004), the number of our Field Assistants started at 19, rose to 38, and ended at 29; and the number of our Church-planters started at 164, rose to 297, and ended at 192. These fluctuations were largely administrative, depending on which workers we chose to recognise. We have since regulated our system.

Besides field assistants and church planters, we also have our Volunteers. The Volunteers, both those under training and those who were trained, are those who have not been recognised as Field Assistants or Church-planters. The number of Volunteers started at 285 and rose to 617. We lost some of them who opted to undergo formal training and take up positions in local churches.

In summary, the total number of our workers was 515 in 1999; this rose as high as 930 in 2003, and levelled off to 865 in 2004.

In this period from 1999 to 2004, the allowances paid to the missionaries kept pace with the Cost of Living Indices. However, allowances paid to other workers became a thing of the past. We are aware that many of our missionaries gave a little pocket money to their workers out of their Ministry Expenses discretionary allowance, but this could only have been paltry. As can be seen, even the paucity of incentives to volunteer workers did not affect their number, and there were increases despite this practice.

Ministry statistics:

The Mission force from COF shared the Gospel with a massive 50,875 persons in 1999. This number dropped to 32,675 in 2004, but the number of commitments to Christ remained steady, 4,278 in 1999 and 4,137 in 2004. What does this mean? Were our missionaries less active?

From 1999 to 2004, as our ministry statistics show, the Mission force was unable to do mass evangelism and they had to concentrate on person-to-person evangelism. We noticed that the absence of mass evangelism had no affect whatsoever on our ministry outcomes. We continued to see a high number of commitments to Christ.

We were also able to evaluate our new methods of evangelism in the figures for new churches planted and new fellowships established. During the five year period from 1999 to 2004, the number of churches planted was 32, 31, 10, 12 and 26 respectively. The numbers for new fellowships over the same period were 48, 61, 55, 38, and 143. Again, our change of focus from mass evangelism to individuals and small group evangelism is apparent.

Conclusion

In conclusion, we can say that Christian Outreach Fellowship has not experienced any serious attrition over the period 1999 to 2004, either in terms of the number of workers, in terms of the number of drop-outs, nor in the commitment of the workers to the task in hand. We can thank the Lord for a dedicated and effective work-force to the glory of God.

Discussion questions:

1. Does your organisation keep good personnel records, including reasons for the placement and attrition of missionaries? If not, what can be done to improve the keeping of personnel records?

2. How does your organisation evaluate its ministry outcomes? What aspects of the ministry should be evaluated on a more regular basis? Who should do the evaluation?

In the real world

A table to stimulate ideas for best practice in mission partnership. For further explanation, see page 7.

This chart has been partially filled in for you. Now you fill in the blanks.

Who? → When? ↓	Home Church	Missionary	Mission Agencies	External Partners
Continuous	➢ Create a culture of purpose driven ministry ➢ Create a culture of excellence in ministry			
Recruitment			➢ Select based on gifts and experience	
Preparation		➢ Train specifically in needed qualities	➢ Ensure clear expectations and goals	➢ Provide training that leads to desired outcomes
On field		➢ Commit to goals and expectations ➢ Develop good relationships with people served	➢ Keep records of ministry outcomes	➢ Provide tools to measure outcomes
Crisis				
Furlough		➢ Evaluate ministry and take measures	➢ Evaluate ministry	
Re-entry		➢ Evaluate ministry and give feedback		

28

Ministry
Individual/Agency Relationship

(OSC)	○○○○○○○●●●●
(NSC)	○○○○○○○●●●●

The facts

The relationship between the individual and the agency is at the heart of the ReMAP II research. This chapter is focused specifically on that relationship in the area of ministry—the work that the missionary actually undertakes. Difficulties arise between individuals and agencies when what an individual understands or intends for their work is different from what the agency intends. These issues include how closely the ministry aims of the individual match those of the agency, how effectively the agency supports the individual in carrying out the ministry, and who sets the agenda and priorities of the ministry.

The data

Q. No.	Factor	OSC Health Indicator	✓	NSC Health Indicator	✓
40	Vision and purpose are shared and understood throughout the agency	○○○○○○○●●●	✓	○○○○○○○●●●	✓
41	Plans and job descriptions are communicated clearly to the missionary	○○○○○○●●●●	✓	○○○○○○●●●●	✓
42	There is a free flow of communication to and from the leadership	○○○○○○●●●●	✓	○○○○○○●●●●	
44	Missionaries are included in major decisions related to the field	○○○○○○○●●●		○○○○○○●●●●	
46	A culture of prayer is actively promoted within the agency	○○○○○○○●●●	✓	○○○○○○○○●●	
51	There are documented and adequate procedures for handling complaints from missionaries	○○○○○●●●●●	✓	○○○○○●●●●●	✓

56	Missionaries are assigned roles according to their gifting and experience	○○○○○○●●●●		○○○○○○●●●●	✓
57	Missionaries are given room to shape and develop their own ministry	○○○○○○○●●	✓	○○○○○○○●●●	✓
59	Missionaries know how to handle spiritual warfare	○○○○○○○○○●	✓	○○○○○○○○○●	✓
60	Missionaries are committed to their ministry	○○○○○○●●●●	✓	○○○○○○○○●●	✓
61	Missionaries are committed and loyal to the agency	○●●●●●●●●●	✓	○○○○●●●●●●	✓
62	Missionaries are generally not overloaded in the amount of work they do	○○○○○○○●●●	✓	○○○○○○○●●●●	
63	Opportunities are provided for a ministry/role for the spouse	○○○○○○●●●●	✓	○○○○○○●●●●	✓
64	Missionaries have adequate administrative and practical support on the field	○○●●●●●●●●	✓	○○○○●●●●●●	
66	Missionaries are developing good relationships with the people they serve	○○○○○○○○○●		○○○○○○○●●●	
70	Missionaries experience a sense of fulfilment in their ministry	○○○○○○○●●	✓	○○○○○○○●●●	✓
72	Effective pastoral care exists at a field level (preventative and in crises)	○○●●●●●●●●		○○○○○●●●●●	✓

 ## *The key findings*

- ✓ Commitment and loyalty to agency (Q60) was rated very high for significance and performance in NSC, and not so high in OSC. It was moderately correlated with total annual retention in OSC and NSC.
- ✓ Communication with leadership (Q42) is rated high; correlation with retention was established only for OSC.
- ✓ Vision and purpose (Q40) is rated very high in OSC and NSC and moderately correlated to total annual retention.
- ✓ Clear plans and job description (Q41) was highly correlated with retention in OSC and NSC.
- ✓ Missionaries are included in major decisions (Q44) proved a moderate negative correlation with retention in NSC.
- ✓ Clear procedure to handle complaints (Q51) was correlated with high retention in OSC and NSC.

✓ Missionaries are provided with administrative and practical support (Q63) correlated with high retention.

✓ Effective member care on the field (Q72) received a very high rating in NSC and strongly correlated with retention.

✓ There is a culture of prayer throughout the agency (Q46) received a very high rating and correlated with high retention (OSC).

What it means

Rob Hay

The relationship between missionary and agency is obviously important for retention; however, it is a complex and multi-faceted relationship. Tensions can and historically often did arise between the mission agency and the individual missionary. From William Carey onwards we have examples of tensions. Many missionaries were strong-minded pioneers who did not take kindly to anyone interfering with "their ministry". Indeed, even today it takes a certain perseverance to endure the rigorous application procedures and support raising required just to join many mission agencies, so perhaps there should be no surprise when tensions arise.

The personal and logistical assistance received from the agency to the missionary in support of their ministry is an important group of questions to consider in this area. Questions 61 [Q61 *Missionaries are generally not overloaded in the amount of work they do*], 63 [Q63 *Missionaries have adequate administrative and practical support on the field*], and 72 [Q72 *Effective pastoral care exists at a field level (preventative and in crises)*] are three forms of support that demonstrate value for the missionary, his/her spouse, and their ministry. The average rating for performance and significance across these three questions was just three out of ten for OSC and five out of ten for NSC, according to the executives' assessment. We suspect that a missionaries' rating is likely to be even lower. These practical areas, which contribute significantly towards how well and how easily a missionary can conduct their ministry, need further improvement as the missionary is likely to feel undersupported. Agencies should discuss these support aspects with mission partners on a regular basis to ensure this crucial area (which correlates strongly across all the questions) is as strong as can be.

The second group of questions includes issues of communication between the missionary and the mission agency and its leadership. This topic is discussed fully in Chapter 20 on communication. These issues correlate with retention and scores are reasonably good (averaging six out of ten) in both NSC and OSC. Thus, if tensions arise from other areas discussed in this chapter, well-functioning communication channels will enable discussion and hopefully resolution of the issue.

The third group of questions asks whose ministry it is, who is a missionary loyal to, and how are these things decided. A number of mission agencies act as little more than facilitators, helping missionaries fulfil their own personal visions of ministry without any requirement to contribute toward a central aim or vision. This is not necessarily wrong; indeed, it often allows a wide range of ministries to flourish. Problems occur when missionaries make ministry an extension of themselves, yet the ministry may no longer be needed and/or wanted by the emerging national church. Is the missionary willing to accept accountability and receive criticism? Mission ministry is not the place for self-realisation and building one's own kingdom. Problems also occur when missionaries are not willing to shape their ministry according to the agency's core vision and contribute towards the overall ministry focus.

Whose ministry? Question 44 [Q44 *Missionaries are included in major decisions related to the field*] and 57 [Q57 *Missionaries are given room to shape and develop their own ministry*] both demonstrate the amount of input the individual missionary has in the ministry. In particular, Question 57 shows a correlation with retention, (the lack of correlation on Question 44 may be due to the majority of mission agencies involving missionaries in decisions of posting, team formation and strategy, so that there was no statistically significant difference between high and low retaining agencies). Question 57, however, had a moderate correlation with retention and encouragingly received good ratings in NSC and OSC alike: seven and eight out of ten, respectively.

Loyalty to agency is in some ways a complex issue. The felt tension between the ministry of the pioneer missionary and the mission agency's goals (the organisation/ministry tension) is a common thread in early missionary biographies. Questions 59 [Q59 *Missionaries are committed to their ministry*] and 60 [Q60 *Missionaries are committed and loyal to the agency*] relate to this tension. Results from both questions showed a moderate or high correlation with retention. Not surprisingly, missionaries have a very high commitment to their ministry, rating this question nine out of ten for both NSC and OSC. As discussed elsewhere (see Chapters 6-9), a missionary's commitment to ministry is tested through a long selection processes and demanding requirements (in many cases) to raise their own support before reaching the field. Also, few missionaries begin service because of a draw to an organisation; instead, most feel a call (however that might be understood—discussed in more detail in Chapter 8) to use their life, skills or profession in ministry. The ministry call then leads them to seek an organisation that will help them fulfil this.

Encouragingly, Question 60 (loyalty to agency) received a reasonably good rating, six for OSC and eight for NSC. The rating demonstrates room for improvement, but there seems to be a workable tension between these two loyalties that sometimes make opposing demands. The lower rating in OSC may reflect the attitudes to organisational loyalty in general. For example, "general gift income" is low in many agencies throughout the West as supporters like to direct their financial support to people or specific projects.

How an agency communicates value and involvement to the missionary can affect the above issues of ministry formation and loyalty to agency. Paying attention to how value is communicated demonstrates how seriously the agency actually does value its people. This value then determines whether the missionaries feel they are fulfilling a calling or feel as if they are a cog in the machinery of a large agency agenda.

Questions 56 [Q56 *Missionaries are assigned roles according to their gifting and experience*] and 62 [Q62 *Opportunities are provided for a ministry/role for the spouse*] demonstrate to missionaries involved how the agency sees them as individuals with God-given gifts and a specific calling that needs to be explored, drawn out and honoured. Inattention to these can sometimes be attributed to the need for a missionary to have flexibility and to sacrifice—to put the needs of the organisation first. Though required at times, this attitude is abused when it becomes the normal mode and an excuse for poor organisational behaviour. A healthy organisation seeks to allow its staff to thrive as individuals. Done well, the organisation will in turn receive maximum benefit from that individual as a result. Filling unexpected roles sometimes leads to developing a new skill or even finding fulfilment in that new role. Problems arise when someone agrees to stand in for a role, then ends up doing it indefinitely without reevaluation, which can cause significant stress and lead to attrition.

In OSC, the lack of established correlation of assigning missionaries according to their gifting with retention most likely speaks to the widespread expectation that a missionary's gifting and experience will be taken into account in determining his or her role (or perhaps there is a gap between self-assessment and practice). In NSC, there was a correlation with retention, demonstrating that high retaining agencies are much more careful in staff assignment. Interestingly though, agencies in both NSC and OSC feel they are only doing adequately in this area, with a rating of six out of ten in both. Reasons for under performance may be due to inadequate communication, lack of priority, or simply the shortage of personnel—for the organisation to maintain its current ministry it must ask unqualified and inexperienced people to fulfil key roles that they feel ill-equipped to do. Whatever the cause, agencies should discuss and explore this key area.

In OSC, there is widespread expectation that just as the "post-holder"[1] will be used in a way that honours their skills and experience, so too will the spouse (still in the majority of situations, the wife). This clearly correlated with retention in OSC, underlining the importance in ensuring that the spouse feels called and in the right place. NSC gave a similar rating (six compared to seven (OSC) out of ten respectively) but no correlation with retention. This fact might indicate the lower role expectancy and/or increased family loyalty in NSC.

Despite the very real challenges outlined above and throughout the book, missionaries do demonstrate flexibility, adaptability and perseverance. In the midst of surviving, they find fulfilment amidst or in spite of the difficulties. Question 70 [Q70 *Missionaries experience a sense of fulfilment in their ministry*] showed a high rating in NSC and a very high rating in OSC.

---

1   This term has been used to try to avoid a pejorative statement. The reality is that in many countries a visa is granted for a couple or family in the name of either husband or wife based on their role and what we are discussing here is the role of the "non-post-holder".

Understanding Bruce

Laurel McAllister[2], ACTS Seminaries of Trinity Western University, Canada

Note: The names used in this case study have been changed to protect the identity of individuals and the mission agency involved.

Lorraine and Bruce saw the pain in each other's eyes. For weeks, they had felt as if they were on a treadmill—going round and round and getting nowhere. Then Bruce put his thoughts into words, "I just can't face going to the office one more day!" His role at the mission's international office had become increasingly stifling and stressful, in spite of his efforts to manage the situation. Bruce had never quit before, but now he thought he had no other alternative. He would tender his resignation to the Director in the morning.

This was a situation Bruce could not have imagined ten years before, when he and his family joined the mission. He had wanted to serve in the mission until his retirement.

Bruce's first assignment was Business Manager in one of the mission's new fields. He and his family had settled down quickly, becoming part of an active missionary community. Bruce enjoyed the challenges of starting the field in the use of computers, establishing a more efficient accounting system, and initiating a budget. All of these "firsts" greatly enhanced the effectiveness of the mission in that field. Lorraine readily found opportunities to use her skills. As a family, they assisted in local church planting efforts.

Being on a new field, Bruce had much personal freedom in how he managed his work. Since many ministries were just getting started, he was able to participate in a variety of activities: from practical building and repair work to the business side of things. Bruce thrived because he could use his creative skills to address various challenges at work. After some years, health concerns and family issues made it necessary for Bruce and his family to return to North America.

The mission, not wanting to lose this family, assigned Bruce to its international office. Lorraine and Bruce were not given much opportunity to discuss his new assignment, but they trusted the mission leadership's decision. Both were glad to stay with the mission. Soon, they were settled into a well-established community close to a supporting church, and they began to get help and answers to their son's difficulties.

After the initial time of "learning the ropes", Bruce found that he missed the variety of challenges he had faced on the field. Now, he worked with a very effective finance director, and the technical area was well managed. In this more structured office environment, Bruce found it hard to use his practical and creative gifts.

---

2   Laurel McAllister served as ReMAP II Canada Coordinator. As a facilitator in Member Care Training Workshops, she encourages healthy relationships. Teaching a missions course at ACTS Seminaries of Trinity Western University also keeps her challenged and builds on her experience as a missionary teacher in Africa and her years in missionary training.

A new General Director was appointed in the mission. His appointment had given Bruce hope at first. Perhaps there would be a change in the office that would allow him to use his gifts more fully. However, the General Director could not understand or appreciate Bruce's unique skills, nor his need for variety and personal freedom to exercise his creativity. Bruce's repeated attempts to communicate with the Director failed, leaving both of them frustrated. At that time, there was no procedure in place for resolving complaints and conflict. Bruce, therefore, saw no alternative but to resign.

About this time, the mission agency appointed a Member Care Director. Among the first practices he initiated, in a fledgling member care department, was a Debriefing Interview for all missionaries at the end of each term of service. The first Debriefing Interview he conducted was with Bruce and Lorraine.

Meanwhile, Bruce had found a new job, so there was little chance of reversing his decision to leave the mission. Nevertheless, the Debriefing Interview gave Bruce an opportunity to tell his story and to be heard. There was no anger or bitterness in his story, just regret that he had to resign in order to use his God-given gifts and skills.

When the General Director read the Debriefing Report, he was initially very defensive. He found it hard to take responsibility for the resignation, but Bruce's story, in written form and signed by both Bruce and Lorraine, had a powerful effect on him. He realised the importance of getting all sides of a story and of listening to those who disagree. He learned from this experience and considered it an important part of his growth as an administrator.

In time, the General Director began to see the need for more adequate member care within the organisation. He recognised that the Debriefing Interview was a very important and effective tool. He also realised the need for missionaries on the field to be nurtured and given opportunities to use their skills and gifts in appropriate roles.

Following his resignation from the mission agency, Bruce worked in the business world. He gained experience in people management and advanced computer financial programmes. Bruce was highly respected and well-paid, and he found a certain freedom in not having to deal with support issues. He was active in his local church leadership, but he continued to have a burden for ministry in his former mission.

Then about five years after Bruce resigned, the mission agency's international office faced a problem. There was a need for a Finance Director. After exploring many possibilities, the General Director remembered Bruce. "Do you suppose he would be willing to leave that good position in business to raise support and come back to us?"

This story has a very happy ending. Bruce decided to return to the mission. Because of the Debriefing Interview and the communication it generated with Bruce, the General Director could better understand and value Bruce's unique strengths and needs. Today, both Bruce and the Director serve God together on the mission's administrative team.

Discussion questions:

1. Does your organisation provide job descriptions and clear plans for each worker?

2. Does your agency or church include the missionary when leaders make major decisions that affect his/her ministry?

3. What procedures, if any, are in place for handling complaints on the field?

In the real world

A table to stimulate ideas for best practice in mission partnership. For further explanation, see page 7.

This chart has been partially filled in for you. Now you fill in the blanks.

Who? → When? ↓	Home Church	Missionary	Mission Agencies	External Partners
Continuous	➢ Maintain prayer as the basis for good relationships	➢ Be committed and loyal	➢ Include missionaries in major decisions regarding the field ➢ Pray for the missionary	
Recruitment		➢ Share vision and purpose	➢ Share vision and purpose	
Preparation				➢ Provide training in maintaining relations
On field	➢ Offer pastoral support	➢ Provide clear feedback	➢ Ensure appropriate and clear communication ➢ Ensure policies and procedures are people orientated	➢ Facilitate meetings
Crisis			➢ Ensure availability of a network of relationships	
Furlough		➢ Evaluate ministry and agency relationship		
Re-entry		➢ Keep in touch with former agency	➢ Keep in touch with former missionaries	➢ Facilitate reunions

29

Finances

The facts

In both OSC and NSC, high retaining agencies provide sustained financial support that is adequate to meet the needs of their missionaries. They use a backup system to respond to low or irregular financial support. In addition, high retaining agencies in OSC handle project finances effectively, and they show financial transparency on how and where finances are spent, both to their missionaries as well as to their donors.

High retaining agencies in OSC and NSC put aside part of missionary allowances for retirement. This contribution is clearly correlated with retention of mission personnel for NSC, and mildly correlated in OSC.

The data

Q. No.	Factor	OSC Health Indicator	✓	NSC Health Indicator	✓
5	Estimate what percentage of your missionaries' allowances are allocated for retirement[1]	○○○○○○●●●●		○○○●●●●●●●	✓
44	Missionaries are included in major decisions related to the field	○○○○○○○●●●		○○○○○○●●●●	
80	Missionaries usually receive sustained financial support that is adequate for their needs	○○○○○○○●●●	✓	○○○○●●●●●●	✓
81	There is financial back-up for missionaries with low or irregular support	○○○○●●●●●●	✓	○○○●●●●●●●	✓

---

1   Adjusted health score formula: with optimum 5-20% of allowance put aside for retirement.

| 82 | Project finances are used effectively | OOOOOOOO●● | ✓ | OOOOOOO●●● | |
| 83 | Agency finances are transparent to the missionaries and donors (how and where money is spent) | OOOOOOO●●● | ✓ | OOOOOOOO●● | |

The key findings

✓ Average rating of financial issues was highly correlated with retention in OSC and NSC.

✓ Effective use of project finances (Q82) received highest ratings and was correlated to retention in OSC.

✓ Transparency of agency finances (Q83) was also rated very high in OSC and NSC. It was correlated with retention in OSC—and so high in low retaining NSC agencies that it could not serve as discriminator.

✓ Sustained financial support (Q80) was rated very high in OSC but not so high in NSC; yet it showed correlation with retention in OSC and NSC.

✓ A back-up system for irregular financial support (Q81) received a considerably lower rating than the other factors (agencies have different financial systems) and was correlated with retention in NSC (and OSC to a lower degree).

What it means

Valerie Lim

Finances for mission is an extremely complex topic. Financial policies and practices differ widely and are shaped by a myriad of factors. Even within the same agency we may observe variations, depending on the local circumstances and customs. But due to the limited space here, it would be impossible to comprehensively cover the many finance related issues that affect cross-cultural mission. In this chapter and the next, we will only highlight our findings on several finance-related practices, outline some financial issues in long-term cross-cultural mission, and suggest topics for further reflection and discussion through the case studies and references.

Our findings confirm the importance of finances not just for missionary sending, but for on-going ministry in the field and other personal expenses in the life of a missionary. Indeed, the finances required go beyond the initial amount of money necessary to relocate a missionary (or missionary family) to the field. Finances are also required to set up a home and to maintain the missionary (or missionary family) on the field.

Expenses on the field can be costly, depending on the country of service, the ministry needs, and the cost of living. Besides basic living expenses (for food, accommodation, and utilities), the missionary may require a budget for ministry expenses, transport or travel, health care, and various other expenses. These additional expenses would include items such as children's education, insurance coverage (for health, life, property, evacuation, etc.), contribution to the administrative office of the sending agency and support structure on the field, home assignment, and retirement funds.[2]

Setting aside funds for retirement is a good practice in the high retaining agencies of both OSC and NSC. (More details in Chapter 30.)

Sustained and adequate financial support

Unlike workers who are employed in other professions with a regular salary and other benefits, missionaries are usually recruited without any promise of a regular income or finances for the work that they will perform. Instead, missionaries and/or their sending agencies are responsible to raise funds in support of their work. Indeed, many mission agencies (or local churches) require new missionaries to raise their financial support before they are sent out to the field. (Exceptions to this general practice are found in some denominational mission agencies.) In some countries, where the people face economic hardship due to weak currency exchange rates and other problems, this process of raising support can be difficult and tedious, sometimes taking many months or even years.

Agency leaders in both OSC and NSC generally recognize the importance of supplying adequate finances to missionaries. Thus, when asked how they rated the provision of sustained financial support that is sufficient to meet their needs, NSC rated this highly while OSC rated it very highly. Sustained financial support was strongly correlated with missionary retention in both OSC and NSC. This meant that regular and consistent financial support positively contributes to high retention of missionaries on the field. (See Chapter 30 for more discussion.)

Back-up system for low or irregular finances

But what happens if some missionaries should face low or irregular support? Would they receive needed finances from another source? Do agencies have a back-up system, that is, a reserve fund and procedures in place to respond to low or irregular finances? Or do agencies expect missionaries to fend for themselves, or to perhaps rely on the kindness of others in the field?

Our survey data showed a considerably lower rating for financial back-up than for the other factors. In other words, most agencies admitted this was something that was not well done, as evidenced by their time, effort and effectiveness. This area warrants further work to establish whether it was time, effort or effectiveness, or a

---

2   Adapted from a Malaysian resource, "Guidelines on budgeting and support for a missionary (family)", Beram Kumar in: "Member Care Handbook -- A guide to caring for our missionaries", 2000, pp. 35-36.

combination of these that resulted in a relatively lower rating. In any case, financial back-up is correlated with retention in NSC, and OSC, although to a lower degree. We would encourage some form of financial back-up system to be developed in all sending agencies.

We note that in some OSC, missionary sending is primarily through denominational agencies, which have contributed to mission efforts since the early nineteenth century. Churches within the same denomination will pool their finances to provide financial and other support (prayer, encouragement, etc.) to the missionaries sent by the denomination. Each church contributes an agreed percentage of their income to the denomination's mission agency (or agencies). Hence, as long as the denominational churches send regular contributions to the agency, the financial support to missionaries remains steady and consistent over long periods of time. This may explain the observed low rating for financial back-up in OSC, because a back-up system may be unnecessary.

What does all this mean for missionaries on the field? Simply this: the missionaries (especially those from NSC) who serve in agencies without a financial back-up system may face intermittent shortage of funds or scarcity of ministry supplies. In such circumstances, they may have to make extreme sacrifices in their daily living for the sake of the work. When missionaries face a prolonged period of low or irregular financial support, they must find a balance between trusting the Lord to provide and worrying about how to make ends meet. Some missionaries may be tempted to compromise their spiritual values in order to boost their low income. For example, they may be tempted to exaggerate their ministry reports or to convey only part of the truth, in order to impress their supporters. Other missionaries may find themselves under enormous pressure to succeed, thus they push themselves harder, and eventually they may suffer from burn-out and over-work.

The case study on "Mission support in the Philippines" captures the plight of many Filipino career missionaries. This case probably echoes similar financial realities for many of the mission agencies and churches in NSC. Missionaries are sent out to the field with less than adequate support. Many continue to serve faithfully, in spite of low or irregular finances.

Mission support in the Philippines

Bibien Limlingan,[3] Philippine Mission Association,[4] Philippines

In 2001, a young Filipino missionary named Vic flew to a city in the Middle East with only US$50 in his pocket. During his stay in that city, his church essentially forgot about him. Financially he was on his own. Remaining faithful to his reason for coming to the Middle East, he did not take up work in addition to his ministry.

---

3 Bibien Limlingan currently serves as the Research Officer of the Philippine Missions Association. Bibien has a Masters degree in Theology from the Asian Theological Seminary. She has just recently finished putting together an extensive study on all the people groups in the Philippines.

4 Philippine Missions Association is a 23 year-old organisation that serves as the missions commission of the Philippine Council of Evangelical Churches.

He simply preached God's Word and won 65 souls to Christ in the one and half years.

Vic survived and flourished in his ministry partly because an Overseas Filipino Worker (OFW) took him into his home. The OFW was working at a European Embassy and serving its Ambassador. The OFW would bring home leftover food to feed Vic, his missionary friend. Whatever the Ambassador ate was what the missionary ate! At one point during his stay, Vic became ill and had to be hospitalised. Other OFWs heard about this and they gave an offering which covered his US$2,000 hospitalisation bill. Vic stayed in that city until he had to return home, when his visa expired at the start of the US-Iraq War.

Vic's story is unique, yet not unlike the stories of other Filipino missionaries. His story reflects some complex issues that face many Filipinos responding to God's call to missions. They sense a personal call to respond to God's heart for the nations. They pursue various options to provide for themselves and family while in ministry. They desire to be fruitful and make an eternal impact.

Like other workers from a New Sending Country, Vic and other Filipino missionaries face challenging realities when seeking financial support. At present, a mission budget or giving to missionaries is seen by some churches as competition to the church budget or internal needs of local churches. Raising "full support" or sufficient support can thus be very difficult, and it often requires many months or even years of effort.

Even those who have received assurances of "full support" may experience difficulties later on. Consider the experience of one family who recently left the Philippines:

In July of 2005, a family of three (one missionary couple with a two-year-old son) left for Central Asia with US$2,600 for their initial set-up budget and US$1,500 for their initial monthly budget. The missionary couple were properly screened, they had sufficient preparation time, and they were happily commissioned by the sending church and agency. They were able to be sent out because they had received the assurance of financial support pledged by church members and other friends. However, in the second month of their stay on the mission field, only 24% of their financial support came in and in the third month, only 21% of their monthly budget came in.

Their experience is not unusual. Giving to missionaries in a regular and sustained manner is a new and infrequent practice for many Filipino churches and individual believers. Through education and encouragement we hope to change this over time, but it is the current reality.

In short, this is the dilemma that many Filipino missionaries and missions executives face in the Philippines. If after a prolonged period of time we do not have adequate and sustained support to meet normal future needs, should we conclude that God is not calling us to missions? Or does God want us to proceed anyway with the expectation that He will provide?

One Filipino mission executive indicates his answer in an e-mail of September 2005:

> "God is good and He is the one who sends people into the mission field. As of now, a team [of three people] from [our agency] is already doing a good job in [one country in Southeast Asia]. They arrived [there] in September 7, 2005 with only 300 dollars in their funds. The three of them … believed that God will supply all their needs. I agreed with them so we sent them even though the funds are not enough. Under God's guidance coupled with right leadership [in our agency], we believe that God will accomplish His purposes with us. (Isaiah 46:11). As of now, the group is already doing Bible studies to more than 20 [locals]."

Indeed, the conclusion of some, if not many, Filipino missionaries mirrors such a response. They believe God does want them to proceed. They may have a partial plan for meeting future needs, but they also believe that having only a partial plan is not reason enough to turn away from a personal call to missions.

Filipino missionaries are meeting and seeing their needs met in a variety of ways. One family, on a day that they had no food because their support had not arrived, received meals from the local people. Another family had money deposited into their account by an unknown person. Housing is sometimes provided to missionaries by Overseas Filipino Workers (such was the case for the three new workers in Southeast Asia mentioned above.) Others may take up preparing and selling food products, or if they have the land, planting crops to provide home-grown food. Yet others proceed to their mission field with plans to work in a "tentmaking" role, or work in a team where some have non-ministry jobs while others more directly do the work of ministry.

Are there no "causalities"? Are there no missionaries without funds to meet emergencies? Are no missionaries forced to return home because of the lack of support? These questions were recently posed randomly to a group of around fifty mission personnel. A few did say that there are missionaries who returned due to a lack of finances and some also told stories of accidents that happened with no emergency funds available to help, or a family that had to fast for three days because they had no support. These also are the realities of Filipino involvement in missions.

Longevity of service and effectiveness in ministry of Filipino missionaries under these conditions is currently under further study by a large partnership of mission groups. Comprehensive answers to those issues are pending. It is known that among several hundred Filipino missionaries working in tribal areas and in translation work, there are missionaries who have served for 10 to 20 years. One missionary family has lived with a support range equivalent to US$10 to US$100 monthly for 22 years. They have testified that although living with a lack of finances is very difficult, they have nevertheless experienced God's faithfulness in enabling all their children to finish school and grow up in good health.

Perhaps effectiveness in ministry is not always related to longevity of service (though it can sometimes be a function of time). Consider Vic's case, who won 65 souls for the Lord in one and half years. Many missionaries would be glad to be blessed with that kind of fruit!

In another incident in the Middle East, eleven Filipinos working 50 plus hours a week in a factory also underwent intensive training in ministry for several months. At the end of one year, they had seen four people come to Christ. This is in a city where eight full-time expatriate missionaries had worked for a number of years, had established hundreds of contacts, but had not yet seen anyone come to Christ.

Financial support for Filipino missionary work is certainly an area of concern and it requires further growth and development. However, many Filipino missionaries have not, and will not, allow low financial support to become a barrier to sustained and effective participation in Great Commission work.

Discussion questions:

1. Is raising adequate funding a great problem in mission mobilisation in your country or your home church?

2. How does your organisation (mission agency or church) ensure that your missionaries receive adequate financial support?

3. What new initiatives has an agency or church in your country implemented to overcome low financial support of its missionaries?

4. What else could be done to help missionaries who are experiencing low or irregular financial support?

5. What are the moral and ethical responsibilities of a church and/or agency when sending a missionary? Does this include a commitment to finance them in an ongoing way?

What it means

In Chapter 30, we will examine how a few mission agencies and churches address low financial support. Meanwhile, let us consider project funding, where the necessary finances (including the financial support for mission workers) are promised for a period of time, usually until the project goals are accomplished.

Effective use of project finances

Some missionaries are sent out to work on specific projects on the field. In fact, the project may not start until the funds are in hand or promised. Thereafter, the sponsors for the project will be interested to follow its progress, and they may request information about the project, including how and where project funding is being spent. Hence, in the ReMAP II survey, we asked two related questions: one on project funds, and another on financial transparency.

Our data showed that effective use of project finances received the highest ratings for significance and effectiveness among the four finance-related practices surveyed. In OSC, this practice could be positively correlated to high missionary retention.

Transparent finances to missionaries and donors

Financial transparency to both missionaries and the donors was also very highly rated both in OSC and NSC. This practice was correlated with retention in OSC. But in NSC, it was rated so high that it could not serve as a discriminator. These facts confirm the importance of financial transparency in mission practice. This is because the embezzlement of funds can be a severe problem in poor countries where corporate governance is lacking; not just among the politicians or business-men, but sadly among some Christian workers. Thus, mission supporters need to know that their donations are being used effectively and appropriately, in accordance with their intended purpose.

Financial integrity is equally important. The handling of finances needs to be beyond reproach throughout a mission agency. Mission leaders should exercise responsible oversight and accountability in their use of finances. There should be careful accounting of the finances received and how finances are employed, with truthful and timely communication of ministry incomes and expenditures. Otherwise, the much-needed funding and financial support will stop.

The case study on "Presenting a Project Budget" provides the story of a young missionary as he prepares to meet the sponsors for his field project. This short case also brings our attention to the question of whether missionaries should be included in making major decisions related to ministry on the field. In the ReMAP II survey, the responses to Question 44 [Q44 *Missionaries are included in major decisions related to the field*] showed that inclusion in decision-making was highly rated in OSC, but not so high in NSC. There was no correlation between this practice and retention.

Presenting a project budget

Ajit Hazra, Methodist Church, Singapore

Note: For security reasons, the name of the missionary in the true story below and his country of service are not given.

Effective use of ministry project finances is a practice that is highly valued in many mission agencies and sending churches. This case study relates what happened when a missionary returned home in two consecutive years to make a budget presentation for his ministry to the mission board at his sending church.

The missionary and his wife had been sent directly to the mission field by their local church. They were sent to pioneer a Christian ministry in an economically deprived and religiously limited-access nation that did not allow open preaching of the gospel. One way that the missionaries tried to minister and reach out to the community was to develop a small orphanage for children from various parts of the country. The children were either orphans or from poor families who were not able to educate or care for their children. Due to civil unrest in parts of the nation, the missionaries decided to house the children in the capital city, which was relatively safe. The children were enrolled in a Christian-based and privately run school.

Below is the case as presented by the missionary to a small group of trusted friends:

> "Budget meetings are times of anticipation for missionaries who want to fulfil the Great Commission at all cost. However, it feels as if my mission board's main concern is to fulfil the Great Commission at the lowest cost!
>
> During my first year of operation of the orphanage, I presented the cost of maintaining a child in the orphanage as $60 a month. That includes housing, schooling, food, medical... basically everything. One board member commented that this amount was way too high when compared to an international organisation which runs a world-wide child sponsorship programme at only $50 per child per month. This board member was sponsoring a child from that organisation.
>
> The discussion then moved to why our monthly cost was $60. Two issues were highlighted: a) sending the children to a private school b) operating the orphanage in the capital city which was more costly. These two activities were considered luxuries and I was told that the activities should be revised.
>
> I responded by explaining that poor government support for education resulted in teachers of government schools often not showing up for work as they wait to be paid. However, in the private school, the children would receive continuous schooling from Christian staff. Additionally, the civil unrest in the country did not make it feasible to run the programme outside the relative safety of the capital. This led to an uneasy stalemate in our discussion. Finally, I claimed "apostolic authority" by saying, "You sent me the field. If you don't trust me with the finances, who will you trust?" I was sent off with a reluctant in-principle approval of my budget for the orphanage.
>
> One year later, the very same mission board invited me to discuss the following year's budget. In that one year, the country had faced tremendous economic problems and inflation went out of control. As I had a limited budget, all I could do was to cut back where possible and to move to a smaller facility at lower cost to house the children. However, due to the inflation rate, our monthly bill for each child was now $90. Before setting off to make the budget presentation, I said to my wife, "A 50% increase from the previous year. How am I going to face the board?"

I came before the mission board feeling rather anxious. When I presented the orphanage budget, I indicated that $90 per child per month was the bottom line. I could not possibly reduce the cost any further. Then I waited for the response. What happened next was a shock to me. The very same member who one year earlier had claimed that $60 was too high responded said: "Wow! $90… that's cheap!" A totally unexpected response! I wondered if his response was the result of prayer. I had sought prayer support from my family."

Discussion questions:

1. What are the main issues and conflicts in this case?
2. How should decisions that directly affect the field operations be made?
3. How can the Mission Board be helped in their decision making for future field project budgets?

What it means

Missions, business, and missionary service

Finally, here are some reflective thoughts from a report[5] by Dr. John Orme, the executive director of IFMA.[6]

"I have recently been reflecting upon missions, business, and missionary service. … What is a mission? Is it like a business? If so, in what ways is it like a business? In what ways is it different from a business? Is it even fair to compare missions and business? Can the one learn from the other? …

In both business and missions, there is loss. In business, if an activity loses money, the business stops that activity. In missions, the activity uses money in order to reach men and women for Christ and in order to disciple the body of Christ. Business worries about loss; missions worries about the lost. …

Business and missions (both) have a bottom line. The bottom line of business is money. The bottom line of missions is the glory of God—to see men and women come to Christ bringing great glory to the Almighty. …

---

5   John H. Orme, "This business of missions – what is the bottom line?", the executive director's report, September 2000, IFMA News, Vol. 51 No. 4, 2000.

6   IFMA is the Interdenominational Foreign Mission Association of North America. Since its beginning in 1917, the Interdenominational Foreign Mission Association of North America has maintained definite requirements of its member missions. In the area of finances, from its beginning, the association has insisted that members demonstrate accountability of all funds received and practice full financial disclosure. Theologically, the IFMA has never wavered from its strong biblical position. The association's high standards have gained, for it and its members, a reputation of proven excellence and integrity. Read more about IFMA at www.ifmamissions.org.

We need to continually ask God for help and wisdom as we consider projects and funding. We need to take care not to slip into the business bottom line when a project becomes more expensive than expected. At the same time, we need to take care not to equate the availability of funds with the will of God. ...

We need to be good managers and stewards of these moneys which are called missionary support. ...

As we look at ourselves, our missions, our association, our doctrine, and our principles and practice, we are reminded from the Scriptures again and again that our principles and our behaviour must correlate. We must take care not to become businesses as we do the work of mission. As we handle the details of mission administration, we must take great care not to become obsessed with forms, obsessed with statistics, obsessed with research, obsessed with numbers while the creativity and adventure of faith ministry fades away. ...

This is the bottom line of missions: While we do lots of other things, there is nothing like the euphoria that we feel when we see someone come to Christ."

Further reading and reflection

"Funding for Evangelism and Mission", Lausanne Occasional Paper No. 56, produced by the Issue Group on this topic at the 2004 Forum hosted by the Lausanne Committee for World Evangelization, http://www.lausanne.org/lcwe/assets/ LOP56_IG27.pdf.

In the real world

A table to stimulate ideas for best practice in mission partnership. For further explanation, see page 7.

This chart has been partially filled in for you. Now you fill in the blanks.

Who? → When? ↓	Home Church	Missionary	Mission Agencies	External Partners
Continuous	➢ Have a culture of giving with joy ➢ Teach financial transparency and accountability		➢ Be transparent about use of finances ➢ Use finances effectively	
Recruitment			➢ Be clear about expectations	
Preparation	➢ Support during training time	➢ Raise needed support		➢ Help to organize finances ➢ Provide training on financial management
On field	➢ Support financially	➢ See chances of tentmaking		
Crisis	➢ Be faithful in support			
Furlough				
Re-entry	➢ Support in needs	➢ Be open and transparent about finances		➢ Provide help in reintegrating

30

Finances
Sustained Financial Support

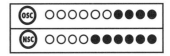

The facts

Sustained financial support is positively correlated with missionary retention in both OSC and NSC. The use of a backup system to respond to low or irregular financial support is also correlated to retention in OSC and NSC.

Part of a missionary's budget should be set aside for retirement. In OSC and NSC, high retaining agencies allocate between 10 to 14% of missionary allowances for retirement. Such allocation is highly correlated with retention of mission personnel for NSC, and mildly correlated in OSC.

The data

Q. No.	Factor	OSC Health Indicator	✓	NSC Health Indicator	✓
5	Estimate what percentage of your missionaries allowances are allocated for retirement.	○○○○○○●●●●		○○○●●●●●●●	✓
44	Missionaries are included in major decisions related to the field	○○○○○○○●●●		○○○○○○○●●●	
80	Missionaries usually receive sustained financial support that is adequate for their needs	○○○○○○○●●●	✓	○○○○●●●●●●	✓
81	There is financial back-up for missionaries with low or irregular support	○○○○●●●●●●	✓	○○○●●●●●●●	✓

The key findings

✓ Sustained financial support (Q80) was rated high for significance and effectiveness by mission executives in OSC, and much lower by NSC.

✓ Sustained financial support (Q80) was correlated with retention in OSC and NSC.

✓ A back-up system for irregular financial support (Q81) received a considerably lower rating than the other factors (agencies have different financial systems) and was correlated with retention in NSC (and OSC to a lower degree).

✓ On average, 10% of missionaries' allowance is invested in retirement funds (Q5) in OSC and NSC as well.

✓ Percentage for retirement allowance (Q5) is highly correlated with retention in NSC.

What it means

Valerie Lim

Our data showed that sustained financial support which is adequate for the missionaries' needs will contribute to their retention on the field.

For many agencies, financial support to missionaries refers only to the basic living expenses and ministry needs on the field. But it should ideally include other expenses, such as: retirement funds, health care, insurance coverage (for health, life, property, evacuation, etc.), children's education, parental support (in cultures where filial piety is important), and home assignment expenses.[1] In ReMAP II, we could have surveyed several other expenses, but we only studied the allocation of retirement funds.

Retirement support is important but often neglected. David Pollock explains the need: "Retiring missionaries or those who conclude their (mission) career because their task is finished or due to health reasons are not throwaways. Too often, the people who have consciously sacrificed economic security for the cause of the gospel find themselves in desperate need because there is little or no provision for retirement (including government-supported supplements) in their closing years. Too often, the church rejects the responsibility to continue support because the person is 'no longer a missionary'. … Retirement support needs to begin long before retirement, through the encouragement and support of both mission agency and church. Financial planning, retirement housing, and useful post-retirement activity are too often ignored until it is too late to provide for these things."[2]

---

1   Adapted from "Guidelines on budgeting and support for a missionary (family)", Beram Kumar in: "Member Care Handbook -- A guide to caring for our missionaries", 2000, pp. 35-36.

2   David Pollock, "Developing a flow of care and caregivers" in *Doing Member Care Well: Perspectives and practices from around the world,*" ed., Kelly O'Donnell (Pasadena, CA: William Carey Library, 2002), p. 31.

Our data showed that high retaining agencies from OSC and NSC allocate between 10 to14% of the missionaries allowance towards retirement. This allocation is clearly correlated with high retention of mission personnel for NSC. In OSC, there is a similar but mild trend, with the correlation being less significant because even low retaining OSC agencies invest 9% of their missionaries allowance to retirement. But why was there a difference between agencies in NSC and OSC? Why would missionaries from NSC serve longer in agencies where funds are allocated for retirement? Perhaps it is because many NSC (in Africa, Latin America and Asia) are not welfare states that provide public health and retirement benefits for their citizens (unlike many OSC in Europe), nor do they have a system for social security payments after retirement (as in the USA). Hence, the provision of funds for retirement is good stewardship. Gracia Wirada recommends that "Mission agencies and churches, especially those in NSC, must plan with their missionaries for retirement needs and provide encouragement to raise support for either pension plans or endowment policies".[3] Such planning for the future will enable their missionaries to live a modest life in dignity in their old age.

Our data also showed that agencies in OSC gave a high rating for sustained financial support, but those in NSC gave a much lower rating. Perhaps this difference is due to the financial realities in NSC where many agencies and churches simply cannot provide sufficient financial support to their missionaries.

What is "sufficient"? How should an appropriate amount be determined for each missionary (or missionary family)? Should support be based on a salary structure for Christian workers in the sending country, or the cost of living on the field, or some other criteria? Should the amount be reviewed yearly in order to adjust for currency fluctuations or changing needs? What items should be included? These and other questions must be carefully considered and clearly documented in the financial policy of each missionary sending agency or supporting church.

Let us look at how some agencies and supporting churches in NSC are addressing the problem of low financial support. The case study from Malaysia explores two recent initiatives in mobilisation. Sending "tentmakers"[4] has largely eliminated or reduced the need to raise sufficient and sustained financial support for ministry. Sending "finishers"[5] has meant encouraging those who can easily raise their support for mission ministry.

---

3   Gracia Wirada, "Challenges and care for Asian missionaries" in *Doing Member Care Well: Perspectives and practices from around the world,*" ed., Kelly O'Donnell (Pasadena, CA: William Carey Library, 2002), p. 60.

4   "Tentmakers" are missionaries who enter the mission field through the employment of their professional skills.

5   "Finishers" is a term used to describe workers who are entering missionary service after having retired from their career jobs. They are usually mature adults and well respected in their home churches. Hence, they may find it relatively easier to raise financial support. Some may also have accumulated adequate savings to support themselves fully or partially, or built up passive income sources. Most finishers would have adult children who are independent, and therefore they need not be concerned about their educational needs. In fact, the children could even contribute to their parents' financial support.

Overcoming low financial support by sending "tentmakers' and "finishers"

Philip Chang[6], Malaysia.

Efforts to mobilise "tentmakers"[7] (as opposed to traditional career missionaries), and "finishers" (mostly senior or retired professionals) are two recent initiatives in mission recruitment in Malaysia. Such efforts represent a significant shift in mobilisation strategy by some mission agencies and churches, which has overcome common obstacles that previously would have prevented some mission candidates from entering the mission field and staying on. These obstacles include certain socio-cultural values.[8]

Lee, the tentmaker

Lee applied for a job in a multinational company in the Middle East. He obtained the job easily due to his work experience. He is now paid a tax-free expatriate salary, provided accommodation, and given several return air-tickets each year. However, had Lee tried to apply to work in a church or Christian organisation in the Middle East, he would have faced many obstacles getting a visa and raising adequate financial support due to the high cost of living there.

Since there were few believers or Christian workers in the country where he works, Lee decided to join a mission agency that could provide him with member care while on the field. From his mission agency's perspective, it is a win-win situation. "We have been trying to place people into that country for some time but without any success. Here we have someone who not only has a job and an employment visa, but all his financial needs are met and with surplus!" says his mission agency director.

In Malaysia, Full Gospel Assembly (FGA) is one of the local churches that have actively sent out many tentmakers in partnership with various mission agencies. Dorai Manikam, Missions Director of FGA shares about their experience. "The majority of our missionaries now are tentmakers. Previously, our mission mobilisation was focused on sending out traditional missionaries, but when we started

---

6   Philip Chang holds a senior management position in the marketplace in the financial services sector. He has over 23 years of cross-cultural experience, having studied and worked in both Europe and Asia. Philip is the Chairman of Interserve Malaysia, a member of the Missions Commission of National Evangelical Christian Fellowship in Malaysia, a member of the Asia Member Care Taskforce and the Missions Commission of WEA. He served as national coordinator for Malaysia in the ReMAP II project.

7   Many tentmakers serve in countries which are not open to traditional missionaries, countries known as "creative access nations". In the past few years, a growing number of missionaries (in particular single men) from Malaysia have been able to obtain reasonably well-paying professional jobs in creative access countries, hence becoming tentmakers in those places.

8   For those professionals coming from non-Christian families, they were able to overcome family objections when they go overseas for work. This is because Malaysian families generally view overseas employment as something positive. Likewise among their family and friends, such a change in profession was more readily accepted, without the usual social stigma associated with someone becoming a full-time missionary and 'living on charity'.

to bring tentmaking into the picture, we saw a large jump in numbers. When mobilisation and tentmaking are brought together, it has a powerful impact. FGA would not have been able to deploy so many missionaries if not for tentmaking."

John and Lucy, the finishers

John and Lucy had already become grandparents. They were both in their 60s when they felt a strong calling to serve overseas. But how could they go, and what could they do? After praying and making enquiries, a friend introduced them to a children's ministry overseas. They decided to go on a short-term stint for six months.

When they returned home, they were convinced that they should return for the long-term. Having both retired from their jobs a few years earlier, and their children already grown-up and independent, Lucy said "We have a calling to serve, and we have skills and experience which can be used by God. We just want to use the remaining years of our working life to do His work." They applied to become partners with Interserve and were sent out by their home church, a Presbyterian Church in Kuala Lumpur, which now supports them financially.

Here is the perspective of one of their church members. "It will always be easier for a church to support a couple who have been church members for a long time, especially if they are mature Christians. People like John and Lucy serve as role models for other working adults in the congregation, who can see them as good examples and will personally consider serving in the mission field upon their retirement."

Dorai Manikam of FGA, having sent out a number of couples who are finishers, shares a similar view. According to Dorai, "Sending out finishers, in itself, has a mobilising effect on other church members." Mission agencies like Interserve, Operation Mobilisation and Wycliffe Malaysia have begun to notice more enquiries from older, mature Christians in recent years.

Joshua Aw, the Personnel Director of Interserve Malaysia, is keen to recruit more finishers. Joshua says "finishers possess valuable work experience and skills which can be used to mentor people they serve in the field. Financially, as many of them are already quite established, they are able to provide for their own basic needs, such as a home for retirement or set aside some retirement funds, such as the Employees Provident Fund and other savings. In some cases, their insurance policies have all been paid for or taken care of. All these items would definitely reduce the overall costs of supporting mission workers, making it easier to mobilise people."

Besides the financial support aspect, finishers would make excellent and natural Tentmakers because of their skills and years of experience. They would tend to command greater respect amongst the people in their workplace and the community where they live and serve.

Discussion questions:

1. What are the advantages of recruiting "tentmakers" (as opposed to traditional career missionaries), and "finishers" (mostly senior or retired professionals) for missions? What are the disadvantages? What could be some areas of concern?

2. How can we help local churches to take seriously the calling and response of Christian professionals to mission, if people view their decision to become "tentmakers" as "simply making a professional move"?

3. Review your organisational policies and publicity material. Do they communicate that older people are welcomed to participate in mission work?

4. How does your organisation address the issue of low financial support of missionaries? Discuss new initiatives that it could consider implementing to overcome the problem of low financial support. What counsel on financial support would you provide to new missionaries and their local churches?

What it means

Business as mission

Tentmaking was mentioned in the case study above. Although a tentmaker might be a part of a business, the business itself might not be an integral part of the ministry. Business as mission, however, sees business both as the medium and the message. Most often, business as mission involves "job-making" as an integral part of its mission. Tentmaking may involve this, but it is more often simply about "job-taking"—taking up employment somewhere in order to facilitate ministry. The methodologies, as well as the business and ministry strategies used, are creatively diverse. The size of the business may vary from micro to small, medium and large size businesses.

On the small end, Christian micro-enterprise programmes can help provide necessary income for families and individuals resulting in community development, churches being planted, and discipleship taking place. Ah Kie Lim explains how income-generating strategies can supplement low financial support in South Asia. "In our organisation, we are working closely with our church planting teams to help them with income-generating projects to earn income for themselves. Some of these small businesses are making Indian pickles, greeting cards, etc. These micro-enterprises allow our workers to be more independent of outside support, as well as being a testimony to the community. We are in no way saying that we do not trust God to provide for all of our needs or that the sending churches or agencies do not need to take more responsibility for missionaries' support. But we need to be creative with whatever means we have, in order that we might continue to stay on the field."[9]

---

9   Ah Kie Lim, in *Doing Member Care Well: Perspectives and practices from around the world*," ed., Kelly O'Donnell (Pasadena, CA: William Carey Library, 2002), p. 88.

Indeed, creativity in mission giving is not lacking in Northeast India. The case study below illustrates how local churches there raise money to support their missionaries.

A little creativity can bring great results

Detlef Blöcher,[10] DMG,[11] Germany

Mizoram is a state in the remote mountain region of the Northeast of India. Due to its extreme geographical location and its delicate security situation (hemmed in between Bangladesh and Myanmar), this region has been basically excluded from the economic development of India.

The mission secretary of the Presbyterian churches, Reverend Vanlalhruaia, says: "Our state is poor. We are not able to export anything of economic value, but, we do export one thing for which we are very proud. That is the Gospel." The churches in Mizoram are sending missionaries in an impressive way. The synod of Presbyterian churches alone has sent about 1,000 missionaries.

The church in Chanmari has 1,855 members, and it is supporting 120 missionaries that it has sent out. A couple of months ago, I met the mission secretary Reverend S. Nengyakhup. He told me more about the impressive missionary movement of evangelical churches in Mizoram,[12] and how the economically poor churches are supporting their missionaries.

How do the poor churches in Mizoram support so many missionaries? They do so mainly through very creative ideas, which have grown out of their love for Jesus and a burden for the lost. These poor churches are a great example to all of us.

1. Vegetable gardens: Many churches have set up a church garden where they plant vegetables, bananas, oranges, grapes, ginger, rice or teak-trees. Church members work there voluntarily. All the profit goes to mission.

2. Chickens for mission: Farmers keep some extra chickens (clearly marked as "missionary chickens"). The money from the sale of eggs and meat goes to support the missionaries.

3. Portion of the field: Farmers designate a portion of their fields to mission. The entire profit from it goes to mission.

4. Collecting firewood: Women collect firewood in the woods or straw on the fields. They carry the goods to a place at the entrance of the village from where it is sold from time to time. The money they earn goes to mission.

5. Collecting crabs and snails: Women collect crabs and snails at the river banks.

---

10 Dr. Detlef Blöcher is chairman of the German Evangelical Mission Alliance, and an Associate of the WEA Mission Commission. From 1991 to 1999, he served as Personnel Director of German Missionary Fellowship (DMG), and since then as its CEO.

11 German Missionary Fellowship (DMG) is one of the largest evangelical mission agencies in Germany with presently some 350 missionaries serving in 70 countries.

12 S. Nengzakhup, "Amazing Mizo Missions", SAIACS Press, 1999, Bangalore Indien

They sell these at the market as a delicacy. They donate whatever they get to mission.

6. Market stalls: Churches open a shop or a market stall to sell tea. All the money earned goes to mission.

7. Wholesale shopping: Church members buy goods in bulk (e.g. a sack of salt or whole animals to slaughter) and then they sell in small portions. All the profit goes to mission.

8. Donation of work: Church members collect stones, work as carpenters, do embroidery, etc. They donate this extra income to mission.

9. Rent for missions: Churches build a shop or flat into their church building and the resultant rental income goes into the mission box. Some church members reduce their own living space so that they can rent out a room in their home. The rent goes to mission.

10. Part of salary: Civil servants and employees give the seventh part of their wages, because they get paid for Sundays without working.

11. Small loans: Church members receive a small amount of money (5 to 100 rupees) and they do business with it. Any profit they make goes to mission.

12. Christmas Feast: Families do without their Christmas dinner and presents. Instead, they give the money to the missionaries.

13. Imaginary field visit: In their imagination, people visit their missionary in his country of service. They calculate the cost for travel, accommodation and food. Then they give this amount to mission.

14. Short term mission trip: Church members make a short-term trip to their missionary and help him to build his house, a school or a church. Through this, they can help with their gifts and experience, while deepening their personal relationship with the missionary.

15. Thank-Offering box: Church members bring collection boxes from house to house and they ask for donations.

16. Day of fasting: Many Mizos fast one day per week. They give the saved amount to mission.

17. Portion for the chieftain: In former times the chieftain in a village received a quarter of the meat of a hunted animal. Today this portion is given to the missionaries.

18. A handful of rice: When preparing a meal, a housewife puts a handful of rice to the side before preparing a meal. This amount saved goes for her missionaries.

These creative ideas, coupled with the ardent desire by families and churches to give as much as possible to mission, characterise the Mizo mission movement.

Good practices in Mizoram

Many believe this impressive movement began with the good practices of the first missionaries to Mizoram: James Lorrain and Fredrick Savidge. They had taught the Mizos to become self-supporting right from the beginning. They had handed over leadership responsibility for churches, schools and for evangelism as early as possible. By 1953, an indigenous mission committee had been founded. In 1961, this was enlarged to a missionary society (SBM). Mizoram was, until recently, a restricted military zone. Foreigners could not enter the state, so the churches had to work without foreign help. In addition, there were several revivals since 1906, through which a great part of the population became Christians. Thus, the local believers depended on their local resources, and they encouraged and supported one another.

Their mission movement is built on the traditional values of their culture such as helping people in need, doing good and sharing generously (even competing with one another for the privilege of giving). The high standard of education (schools had been introduced by missionaries) contributed to good theological training. Mizos have an emphasis on lay preachers, God's love and prayer, writing their own songs, the expectation of Jesus' Second Coming, and thankfulness for their salvation.

Out of their poverty and need, the Mizoram churches have been involved in world mission. Pastor Nengzakhup writes: "Mizos have never considered poverty an excuse to avoid participation in world evangelisation. If the church in Jerusalem had looked at its poverty and concluded that it could not afford to send out missionaries, the Gospel would not have gone out from that city. It is not affluence but zeal and gratitude to God that drives Mizos to maintain their enthusiasm and active participation in world evangelisation." And he concludes that: "Any church can be a missionary church, irrespective of its economic situation. Poverty need not inhibit a church from participating in world evangelisation. This attitude is biblical. Although money plays a vital role in missions, it is not the primary need."

Discussion questions:

1. Discuss some of the creative ideas by the Mizoram churches to raise money to support their missionaries. Which of these ideas could be adapted and used in your situation to sustain regular financial support of your missionaries?

2. How could you encourage local church members to contribute more regularly to the financial support for your missionaries? Who could be involved in teaching good stewardship of financial and other resources to the families in your local church?

In the real world

A table to stimulate ideas for best practice in mission partnership. For further explanation, see page 7.

This chart has been partially filled in for you. Now you fill in the blanks.

Who? → When? ↓	Home Church	Missionary	Mission Agencies	External Partners
Continuous	➢ Be creative in bringing in money ➢ Have a vision for "finishers"			
Recruitment		➢ Be open about willingness to gain support	➢ Be open about expectations	
Preparation	➢ Provide funds for training			➢ Provide training on financial management ➢ Provide help for retirement funds
On field		➢ Handle finances in an adequate way ➢ Be open and transparent	➢ Have a back-up system for poorer times ➢ Set aside money for retirement time	
Crisis	➢ Be faithful in supporting			
Furlough	➢ Provide money for holiday time			
Re-entry	➢ Take responsibility for former missionaries			➢ Provide help in obtaining retirement money

31

Home Office

The facts

Home office operations received a reasonable rating in significance and performance from the mission executives. By this, mission executives show they believe the home office plays a very important role in retaining missionaries. In OSC, the ReMAP II data confirmed a correlation with retention.

The home office coordinates communication between the field and sending base. This element is one of the characteristics of high retaining agencies. Not only is "horizontal" communication valued, but prayer, being our "vertical" way of communicating with the Sender, is vital, and this has been emphasised by all agencies in NSC. In OSC, emphasis on the vertical aspect of communication set the high retaining agencies apart from the low retaining agencies.

Thorough communication and guidance of the (candidate) missionary before (during pre-field screening) and after field assignment (re-entry arrangements including debriefing) are highly rated. NSC did not value re-entry arrangements as highly, but this may be due to their lack of experience in that area.

The data

Q. No.	Factor	OSC Health Indicator	✓	NSC Health Indicator	✓
43	There is effective communication between sending base and field	○○○○●●●●●●	✓	○○○○○○○●●●	✓
79	Home churches are encouraged to be involved in the life and ministry of their missionary	○○○○○○○○●●	✓	○○○○○●●●●●	✓
84	Pre-field screening prevents unsuitable persons proceeding to the field	○○○○○○○○●●	✓	○○○○○●●●●●	✓
85	Pre-field orientation prepares missionaries for adjustment to cross-cultural life and ministry	○○○○○○○●●●		○○○○○○●●●●	
86	Staff in the home office pray regularly for the missionaries	○○○○○○○○●●	✓	○○○○○○○○○●	
87	Re-entry arrangements/ programmes are provided for missionaries commencing home leave	○○○○○●●●●●	✓	○○○●●●●●●●	
88	Formal debriefing is undertaken during home leave	○○○○○○○●●●	✓	○○○●●●●●●●	

The key findings

✓ Home office operations, in general, received a high rating for significance and effectiveness.

✓ The rating of home office operations was correlated with retention in OSC.

✓ Effective communication between field and sending base (Q43) was strongly correlated with high retention.

✓ Staff in home office regularly praying for their missionaries (Q86) received a very high rating. It was also correlated with retention in OSC (no distinguishable correlation for NSC as it was highly rated in all agencies).

✓ Pre-field screening of candidates (Q84) was rated high and is correlated with retention in OSC and NSC.

✓ Re-entry arrangements and debriefing (Q87, 88) were rated high in high retaining OSC agencies only. There was a clear correlation with retention for OSC; and low rating (and no distinguishable correlation) in most NSC agencies (lack of experience in NSC).

What it means

Jaap Ketelaar

While the home church has a unique role in the sending and care of a missionary, so the mission agency also has a key supporting role in the sending process. God has used the mission agency to have a tremendous impact in the world. Even though the importance of the involvement of the church is now recognised and desired, the mission agency should remain a key partner because of its knowledge and experience. The home office of the agency becomes the sending base of the missionary, and once a missionary has been deployed, creates a "spider in the web" effect, which links the different partners together. And when the agency is part of an international organisation, the agency on the field and the "headquarters" are also included. Cooperation and communication between all the links should not be underestimated, as is shown by ReMAP II results summarised in "The facts" above.

Since the home office is so crucial, forming a new one should not be taken lightly. As has been discussed earlier, the size of an agency has an effect on its actual performance (see Chapter 4). A high level of expertise and many skills are required to run and lead a sending base. The role and function of a home office should not be ignored, for ReMAP II highlights the crucial role it plays.

Operation Mobilisation has clear criteria before they organise operations in a new field. They make sure the following is in place:

- A strategic plan—what will be done and how will it actually be accomplished?
- A mother field—who will be the supporters?
- Committed leadership—good, dedicated leadership is essential
- Financial stability—what about the resources... did faith prove itself in this?
- Board or accountability structure—a group of people who are critical in a positive way
- Sufficient activity to warrant field status—a field should not be a goal in itself

Recognition that a home office is so important should cause careful consideration and attentive prayer to confirm that God wants something new, or if joining and partnering with an already existing agency is a better option. The goal, of course, is not about us, but about God and serving Him in a way that is as effective as possible.

Issues to deal with

Thoughtfully and prayerfully consider the following questions to work into a vision and policy document:

Strategic items (for the longer-term):

- What is the history of our agency and how has God guided us until now?
- What values are important for us personally, the people we serve, and the services we offer?
- Who do we want to serve? What is needed in the area where we feel called?
- With what do we serve? What is our unique contribution? What are our strengths, weaknesses, opportunities, threats? Who are our partners?
- Where exactly do we serve and what are the characteristics of that place?
- What is our dream and vision for the (near) future?
- What is our mission statement in a few words or sentences?
- What should be our priorities be, given the stage of development of the organisation?
- What goals can we describe with our mission statement and vision in mind?
- What are our critical success factors and how do we measure if we have reached our goals?

Operational items (for the coming year):

- What are our goals? Make them specific, measurable, active, realistic, time-bound (SMART).
- What sub-goals of the bigger goals do we have? Make them SMART also.
- Develop an action-plan. Who is doing what, when?
- What resources do we need? Think of time, competencies, equipment, facilities, money.
- Who is going to measure what success we have, and when? How is that going to be done?
- What risks do we have when we start working on this? How are we going to manage them?

Items regarding personnel (missionaries at the home office and on the field), to be evaluated/adjusted every year:

- What values do we have in how we want to work with and treat our personnel?
- Which roles do we have in our organisation? Who has what authority with which responsibility, and how is he or she accountable for that to whom?
- What competencies are needed where? How are we going to develop them?
- How do we get new personnel (recruitment and selection, initial training)?
- How do we develop our personnel (appraisal, ongoing training possibilities)?
- How do we reward our personnel (materially, non-materially)?

- How do we end the relationship with our personnel (when they resign, when we (have to) fire them)? Do we have exit-interviews?

Organisational items, to be evaluated/adjusted every year:

- What is our stage of development as an organisation? What specific type of leadership does this require?
- How are the lines of communication regarding work-flow towards the partners we work with and the people/target groups we want to serve? Do we communicate well or do we see hindrances? How can we solve them?
- What is the organisational/structural picture of how we work (organagram/ organisational chart)?
- What about our communication lines? Who has to discuss what, with whom, when and how?
- Finances/budget: how do we get our money? Who has what authority with which responsibility and how is he or she accountable for that and to whom? How transparent can or should we be to key people and how are we going to do that?

Clearly, in a fast moving world (think of the broad changes in missiology, sociology, politics, and economics), a high level of expertise and many skills are required to run and lead a sending base. There is a special responsibility for the board of an agency to help the CEO, so he or she can in turn help staff to function well.

Mutual learning

Because we have such a task to fulfil, it is essential that we think and work in terms of partnership. We can think of partnership in several arenas:

- Missionaries and mission agencies need the support of local and national churches. This could also work conversely (see Chapter 32). Agencies can also work with partners that do not send out people themselves, but offer help in special areas, including training institutes, specialist organisations on member care, and also umbrella organisations that can bring all the partners together, like national, regional or global mission movements. In this way, support services can be offered and time, money and energy can be saved. Also, the quality of the work would improve by using each other's expertise
- Agencies could partner with other agencies, churches, etc., in sharing office facilities.
- Different generations working together can form interesting partnerships. How can the younger generation learn from the older and how can the older generation learn from the younger? And how can space be created for this when our times focus on efficiency?

In summary, ministry, gifting, and experience are being shared while different partners are each fulfilling their own role in the one calling.

Ministry to the elderly parents of missionaries

Dong-Hwa Kim,[1] Global Missionaries Fellowship,[2] Korea

The population in South Korea is rapidly aging. About 8% of Korea's population is 65 years old and older. The current average lifespan of a South Korean is 76. Unlike many Western countries that provide a social infrastructure for elderly senior citizens, the majority of elderly people in Korea are cared for by their children.

Taking care of one's elderly parents is a very important social value in Korea, as it is in many Asian countries, and this has a long tradition. Many Korean missionaries have a great burden for their parents back home, especially those who have unbelieving parents. Our most senior Korean missionaries are now in their fifties, so the care of their elderly parents is of great concern to them,

About four years ago, Luke Yoon became the assistant director for member care of Global Bible Translators (GBT), the Wycliffe organisation in Korea. Luke had to leave his elderly mother at home when he left for overseas ministry. He and his wife had served for several years in a country in central Asia as linguists and translators, before they were reassigned to work at the agency's Korean home office. Prior to his return, Luke remembered that his mother was very much encouraged whenever a colleague from the same mission field called and visited her.

When Luke returned to Korea, he initiated a new ministry for the elderly parents of his agency's missionaries. In 2003, Mr. and Mrs. Kang, a Korean-American couple in their sixties, were looking for a new assignment. They had previously served in Papua New Guinea as support workers. They were invited to serve in Korea, specifically to help Korean missionaries by caring for their elderly parents.

The Kangs came to Korea in 2003. For one and half years before they went on furlough, the Kangs served faithfully in their ministry to the elderly parents. Some of their activities included:

- Making phone calls: They called the parents regularly and found out how they were doing. They provided news from their sons and daughters and grandchildren. They also made phone calls to each parent on his/her birthday and sent greeting cards to them.

- Visitation: With the help of a local Korean office staff member of GBT, the Kangs visited the parents who were sick or hospitalised.

---

1 Dong-Hwa Kim has been the director of the corporation office of Global Missionaries Fellowship (GMF) of Korea since 2003. Dong-Hwa was one of the founding members of Global Bible Translators and Global Missionaries Fellowship. He was formerly the executive director of GBT for several years until 2002. He has also served as the coordinator of Sorak Mission Forum, which seeks to discover non-Western missionary models for the 21st century among Korean sending agencies. Dong-Hwa and his wife Hyun-Sook have two adult sons.

2 GMF is the umbrella organisation of three sending agencies including Global Bible Translators (GBT), a Wycliffe organisation in Korea, and five supporting agencies including MK NEST and Global Missionary Training Centre (GMTC).

- Arranging meetings: The Kangs organised meetings for the parents in the major cities of Korea. The Yoons and Kangs, together with some members on furlough, participated in these meetings. They explained to the parents how their children were serving on each field, how significant their ministry was, and what kind of contribution they were making. They also assured the parents about how their children serving as missionaries were taken care of as a part of a larger family, and how their grandchildren were being educated. They would pray together with the parents for their children and their ministry.

- Building networks: The Kangs helped parents to connect with other parents, so that the parents could encourage each other and to meet together themselves. Luke said that they wanted to see the parents eventually become mobilisers for the cause of the Bible translation missions and to be faithful prayer supporters.

Missionaries of GBT have really appreciated the new ministry of the home office to their parents. They feel that their burden for their parents has been lightened in many ways. Some unbelieving parents have become believers and now attend church regularly as a result of this ministry. One missionary said that he was relieved from great concern for his parents: "They [my parents] are not worriers anymore. They have become true supporters. It gives my family on the field a sense of stability and confidence."

When GBT celebrated its 20th anniversary in December 2004, all of the parents were invited and a special meeting was arranged for them.

The main challenge for this new ministry is to find suitable staff that can really get along with the elderly. Such a ministry requires staff who have obtained specialised training in caring for elderly people.

Discussion questions:

1. What does your organisation do to show member care to the elderly parents of your missionaries?
2. What can be done to improve such member care?

Sustaining a culture of prayer

LeMei Littlefield[3], OMF International[4], USA

Please note that the names used in this case study have been changed to protect the identities of persons involved in these real-life events.

How does one promote and sustain a culture of prayer? Most agencies would agree that it is far easier to *talk* about the importance of prayer than to *demonstrate* it by implementing a system to disseminate prayer requests and schedule corporate prayer times. Even when such a system is in place, it can be a challenge to sustain effective, Spirit led prayer.

Grace walked quickly down the street. She was on her way to attend a weekly Agency prayer meeting at her team leader's home. Grace has been in Taiwan for six months as a new missionary in full-time language study and cultural orientation. One factor that contributed to her choice of mission agency was its emphasis on prayer. Listed within the Agency handbook was this core value: "We acknowledge prayer as a vital part of our fellowship together and thus we set aside times for both individual and corporate prayer. We recognize that we are engaged in spiritual warfare and depend upon the prayers of our supporting churches and friends to see spiritual breakthrough and victory in ministry." Both Candidate and Orientation Courses in her home country had begun with scheduled corporate prayer each day. When she arrived on the field, Grace was expected to attend a weekly Agency prayer meeting. Grace was encouraged by this time of interceding prayer with other missionaries in the area. She was also encouraged to know that her prayer partners, along with Agency personnel in the Home Office, were praying for their Taiwan team.

Meanwhile, back at the Home Office, it was Pat's turn to lead the daily 30 minute morning prayers. She turned to the Agency prayer book, which serves as a guide for these prayer times. For each of 31 days, the book targets a different field or home country, providing general requests that are specific to that region as well as the names of Agency members serving there. Pat worked in the Partnership Services Department, which prints and distributes prayer letters for missionaries. She regularly expanded on the general requests with portions from current prayer letters. She also added prayer items from monthly "Prayer Powerlines" written by the Home Office Prayer Coordinator, and from prayer bulletins distributed by each field. As she looked at the range of prayer requests to choose from, the challenge was how to present the information creatively and concisely, leaving quality time to pray. Pat noted that today was Day 25 and Taiwan was the field of focus. They

---

3   LeMei Littlefield and her husband Michael serve at the US office of OMF International, where Michael is Director for Personnel for the OMF-US homeside. Michael and LeMei draw on their experiences as missionaries to Taiwan (1987 to 1997) and Singapore (1998 to 2004) to oversee the selection, training and ongoing enablement of missionaries to East Asia. .

4   OMF International, formerly the China Inland Mission, has been sending missionaries to East Asian countries for 140 years. Today, OMF International has approximately 1,000 adults and 600+ children, representing around 30 different nationalities. The missionaries are being sent from 18 sending bases, both Asian and non-Asian, and they work mainly in East Asia.

would certainly remember their new missionaries starting out in language school, missionaries like Grace.

After the morning prayer time, Pat began planning ahead for the Agency's year-end Day of Prayer. This was one of two days in the year which is set apart. Everyone throughout the Agency would spend a half day in prayer. She had been given a structured prayer guide, targeting each field and home centre with specific praises and requests. For her half-hour segment, Pat decided that she would ask Walt to share. He was a volunteer who had just returned from visiting a dynamic new field centre.

Walt was eager to report on what he had observed. At the new field centre, the weekly Agency prayer meetings had been replaced by daily noon time prayers, with intercession for local needs and specific people groups. A prayer room had been set up in the team centre and it was available for ongoing use. The noon time gatherings offered a sense of urgency to prayer. Walt was inspired by the culture of prayer that had developed. The missionaries had come to a point of humility, discernment and reliance upon God. This showed up dramatically in the way they interceded for others as well as in the way they prayed for one another.

Walt was also looking forward to reporting this new development at the upcoming annual Regional Prayer Conference. This gathering of Agency prayer partners would be held in another part of the home country. While at the Regional Prayer Conference, Walt planned to distribute a colourful 31-day People Group prayer booklet. This booklet had been specially prepared by missionaries at the field centre he had visited. He would make copies available to these prayer partners. He would also encourage them to check the Agency website for other new prayer resources.

Discussion questions:

1. How would you describe the current culture of prayer in your agency or church? What next steps could be taken to practically implement regular opportunities for corporate prayer? How can prayer requests be communicated and updated regularly?

2. Consider the "why, when, where, what and how" of sustaining an ongoing dynamic culture of prayer in your agency. If regular corporate prayer is already structured, are the prayer meetings simply "information-processing" sessions where prayer requests are exchanged? How can prayer meetings become vital and Spirit led?

In the real world

A table to stimulate ideas for best practice in mission partnership. For further explanation, see page 7.

This chart has been partially filled in for you. Now you fill in the blanks.

Who? → When? ↓	Home Church	Missionary	Mission Agencies	External Partners
Continuous	➢ Have a culture of prayer		➢ Have a culture of prayer	
Recruitment			➢ Have adequate pre-field screening	
Preparation		➢ Build relationship with the home office	➢ Give opportunities for orientation	➢ Provide training on maintaining relations
On field	➢ Take care of the family that is left behind	➢ Be informative about blessings and needs ➢ Communicate regularly		➢ Facilitate communication
Crisis		➢ Keep home church and agency updated		
Furlough		➢ Take time to work on relationship with agency	➢ Take time to work on relationship with missionary	
Re-entry		➢ Keep in contact with agency	➢ Keep in contact with missionary	➢ Facilitate reunions

32

Home Office
Church and Missions

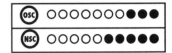

The facts

The home office has a role in coordinating and affirming a good relationship between local church, home office and missionary. All three work together for the retention and success of a missionary. The local church has to recognise and affirm the calling of a candidate-missionary. Likewise, ministry experience in a local church is of great importance. If this is done, retention rates are significantly better in OSC and NSC.

Effective communication between sending base and field is considered to be a key factor for retaining missionaries, especially in OSC. But communication to missionaries from home churches is also essential. When home churches are actively involved in the life and ministry of the missionary, this also correlates with retention. The home office can facilitate such communication.

The data

Q. No.	Factor	OSC Health Indicator	✓	NSC Health Indicator	✓
16	Has committed endorsement from his/her pastor/local church for missionary service	○○○○○○○○○●	✓	○○○○○○○○○●	✓
18	Has ministry experience in a local church	○○○○○○○●●●	✓	○○○○●●●●●●	✓
43	There is effective communication between sending base and field	○○○○●●●●●●	✓	○○○○○○○●●●	✓
79	Home churches are encouraged to be involved in the life and ministry of their missionary	○○○○○○○○●●	✓	○○○○○●●●●●	✓

84	Pre-field screening prevents unsuitable persons proceeding to the field	OOOOOOOO●●	✓	OOOOO●●●●●	✓
85	Pre-field orientation prepares missionaries for adjustment to cross-cultural life and ministry	OOOOOOO●●●		OOOOOO●●●●	
86	Staff in the home office pray regularly for the missionaries	OOOOOOOO●●	✓	OOOOOOOOO●	
87	Re-entry arrangements/ programmes are provided for missionaries commencing home leave	OOOOO●●●●●	✓	OOO●●●●●●●	
88	Formal debriefing is undertaken during home leave	OOOOOOO●●●	✓	OOO●●●●●●●	

The key findings

✓ Pastor's committed endorsement of a new candidate (Q16) was rated very high for significance and performance by mission executives and correlated with retention.

✓ Candidates' ministry experience in a local church (Q18) was rated high in OSC agencies only, and highly correlated with retention in OSC (and NSC regarding preventable attrition).

✓ Home church involvement in the life of their missionary (Q79) received a high rating in OSC and it is correlated with retention in OSC (and NSC regarding preventable attrition).

What it means

Jaap Ketelaar

The ReMAP II data confirms the importance of a good relationship between the missionary, mission agency and the local church. Though all agree to its importance and see the potential, what about practice? Is the fact that this book contains "only" one chapter on church and missions a reflection of low priority in practice? Is the church just one of the many topics mission agencies have to deal with? In reality, a lot of missionary work worldwide is done by missionaries sent by mission agencies, and if a local church is involved, involvement is often only by support through prayer and financial support. What could be the vision for the active involvement of the church?

The common missional structure was shaped through the "two structure theory": the local church works at "home", while the mission agency does the work "overseas".

David Tai Woong Lee has written a very good article about our need to rethink missional structures in the globalised mission context, both church and mission societies.[1] On one hand, there is the unique calling of mission agencies and their knowledge and experience. On the other hand, there is the challenge of getting the global church involved and active world-wide. In a lot of areas, chances are missed when the church is left out. Conversely, it is sad to see (maybe as a reaction to this) more and more churches leave the agency out. They wonder why they would need the agency when they can have easy contact with their missionaries through fast travelling and e-mail communication, or they think they can save money. However, church and mission agencies need each other's calling, knowledge and experience to improve in all the areas mentioned in this book. But how is this done?

Issues to deal with

A willingness to cooperate is crucial. Are church and mission agency willing to fully recognise each other as partners in God's calling and give each other room to work out the unique role God has given each? Churches and agencies must understand what their particular role in the missionary process can be. What is one's calling and what if the other partner can do something better? Can the church not do more? The question should be asked, Am I willing, for the sake of the Kingdom, to give up my place? Or, have I become a goal in myself and do I keep doing certain things to avoid the reality that the organisation should cease?

Choosing partnership requires excellent communication. Poor communication is fatal to partnership. Are there direct lines between the local church and the mission agency, or is the missionary the only means through which communication happens? And why is that? What a challenge it is and how motivating it would be if churches, agencies, missionaries and other partners would sit around the same table to discuss who is doing what in specific situations.

It is encouraging to see that where churches and agencies embrace this vision and start working as partners on new ways to do mission, God uses this to bless the local church itself. This pattern of mission agencies serving the local church presents a much more biblical picture than that which we have seen in recent years.

Mutual learning

- In general in NSC, mission is more a part of the total church life. OSC can learn from this and be enthused by their zeal to reach the world for Christ.
- Churches can learn from the knowledge and experience of mission agencies, and mission agencies can make use of the potential of local churches. However, it takes time, energy and commitment to achieve this.

---

1   David Tai Woong Lee, "Rethinking Missional Structures," Connections, The Journal of the WEA Mission Commission, April 2005, p. 18.

Advocacy teams in church

Thomas Sanchez,[2] Grace Covenant Church, USA

Dwight and Sandi Ekholm were the first missionaries released to the mission field more than 30 years ago from Grace Covenant Church in Austin, Texas. As with many long-term missionaries, the Ekholms have changed roles several times, often being away for long periods of time. As the constituency of the church changed dramatically over the years, Dwight and Sandi lost contact with the church family in many ways.

Some years ago, Grace Covenant Church began to build Advocacy Teams for our long-term missionary families.

The concept of "A-Teams" is built around Colossians 2:19, "...*from whom the entire body, being supplied and held together by the joints and ligaments, grows with a growth which is from God.*" The simple biological reality is that the body is held together by certain physiological parts that exist precisely for that function. These are the joints and ligaments that link it all together and allow it to work in harmony, being constantly supplied with directions by the head, who is Christ.

We (at Grace Covenant Church) had concluded that our long-term missionaries had become disconnected from us because we didn't have people performing this function of linking us to them. Thus, the idea of Advocacy Teams was born. Each of our "A-Teams" is "a group of three to five families (or more) who choose to champion and support a missionary on long-term assignment."

As we have trusted God with this idea, we have seen close to thirty A-Teams develop to one degree or another within the church family. The Ekholms have such a team: a home group of five or six families chose to adopt them a couple of years ago, though they did not know the Ekholms well. This A-Team has communicated faithfully with Dwight and Sandi. On several occasions, they have reached across the world to touch them in very specific ways, and in times of crisis.

Dwight and Sandi are now ministering with Entrust International in Athens, Greece. While they also minister to the diplomatic community in Athens, one of their primary ministry roles is to serve the thousands of refugees who populate that city. Dwight helps in leadership development among the new believers, so that they have sound doctrine and good basic Bible study methods. A good number of the refugees share the Farsi language as a common language for communication.

Several months ago, Dwight and Sandi informed their A-Team of the need for a laptop computer at the refugee centre. Among other tasks, the computer would be used for the translation of material from English into Farsi. The families in the A-Team raised and donated funds for the purchase of a laptop, which was hand-carried to the refugee centre in Athens, Greece. The person put in charge of

---

2 Thomas Sanchez is currently the Pastor of Global Outreach at Grace Covenant Church in Austin, Texas, USA. He and his wife Brenda had served for 27 years as missionaries in Latin America.

the purchase is a computer specialist, who understood how the computer would be used. He was able to match specifications such that both hardware and software were suitable for language translation from English to Farsi.

At Grace Covenant Church, we celebrated this project by showing a video from Dwight during our Sunday morning Missions Emphasis Service. Dwight thanked the A-Team for the part they were playing in his life and ministry, and specifically for the laptop which is being used for a variety of refugee ministry projects. Thus, our whole body was built-up and encouraged through the service and sacrifice of an A-Team, who met a specific and very tangible need on the mission field.

This is just one of many stories of how our A-Teams are responding to the needs of our missionaries. We marvel at the sense of family that this creates, and the mutual blessing that is being experienced.

In our 27 years of serving on the mission field in Latin America, my wife Brenda and I had a great mission agency ministry team. Now we realise that we missed "family". Ministry teams are important for accomplishing the task God has given us, but a church family is essential for restoration, refreshment, encouragement and rest.

Each local sending church can, and should, offer this kind of a "family" that is rarely provided by mission agencies. Each missionary can be blessed, not only materially, but with the sense of being loved and cared for. The local church will be blessed by extending its emotional commitments around the world to match its spiritual ones, and most importantly God is glorified at the unity and functioning of the body responding to the headship of Jesus Christ in loving one another.

Discussion questions:

1. What are the advantages of advocacy teams? What could be some disadvantages?

2. How does your local church currently relate to its missionaries? Are there groups of people in the church who provide a sense of "family" to each missionary and missionary family?

3. Do you currently support missionaries who are "disconnected" from the church?

Arab church and missions

Fayez Ishak,[3] Kaser El Dobara Church, Egypt

As a representative of a Middle Eastern church which both receives expatriate missionaries and sends Egyptian workers, I wish to share a summary of several factors which have aided in the retention of Arab workers. In our own pioneering efforts to send Arab missionaries, we have experienced many growing pains, including a few cases of attrition.

Over the years, we have learned several basic factors which help in the retention of Arab workers.

Adequate preparation

One of the most key contributors to retention is ensuring that each worker receives sufficient training and preparation before being sent to the field, despite the overwhelming needs in the field and the pressure to send more servants. We are learning that these needs cannot be given greater importance than careful planning, foresight and preparation of the workers themselves. In addition, resources and opportunities for strong missionary training are still developing in this region of the world. After realising how crucial thorough preparation is, we formed a special committee to develop a training school for potential missionaries. In January 2006, the first class of students will have completed this school.

Member care

Though it is still in the development stages, forming a Member Care system has played a major part in the retention of some missionaries. Some of the fields where we have or have had workers are extremely difficult, and the workers are under a great deal of spiritual, psychological, or emotional stress. Providing adequate support and resources to address the unique trials these workers face is quite a challenge. However, supplying this kind of support makes all the difference in many cases!

Faith and financial support

Another major challenge in keeping the workers in the field is lack of sufficient financial support. Though the record of local giving and support from abroad has increased dramatically in the last few years, raising sufficient financial support for workers has always posed a great challenge, and in some cases been the sole factor in bringing workers back from the field.

---

3 Fayez Ishak graduated from law school. He has been an Elder and the Director of the Mission Department at Kaser El Dobara Church in Cairo, Egypt for the last 14 years. He currently supervises, encourages, and ministers to 35 missionaries in several different countries.

As an example, one Egyptian couple felt a deep call on their lives to serve God by ministering to North African immigrants in Spain. The mission board met and prayed with them, and took a step of faith in sending this couple and their young son to Spain, despite the fact that they were going alone and without their full support in place. After the first year, it became clear the timing was not right. Because of insufficient support, they had to share an apartment with another couple. In addition, they found themselves overwhelmed by the needs of the ministry, with few resources for support from other team members.

Following their first year, they returned to Egypt, making it clear that they would never return unless accompanied by more team members and until enough support had been raised for them to live in their own apartment. Thankfully, God provided both of these, and they were able to return to the field, where they have been serving now for ten years. In their case, we were challenged to live by faith, trusting in God's provision for our financial needs without being presumptuous and hasty in sending servants to the field. As in most cases in the Third World, all our projects are faith-based and we are often put to the test in making choices that often fall on a thin line between faith and presumption.

Community and pastoral care

An important lesson we learned in this and other cases is the vital role of community in the lives of our workers. Egyptian culture is intensely community oriented, a fact which has been shaped by its history and geography. Egyptians have lived in the same narrow valley for over 5,000 years, using only 4-5% of the land. In general, no one travels a great distance; usually you're born, raised, and married in the same small village or city. Travelling even to the next city may call for an extravagant farewell party! This has changed somewhat in the last three or four decades, as many Egyptians have sought opportunities for employment in the Gulf. Yet the idea of going to serve far from your community in a mission context is still quite radical.

For our workers, we have seen how important it is for each of them to have strong relational ties with their church body, and to be a part of a small group. For one couple in particular, their continued service despite extreme difficulties and challenges in a Gulf country has been mostly due to the wider circle of relationships and support within their home church. Even though they do not attend their cell group on a weekly basis, they are still considered part of the group, and prayed for on a regular basis. Their cell group leader and other members of the group communicate with them on a regular basis.

Furlough

Finally, a regular furlough plays an important part in the overall health and retention of the Egyptian missionary. Some mission agencies require the missionary to stay in the field for three years before a visit home. Such a policy would likely result in the assured attrition of the typical Egyptian! He/she needs to be part of a team in the field and come home for a short period once a year. We found this helps our missionaries stay refreshed and focused.

Discussion questions:

1. What lessons can your organisation (agency or church) learn about missionary retention from this case?

2. How important is a sense of community to your missionaries? What could your organisation do to develop a sense of belonging to a home-based community among your field missionaries?

In the real world

A table to stimulate ideas for best practice in mission partnership. For further explanation, see page 7.

This chart has been partially filled in for you. Now you fill in the blanks.

Who? → When? ↓	Home Church	Missionary	Mission Agencies	External Partners
Continuous	➢ Choose to be the base for mission ➢ Have mission as a mission statement ➢ Have all church members involved somehow ➢ Give opportunities for training	➢ Stress the importance of the relationship between local church and mission	➢ See the agency as a partner for the local church	➢ Offer programmes to mobilize the local church
Recruitment	➢ Have a culture of recruitment		➢ Seek endorsement of pastor	
Preparation	➢ Have a culture of training potential missionaries			
On field		➢ Be open and transparent ➢ Communicate on a regular basis to keep church involved	➢ Work on relations with home church	➢ Train on specific issues
Crisis	➢ Offer pastoral support			
Furlough	➢ Support time of vacation	➢ Take time to build and maintain relationships	➢ Take time to build and maintain relations	
Re-entry	➢ Help to integrate back into home church			

33

Home Office
Debrief and Re-entry

	OSC	NSC
	OOOOOO●●●●	OOOO●●●●●●

The facts

Debrief and re-entry proved to be an immensely important area for retention, particularly in OSC. Encouragingly, the area received a generally good rating, although there is room for further improvement. In NSC, there was not a strong correlation across the board and some areas may as yet be undeveloped in NSC as a whole. OSC and NSC can learn from each other's strengths in this area and together tackle the weaknesses highlighted.

The data

Q. No.	Factor	OSC Health Indicator	✓	NSC Health Indicator	✓
43	There is effective communication between sending base and field	OOOO●●●●●●	✓	OOOOOOO●●●	✓
79	Home churches are encouraged to be involved in the life and ministry of their missionary	OOOOOOOO●●	✓	OOOOO●●●●●	✓
87	Re-entry arrangements/ programmes are provided for missionaries commencing home leave	OOOOO●●●●●	✓	OOO●●●●●●●	
88	Formal debriefing is undertaken during home leave	OOOOOOO●●●	✓	OOO●●●●●●●	

The key findings

✓ Re-entry arrangements (Q87) was rated high for performance and significance only in OSC regarding preventable attrition, and was highly correlated with retention (OSC). NSC agencies gave a much lower rating than to the other home office operations, and no correlation with retention was found (probably lack of experience).

✓ Debriefing during home assignment (Q88) was rated high in high retaining OSC agencies only, and there was a moderate correlation with retention for OSC. It received a low rating from NSC agencies and a weak negative correlation with retention.

✓ Re-entry arrangements and debriefing during home assignment are lacking in NSC due to the young mission movement.

What it means

Sarah Hay

Literature review indicates that re-entry arrangements and debrief provisions have been the focus of many workshops and conference time in recent years (ReMAP I did not look into this issue so there is no statistical comparison). One organisation, Care for Mission—based at the Edinburgh International Health Centre in Scotland, has seen steady growth in the number of agencies utilising their debriefing services. As awareness has grown of the cultural gap experienced by people entering a new environment, pre-field preparation has increased. Logically, one would expect awareness of a similarly wide gap for home return would also grow, and with that, understanding of the need for debrief and re-entry arrangements.

No country remains the same—a home country changes while a mission partner is away. Added to this, a mission partner is also changing, and he or she will look at "home" through very different eyes upon return. I remember talking to a dear friend who had been a mission partner for over 20 years, first going overseas by a six-week boat trip. On one home leave, she was confronted with a cash machine ("hole in the wall") when seeking to withdraw some cash. No-one had thought to tell her of the cash machine revolution while she had been away and she had no idea what to do!

In OSC, ReMAP II results show communication between the base and the field, home church involvement, re-entry arrangements/programmes during home leave, and debriefing during home leave are correlated with retention of a mission partner. They are all important, but while OSC agencies are good at home church involvement and debriefing (to a slightly lesser extent), surprisingly, re-entry arrangements do not appear to be carried out effectively and communication needs improvement. This is notable because, as mentioned, there has been a lot of discussion on re-entry in recent years and good communication always seems to be on the agenda.

NSC agencies show slightly greater health in terms of communication between home and field, which correlates with retention. Home church involvement is also correlated, but has a lower score for performance and significance. Yet, re-entry arrangements and formal debriefing receive a very low score. The poor score is probably indicative of relatively young organisations with either no re-entry/debriefing plans, or plans in embryonic format. Perhaps once they are introduced, an increase in retention will be demonstrated. Clearly, both OSC and NSC need to improve their arrangements for re-entry and debriefing.

How does re-entry and debriefing have an effect on retention? These are often associated with a mission partner having already left the field (and therefore not able to be retained!). However, debriefing should take place during every home leave to ensure that field experiences are regularly discussed and processed in a healthy way. Re-entry stresses will also affect an individual during home leave (although to a lesser extent if the individual knows they are returning to the field within a matter of months). The issues discussed in this chapter will affect a mission partner whenever they return home, and are therefore relevant to retaining people. Furthermore, it is an important discussion to be had since the focus of this book is valuing people.

Before further discussion on best practice for re-entry and debriefing, those who are new to this concept might appreciate a look at the basic details. Re-entry is the term used to describe a space rocket returning into the earth's atmosphere—it describes a very bumpy, turbulent, dangerous time, which could result in the rocket disintegrating spectacularly, yet tragically, into flames. As Peter Jordan points out in his book "Re-entry",[1] this word applies aptly to the experience of returning mission partners as they adjust to life back home after time overseas. The dangers may seem different, but there is a great risk of disintegration through emotional, spiritual, relational, and even physical damage. A returning mission partner must have the correct care and support if they are to survive their own re-entry and remain both physically and psychologically well.

Re-entry: Stressors and support

What are the dangers on re-entry? Why should it be so difficult coming "home"? Authors Neal Pirolo and Peter Jordan provide some excellent reading on these issues.[2] There are so many potential areas of re-entry stress. In general, however, re-entry is difficult because the mission partner has changed, or is changing, in terms of attitudes, values, and beliefs, and is returning to a previously familiar environment which has changed as well. For example, a major re-entry stress for me was the sheer volume of choice and luxury available in the supermarkets. I was so totally immobilised by trying to decide which brand/type of toilet paper and toothbrush to buy that I ended up walking out of the store empty-handed. Five years later, I now do my grocery shopping on-line and have it delivered to my door!

---

1   Jordan, Peter, Floyd McClung, and Youth with a Mission Inc., *Re-entry: Making the transition from missions to life at home*, (Seattle, WA: YWAM Publishing, 1992).

2   Neal Pirolo, *The Re-entry Team: Caring for your returning missionaries*, (San Diego, CA: Emmaus Road International, 2000), and Jordan, 1992.

This would be an especially unfamiliar concept for someone used to shopping daily in a local market for 20 years!

Neal Pirolo, in "The Re-entry Team,"[3] highlights a number of factors that impact a returning mission partner. These include length of time away, degree of change in the home environment, degree of change in the mission partner, attitude of the church, amount of time given to prepare for re-entry on the field, length of time taken to return home, and the uniqueness of the mission partner's personality, to highlight just a few.

There are physical stresses initially, even if only jet-lag. Professional stresses can be overwhelming—perhaps of finding a job in a secular organisation or being part of a hierarchical structure as opposed to being part of a dynamic team. There are also stresses of deputation—many mission partners find it difficult to visit lots of groups/churches and stand in front to present their whole term's work in 20 minutes, or less!

Many find financial pressures stressful. Depending on others for support is often uncomfortable. On return home, this pressure may continue (if the individual is continuing in mission work at home) or change. Financial values may have changed—the individual could struggle with return to a materialistic society (in the West or some Asian countries) and fight against it, or find themselves embracing it wholeheartedly.

Cultural issues must be re-examined. In my case, it took a long time to reprogramme myself not to give everything only with my right hand and to use my left hand to touch my right arm as I gave over cash in a shop. While considered very polite in Asia, this had no meaning in leafy, suburban England. Social stresses crop up, such as being placed on the "missionary pedestal" (which can only end in falling off it!) or, perhaps worse, finding that your family, friends, or even your church may not be that interested in what you've been doing. How much have you and your best friend changed? Can you just pick up where you left off? Relationships need a lot of work and may never be the same again.

Pirolo also looks at language, national/political, educational and spiritual stresses. A common form of spiritual stress happens when mission partners feel that their home church has a lower level of spirituality than they have. Their whole focus has been on God's ministry. Yet back home, the church may be in a great debate about peripheral faith issues. Or worse. A friend of ours returning after a time overseas found her church meeting discussing heatedly which version of the Bible they should adopt. After a few minutes she stood up exasperated and said, "At least you have Bibles and know how to read!"

Pirolo goes on to identify five re-entry behaviour patterns: Alienation; Condemnation; Reversion; Suicide; and Integration. Alienation describes a mission partner not knowing how to integrate and therefore withdrawing. Condemnation goes a step further, where the individual is very negative about the home culture,

---

3   Pirolo, 2000.

church, friends, etc. Reversion is an attempt to deny that anything has changed and try to fit back in exactly where they left off. While these are all dangerous, the ultimate danger is suicide and it is a tragic reality that some people took this route to escape their re-entry shock. The hope is that a mission partner would engage in integration, where a mission partner is proactively, rather than reactively, supported and helped to integrate fully.

How can a mission partner be supported so as to integrate fully upon their return home? Just as there are different re-entry stresses, so there are different ways in which support can be given and different parties who can help facilitate this. The involved parties include the mission partner (and family), field leader, home office, and the home church. These parties will have different roles in the process but each has an integral and vital role to play.

For example, note how different parties can play a role in helping a missionary prepare mentally and emotionally for major change by forming realistic expectations (discussed in Chapter 10, Orientation). The mission partner and family need to have realistic expectations of what returning "home" may be like. They need to know that it will be hard, that people may not be interested in what they have been doing, and that there will be other stressors. Preparing children to return is particularly important, especially if they have no real memory of "home". Field leaders can begin the process of forming realistic expectations on the field, perhaps during an operational debrief or exit interview with the field leader or personnel representative. The home office should also play an important role to assist transition immediately upon return. Home church members can be aware and sensitive toward the missionary as they adjust.

The role of debriefing

Debrief allows a mission partner to explore in detail issues faced during their term on the field. Debriefing literally means talking through an experience after it has taken place. Dr. Debbie Lovell-Hawker, in "Crisis and Routine Debriefing",[4] describes three types of debriefing:

Operational debriefing:	Asking how the work was performed and what was achieved
Personal debriefing:	Asking how the experience was for the individual and how it has affected them. The aim is to offer any necessary support and help with the readjustment process, bringing about integration.
Critical Incident debriefing:	A highly structured form of personal debriefing which usually takes place after a traumatic experience, such as a natural disaster, violent incident, or accident. The aim is to help with recovery

---

4   Debbie Lovell-Hawker, in "Crisis and Routine Debriefing," in *Doing Member Care Well: Perspectives and practices from around the world,*" ed., Kelly O'Donnell (Pasadena, CA: William Carey Library, 2002).

and prevent post-traumatic stress reactions from developing.

All mission partners should undergo an operational debrief so the organisation can evaluate the project they have been involved in, its progress and any issues of concern which may require change. Another type of debriefing some organisations use is an exit interview, a cross between operational and personal debriefing, done at the end of an employment contract. While done to aid the individual in readjustment and moving on, exit interviews can also be helpful for the organisation to help identify areas requiring change or development.

Personal debriefing is important for all mission partners, yet, the ReMAP II data shows this is not always happening. Why should personnel undergo debriefing? As discussed above, huge stresses are placed upon people at re-entry, but stresses also emerge throughout an individual's service period. These could include cultural, relational, spiritual, emotional (e.g., homesickness) or physical. Studies show that around 40% of aid workers develop a psychological disorder (such as depression) while on the field or shortly after returning home.[5] Allowing an individual to talk about issues in a confidential, caring environment may significantly reduce this figure.

Debriefing allows missionary partners to feel listened to and valued, reassured that the difficulties faced are common, helped to identify stress symptoms, and given ways to cope. Debriefing can help provide missionary partners with practical information and, in a small number of cases, may be able to refer people for psychiatric help. Ultimately, debriefing allows an individual to integrate their mission experience into their whole life and view it meaningfully, which allows closure and brings about a readiness to move on. Only providing debriefing for those that ask usually means that those who really need it won't get it! Better to arrange debriefing for all and let people opt out. An informal opportunity to allow children to share their feelings (e.g., through play or drawing) is also very beneficial.[6]

When conducting debriefing, there are a number of issues to consider. Debriefing should happen fairly soon after the mission partner has returned home, ideally within one to three weeks. The meeting should take place in a quiet room, free from interruption. Confidentiality is paramount. Confidentiality should only be broken where the individual is likely to seriously harm themselves or someone else or if they disclose that a child is being abused. The person who conducts the debrief may be someone from the organisation or an external partner. Gender, age, ethnicity of the debriefer and even the location of the interview should be taken into account. In my own situation, I requested a debrief with an external person

5   Debbie Lovell, "Psychological adjustment among returned overseas aid workers." Unpublished D. Clin. Psy thesis, University of Wales, Bangor, 1997 and C.B. Eriksson, C.B. et al., "Trauma exposure and PTSD symptoms in international relief and development personnel," *Journal of Traumatic Stress*, 14, 1, 2001, pp. 205-212. Accessed on 2-17-07 from: http://www.peopleinaid.org/pool/files/publications/effective-debriefing-inote. pdf.

6   For more information on dealing with children, please look at Kelly O'Donell, ed., *Doing Member Care Well: Perspectives and practices from around the world*," (Pasadena, CA: William Carey Library, 2002), p 469-70.

because my work was often within the organisation and I felt more comfortable talking to someone who did not know the people involved.

A debrief should be structured. This ensures consistency and provides regular prompts to direct the conversation. Structure also prevents the interview from becoming a counselling session. Again, Dr. Lovell-Hawker outlines a structure for debriefing.[7] The worth keeping website (www.worthkeeping.info) contains links to several of her articles, and provides her debriefing guidelines.[8] Wherever possible, a person conducting debriefs should undergo at least a one-day training course. Debriefers should also have supervision and support themselves.

The field leader should be aware of any traumatic incident which may require critical incident debriefing. They should also be aware of any health issues (physical or mental) and also any family needs and will need to communicate these with the mission partner and home office. In Nepal, INF usually begins the debriefing process on the field in order to help the mission partner form correct expectations for returning and to begin thinking through experiences. Notes, with permission granted by the individual, are then forwarded to the person who will carry out the debriefing at home.

The home church also has a large role to play, and not just in helping with logistical and practical issues. They will have the greatest day-to-day contact with the mission partner and family and are therefore best placed to identify any issues where there may be struggles. They can provide support in many different ways, such as finances, prayer and logistics. Our home church managed to furnish a small flat for us when we returned in order that we could have our own space rather than lodging with someone—which was such a gift as our first child was due within eight weeks of being home! The church may just be there for people or someone may drop in with a meal or a cake to say "hi, we haven't forgotten about you and are here for you". They can help pastorally and encourage communication between the mission partner and home office. Communication throughout re-entry with all of the main parties is vital. This will ensure the successful integration of the mission partner.

As with many of the chapters in this book, the issues are vast and a short chapter cannot comprehensively address the issue. Hopefully, this discussion has highlighted the problems and opened up the issues. For OSC, the message is to keep going, invest in better communication and training and encourage all to be involved. For NSC, the message is to start on a programme of re-entry and debriefing and use whatever resources are available to help people to integrate back home. For the mission partner, the message is to ask for debriefing if it's not offered and remember that you are valued and your service has helped to bring glory to God. For the retention statistics, the message is to watch this area as there is room for improvement and it can take place!

---

7   Guidelines from her article in Kelly O'Donell, ed., *Doing Member Care Well: Perspectives and practices from around the world*," (Pasadena, CA: William Carey Library, 2002), pp. 461-468.
8   As well, the website provides helpful articles on debrief for families, teams, and Critical Incident Debriefing from a variety of organisations.

Debriefing through missionary retreats and restoration camps

Rachel Murray,[9] New Zealand, and Dong-Hwa Kim,[10] Global Missionaries Fellowship,[11] Korea

After a few years of cross-cultural ministry overseas, missionaries generally return to their country for home assignments or furloughs. On arrival, the missionaries have to adjust to their local home culture and environment, and this re-entry process is always challenging. Additionally, the time at home gets invariably filled with meetings, where missionaries are expected to talk with supporters in different places around the country.

During home assignment, missionaries need an opportunity to rest. Many missionaries return home feeling burned-out or close to it. Therefore, missionaries should be given time to recuperate and be refreshed both physically and spiritually.

Missionaries also need opportunities for reflection and debrief. They need time to reflect on the term that has been completed. Nearly everyone can benefit from having a skilled listener to help them explore their experiences and reactions.

In this case study, we shall briefly describe two helpful programmes for the debriefing of returning missionaries. Both are residential programmes of five days duration, which are offered through the partnership of several sending agencies or training agencies. Both programmes are held in a relaxing environment where missionaries can enjoy nature, spend time in reflection and to be debriefed.

Missionary Enrichment Retreats in New Zealand

Missions Interlink (MI) in New Zealand (NZ)[12] offers Missionary Enrichment Retreats (ME Retreat) to those in New Zealand on home assignment as well as those who have recently retired from the field. Two retreats are held each year,

---

9   Rachel Murray was the New Zealand coordinator for the ReMAP II project. Rachel was formerly the short term missions coordinator for Interserve (NZ), an agency facilitating individuals into positions related to their professional skills for one to 12 months throughout Asia and the Middle East. In her role at Interserve (NZ), Rachel worked with enquirers regarding service with the agency and was involved with the orientation and preparation of short-termers, many of whom went on to be long term mission partners. Rachel is currently the Executive Assistant at Carey Baptist College in Auckland, New Zealand. In her new role, she assists the Principal in leadership of a growing Bible and theological college where people are trained for mission, ministry, and the marketplace.

10   Dong-Hwa Kim has been the director of the corporation office of Global Missionaries Fellowship (GMF) of Korea since 2003. Dong-Hwa was one of the founding members of Global Bible Translators and Global Missionaries Fellowship. He was formerly the executive director of GBT for several years until 2002. He has also served as the coordinator of Sorak Mission Forum, which seeks to discover non-Western missionary models for the 21st century among Korean sending agencies. Dong-Hwa and his wife Hyun-Sook have two adult sons.

11   GMF is the umbrella organisation of three sending agencies including Global Bible Translators (GBT), a Wycliffe organisation in Korea, and five supporting agencies including MK NEST and Global Missionary Training Centre (GMTC).

12   Missions Interlink (MI) in New Zealand (NZ) was established to connect and resource agencies, churches, training organisations and individuals with the tools for more effective and beneficial mission service.

with one in each half of the year. Having two retreats maximises the opportunity for those returning to NZ at different times. Each retreat is residential and is run over five days for a fee which many agencies will subsidise or pay fully for the missionaries.

The ME Retreat begins each day with worship and Bible teaching, followed by two workshops. Topics include the development of skills, such as communication, conflict resolution, teamwork, and spiritual resourcing. Additional workshops may focus on issues such as past concerns, unfulfilled expectations, stress and burnout, forgiveness and anger, singleness and marriage challenges. Participants have opportunity to indicate which topics would be particularly useful and relevant to them, and these topics are then factored into the workshops.

Plenty of personal time is given each day to allow for individuals to spend alone with the Lord for their own worship and reflection. This complements the corporate worship at the beginning of each day. Free-time is included so that missionaries can enjoy the surroundings, or simply get to know others at the retreat.

Besides guiding and leading sessions, the facilitators and counsellors are also available for private discussions on personal issues throughout the week. Retreat facilitators come with extensive experience, including overseas assignments. They are highly respected in their areas of expertise. For example, those involved in MI's ME Retreats include the following:

- A medical missionary couple who spent over 20 years in the South Pacific and returned to NZ to a further 20+ years in counselling ministries.

- A medical missionary in South Asia for over 30 years, including five years as the international medical advisor for her sending agency.

- A couple who run a ministry dedicated specifically to caring for cross-cultural workers.

- A pastor and doctor couple who completed their mission years in an international school in South Asia and returned to NZ to pastor a local church and continue in medical practice.

- A pastoral/counselling couple involved in leading a local Brethren church after six years in the South Pacific.

- A couple with 32 years mission experience in Africa, Australia, Oceania, and the United States who remain involved in personnel management, care policies and programmes.

The evening sessions are often spent in story-telling. This is a time for missionaries to share their journeys and personal life experiences. Such time helps to create an atmosphere where participants recognise that they are not alone in their situation and that support is available. These sessions are also designed to encourage missionaries from different agencies to learn about what others are doing overseas and to help them to network further.

Child-care is not normally provided, and parents are encouraged to leave their children with friends or family. Because there are no children on-site, parents can relax and get maximum benefit from the retreat. Single missionaries are provided individual rooms wherever possible. Before attending the retreat, as part of the preparation, each participant is asked to complete a personality profile test. By answering questions in the profile test, each individual will understand a little more about how they have structured their own lives. This confidential profile will form a basis for the personal interviews or private discussions with the qualified counsellors, as requested by the individual.

The ME Retreats in New Zealand have been well received by both agency and missionaries. Small agencies are grateful to have access to a well-planned programme, which an agency may not be able to organise alone on a regular basis. In addition, the agency leaders appreciate being able to network with leaders from other agencies. Missionaries have also welcomed attending these retreats. Besides being encouraged, refreshed, and revitalised during their well-deserved break, the retreats offer options for them to deal with any concerns that may have arisen during their recently completed term. These retreats have set many workers in good stead for future terms of service.

Rest and Restoration Camps in Korea

Dr. Sohn Eun-Sup, a clinical pathologist, has been helping Korean missionaries by giving medical check-ups and counselling. After serving in the mission community for several years, he realised that a brief session of counselling does not provide sufficient help to returning missionaries. Many missionaries bring home with them interpersonal relationship problems and/or emotional problems, including depression and anxiety. Therefore, he started a new re-entry programme called "Rest and Restoration Camp" some three years ago. He did this with the help of a Christian business group and Global Missionary Fellowship, an umbrella organisation for three sending agencies and five supporting and training agencies.

Here are some details of the camp:

- Location: A hotel in the Sorak Mountain area which is owned by a Christian business group. Much of the financial cost for each camp is sponsored.
- Duration of the programme: Five days
- Number of participants: Maximum 35 persons, including children.
- Staff of the programme: Two medical doctors, plus a psychiatrist, two counsellors, one speaker, and a child-care team of five people and two administrative workers. Besides these resident staff, the executive staff of mission agencies are invited to meet their missionaries during the camp.

On the first day, participants get to know one another through games. During the evening concert, families are introduced to each other. All the other days begin with prayer and meditation, followed by physical exercise. After breakfast, there is a lecture and a workshop. Then after lunch, time is set aside for outdoor activities.

In the evening, everyone gathers for worship or some group activity, such as fellowship, singing or sharing. Almost one whole day is set aside for silent meditation and counselling. On the last day, there is a closing service and farewell party during which the missionary children present items. The camp ends with a review and evaluation time.

According to Dr. Sohn, the main purpose of the camp is to help returning missionaries reach a turning point in their lives and ministries. Each missionary is given an opportunity to reflect by himself/herself, and then to share freely his or her painful experiences and fears. Besides the counselling with a psychiatrist or counsellor, participants may have debriefing sessions with their home office staff during the camp.

"It is the beginning of an ongoing process. I hope that missionaries will learn how to help themselves, especially how to keep themselves and their families healthy spiritually, physically and emotionally", said Dr. Sohn. Those who need more counselling sessions after the camp are given a list of Christian counsellors who can help them.

Ten different "Rest and Restoration Camp" sessions have been held since 2002. More than 200 missionaries have obtained great benefit from participating in the camp. Many participants expressed how much they were helped by the lectures, sharing each others' experiences, and receiving counselling during the camp. Some said that it was first time that they felt they were really cared for.

Discussion questions:

1. How could a similar five-day retreat or camp encourage the retention of missionaries returning to your country after serving on the field?

2. Are there agencies or churches in your country that could partner with your organisation to offer such a retreat or camp for returning missionaries?

3. What obstacles might have to be overcome for different agencies to organise a common retreat or camp? What staff will need to be recruited to facilitate such an event?

Our missionary returns for home assignment

Detlef Blöcher,[13] DMG,[14] Germany

After several years of service, one of our missionaries is returning for home assignment. As we await Christine's arrival, we wonder: What should we expect? What does she expect? What will be helpful to us as a church? What will be helpful to her? Will we still understand each other? It is normal that both sides should feel insecure.

Perhaps we can learn something from what happened at the church in Antioch when the Apostle Paul came back from his first missionary journey. In Acts 14:26-28 we read: "From there they sailed back to Antioch, where they had been committed to the grace of God for the work they had now completed. On arriving there, they gathered the church together and reported all that God had done through them and how He had opened the doors of faith to the Gentiles. And they stayed there for a long time with the disciples."

Upon their return, the two missionaries gathered the whole church. They reported in detail about their experience with God. Paul and Barnabas reported all. This would have been much more than forty minutes of a slide presentation, or a short talk during the church worship service.

Similarly, when our missionary returns for the home assignment, there will be so much to tell and so much to learn from each other, in order to reestablish personal relationships. When a large cultural gap exists between the country of service and the home country, such communication may not flow easily at first. Therefore, our missionary will need our help, patience and compassion. She will go through many transitions simultaneously. We need to understand and consider each of these transitions.

The most immediate transition is physical change. On her return, Christine is exhausted from her long journey, and she feels the effects of jet-lag. Christine had started her journey two days earlier. She had passed through several different time zones to reach her home country. When in the country of service, Christine had served in a small village where the climate was mild throughout the year. Now, she is arriving in the middle of winter. Our missionary needs rest and recovery, especially after intensive weeks of packing, handing over of responsibilities, and completion of projects. She needs to adapt to new routines and to our cold climate.

While she was away, new technologies have been introduced. Christine is puzzled by the changes: how to buy a bus ticket, how to withdraw money from a bank

---

13   From 1991 to 1999, Dr. Detlef Blöcher served as Personnel Director of German Missionary Fellowship (DMG). Since then, he has been its CEO. He is also chairman of the German Evangelical Mission Alliance, and an Associate of the WEA Mission Commission. Detlef is a physicist by training, and he had previously worked in medical research at German universities and in the Middle East.

14   German Missionary Fellowship (DMG) is one of the largest evangelical mission agencies in Germany with presently some 350 missionaries serving in 70 countries.

account, new procedures at the doctors, new roads and traffic regulations, and new tax forms. Everything looks so different. Christine feels lost.

Christine goes through a mixed bag of emotions. When she went overseas, our missionary had left behind many friends and relatives. Where are they now? Will they still share the same friendships and emotional ties? She looks forward to the opportunity to reconnect with them.

Sadly, one of Christine's childhood friends and also her grandfather both died in recent years. Only now, upon the arrival at the location of cherished memories and personal encounters with these loved ones, does the loss actually take hold of her. Our missionary goes through a period of mourning and bereavement to bid farewell and to bring thoughts and memories to closure.

Our missionary has to adjust to social changes. In the country of service, the social behaviour had been different. As a teacher, Christine was expected to provide employment for household helpers to do the cleaning, washing and cooking—and their salaries are very reasonable—but now she has difficulties doing everything by herself and keeping a balanced life. Christine had a privileged role in the small village, and she was a highly respected person in the community. Now, she is one among hundreds in our church, where interest in her mission work is limited. Our missionary sees many new faces in the church because some old familiar friends have moved elsewhere.

Perhaps the most difficult adjustment is to economic changes. In the small village where Christine had served, the economy was based on agriculture. Life was simple and she always had enough to meet her daily needs. What a contrast it is to adjust to the affluence in our developed society. In addition, she finds that she has limited financial resources. Everything seems so expensive in the home country. Like other missionaries returning to a fast-pace modern city, our missionary is simply overwhelmed by the variety of products in the supermarket and she is unable to make choices.

If our missionary has become well immersed into the culture in the country of service, then she will experience reverse culture shock when returning to the home country. The culture in the country of service may be very different from that in our home country. Many cultures put a strong emphasis on personal relationships: it is not so important how much you possess, but whom you know. They live in a community and they share close personal relationships. Going shopping means meeting people and making friends. However, in Western, and some Asian, societies, "time is money". Labour costs are expensive, so relationships are cut down to the minimum. Everything needs to operate quickly and with a minimum of personal contact. Our missionary can feel lonely and uncomfortable even though she is back in her home country.

Over the past few years, Christine has communicated mainly in a different language. Now, she has to make a conscious effort to communicate in the language of the home country. Some words in the mother tongue may have been dropped from her memory. In addition, the mother tongue has been further developed while she was away. New words have been added, while others have changed their meaning. Our missionary feels confused.

Having experienced a different type of political government, our missionary now identifies with her country of service and with their politics. She will now see the world with other eyes. She may judge some social and political events, including the foreign politics of our country, differently.

Christine may have to adjust to spiritual changes. The churches in the country of service had a different cultural flavour than ours. Some biblical values have become particularly precious to our missionary, while others, which are important in her home country, have lost their significance. Her concept of church has been developed while she was overseas.

From the above, we see that our missionary goes through many transitions. Some of the changes may cause her to feel lonely, alienated, disappointed, and foreign. During this time, she may even judge our culture: the waste of resources, superficial relationships, lack of devotion and sacrificial giving, unspiritual behaviour in church. However, this is a normal human reaction. It may result in a transient withdrawal from the home culture. This process typically lasts several months, until the old and new impressions are fully processed and integrated into the world view and God's working in the life.

During this adjustment time, our missionary will need our help. For this reason, the mission agency invites our pastor, or a representative from our local church, into the formal debriefing interview. This will allow us to listen and learn first-hand what the missionary has gone through, what she expects from the church in the coming months, and how she can serve us with her rich gifting and experience.

Missionaries are normal humans, with the same needs and concerns that we have. They are grateful for personal care, and they will certainly appreciate our expressions of love. They are a great enrichment to our local church, especially during their home assignment. They bring their gifts and experience. They take a fresh look at our challenges and they may have some creative ideas. By making our small contribution as a home church, we can be a great help to our missionary. We can help each missionary to have a significant impact in world missions.

Discussion questions:

1. To what extent do you give your missionaries the opportunity to report *all* that they have experienced?

2. What issues would be helpful for each missionary to work through? What issues would be beneficial or appropriate for the sending church to consider?

3. It is important for each missionary to readjust to the home culture during home assignment. In what practical ways can you or your family help? What are the specific roles of the missionary's relatives, church members and church leadership to the missionary during home assignment?

In the real world

A table to stimulate ideas for best practice in mission partnership. For further explanation, see page 7.

This chart has been partially filled in for you. Now you fill in the blanks.

Who? → When? ↓	Home Church	Missionary	Mission Agencies	External Partners
Continuous				
Recruitment				
Preparation	➢ Be trained about re-entry	➢ Know about reverse culture-shock		➢ Teach about the impact of re-entry
On field	➢ Prepare well ➢ Pray	➢ Prepare up-front for re-entry	➢ Help to prepare for re-entry	
Crisis				
Furlough				
Re-entry	➢ Be interested in the experiences of the missionary ➢ Help to re-integrate practically ➢ Provide pastoral support ➢ Give opportunities for involvement in ministry in home church	➢ Be open and transparent ➢ Take time to adjust	➢ Evaluate ministry ➢ Do internal debriefing	➢ Offer external debriefing ➢ Organise rest and restoration camps ➢ Organise retreats

Section C

Construction... in the real world:

This section has three key resources for you. The first is a case study on the development of a Code of Best Practice. Here, using the example of the UK Short-Term Mission Code, the study outlines the process used to develop it as well as the code itself. We hope that others will be helped to develop Codes of Best Practice for their own context. Second, we give you the full questionnaire utilised in the ReMAP II survey. Finally, we offer an index of key words and concepts to aid you in your use of this book.

34

Code of Best Practice

Promoting good or best practice: Lessons from the Global Connections' Code of Best Practice in Short-Term Mission

Richard Tiplady[1]

"Codes of Practice don't work. They don't help people to improve their performance or to minimise bad practice." I was having lunch with Alex Lynch, a university lecturer doing Ph.D. research into codes of practice and their effectiveness, when he dropped this bombshell. Thankfully, for the sake of my self-esteem and for the purpose of this chapter, he continued talking. "But yours is different. It's one of the few I've found that has made a difference."

This chapter tells the story of the Global Connections' *Code of Best Practice in Short-Term Mission*, and draws out some principles about why it works and what this means for promoting good (or best) practice in other areas of mission agency practice.

The background

In 1995, a small group of mission agency leaders and others got together to discuss the rapid growth of short-term mission programmes, which took off in the UK during the first half of that decade. One of the concerns raised was the question of quality. It was felt that many of the people starting up these programmes were inexperienced and there was the potential for some "horror stories" to emerge, with young people left exposed in vulnerable situations where things could go seriously wrong. One solution that was proposed was the formation of an Association of

---

1   Richard Tiplady is British Director of European Christian Mission, a church-planting mission agency with over 150 missionaries working in 19 European countries. He is author of several books on world mission, including "One World or Many? The impact of globalisation of mission" (William Carey Library, 2003). From 1996 – 2002 he was Associate Director of Global Connections, the UK evangelical network for world mission. (www.ecmbritain.org, www.tiplady.org.uk)

Short-Term Agencies. This would require its members to meet certain standards before being accepted into membership, thus reassuring worried parents that their beloved son or daughter would not be abandoned in the middle of nowhere for a few months by a bunch of mission cowboys who didn't know what they were doing. However, both the Evangelical Alliance (EA) and Evangelical Missionary Alliance (EMA, now Global Connections) expressed reservations at the ethos of the proposed association, which seemed to be primarily concerned with policing and working under the assumption that these new programmes needed a heavy hand and couldn't be trusted to run their own affairs.

The group that proposed this Association was asked by EA and EMA to continue its work and to rethink the question of how quality could be improved in short-term programmes. It was at this point in mid-1996 that I joined the group as the newly appointed EMA Associate Director.

Listening to the discussion, I concluded that a key assumption to be confronted was that the organisers of short-term programmes could not be trusted and had to be monitored. I had set up a short-term mission programme in the previous two years, sending people from Britain to Nigeria, and had benefited from advice freely given to me by Latin Link and Tearfund, who were ahead of the pack in the quality of their programmes. I believed (and still do) that most, if not all, of those who were setting up short-term programmes were (often young) people of good will who wanted to do the best job they could. But they sometimes struggled with the variety and complexity of matters to be considered in even the smallest of these programmes (including strategy, budgeting and financial management, marketing and recruitment, leadership and pastoral care, field and partner liaison, and programme evaluation). But I also believed that there was a lot of good practice going on "out there" that we had to find, capture, and share for the benefit of others. And it was time that EMA/GC stepped in to take a lead in these matters.

First steps

In February 1997, I invited all EMA/GC members (and others) to attend a one-day consultation on the issue of quality in short-term mission programmes. Over 80 people from 50 different organisations attended and took part in a series of small-group and plenary discussions, in which they identified examples of current good practice and their aspirations towards the best practices they would like to achieve.

I then worked with the original small group of leaders to draft their comments into a summary statement that included all that those who attended the consultation had considered to be good practice. I circulated it (twice) to the wider group that attended the original consultation, taking feedback and making amendments to the summary each time on the basis of comments received.

Then, in October 1997, I reconvened the wider group, and proposed a final draft summary. It went through some final amendments at that meeting and was accepted by those present as a reasonable summary of their aspirations for the quality of their programmes. We discussed whether this should remain an internal working standard, for those concerned to work to, or whether we should go public with the summary and become accountable to the wider Christian church for the standards that we espoused for ourselves. While some wanted to keep it private, a large majority favoured making themselves accountable to participants, parents, and churches by publishing the Code (as it was now called) and allowing others to hold them to account if they failed to live up to its standards. I considered this to be a very healthy and open attitude, and it reinforced my belief that those who ran the short-term programmes were people of good will who wanted to do the best job they could.

What was even more important for me was that the resulting Code was not a series of standards dreamed up by a self-appointed group to impose on the wider sector. It was a series of promises and aspirations created by the programme organisers themselves. I can't overemphasise the importance of this, and I believe it played a significant part in the overall future success of the Code.

Helping people to live up to their own standards

One of Alex Lynch's points was that most codes of practice stop with the creation of the code itself, as though the mere publication of a code will motivate and help people to live up to its standards. But that doesn't happen. They ignore it. Or people don't know how to improve what they do, even though they want to.

I felt the same way regarding the *Code of Best Practice in Short-Term Mission*. Having worked together to agree what we wanted to live up to, I had to find a way of helping people to do this, otherwise they would get disillusioned and frustrated and the whole process would have been an almighty waste of time.

So Global Connections began to host twice-yearly forums for short-term programme organisers, at which they would discuss certain aspects of the Code, share good practice, and work together to identify current best practice standards that all could aspire to, learn from and copy. Right from the start, and all the way along, I emphasised that you cannot separate the Code from the Forum. The Code gave the Forum something to discuss, and the Forum gave the Code a way of having an impact. And we didn't import outside experts into the Forum either. Because there were none. The experts were the programme organisers themselves, who were working on management and quality issues all the time. So the Forum was a peer-learning group. I said that each person present had things to learn from others, and that others had things to learn from them. This created a very positive dynamic of mutual learning, trust and knowledge creation, as practices and lessons were shared and refined by short-term programme organisers themselves.

For the Code to have integrity, we had to have some kind of monitoring system, so that those who publicly committed themselves to the Code could demonstrate how it was helping them to improve what they were doing. But I didn't want to introduce a whole new level of bureaucracy, and I really didn't want to get bogged down in close monitoring of it myself. So we devised a light-touch system that balanced the need for integrity and monitoring with a desire to keep the paperwork down to a minimum. It went like this:

- Short-term programme organisers would sign a statement committing them to the Code. This was signed by both the programme organiser and their line manager or chief executive, so that the organisation as a whole knew what it had signed up to.

- All Code signatories had to send at least one person to each of the biannual Forums, so that they could share and learn good practice.

- Each year, all signatories would complete a brief statement showing where they had improved their programmes during that year, and also stating which areas they had identified as needing improvement and on which they would work in the coming year.

And that was it. Light touch, helping organisations to think about where they could improve, and looking for evidence of good will and commitment to the spirit of the Code, which was about continually improving quality, rather than meeting some minimum standards and then sitting back to rest on their laurels.

The principle of continual improvement was enshrined in every aspect of the Code, the Forums, and the monitoring/feedback system. It was emphatically *not* about reaching a set of minimum standards and resting there. One of the reasons for this was the diversity of programmes that the Code embraced. How can you define good standards for different short-term programmes that last for anything between two weeks to two years, and which might be for an individual but may equally involve a team of five, ten or twenty-plus people? So it was never about minimum standards. It was about creating a culture and an ethos of continual improvement, regardless of the size and complexity of the short-term mission programme itself. That's why we chose the title "Code of *Best* Practice", rather than "Good Practice". The Code wasn't about helping people to do good work; it was about helping them to be the best they could be, and as standards rose, what was defined as 'best' would keep on improving.

I drew on Quality Assurance (QA) thinking to help people understand what was expected. QA works by identifying key measurable "quality standards". The gap between current practice and the quality standard (such as the Code) is noted. Training and systems development then ensures that the standards can be met. It is important in QA to focus not just on what needs improvement, but also to look at existing best practice, i.e., what you do well. This is used as the basis for good standards (otherwise you can end up just looking at the faults and not recognising what is good, or you can set the quality standard too low). Quality standards need to be clear, specific, measurable and attainable.

We also encouraged programme organisers to benchmark. Benchmarking is the selection and application of excellent practice, often from elsewhere, as standards for my own organisation's performance. It aims to put improvements into action in the following way:

1. Identify what makes the difference between ordinary and excellent.
2. Set standards according to the best practices that can be found.
3. Research how others meet their challenging standards.
4. Apply the best of other's ideas, and your own, to meet new standards, and improve upon them if possible.

I also drew on Total Quality Management (TQM) principles to help people to understand the ethos of continual improvement. One of my favourite sayings, both then and now, is "1% improvement, 100% of the time". TQM ideas underlie the Code's annual feedback mechanism, by looking for evidence of improvement in procedures, such as the attaining of previously set benchmarks, etc.. It does not look at standards attained so much as concern about general direction (although the benchmarks were expected to be aimed at best practice, not minimum effort).

So what was the impact?

The Code was widely accepted by organisers of short-term mission programmes, and during 1998, the first year of operation, 28 organisations publicly signed up to the Code. By 2000, this had risen to 60. The biannual Forums were well attended and became a highlight of my year, as 50+ programme organisers got together to discuss best practice and to learn from each other. My conclusion was that by 2000, issues of quality and continual improvement had become part of the culture of short-term mission organisers in the UK. Which is what we had set out to achieve.

Geoff Tunnicliffe, previously coordinator of the Evangelical Fellowship of Canada's Global Mission Taskforce (and now International Director of the World Evangelical Alliance) picked up on the Code during one of his visits to England. He took the concept back to Canada, and I was delighted when they adopted the Code and its systems (forums, etc.) pretty much wholesale (with a few minor changes in terminology to suit the Canadian context). They say that imitation is the sincerest form of flattery. It was great that another national missionary alliance took up the issue of quality in short-term mission, and it was tremendously encouraging that they considered our Code and its supporting systems to be of such quality that it didn't need much changing for use in another country.

Roger Peterson of STEM Ministries, who has done so much to research and demonstrate the effectiveness of short-term mission programmes, contacted me and drew on our ideas, and then developed a set of standards suitable for the US context, which can be found at www.stmstandards.org. The *Standards of Excellence in Short-Term Mission* have been adopted by 88 US short-term programme organisers since their launch in 2003.

One lesson I learned is that you cannot stand still/sit back and expect a code of practice to do its work. This was what Alex Lynch had told me during our lunch meeting in 2000, and evidence of this arose after I left Global Connections in 2002. Without an advocate maintaining an awareness and interest in quality issues, and bringing together interested parties like the short-term mission programme organisers, the whole process loses momentum. To their credit, recently-appointed staff at Global Connections have picked up on the Code again, made some small amendments to its content to reflect changes in the UK short-term mission sector in the eight years between the first drafting of the Code and its relaunch, and at the time of writing 20 organisations (including the one of which I am chief executive) are signed up to the Code.

Lessons learned

Looking back over the last decade of work on quality standards in short-term mission in the UK and beyond, we have learned some lessons that I think are relevant to anyone trying to find ways of improving practices and raising standards in any aspect of human resource management in mission agencies.

1. A small group of self-appointed "experts" should not, cannot and must not think that they can produce a list of standards that others will then be expected to live up to. My question to any such group is "who on earth do you think you are to presume this right?" Try reading what Jesus said in Luke 12:14 sometime. Let those working on and struggling with the issues share their questions, experience, wisdom and insight. Remember, most (if not all) of them are God's servants trying to do their best to please him in their work. So listen to them and let them decide what best practice is. And make it your job to serve them and help them achieve it.

2. Pay as much attention to the process by which you will help people to improve the quality of what they do as you do to the initial defining of good standards. Ask not only the "what should we do?" question, but also the "how will we do it?" question.

3. Aim high. It is not about achieving the minimum and sitting back. It is about continual improvement, striving to be the very best we can for Christ's sake, not resting in the management, development, care and support of our missionaries, just as we don't rest in our desire to be more Christ-like.

4. Draw on good ideas from elsewhere. The desire for excellence is not an exclusively Christian one. There are a lot of good ideas out there that we can draw on and use to be more effective. That is what benchmarking is about—taking ideas and practices from others, learning from them, and adopting them for ourselves.

5. Good ideas will be copied. Be prepared to have an impact beyond what you expected. God is like that. That is a good thing.

The Global Connections Code of Best Practice in Short-Term Mission

(produced 1997, revised 2005)

Introduction

The Global Connections' *Code of Best Practice in Short-Term Mission* is designed to apply to all gap year, individual placements, electives, and team trips of up to two years duration organised by UK mission agencies, churches and other Christian organisations.

Though formed initially with cross-cultural contexts in mind, it can apply to both UK and overseas situations, both same-culture and cross-cultural.

It is a Code of *Best* Practice. Our motivation is based on our desire that God is glorified in all that we do. We also recognise our responsibility toward all participants and partners in our programmes, that we serve them to the highest standards possible. The Code does not necessarily indicate current achievement, but rather our aspirations toward high standards in short-term mission practice. It is recognised that not every situation permits a literal application of every element of the Code. Nonetheless, some minimum accomplishments are implied in the Code.

Core values within the code:

Importance of partnership
The partners in a short-term mission programme are participant(s), senders (church and/or agency), and hosts (church, individual and/or agency). Under God, all partners have a significant contribution to make.

There are also other interested parties involved. These include the participant's family, friends and local Christian community (home church, Christian Union, and/or other). They need to be recognised and included as appropriate.

Commitment to excellence
The code affirms the need for standards in short-term mission and provides a means of demonstrating a commitment to excellence.

Biblical mandate
A distinctive element of short-term mission programmes is an emphasis on biblical principles and the mandate to be involved in mission.

Biblical attitudes
It is recognised that the attitudes of all involved are important and that they need to be grounded in biblical truth and spiritual integrity.

Discipleship of participant
In recognising the potential of short-term mission trips on the participant's faith and personal development, the need for positive discipleship is affirmed.

Facilitating senders
Although the code seeks to outline best practice in all areas of short-term mission, it is specifically designed to help senders explore ways of improving what they do.

Long-term vision
This value recognises that short-term mission activity needs to fit into the long-term aims of the project and so affirm the long-term objectives and activities of the hosts.

Section one: Aims and objectives

1.1 A short-term mission programme will have clear aims and objectives. These will be realistic, measurable and reflect the long-term objectives of the partners. The project's aims should clearly reflect that this is distinctive Christian mission.

1.2 The benefits to and responsibilities of all the partners should be clearly identified.

1.3 Through consultation between the senders and hosts, there should be shared ownership of the short-term programme. Care should be taken not to undermine the hosts' ownership of the longer-term project.

1.4 Projects will be appropriately contextualised.

1.5 There will be a commitment to disciple and develop the participant through the experience.

Section two: Publicity, selection and orientation

To ensure clear communication of aims and expectations, appropriate matching of people to projects, and adequate briefing and equipping of all partners,

2.1 Publicity materials will be accurate and truthful. They will be targeted appropriately, and used with integrity.

2.2 All forms of communication will clearly represent the ethos and vision of the senders, and will define the purpose of the programme in terms of service, discipleship and vocation.

2.3 The application process, including timescale and financial responsibilities, will be clear and thorough.

2.4 A suitable, transparent selection process will be established, including selection criteria and screening. A pastoral element will be included, regardless of the outcome of selection.

2.5 Church involvement in the selection process will be sought, as appropriate.

2.6 Preparatory information (between selection and formal orientation) will be provided as early and as fully as possible.

2.7 Orientation prior to the project and induction at the start of the project will be given to all participants. This should include all procedures outlined in 3.5 and, for example: project brief, location and tasks; structures and lines of accountability: biblical mandate; job descriptions; child protection; health and safety, security and risk assessment; team dynamics and conflict resolution; finances, legal liability and insurance; cultural issues; guidelines on behaviour and relationships; communication policy with home: expectations regarding debriefing.

2.8 Responsibilities of all partners regarding practicalities, job descriptions and supervision will be made clear and agreed prior to placement.

2.9 Placement decisions will be clear and transparent, will be made with integrity, and will be communicated to all involved (including when changes are made).

2.10 Where participants are working with children and vulnerable adults, police checks will be made.

2.11 Any participant under the age of 18 needs to have parental consent. Senders need to clearly define their lower age limit and who is responsible for under-age participants. Groups with under-age participants need to seek legal and insurance advice.

Section three: Field management and pastoral care

To ensure the aims and objectives are met for all partners, and the care and development of the participant is provided for,

3.1 Clear task aims and objectives will be re-emphasised (see 2.8). The ongoing responsibilities and expectations of the participant will be reviewed.

3.2 Suitable supervisors will be in place and there will be clear lines of authority, supervision, communication, responsibility and accountability.

3.3 Pastoral care and support structures will be established and implemented.

3.4 Opportunities for personal and spiritual development of the participant will be provided.

3.5 Practicalities and procedures will be established, communicated and implemented as appropriate. These would include: healthcare, medical contingencies, security and evacuation; risk assessment; stress management and conflict resolution; misconduct, discipline, and grievances.

Section four: Re-entry support, evaluation and programme development

To ensure the participant is supported post-assignment, and all partners are able to give feedback, leading to improvement of future programmes,

4.1 Debriefing and support for the participant will be seen as an integral part of the short-term "package" (in addition to orientation, task supervision and pastoral care), and the process will involve all partners.

4.2 Re-entry preparation, including placement appraisal, will begin before the end of the project.

4.3 The senders will assist the participant through post-assignment readjustment.

4.4 Advice and guidance will be offered to participants to find the next step in their Christian life following the programme. Where appropriate, this will be done in liaison with the participant's home church.

4.5 An evaluation of aims, responsibilities and procedures will be undertaken, inviting comment from all partners. Culturally appropriate ways of feedback will be sought.

4.6 The results of evaluations will be communicated to relevant managers, for the improvement of future projects.

35

The ReMAP II
Questionnaire

The following is the original ReMAP II questionnaire, sent out to mission agency executives in 2003.

ReMAP II: An international study on missionary retention

Eight years have elapsed since ReMAP I, the study of the World Evangelical Alliance Mission Commission on "missionary attrition" (see Taylor W.D., *Too Valuable to Lose: Exploring the Causes and Cures of Missionary Attrition*, 1997, William. Carey Library). This led to much creative thinking among mission executives resulting in significant changes in the international mission movement. ReMAP I focused primarily on personal factors of individual missionaries. Now missionary leaders see the need to focus on organisational factors that lead to stronger retention. The current study is on "missionary retention", that is: "What keeps them in active service?" We trust the results of the study will identify practices for supporting our missionaries so that they can do their ministry well and see His kingdom extended.

Because of the importance of this study, we are asking you, the mission leader, to fill out the following questionnaire. Your responses will be treated with the utmost confidentiality. Results will be reported in the form of summary statistics so that no individual or mission can be identified. National and international results will be made available to participating agencies. Thank you for your prompt cooperation.

Please send in your response before *31 MARCH 2003*. Confidential.

Definitions:

This study is about long-term, cross-cultural missionaries who serve in the name of Christ.

- Long-term missionaries are defined as "career" missionaries who are expected to serve for at least three years. Missionaries who intend to serve for shorter periods of time would not be included in this study.

- Cross-cultural missionaries serve full-time in a culture other than their own. Normally, they learn a different language and/or make significant cultural adjustments. They may serve within their national borders or internationally.

- Missionary couples are counted as two persons.

- Agency refers to a sending base that is: a) an independent mission, b) a denominational mission's department or a c) church that sends out missionaries without the assistance of another organisation.

- If your agency is part of an international organisation, please give the number of missionaries sent out from your national sending base only.

A. Background Information About Your Agency

To enable us to understand your agency, please provide the following background information about your organisation at the national level (international agencies: report **your national figures only**).

1. How many years have you been sending out missionaries from your **national base**?

2. How many *active* long-term, cross-cultural missionaries sent from your **national sending base** did you have as of 31 December 2002? (Include those on home leave)

3. Of these, how many have children aged 0-21 years? (Couples count as two persons)

4. How many full time (or equivalent) workers/employees serve in the **national** home office?

5. Estimate what percentage of your missionaries' allowances are allocated for retirement.   %

Please provide an estimated break-down of your missionary task force, indicating the approximate percentage of your missionaries primarily involved in the following areas:

6. Evangelism & Church planting among "Unreached Peoples" (less than 1% Evangelicals)   %

7. Evangelism & Church planting among peoples with more than 1% Evangelicals   %

8. Support of existing churches (Bible teaching, pastoral, etc.)   %

9. Social and community work (agriculture, medical, relief & development, etc.)   %

10. Service (translation, missionary children's education, aviation, administration, etc.)   %

B. Screening Procedure

Please indicate the extent to which your mission considers the following factors before accepting an applicant for cross-cultural service. Circle the most appropriate response from 0 to 6 where: 0 = not assessed, 1 = assessed but not given a great deal of weight in the final decision, up to 6 = assessed and given a great deal of weight in the final decision.

		Not assessed	Not given a great deal of weight				Given a great deal of weight	
11.	Expresses a clear calling to missionary service	0	1	2	3	4	5	6
12.	Agrees with the agency's doctrinal statement	0	1	2	3	4	5	6
13.	Knows and is committed to the agency's principles and practices	0	1	2	3	4	5	6
14.	Demonstrates mature Christian character and discipline (prayer & devotional life)	0	1	2	3	4	5	6
15.	Has good character references	0	1	2	3	4	5	6
16.	Has committed endorsement from his/her pastor/local church for missionary service	0	1	2	3	4	5	6
17.	Has the blessing of their family	0	1	2	3	4	5	6
18.	Has ministry experience in a local church	0	1	2	3	4	5	6
19.	Has had previous cross-cultural experience	0	1	2	3	4	5	6
20.	Has demonstrated ability to cope well with stress & negative events	0	1	2	3	4	5	6
21.	Meets health criteria determined by a physical examination	0	1	2	3	4	5	6
22.	Meets health criteria determined through a psychological assessment	0	1	2	3	4	5	6
23.	Exhibits contentment with present marital status (single, married)	0	1	2	3	4	5	6
24.	Has good potential for financial support	0	1	2	3	4	5	6
25.	Has firm/stable prayer support	0	1	2	3	4	5	6

C. Educational Level

Please *estimate* the percentage of your missionaries whose highest level of education is:

26. 6 -10 years of schooling   _____ %

27. High school diploma (12th grade or equivalent)   _____ %

28. Trade school/apprenticeship   _____ %

29. Bachelor degree, diploma, or equivalent   _____ %

30. Master's degree or equivalent   _____ %

31. Doctorate or equivalent   _____ %

Must add up to 100%   100 _____ %

D. Pre-field Training Requirement

How many years, months, or weeks full-time training does your agency *generally* require from new long-term cross-cultural missionaries before sending them to the field?

	Years	Months	Weeks	Not Required
32. Bible school or seminary training				
33. Formal academic missiological training				
34. Practical pre-field missionary training				
35. Structured cross-cultural missionary internship or apprenticeship				
36. Mission agency's own orientation				

E. Pastoral Member Care

Please provide an estimate/ best guess by circling one of the options:

37. Estimate the percentage of total time spent in pastoral care of missionaries (include both home and field workers).	0 -2%	2 -5%	5 -10%	10-20%	20-30%	> 30%
38. Estimate the percentage of budget/total finances spent on pastoral care.	0 -2%	2 -5%	5 -10%	10-20%	20-30%	> 30%
39. How much of these resources are preventative member care: prevention, personal development, support, etc. (*versus* responsive, crisis resolution)	0 -5%	5-10%	10-30%	30-50%	50-70%	70-100%

F. AGENCY OPERATION

Please evaluate your mission agency's **practices** in the following areas (as evidenced by time, effort, and effectiveness). Circle the appropriate answer.

		N/A	Not well done					Very well done
COMMUNICATION								
40.	Vision and purpose are shared and understood throughout the agency	0	1	2	3	4	5	6
41.	Plans and job descriptions are communicated clearly to the missionary	0	1	2	3	4	5	6
42.	There is a free flow of communication to and from the leadership	0	1	2	3	4	5	6
43.	There is effective communication between sending base and field	0	1	2	3	4	5	6
44.	Missionaries are included in major decisions related to the field	0	1	2	3	4	5	6
45.	Policies are well documented and understood	0	1	2	3	4	5	6
46.	A culture of prayer is actively promoted within the agency	0	1	2	3	4	5	6
LEADERSHIP								
47.	Most leaders are a good example of the agency's beliefs and values	0	1	2	3	4	5	6
48.	Most leaders identify problems early and take appropriate action	0	1	2	3	4	5	6
49.	Good on-field supervision is provided (quantity and quality)	0	1	2	3	4	5	6
50.	Leaders conduct an annual performance/ministry review with each missionary	0	1	2	3	4	5	6
51.	There are documented and adequate procedures for handling complaints from missionaries	0	1	2	3	4	5	6
ORIENTATION & CONTINUOUS TRAINING								
52.	Effective on-field orientation is in place for new missionaries	0	1	2	3	4	5	6
53.	Language learning arrangements are provided that enable new missionaries to learn the local language well	0	1	2	3	4	5	6
54.	Ongoing language and culture training are actively encouraged	0	1	2	3	4	5	6
55.	Missionaries are provided with opportunities for continuous training and development of gifts and skills	0	1	2	3	4	5	6

MINISTRY

56.	Missionaries are assigned roles according to their gifting and experience	0	1	2	3	4	5	6
57.	Missionaries are given room to shape and develop their own ministry	0	1	2	3	4	5	6
58.	Missionaries know how to handle spiritual warfare	0	1	2	3	4	5	6
59.	Missionaries are committed to their ministry	0	1	2	3	4	5	6
60.	Missionaries are committed and loyal to the agency	0	1	2	3	4	5	6
61.	Missionaries are generally not overloaded in the amount of work they do	0	1	2	3	4	5	6
62.	Opportunities are provided for a ministry/role for the spouse	0	1	2	3	4	5	6
63.	Missionaries have adequate administrative and practical support on the field	0	1	2	3	4	5	6
64.	Missionaries regularly evaluate and seek to improve the agency's ministry	0	1	2	3	4	5	6

MINISTRY OUTCOME

65.	Missionaries are actually achieving the agency's goals and expectations	0	1	2	3	4	5	6
66.	Missionaries are developing good relationships with the people they serve	0	1	2	3	4	5	6
67.	The people our missionaries serve are becoming followers of Christ	0	1	2	3	4	5	6
68.	The church on the field values the ministries of our missionaries	0	1	2	3	4	5	6
69.	Missionaries are developing leadership among the people they serve	0	1	2	3	4	5	6
70.	Missionaries experience a sense of fulfilment in their ministry	0	1	2	3	4	5	6

PERSONAL CARE & FAMILY SUPPORT

71.	Missionary teams are effective in providing each other with mutual support	0	1	2	3	4	5	6
72.	Effective pastoral care exists at a field level (preventative and in crises)	0	1	2	3	4	5	6
73.	Interpersonal conflicts are resolved in a timely and appropriate manner	0	1	2	3	4	5	6
74.	Emphasis is placed on the maintenance and growth of personal spiritual life	0	1	2	3	4	5	6
75.	There are satisfactory schooling opportunities for missionaries' children	0	1	2	3	4	5	6

76.	Health care services for missionaries/missionary families are satisfactory	0	1	2	3	4	5	6
77.	Time for an annual vacation or holiday is provided	0	1	2	3	4	5	6
78.	Risk assessment and contingency planning is in place in all fields	0	1	2	3	4	5	6
79.	Home churches are encouraged to be involved in the life and ministry of their missionary	0	1	2	3	4	5	6

FINANCES

80.	Missionaries usually receive sustained financial support that is adequate for their needs	0	1	2	3	4	5	6
81.	There is financial back-up for missionaries with low or irregular support	0	1	2	3	4	5	6
82.	Project finances are used effectively	0	1	2	3	4	5	6
83.	Agency finances are transparent to the missionaries and donors (how and where money is spent)	0	1	2	3	4	5	6

HOME OFFICE

84.	Pre-field screening prevents unsuitable persons proceeding to the field	0	1	2	3	4	5	6
85.	Pre-field orientation prepares missionaries for adjustment to cross-cultural life and ministry	0	1	2	3	4	5	6
86.	Staff in the home office pray regularly for the missionaries	0	1	2	3	4	5	6
87.	Re-entry arrangements/programmes are provided for missionaries commencing home leave	0	1	2	3	4	5	6
88.	Formal debriefing is undertaken during home leave	0	1	2	3	4	5	6

G. CONTRIBUTIONS TO PRESENT EFFECTIVENESS

Which factors **contribute most** to your missionaries attaining their **on-field** objectives? Please list the top four factors from your experience. If you choose a factor given in **Section F,** then use the number of this item.

89. _____

90. _____

91. _____

92. _____

H. HINDRANCES TO EFFECTIVENESS

Which factors **most hinder** your missionaries attaining their **on-field** objectives? Please list the top four factors from your experience.

93. _____

94. _____

95. _____

96. _____

I. LENGTH OF SERVICE RECORD

97. How many of your active long-term missionaries left their field of service for all reasons during the two-year period between 1 January 2001 and 31 December 2002? Include those who retired as well as those who left for both unavoidable and potentially avoidable reasons.

98. What was the average length of service of this group of missionaries? Calculate this number by adding the total years of service of everyone in this group (couples counted as two people) and then dividing the grand total by the number of people in this group.

Thank you for completing the survey to this point. The following section is of great importance to the success of this research, as this information will be used to calculate retention rates. The retention rates for your agency can be made available to you, provided you keep a copy of the research code given on the front page of this survey.

J. RETENTION RECORD

Please indicate the present status (as at 31 December 2002) of the missionaries sent out by your agency over the past twenty years by completing the table on the following page. If you don't have a 20-year history or don't have accurate data that far back, please provide the information for as many years as possible. If completing the table requires an inappropriate amount of work, we would very much appreciate you providing figures from at least a few representative years.

Column A: _Year of first departure of these missionaries_

Column B: _Number of missionaries you sent out for the first time during that year (between 1 Jan and 31 Dec)_

Column C: _Number of the missionaries from column B who are **still in active service** with your agency on 31 Dec 2002_

Column D: _Number of missionaries from column B who have left your agency but are **still working on the field**_ now under the auspices of another organisation (e.g. harmonious change to another organisation or sending base, merger of agencies, marriage to a missionary of another agency or to a national). Workers involved in non-harmonious change should be included in column F.

Column E: _Number of missionaries from column B who have since left your agency for **unavoidable reasons**_ (e.g. normal retirement, death in service, loss of visa, expulsion from the country, disability due to illness, appointment into a leadership position in your agency's home office, completion of a pre-determined, limited length assignment).

Column F: _Number of missionaries from column B who have since left your agency for **potentially preventable reasons**_ (e.g. personal, agency, work or team-related reasons or dismissal by your agency – even if they remained on the field).

An example:

Let us assume that between 1 Jan 1991 and 31 Dec 1991 (column A) your agency sent out 23 new career missionaries to the field for the first time (column B). Now check your records as to what happened to them since that time. Let us assume that 11 of them are still serving with your agency on 31 Dec 2002 (column C), 2 left your agency at some point in the past but are still working in the same country (with a different agency) (column D); 3 have left the field for unavoidable reasons (column E) and 7 for potentially preventable reasons or have been dismissed (column F). Thus you enter the following numbers into the row for the year 1991:

A	B	C	D	E	F
Year of first departure	Number of new missionaries in that year	Number of these missionaries still in active service with you on 31 Dec 2002	Number of these missionaries who transferred to another agency but are still working on the field on 31 Dec 2002	Number of these missionaries who left your agency for unavoidable reasons	Number of these missionaries who left your agency for potentially preventable reasons or were dismissed
1991	23	11	2	3	7

As you see, the sum of columns C, D, E and F (11 + 2 + 3 + 7) equals the number in B (23).

PLEASE SEE NEXT PAGE FOR THE TABLE

A	B	C	D	E	F
Year of first departure	Number of new missionaries in that year	Number of these missionaries still in active service with you on 31 Dec 2002	Number of these missionaries who transferred to another agency but are still working on the field on 31 Dec 2002	Number of these missionaries who left your agency for unavoidable reasons	Number of these missionaries who left your agency for potentially preventable reasons or were dismissed
2000					
1999					
1998					
1997					
1996					
1995					
1994					
1993					
1992					
1991					
1990					
1989					
1988					
1987					
1986					
1985					
1984					
1983					
1982					
1981					

Many thanks for your help—your insights will contribute greatly to this study, which is intended to strengthen the global evangelical mission movement. Your responses will be treated confidentially.

Your position in the Agency: _____

How long have you held this position?: _____

Index